CHILDREN OF THE 21ST CENTURY

The first five years

Edited by Kirstine Hansen, Heather Joshi and Shirley Dex

This edition published in Great Britain in 2010 by

The Policy Press
University of Bristol
Fourth Floor
Beacon House
Queen's Road
Bristol BS8 1QU
UK

Tel +44 (0)117 331 4054
Fax +44 (0)117 331 4093
e-mail tpp-info@bristol.ac.uk
www.policypress.co.uk

North American office:
The Policy Press
c/o International Specialized Books Services (ISBS)
920 NE 58th Avenue, Suite 300
Portland, OR 97213-3786, USA
Tel +1 503 287 3093
Fax +1 503 280 8832
e-mail info@isbs.com

British Library Cataloguing in Publication Data
A catalogue record for this book is available from the British Library.

Library of Congress Cataloging-in-Publication Data
A catalog record for this book has been requested.

ISBN 978 1 84742 475 4 paperback
ISBN 978 1 84742 476 1 hardcover

Cover design by The Policy Press
Front cover: image kindly supplied by I-stock
Printed and bound in Great Britain by MPG Book Group

Mixed Sources
Product group from well-managed
forests and other controlled sources
www.fsc.org Cert no. SA-COC-1565
© 1996 Forest Stewardship Council

Contents

List of figures

List of tables

List of boxes

Acknowledgements

We wish to acknowledge the funding of the Millennium Cohort Study (MCS) by the Economic and Social Research Council (ESRC) and the consortium of government departments (led by the Office for National Statistics [ONS]) including the Department for Children, Schools and Families (DCSF), Department for Work and Pensions (DWP), Department of Health (DH), Sure Start and the governments of Wales, Scotland and Northern Ireland).

We would also like to thank the children who form the Millennium Cohort, their mothers, fathers and other family members for giving up time for the interviews.

Thanks are also due to Chris Baker for editing and formatting work and to Mina Thompson for collating references and lists.

List of contributors

Name	Title	Institution
Alice Sullivan	Research and Teaching Fellow	Centre for Longitudinal Studies, Institute of Education, University of London
Anna Vignoles	Professor of Economics of Education at the Institute of Education, and Director of the Centre for Economics of Education	Department of Quantitative Social Science, Institute of Education, University of London
Carol Dezateux	Professor of Paediatric Epidemiology, and Director of MRC Centre of Epidemiology for Child Health	Institute of Child Health, University College London
Catherine Law	Professor of Public Health and Epidemiology, and Director of the Centre for Policy Research	Institute of Child Health, University College London
Elizabeth Jones	Research Officer	Centre for Longitudinal Studies, Institute of Education, University of London
Fiona Mensah	Research Fellow	Department of Social Policy and Social Work, University of York
Fiona Roberts	Research Officer	Department of Education, University of Oxford
Heather Joshi	Director of the Centre for Longitudinal Studies, and Professor of Economic and Developmental Demography	Centre for Longitudinal Studies, Institute of Education, University of London
Helen Cheng	Research Officer	Department of Quantitative Social Science, Institute of Education, University of London
Ingrid Schoon	Professor of Human Development and Social Policy	Department of Quantitative Social Science, Institute of Education, University of London
Jo Blanden	Lecturer in Economics	Department of Economics, University of Surrey, and Centre for the Economics of Education and Centre for Economic Performance, London School of Economics and Political Science
John Holmes	Research Associate	Institute for Social Change, University of Manchester
John McDonald	Professor in Longitudinal Social Statistics	Centre for Longitudinal Studies, Institute of Education, University of London
Jonathan Bradshaw	Professor of Social Policy	Department of Social Policy and Social Work, University of York

Name	Title	Institution
Kathleen Kiernan	Professor of Social Policy and Demography	Department of Social Policy and Social Work, University of York
Kathy Sylva	Professor of Educational Psychology	Department of Education, University of Oxford
Kelly Ward	Senior Database Manager	National Centre for Social Research, London
Kirstine Hansen	Research Director, Millennium Cohort Study	Centre for Longitudinal Studies, Institute of Education, University of London
Lorraine Dearden	Professor of Economics and Social Statistics	Department of Quantitative Social Science, Institute of Education, University of London, and Institute for Fiscal Studies, London
Lucy Jane Griffiths	Senior Research Fellow	Institute of Child Health, University College London
Luke Sibieta	Senior Research Economist	Institute for Fiscal Studies, London
Melanie Bartley	Professor of Medical Sociology	Epidemiology and Public Health, University College London
Sandra Mathers	Senior Research Officer	Department of Education, University of Oxford
Shirley Dex	Professor of Longitudinal Social Research in Education	Centre for Longitudinal Studies, Institute of Education, University of London
Sosthenes Ketende	Research Officer	Centre for Longitudinal Studies, Institute of Education, University of London
Stephen Machin	Professor of Economics and Director of the Centre for Economics of Education and Programme Director, Skills and Education, Centre for Economic Performance	Department of Economics, University College London, and Centre for Economics of Education and Centre for Economic Performance, London School of Economics and Political Science
Summer Sherburne Hawkins	Robert Wood Johnson Foundation Health and Society Scholar	Harvard School of Public Health
Tim Cole	Professor of Medical Statistics	Institute of Child Health, University College London
Yvonne Kelly	Senior Lecturer	Research Department of Epidemiology and Public Health, University College London

Glossary

AHC	after housing costs
ALSPAC	Avon Longitudinal Study of Parents and Children
BAS	British Ability Scales
BCS 70	British Cohort Study of 1970
BHC	before housing costs
BMI	body mass index
BSRA	Bracken School Readiness Assessment
CCTC	Childcare Tax Credits
CI	confidence interval
CM	cohort member, or the cohort child in MCS
CP	*The Children's Plan* (2007)
CTB	Council Tax Benefit
CTC	Child Tax Credits
DCSF	Department for Children, Schools and Families
DfES	Department for Education and Skills
DH	Department of Health
DWP	Department for Work and Pensions
ECERS-E	Early Childhood Environment Rating Scale – Extension
ECERS-R	Early Childhood Environment Rating Scale – Revised
ECM	*Every Child Matters* (2004)
ELB	Education Library Board
ERA	Employment Retention and Advancement initiative
ESRC	Economic and Social Research Council
F-statistic	statistic used to test overall fit
FRS	Family Resources Survey
FSP	Foundation Stage Profile [subsequently Early Years Foundation Stage Profile, EYFSP]
GIRFEC	Getting it Right for Every Child (Scottish Government)
HBAI	Households Below Average Income
HLE	home learning environment
IMD	Index of Multiple Deprivation
IOTF	International Obesity Taskforce
JSA	Jobseeker's Allowance
Kessler 6	scale measuring non-specific psychological distress
LCA	latent class analysis
LEA	local education authority
LSOA	lower super output area
MSOA	middle super output area
MCS	Millennium Cohort Study
MCS 1	Millennium Cohort Study, first survey at 9 months
MCS 2	Millennium Cohort Study, second survey at 3 years

MCS 3	Millennium Cohort Study, third survey at 5 years
MCS 4	Millennium Cohort Study, fourth survey at 7 years
NCDS	National Child Development Study (1958)
NISRA	Northern Ireland Statistics and Research Agency
NNEB	National Nursery Examination Board – awards diplomas in childcare
NNI	Neighbourhood Nurseries Initiative
NSHD	National Survey of Health and Development
NS-SEC	National Statistics – Socio-Economic Classification
NVQ	National Vocational Qualification
NVQ 1	National Vocational Qualification Level 1 or GCSE equivalent grades D–G
NVQ 2	National Vocational Qualification Level 2 or GCSE equivalent grades A–C
NVQ 3	National Vocational Qualification Level 3 or A-level equivalent
NVQ 4	National Vocational Qualification Level 4 or Degree equivalent
NVQ 5	National Vocational Qualification Level 5 or Higher Degree equivalent
OECD	Organisation for Economic Co-operation and Development
ONS	Office for National Statistics
OR	odds ratio
PCA	principal components analysis
PSA	public service agreement
PSE	personal, social and emotional
PSU	primary sampling unit
QTS	qualified teacher status
SDQ	Strengths and Difficulties Questionnaire
SOC	standard occupational classification
SRMI	sequential regression multiple imputation technique
SSLP	Sure Start local programme
Stata	data analysis and statistical software
T-score	transformation of continuous score (adjusting for age at interview)
t-statistic	Statistic used to test the significance of a single estimate
UK	United Kingdom, i.e. England, Wales, Scotland and Northern Ireland
UKDA	UK Data Archive
UNICEF	United Nations Children's Fund
WAG	Welsh Assembly Government
WFTC	Working Families' Tax Credit
WTC	Working Tax Credit

ONE

Introduction

Heather Joshi, Kirstine Hansen and Shirley Dex

Introduction

This book takes up the story of the 19,000 children recruited into the UK Millennium Cohort Study (MCS) at the beginning of the new century, following their progress from birth to primary school. The origins and objectives of the study, along with the results of its first survey, were covered in a companion volume, *Children of the 21st century: From birth to nine months* (Dex and Joshi, 2005). In brief, the MCS is the fourth of a set of world-renowned national cohort studies in Britain, each following a group of individuals drawn from the population at large from the time of their birth and onwards through later life. The first of these nationally representative cohort studies, the MRC's National Study of Health and Development, is still following people born in 1946, who by 2010 are well into their 60s. This was followed by the National Child Development Study (NCDS), a 1958 cohort, and later by the British Cohort Study of 1970 (BCS 70), which are following cohort members into mid-life, complete with records of their childhood, education, health, employment and family formation.

Each cohort study forms a resource for a wide range of research into many social and medical areas. They all offer material for a holistic account of the dimensions of change as individuals grow older, and a view of the social dynamics as individuals move between stages of life and their positions relative to others. This provides a moving picture of the social mosaic, rather than a series of unlinked snapshots available from sources such as censuses or one-off cross-sectional surveys. These British studies, viewed together, offer an opportunity for understanding social changes, the processes behind them and the impact of policy (Bynner and Joshi, 2007). One example of inter-cohort comparison is contained in Chapter 9 of this volume, linking children's achievement to parents' resources.

The MCS has several new features. It has a clustered sample design, featuring over-representation of children living in areas of high minority ethnic populations and high poverty rates, and the smaller countries of the UK, with Northern Ireland covered in the follow-up for the first time. It sought interviews from fathers as well as mothers, and its content was adapted to the 21st-century context. More details on the content, size and design of the first three surveys are provided later in this chapter. A key innovation was to recruit the families for the study from a sample of births spread over a year, rather than to take everyone born in one week, as the previous national cohort studies had done. One reason for this was to allow research into the possible consequences of being born at different times of the year.

The children recruited into MCS were born over 16 months, starting in September 2000. Their families were first surveyed when the children were aged 9 months, during 2001 and 2002. They were followed up again around the time that the children were aged 3, most interviews taking place in 2004, and around age 5, when they had just started compulsory schooling, in 2006. This volume covers all of the first three surveys, up to age 5, exploiting the longitudinal linking of each child's multifaceted history. Follow-up has continued with a fourth survey at age 7 in 2008; a fifth survey is planned for age 11, and the intention is to continue following these individuals into adulthood.

The first five years of life

The stage of the life course which this book covers is one of great advances in child development – the most rapid since the 9 months before their birth. As they grow from babies into children they have been weaned, learned to walk, talk and play. Height at age 5 is around double their length at birth. They grow out of nappies. Their bodies strengthen and their faces change. Differences between boys and girls are reinforced by gendered clothing and, often, gendered toys. Identity and personality emerge, along with relationships with other family members. They have been prepared for later years by immunisations against childhood infections. They acquire their first set of teeth and learn to brush them. They also learn to sing, draw and paint, to listen to stories, to count and to recognise symbols. Many, but not all, start reading and writing by age 5. By the end of the study period we observe that they are sufficiently independent of the parental nest to attend school, to learn from other adults and to interact with other children. They have acquired knowledge and skills through learning at home, and pre-school provisions, which will also stand them in good stead in later life. It is also thought that negative experiences and hardships at these early ages will prove an impediment to their later development.

The opening years of the century

The global backdrop to the period through which the children have made these transitions has been a growing world economy, increasing digitisation of everyday technology, growing concerns about climate change and the emergence of conflict in Iraq and Afghanistan after the events of 11 September 2001. Concerns about security from terrorism have been mounting on a worldwide scale, especially after the London bombings on 7 July 2005. Despite some occasional manifestation of community tension, international migration to the UK reached high levels. Many came from new countries in Eastern Europe entering the European Union (EU) and filling the demand for labour. Births in the UK also rebounded from the record low fertility rate of 1.63 in 2001, around the time the cohort was born, to 1.83 births per woman in 2006. More young people than ever went to university during this period – with over half a million people applying for places through UCAS and over 400,000 successfully securing places. The expansion of higher education that had already occurred meant that more of the parents from the MCS were graduates than in previous generations. Throughout these years, the UK was under the New Labour government of Tony Blair, with Gordon Brown as the Chancellor of the Exchequer. They presided, at this time, over a period of general prosperity, including the expansion of education and health services, unprecedented spending on Early Years services, childcare and attempts to reduce child poverty, and falling unemployment (until 2005). At the same time house prices rose close to a peak, leaving house purchase out of the reach of many parents with young families.

The New Labour government introduced a whole raft of initiatives to improve the quality of life of children and families, and a commitment to tackle child poverty in particular. As already outlined in the introduction to the previous book, these included a series of tax credit schemes, raising Child Benefit, Sure Start, the Children's Fund, the National Childcare Strategy, improvements in maternity, paternity and parental leave, the provision of free nursery school places for 3- and 4-year-olds, and Child Trust Funds. The Children Act of 2004 implemented a document to promote interagency cooperation in services for children, *Every Child Matters* (ECM), and appointed children's commissioners to champion children's rights in all UK countries.

Despite the introduction of the National Minimum Wage in 1999 and the expansion of tax credits for families (Working Families' Tax Credits [WFTC] in 1999 followed by Working Tax Credits [WTC], Child Tax Credits [CTC] and Childcare Tax Credits [CCTC] by 2003), income inequality began to rise in 2004 to 2006. It had been relatively stable between 1992 and 2004, after a period of rising inequality between 1977 and 1991. Child poverty had followed a similar course, rising across the 1980s to a plateau in the 1990s. In 1999, the government announced its aim to eradicate child poverty by 2020, and since then the numbers of children (all ages) in poverty have fallen steadily. In 1998/99 there were 3.4 million children (26%) living in poverty. By 2006/07 this figure had fallen by 500,000 children, to 2.9 million (DWP, 2009).

The policy environment had many features which should have meant the new century was a good time to have been born for British children, or for people to become parents, at least in comparison with those born into the era when child poverty was rising in the 1980s and 1990s. However, the pro-child policies seem to have been impeded in their impact by forces of growing inequalities pulling in the opposite direction. This is evident in the international comparisons where the well-being of British children turns out to be at, or near, the bottom of the distribution in a league table of rich (or European) countries (UNICEF, 2007; Bradshaw and Richardson, 2009). Although the first of these studies could have been dismissed on the grounds that much of the data used came from the late 1990s, before New

Labour policies had taken root, the second study, based on more recent evidence, mostly from 2006, shows little relative improvement. The UK comes 24th out of 29 European countries, on average, over seven dimensions comprising material resources, health, subjective well-being, children's relationships, behaviour and risk, education and housing, and environment, as measured across children of various ages up to age 18 in various cross-sectional snapshots.

In the last 20 or 30 years the sociology of childhood has grown as an academic area and produced theoretical debates and numerous empirical studies. Key players in this field (such as Qvortrup et al, 1994; Jenks, 2001; Prout, 2004) argue that children are social actors, active participants rather than emergent members of society. Reflecting this perspective, the Children's Society launched The Good Childhood® Inquiry in September 2006 to examine societal understanding of modern childhood. Recommendations were made to parents, teachers, the government, the media, advertisers and society as a whole about best practice when it comes to children. These ranged from reducing child poverty to taking a more positive attitude to children (Layard and Dunn, 2009).

The MCS children had reached age 5 by the time the snapshots used by Bradshaw and Richardson (2009) were taken, so were not old enough to be counted on all of that study's dimensions of well-being. But the evidence accumulated over their first five years can bring valuable insight into diversity and disadvantage as experienced by children in the UK. It provides a longitudinal perspective on the pathways followed to reach age 5 by 2006. It records how far a status recorded at any one time, say income poverty in 2006, had persisted since earlier dates and how far the experience is transitory. Because the study is multifaceted as well as longitudinal it offers depth to the measurements, and evidence about how far the different facets of advantage and disadvantage are found in the same families, and how the earlier circumstances, during and before the child's life, contribute to explaining or predicting individual variations in disadvantage, on the one hand, and positive, healthy developments, on the other.

On a longer-term perspective, the early years of the 21st century produced the somewhat surprising finding that intergenerational social mobility had levelled off (Blanden and Machin, 2008). This involved the establishment of advantage at various points of pre-school, school and post-school stages, comparing childhoods spent mostly in the 1960s with the 1970s. It is too early to say whether the MCS children will follow their parents' position in the labour market, but the data from the first five years can be used in a new intercohort comparison of the importance of parental socioeconomic status in predicting child academic attainment. This careful comparison of some of the MCS children with offspring of members of the 1958 and 1970 cohorts forms part of the contribution of Jo Blanden and Stephen Machin to this book, in Chapter 9. They conclude that social mobility in the millennium generation is, so far, maintaining the level experienced by those born in the last couple of decades of the previous century.

Although the MCS is designed to observe the progress and diversity of children starting out in life in the 21st century, along with the experience of their families, it was not designed explicitly to evaluate the policies put in place to enhance that experience, which would have involved some sort of controlled experiment. What it can do is monitor what sorts of progress were made by whom, and for which groups of families they appeared to be particularly high or low. The dataset also offers the possibility of making comparisons with similar data collected in different policy regimes. In Britain, as well as the earlier cohort studies of births in 1946, 1958 and 1970, there is a study of the Avon area (ALSPAC – Avon Longitudinal Study of Parents and Children). Other countries (including Australia, the US, France and Ireland) have more recently launched multipurpose national child cohort studies, which offer an opportunity for international comparison (or pooling of data). It was not possible to explore these possibilities in this volume, however.

The purpose of the chapters in this volume is to show readers a selection of the patterns and regularities in the lives of this generation of UK children over their first five years. Each chapter focuses on a particular topic, but links it to other domains, and across time. Although each chapter offers answers to its own questions, more questions are raised. As the data are available to researchers at the UK Data Archive (UKDA), a second aim of this volume is to stimulate further investigation of the MCS, either itself, or by making comparisons with other sources.

Chapters at a glance

The contributors to this volume offer diverse perspectives on the homes in which children are growing up and the variations among children in the different dimensions of their development. The earlier chapters are mainly about the family context; the middle section deals more with child developmental outcomes and educational experience; and three chapters at the end focus more on health and behaviour. However, as befits a holistic study, most chapters reach out across these boundaries and they do not therefore have to be read in any particular order.

The contributions start with the policy priority issue of child poverty, still a disappointingly common experience for children born in the UK and which reappears throughout the contributions. In Chapter 2 Jonathan Bradshaw and John Holmes look at the incidence of child poverty, and the extent of its persistence over time, taking a range of approaches to its definition. They (and also Kathleen Kiernan and Fiona Mensah in Chapter 5) identify social and demographic groups at the highest risk of poverty, such as the least educated and young lone mothers. In Chapter 9 Jo Blanden and Stephen Machin's search for signs of intergenerational stability or mobility in life chances is one of several chapters to provide evidence on the association of family economic resources with children's cognitive and behavioural scores at ages 3 and 5. Several other chapters are concerned with the outcomes of poverty, or family economic resources more generally, for child development (Chapters 10, 12 and 14). These chapters also consider other, possibly more modifiable, factors that may explain how families influence child development or may moderate the impact of a lack of resources. In Chapter 14 Ingrid Schoon, Helen Cheng and Elizabeth Jones look at the longitudinal experience of persistent poverty severe enough to put a family on means-tested benefits. They find mothers' psychological resources as possible mediators, some might say protective factors, helping children to grow to be more resilient. In Chapter 12 Kirstine Hansen's account of the ratings given by teachers at the end of the first year of school fits into a very similar pattern.

Similar predictors of child development are in the background of the chapters that focus on the relationship of child development with changing patterns of married, cohabiting and lone parenthood (Kathleen Kiernan and Fiona Mensah, Chapter 5); ethnic groups (Lorraine Dearden and Luke Sibieta, Chapter 10) and parents' physical and mental health (Yvonne Kelly and Melanie Bartley, Chapter 15). In Chapter 4 Elizabeth Jones focuses on the links between quality of parental relationships, parenting practices and child outcomes. The analyses of overweight (Lucy Jane Griffiths, Summer Sherburne Hawkins, Tim Cole, Catherine Law and Carol Dezateux, Chapter 13) and its more serious form, obesity (Yvonne Kelly and Melanie Bartley, Chapter 15), also show some socioeconomic patterning, but additionally find associations with infant feeding, eating habits, sedentary behaviour and parental body mass.

Ethnic variations run through many chapters. In Chapter 3 Alice Sullivan focuses on the cultural context and climate of racial discrimination reported by some, but not all, of the minority group of mothers represented in the study. Another feature of the new century, which is itself subject to ethnic diversity, is the now common experience of employment for mothers of pre-school children. In Chapter 6 Shirley Dex and Kelly Ward report the complex histories of parents moving in and out of employment which helps account for the movement of families in and out of poverty over the pre-school years. Mothers' employment has been accompanied by a growing array of childcare arrangements, reviewed by Fiona Roberts, Sandra Mathers, Heather Joshi, Kathy Sylva and Elizabeth Jones in Chapter 8, attended by most MCS children at some point, whether or not their mother was employed. Chapter 8 also reports on a detailed set of observations on a sub-sample of childcare settings.

The sorting of children from advantaged homes into the better schools is felt to be another route by which economic privileges are transmitted across the generations. Whether or not families have been moving home to facilitate getting their children into a school of their choice, the evidence assembled by Kirstine Hansen and Anna Vignoles in Chapter 11 shows that for this cohort most parents got the school of their first choice, and that whether or not school choice had been exercised, most parents were satisfied with their child's first school, where most children were reported to be happy.

Besides a relatively small number of moves motivated by school choice, residential mobility is a common experience for families with small children. In Chapter 7 Sosthenes Ketende, John McDonald and Heather Joshi relate the moves of MCS families to the nature of the places they inhabit, drawing attention to the role spatial mobility plays in the polarisation of family fortunes within these early stages of the cohort's life course over the period.

The complex patterns revealed in these chapters of social and ethnic variation in the children's development so far, or of the role that parenting behaviour plays, do not amount to an account of how differences between these ages have been determined. Nor does it suggest that these children's futures are set in stone. For one thing, there is plenty of variation between children that has not been statistically accounted for. Some predictors of disadvantage for children, such as parents not being legally married, or early motherhood, may be markers of disadvantage and not necessarily its 'makers', if they themselves are the outcomes of earlier disadvantage.

MCS content, size and design

Table 1.1 shows the numbers of families who provided information at each survey contact. At each survey there was a home interview where the main respondent was almost always the child's natural mother, with a shorter interview with the

Table 1.1: MCS: contents of the first three surveys at a glance

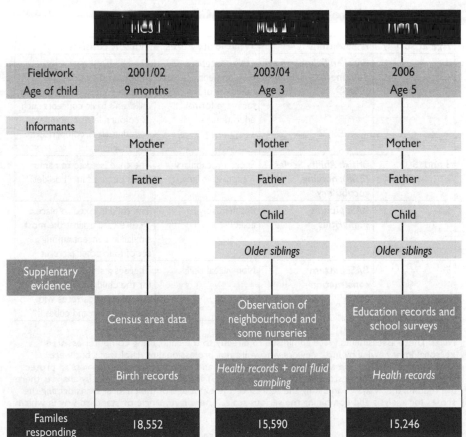

	MCS 1	MCS 2	MCS 3
Fieldwork	2001/02	2003/04	2006
Age of child	9 months	Age 3	Age 5
Informants			
	Mother	Mother	Mother
	Father	Father	Father
		Child	Child
		Older siblings	*Older siblings*
Supplentary evidence			
	Census area data	Observation of neighbourhood and some nurseries	Education records and school surveys
	Birth records	*Health records + oral fluid sampling*	*Health records*
Familes responding	18,552	15,590	15,246

Note: Elements in italics are not covered in this volume, but are included here for completeness.

main respondent's resident partner, if any. Around 5 out of 6 families had two resident parents, and around 9 out of 10 resident partners responded. These two elements of the survey are labelled 'Mother' and 'Father' for simplicity. Each parent answered questions about their own health and health-related behaviour, demographics, relationship to each other, parenting and attitudes. In addition, the main respondent answered questions about pregnancy and the cohort child's birth, subsequent health, activities with the child, family income, housing and neighbourhood. As early as age 3 the child became an active participant in the survey, undertaking two cognitive assessments, and being measured by the specially trained interviewer for their height and weight. At age 5 the child assessments were increased to three of the British Ability Scales (BAS), and the anthropometric measurements included waist as well as height and weight. Box 1.1 gives details of all the cognitive instruments used in MCS 2 and MCS 3, while Box 1.2 describes the main indicator of child behavioural development used in this book, the Strengths and Difficulties Questionnaire (SDQ).

Box 1.1: Cognitive assessments in MCS

Age at survey	Assessment	What it measures	What it consists of
3	*Bracken School Readiness Assessment (BSRA)*	Basic concept development; readiness of the child for more formal education	The child is shown a set of coloured pictures that contain six sub-tests to assess children's basic concepts such as colours, letters, numbers/ counting, sizes, comparisons and shapes
3 and 5	*British Ability Scales (BAS): naming vocabulary*	Spoken vocabulary – expressive language	The child is asked to name items pictured in a booklet
5	*BAS: picture similarities*	Problem-solving ability	The child is asked to place a picture card against the most similar in concept among a set of four other pictures
5	*BAS: pattern construction*	Non-verbal skills	There is a set of timed tasks for the child, copying and constructing patterns with coloured tiles and cubes.

Notes: These assessments were administered directly to the child, using computer assisted personal interviewing by interviewers who were not professional psychologists, but were specially trained. They use age-related starting points, and alternative stopping points to protect the motivation and self-esteem of the child (Hill, 2005). In the use of the scores by analysts there are then further ways of adjusting the scores for the exact age of the child or transforming the scores for analysis and combining the various scales. There is no single or standard way in which this is done.

Sources: BSRA: Bracken (1998); BAS (second edition): Elliott et al (1996); Hill (2005).

Box 1.2: The Strengths and Difficulties Questionnaire in MCS

At the age 3 and age 5 surveys behavioural adjustment was assessed using the Strengths and Difficulties Questionnaire (SDQ) devised by Robert Goodman. This standard instrument is well validated for screening psychiatric disorders. The version about children aged 4-15 was included in the self-completion module usually answered by the child's mother. It covers five domains. The respondent is asked about the following statements grouped into the five scales:

1. Emotion symptoms scale
  1. Complains of headaches/stomach aches/ sickness
  2. Often seems worried
  3. Often unhappy
  4. Nervous or clingy in new situations
  5. Many fears, easily scared
	2. Conduct problems
	  1. Often has temper tantrums
	  2. Generally obedient
	  3. Fights with or bullies other children
	  4. Can be spiteful to others
	  5. Often argumentative with adults

3 Hyperactivity scale
  1. Restless, overactive, cannot stay still for long
  2. Constantly fidgeting
  3. Easily distracted
  4. Can stop and think before acting
  5. Sees tasks through to the end
	4. Peer problems
	  1. Tends to play alone
	  2. Has at least one good friend
	  3. Generally liked by other children
	  4. Picked on or bullied by other children
	  5. Gets on better with adults

5. Pro-social scale
  1. Considerate of others' feelings
  2. Shares readily with others
  3. Helpful if someone is hurt, upset or ill
  4. Kind to younger children
  5. Often volunteers to help others	

Replies that adverse statements are 'certainly true' score 2, 'somewhat true' score 1 and 'not true' score 0. The reverse applies to 'positive statements' like pro-social behaviour.

The resulting scores have been combined and transformed in various different ways by the contributors to this volume; most of them extract the total difficulties score, which is the sum of the first four sub-scales without the pro-social items.

For further details see www.sdqinfo.com, and Goodman (1997, 2001); Goodman et al (1998).

Interview data have been supplemented from auxiliary sources, as shown in Table 1.1. Among those used in this volume are the 2001 Census evidence on the ethnic composition of the place of residence in 2006 (see Alice Sullivan, Chapter 3). Teacher assessments of the 5-year-olds' performance in their first year at school used in Kirstine Hansen's Chapter 12 come partly from linkage of administrative records on the Foundation Stage Profile (FSP) from England and partly from an auxiliary postal survey of teachers in Scotland, Wales and Northern Ireland. The linkage of birth registration and hospital records from 2001/02 has helped validate data on birth weight which enters as a control in many analyses in this volume, besides offering material for other studies that are not included here.

The number of families responding to each of the three surveys, shown in the last row of Table 1.1, understates the number of children in the survey to the extent that some families, with twins and triplets, have more than one child in the survey (for example, the 18,522 families responding to the first survey had 18,818 children).

The second MCS survey managed to recruit an extra 692 families in England who would have been eligible for the first survey by virtue of where they were living in 2001/02, but whose addresses became known too late. This additional sample, known as 'New families', was asked some additional questions to 'repair' missing information. At the same time the age 3 survey lost 3,654 cases who had been interviewed at MCS 1, so the number of 'productive' interviews was 15,590. The number of productive interviews achieved at age 5, 15,246, is the net result of losing 1,788 families from MCS 2, and gaining 1,444 MCS 1 respondents who did not respond at MCS 2. Further details on attrition can be found in Ketende (2008).

Table 1.2 shows the distribution of the achieved sample over the four countries of the UK. At the start of MCS all except England were relatively over-sampled compared to their population size, particularly Wales. Readers are referred to other sources for further details on MCS: there are three user guides to initial findings (Dex and Joshi, 2004; Hansen and Joshi, 2007, 2008); a guide to the datasets (Hansen, 2008); and technical reports on sampling and response (Plewis, 2007; Ketende, 2008).

Table 1.2: Number of families participating in the first three surveys of the MCS

Pattern across MCS surveys	Response at each MCS survey			Achieved sample numbers				
	1	2	3	UK	England	Wales	Scotland	N. Ireland
All	●	●	●	13,234	8,314	2,002	1,596	1,322
1 and 2 but not 3	●	●	○	1,664	1,044	259	218	143
1 and 3 but not 2	●	○	●	1,444	835	179	218	212
1 only	●	○	○	2,210	1,340	320	304	246
New families: 2 and 3	○	●	●	568	568	NA	NA	NA
New families: 2 only	○	●	○	124	124	NA	NA	NA
At least one survey	18,552	15,590	15,246	19,244	12,225	2,760	2,336	1,923

Notes: The MCS cohort for follow-up is all who responded at MCS 1 plus 'New families' recruited, for the only time at MCS 2.

A family is counted as responding (●) if they provided information on at least one instrument at the relevant sweep. Families with twins and triplets are counted only once.

The breakdown into countries of the UK is based on residence at MCS 1.

Complex survey design

The MCS design is complex and therefore requires analysts to correct for its clustering into electoral wards at the outset. Without some correction, standard tests of statistical significance may be biased upward, as explained in the technical report on sampling (Plewis, 2007). Most authors have chosen to address this issue by using the 'Survey' commands in the Stata package which allows for the use of weights to redress the disproportionate sampling as well as providing correction for clustered survey design. Some authors have used an amended set of weights as a way to adjust for attrition along lines explained in Hansen (2008, pp 71-2).

A reader's guide

Following chapters in the sequence in which they appear will take the reader through the child's home and neighbourhood, with an excursion to the parents' workplace, then to daycare providers, and schools, and back home again in Chapters 13, 14 and 15 on 'healthy development'. The journey affords several perspectives on how the children are progressing at the start of their school years, and, especially in the earlier chapters, of the lives of their parents. The intergeneration transmission of resources, health and care from parent to child is a recurring theme – the opportunities and handicaps linking children's life chances to those of their parents will appear again and again. Another leitmotif will be diverse ethnic variations in these circumstances and processes. The concluding chapter (Chapter 16) will pick up these, and other cross-cutting themes, and return to the changing policy and macro-economic context in which these children are passing their primary school age years, and in which another generation of babies and their parents are setting out.

TWO

Child poverty in the first five years of life

Jonathan Bradshaw and John Holmes

Introduction

The children in the Millennium Cohort Study (MCS) were born around a year after the then Prime Minister Tony Blair announced that it was the government's intention to eradicate child poverty in a generation by 2020. In fact these children are the generation over which it is hoped child poverty will be eradicated. In Figure 2.1 we can see that child poverty fell after 1998/99. However, the government just missed the first five-year target to reduce child poverty by a quarter by 2004/05, and, according to the latest data available, there has been no further improvement.[1]

Figure 2.1: Child poverty rates 1998/99–2006/07: % of dependent children (all ages) in households with equivalent income less than 60% median

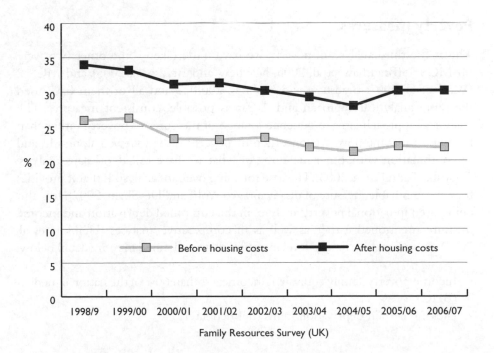

Family Resources Survey (UK)

This chapter explores family poverty in the MCS 3 when the children were aged 5 and traces changes in poverty between MCS 1 and 3, from 9 months to age 5. It is not possible to replicate exactly the measures that the government has been using to monitor the child poverty strategy using the MCS data, however.[2] The MCS collects income data but records the responses in income bands, before housing costs (BHC). Over the three MCS surveys, data on deprivation has also been collected although there are differences between the MCS and the 'official' measures based on the Family Resources Survey (FRS)[3] as well as with the nature of the samples. The MCS is a sample of families with a child of a certain age and cannot be used to compare with the results of the Households Below Average Income (HBAI) analysis of the FRS that produces data on the proportion of all dependent children in poverty.

Nevertheless there are a number of reasons why it is important to analyse poverty in the MCS:

- The children are being surveyed repeatedly over their childhood. The MCS therefore represents an opportunity for the analysis of change over time and in particular the persistence of poverty and the factors associated with movements into and out of poverty.
- The children constitute a very large sample that is deliberately stratified to include a large ethnic sample and families living in poorer areas.
- Poverty is an important variable in understanding other aspects of the development and well-being of children. Others who study the cohort children can use the variables created in this analysis.

Poverty measures

This is the third analysis of poverty we have undertaken – the other two were on MCS 1 (Bradshaw et al, 2005; Mayhew and Bradshaw, 2005) and MCS 2 (Ward et al, 2007; Bradshaw and Holmes, 2008) – and all of them have used the same analytical approach and, as far as possible, consistent measures. The analytical approach aims to generate a range of measures of poverty, rather than relying on income poverty alone. Income poverty is then viewed alongside, and in combination with, other measures, in what we have called 'overlaps analysis' (Bradshaw and Finch, 2003). The case for using overlaps analysis is that it provides for a more reliable measure of disadvantage (Wolff and De-Shalit, 2007). It is also being used in national poverty analyses in the combined deprivation and income measure mentioned earlier, as well as in comparative analyses (Heikkila et al, 2006). So we use four family-level measures that are defined in more detail below:

- Income poverty: family equivalent income less than 60% of the national median (BHC)
- Lacking certain deprivation items (defined later)

- Subjective poverty
- Being in receipt of income-related welfare benefits.

In this chapter we give family poverty rates using each of these measures, and we describe the overlaps between the different measures. In addition, we estimate the odds of a family in MCS 3 being 'reliably' poor and explore how family poverty has changed between MCS 1 and 3.

The analysis is based on the family unit and the sample used is confined to families with singleton births (that is, not twins or triplets) where the mother remained in the household and was the main respondent at the relevant MCS survey.[4] Sampling weights are applied to percentages throughout and attrition weights are used for the MCS 3 analysis.

Income poverty

Using *household income* to define poverty is the conventional measure of relative poverty. Income poverty is defined as having a net equivalent (taking account of household size and composition) family income below 60% of the national median. For the calculation of equivalent income we used the modified Organisation for Economic Co-operation and Development (OECD) equivalence scale, which has also been used by the government in its annual analysis on poverty – HBAI – since 2004/05 (Hagenaars et al, 1994; DWP, 2006, Appendix 3). The derivation, using MCS data, of equivalent family income was problematic because of the nature of the income data collected in the MCS. In order to encourage responses, instead of asking people to reveal their actual family income, respondents were asked to specify which of 18 income bands their family income belonged to. The survey questionnaire used separate income bands for lone parents and for couples. In order to determine equivalent family income, we assigned the mid-point of the income band to all the families belonging to that particular band. For the top and bottom bands we took respectively the bottom and top thresholds as the family income. Next we applied the equivalence scale to the family income for each family type and created one common income variable containing the equivalent family income of both couples and single parents. Where income was missing in MCS 3, it has been imputed using a sequential regression multiple imputation (SRMI) technique (Ketende and Joshi, 2008).

The proportion of families in our sample living below this poverty threshold at MCS 3, mostly in 2006, was 30%. This was very little change from earlier MCS surveys: 29% of families were in poverty in MCS 1 (2001/02) and 29% in MCS 2 (2003/04). Although the three samples are not identical, it suggests a similar pattern of fluctuation as observed for children of all ages in Figure 2.1.[5]

Deprivation

The *deprivation* measure used here follows the principle of measuring poverty as a lack of (socially perceived) necessities (Gordon et al, 2000). The deprivation indicators in MCS have changed across the various surveys. MCS 1 merely asked respondents about the availability of a number of appliances in working order in the household. By the time that MCS 2 was being designed it was possible to draw on progress that had been made in the development of indicators of material deprivation and nine deprivation items were included. In MCS 3, the nine items were replaced by five, and unfortunately none of them were identical to the items in MCS 2 and neither were they identical to the deprivation questions in the FRS. Table 2.1 gives the proportion lacking each of the items included in the MCS 3 questionnaire and compares these with the FRS 2006/07. It is difficult to interpret the differences between the MCS 3 and FRS because the questions are not the same and the samples are not comparable.[6]

Table 2.2 gives the proportion of MCS 3 families lacking one or more of the five items. Taking a threshold of lacking at least one item gives us 38% of families as materially deprived.

Subjective poverty

Subjective poverty is an indicator of respondents' own assessments of their poverty status. The question used here is: 'How well would you say you (and your partner) are managing financially these days?'. The answers given are presented in Table 2.3. We decided to define as subjectively poor those who were finding it quite or very difficult to manage plus those who said they were just about getting by. This

Table 2.1: Deprivation items lacking in MCS 3, and the FRS

Item	MCS 3 % families lacking this item in the sample	Item	FRS 2006/07 % children in households want but cannot afford
Celebrates birthdays/ festivals	1.7	Celebrations on special occasions	4
Annual holiday not staying with relatives	29.4	Holiday away one week a year not with relatives	38
Small amount of money to spend on self weekly	23.1	Money to spend on mother herself each week	32
Two pairs of all-weather shoes for the child	2.1	Two pairs of all-weather shoes for each adult	9
Weather-proof coat for the child	1.0		

Table 2.2: Number of deprivation items lacking, MCS 3

Number of items lacking	% families lacking
0	61.6
1	22.9
2	12.7
3	2.4
4	0.4
5	0.0
Total %	100
N	14,500

Notes: Sample = all MCS 3 main respondents. These are weighted percentages and unweighted numbers.

Table 2.3: Subjective poverty among MCS 3 families

	% of families	Number
Living comfortably	24.0	3,371
Doing alright	37.7	5,543
Just about getting by	27.8	4,070
Finding it quite difficult	7.7	1,130
Finding it very difficult	2.8	399
Total	100.0	14,513

Notes: Sample = all MCS 3 main respondents. These are weighted percentages and unweighted numbers.

gives us 38% of families defined as subjectively poor. The equivalent proportion in MCS 1 was 37% and at MCS 2, 36%, again a slightly dipping sequence of cross-sectional estimates.

Receiving means-tested benefits

The other datum that was available, which is a useful indicator of living on a low income, was being in receipt of various income-tested benefits. We explored the overlap in the receipt of benefits (see Table 2.4), and decided to include as poor those receiving any of the following: Income Support, Working Tax Credit (WTC), Housing Benefit or Council Tax Benefit (CTB). Those receiving Jobseeker's Allowance (JSA) are included, therefore, if they were also receiving either Housing Benefit or CTB. Those with Housing Benefit/CTB are more likely to be receiving income-tested JSA rather than contributory JSA. This definition gives 37% of MCS 3 families in poverty when defined as dependent

Table 2.4: Overlap between means-tested benefits, MCS 3

			Row percentages			
	Income Support	*Housing Benefit*	*Working Tax Credit*	*Council Tax Benefit*	*Number in receipt*	*% of total in receipt of benefit/credit*
Income Support	–	77.4	0.3	73.4	2,280	14.6
Housing Benefit	70.7	–	13.9	86.7	2,383	16.0
Working Tax Credit	0.2	9.7	–	10.9	3,494	22.8
Council Tax Benefit	66.7	86.2	15.4	–	2,261	16.0

Notes: Sample = All MCS 3 main respondents. These are weighted percentages and unweighted numbers.

on some form of means-tested benefits. Analyses in Chapter 14 take a slightly broader version of benefit–defined poverty.

Sensitivity analysis of the four poverty measures

None of the four poverty measures is by itself entirely satisfactory. For example, lacking one or more necessities could be a lifestyle choice; the grouped income variable is not very precise and it was imputed for the 1,534 cases where it was not given; people may or may not feel poor due to 'false consciousness' or because they are living in a household with better-off adults (such as their own parents) whose income we do not know; and there may be confusion in the reports of benefits received.

We therefore set about deriving a poverty indicator that combines the information on the separate elements to produce a more reliable and valid overall indicator. This was done using the technique of overlaps analysis (Bradshaw and Finch, 2003). Table 2.5 shows the relative size of our separate poverty domains. The four different measures of poverty produce different proportions of families living in poverty.

Table 2.6 shows the degree of overlap between the measures. The most overlap is between those receiving means-tested benefits and those that are income poor

Table 2.5: Percentage of mothers defined as in poverty on four measures, MCS 3

Poverty measure	% of MCS 3 families poor on each measure	Observation	Base n
Deprived	38.4	5,681	14,513
Income poverty	30.1	4,858	14,582
Subjective poverty	38.3	5,599	14,513
Receiving means-tested benefits	37.4	5,768	14,511

Notes: Sample = All MCS 3 main respondents. These are weighted percentages and unweighted numbers.

Table 2.6: Overlap between the different measurements of poverty, MCS 3

	Row percentages					
	Deprived	Low income poor	Subjectively poor	Receiving means tested benefits	Obs	n
Deprived	–	54.0	69.1	58.2	5,681	14,513
Income poverty	68.8	–	62.3	72.2	4,858	14,582
Subjective poverty	69.2	48.9	–	53.3	5,599	14,513
Receiving means-tested benefits	59.9	58.2	54.7	–	5,768	14,511

Notes: Sample = All MCS 3 main respondents in receipt of one or more benefit. These are weighted percentages and unweighted numbers.

(72%), which is to be expected since the latter is the prerequisite of the former. There is relatively less overlap between the deprived and those who are subjectively poor or receiving means-tested benefits. Nevertheless 69% of the subjectively poor are 'deprived' and nearly half are income poor.

Sixty-three per cent were poor on at least one of the definitions, 43% were in poverty on two definitions, 26% on three, but only 12% were poor on all four definitions. We describe those who were poor on at least three out of four measures as 'reliably poor'.

Latent poverty measure

Another means of exploring the relationship between the four poverty measures is to use latent class analysis (LCA) (McCutcheon, 1987). LCA is a market segmentation technique used for exploring latent concepts underpinning observed relationships between categorical data. It allows for the derivation of probabilistic models of variables that describe the underlying concept.

In this instance, our deprivation, subjective and benefits measures were used in conjunction with income quintiles to derive a probabilistic variable describing poverty as observed by these measures. The resultant groupings give us a new way of looking at the relationship between our measures. Although less parsimonious, it has greater statistical rigour and also offers opportunities for longitudinal analysis which will be explored in future work.

It should be noted that while the indexing of overlaps in poverty measures (as mentioned earlier) is an incremental approach to combining the measures, LCA is a typological approach. This means that, in overlaps indices, those in the most severe poverty are a sub-set of those poor on fewer measures whereas, in LCA, those in the most severe poverty are not a sub-set, but a distinct group solely defined by the structure of the data, not a cumulative process. The only restriction on the probability of being in a particular group is that the probabilities of being in each group sum to one.

Table 2.7 shows the best fitting model that has four latent groups. The groups suggested are:

- Experiencing poverty on all four measures ('truly poor')
- Others on low income and being on benefits ('money poor')
- Others lacking 'deprivation' items and feeling poor ('deprived poor')
- Not poor.

The bottom row of Table 2.7 displays the probability of being in each latent class (that is, the probability of being in a particular group); these sum to one. The main body of the table gives the probability of a group member being in each income quintile *given they are in a particular latent class*. With consistent variables across time, this model can be used to explore changes in poverty composition and the relative influences of our measures on that composition in future MCS surveys. By calculating the modal probabilities (that is, the most likely latent class for every possible response pattern) we can also assign individual cases to groups, although the validity of this approach is disputed (Heinen, 1996). Using this approach, 40% of MCS 3 families were not poor on any of these LCA measures, and 28% were truly poor, 16% were money poor and 16% were deprived poor.

Table 2.7: LCA of poverty, MCS 3

		Truly poor[a]	Money poor	Deprived poor	Not poor
Income quintile poverty	1st (low)	0.54	0.19	0.07	0.02
	2nd	0.31	0.35	0.21	0.06
	3rd	0.11	0.28	0.35	0.17
	4th	0.03	0.15	0.27	0.30
	5th (high)	0.01	0.02	0.09	0.45
Subjective poverty	No	0.21	0.77	0.36	0.93
	Yes	0.79	0.23	0.64	0.07
Benefit poverty	No	0.18	0.09	1.00[b]	0.94
	Yes	0.82	0.91	0.00[b]	0.06
Deprivation poverty	No	0.09	0.83	0.38	0.97
	Yes	0.91	0.17	0.62	0.03
LCA probability		0.28	0.16	0.16	0.40

Notes: Sample = All MCS 3 main respondents in receipt of one or more benefit.

[a] While those defined here as 'truly poor' are not necessarily poor on all four measures, they are the most likely to be poor on each of the other individual measures considered in this chapter (except means-tested benefits) and as such are also the most likely to be categorised as poor on any given combination of measures.

[b] Fixed value restrictions applied due to boundary estimates.

$L^2 = 22.07$, df = 9, AIC = 4.11, BIC = -64.12, $n = 14,488$

Characteristics of poor families

Using correlations between being in poverty on each definition and other characteristics (presented in Appendix Table A2.1 at the end of this chapter) we found that families were generally more likely to be poor if there was only one parent, a large number of children or no earners. Families were significantly less likely to be in poverty, by any definition, if they had two married natural parents, the MCS mother was of white or Indian ethnicity, the family lived in owner-occupied housing, there were two earners in the family, the mother had tertiary level education or the mother was over 30 years old at the MCS child's birth.

In Table 2.8 we present the findings from multivariate logistic regression, calculating the odds of being poor, having controlled for the other variables. In order to minimise interaction effects between family type and number of earners we dropped the variable indicating number of adults in the family and combined the number of earners with the family type variable.

After controlling for other characteristics, the odds of being poor were higher, if:

* there were two or more children in the household compared with only one child (in the case of benefit receipt poverty, having four or more children was significantly associated with higher odds of being poor);
* the family had two natural parents where at least one parent was not employed compared to if two parents were employed;
* natural parents were cohabiting rather than married (this result holds up even after controlling for number of earners on two out of four of the poverty definitions);
* a natural mother was living with a stepfather compared with married natural parents, particularly if they were not both employed (and this is significant on two poverty definitions even if they were both employed);
* the child was living with a lone mother compared with natural married parents, whether or not she was in employment;[7]
* the mother was aged[8] under 30 compared with being 35 or older at the birth of the cohort child;
* the mother was of Pakistani, Bangladeshi, black or black British ethnicity rather than white or Indian ethnicity;
* the mother's educational level was less than lower tertiary (NVQ Level 3 or below) compared with NVQ Level 5;
* the family was not an owner-occupier.

These are very similar to the results derived from the bivariate analysis although the coefficients tend to be attenuated and there are fewer significant results having controlled for the range of other factors.

Further multivariate analyses were carried out where the definitions of poverty derived from the LCA were the three dependent variables, namely 'truly poor',

Table 2.8: Multivariate logistic regression of the family being poor at MCS 3

	Income <60%	Deprivation	Benefit	Subjective	Reliably poor (3 or more)
Number of children					
1	1.00	1.00	1.00	1.00	1.00
2	1.55**	1.19**	1.10	1.11**	1.18**
3	2.63**	1.35**	1.13	1.14**	1.58**
4+	4.82**	1.57**	1.45**	1.19**	1.93**
Family type and earners at MCS 1					
Married natural parents – 2 earners	1.00	1.00	1.00	1.00	1.00
Married natural parents – 1 earner	2.77**	1.41**	1.68**	1.29**	2.70**
Married natural parents – 0 earner	9.73**	2.64**	1.73**	2.13**	6.18**
Cohabiting natural parents – 2 earners	1.11	1.62**	1.08	1.47**	1.38**
Cohabiting natural parents – 1 earner	3.31**	2.17**	2.07**	1.44**	3.34**
Cohabiting natural parents – 0 earner	12.19**	3.87**	2.01**	2.67**	9.66**
Natural mother & stepfather – 2 earners	1.44	1.90**	1.96**	1.31	2.31**
Natural mother & stepfather – 1 earner	4.28**	2.10**	2.29**	1.64**	4.85**
Natural mother & stepfather – 0 earner	12.42**	3.36**	2.27**	2.40**	7.67**
Lone natural mother – 1 earner	9.87**	2.94**	8.40**	2.53**	8.65**
Lone natural mother – 0 earner	63.45**	5.65**	10.27**	3.66**	25.38**
Mother's age at birth					
35+	1.00	1.00	1.00	1.00	1.00
30-34	1.03	0.91	1.06	0.91	0.88
25-29	1.30**	1.14**	1.33**	0.86**	1.03
20-24	1.65**	1.23**	1.82**	0.91	1.29**
Under 20	2.03**	1.17	2.03**	0.71**	1.14
Mother's ethnicity					
White	1.00	1.00	1.00	1.00	1.00
Mixed	1.29	1.50	1.03	1.31	1.23
Indian	2.05**	1.07	0.85	0.87	1.20
Pakistani and Bangladeshi	6.08**	1.95**	2.00**	1.63**	3.08**
Black or Black British	1.40**	1.84**	0.67**	1.81**	1.31**
Other ethnic groups	2.61**	2.29**	1.11	1.56**	2.60**
Mother's highest qualification at MCS 1					
NVQ level 5	1.00	1.00	1.00	1.00	1.00
NVQ level 4	1.14	1.15	1.24**	0.95	1.05
NVQ level 3	2.12**	1.67**	1.98**	1.37**	1.83**
NVQ level 2	2.51**	1.91**	2.10**	1.40**	1.99**
NVQ Level 1	3.48**	2.06**	2.59**	1.44**	2.24**
No recognised qualifications	4.58**	2.55**	2.62**	1.62**	2.93**
Housing tenure at MCS 1					
Owner-occupier	1.00	1.00	1.00	1.00	1.00
Social housing	3.09**	2.46**	2.77**	2.13**	3.46**
Private rented/other	2.24**	1.68**	1.77**	1.70**	2.21**
n	14,056	14,049	14,044	14,048	14,030

Notes: Sample = All MCS 3 main respondents

Significance ** p<0.05

'money poor' and 'deprived poor'. The same sociodemographic predictors were used as displayed in Table 2.8. The conclusions from these analyses are summarised below (results not shown):

- those classed as 'truly poor' were more likely to live in the most disadvantaged social circumstances;
- being 'deprived poor' was significantly associated with the sociodemographic variables. However, this set of sociodemographic variables were stronger predictors of being 'money poor';
- being 'deprived poor' was strongly associated with being from a black ethnic group;
- the number of earners in the family and its partnership structure were the best at distinguishing between the different types of LCA poverty.

So being 'money poor' appears to be related to social background, whereas being 'deprived poor' seems to emphasise a cultural element. However, family status and number of earners remained the strongest predictors of all types of poverty.

Poverty over the MCS surveys

We are able to trace changes in poverty over the MCS surveys using two of our four dimensions: income poverty and subjective poverty.[9] There is a remarkable consistency over MCS surveys. Poverty rates went down between MCS 1 and 2 surveys and up again between MCS 2 and 3 but the differences are very small and not statistically significant (see Table 2.9). It is likely that there was no reduction in poverty for this cohort as a whole in the first five years of the lives of these children. However, individual families had quite varied experiences.

In terms of persistence, 39% of families experienced income poverty, 58% subjective poverty and 28% were poor in both respects in at least one of the first three MCS surveys. However, only 14% were income poor, 16% subjectively poor

Table 2.9: Proportions of MCS families in poverty, by MCS surveys and poverty dimension

	Income poor	Subjective poverty	Neither income nor subjective poor	Either income or subjective poor	Both income and subjective poor
MCS 1	29.4 (16,677)	37.1 (18,202)	50.9 (16,673)	49.1 (16,673)	17.5 (16,673)
MCS 2	28.8 (12,687)	36.4 (15,006)	52.0 (12,687)	48.0 (12,687)	17.6 (12,687)
MCS 3	30.1 (14,582)	38.3 (14,513)	50.3 (14,508)	49.7 (14,508)	18.7 (14,508)

Notes: Sample = All MCS 3 main respondents
Weighted percentages – weighted by each sweep's relevant weight; (unweighted numbers).

and 5% were poor in both respects in all three MCS surveys (see Table 2.10). These can be described as the persistently poor.

Approximately one fifth of families with income data at both MCS 1 and MCS 3 surveys were income poor in both surveys. A further 10% left income poverty, which was almost exactly matched by 10% who became income poor between those particular surveys. Twenty-two per cent of those for whom an indicator of subjective poverty was known were subjectively poor at both points and again nearly the same proportions left poverty as moved into poverty (see Table 2.11).

Table 2.12 shows the odds of being poor on two dimensions and at three time points. The first in sequence is at three MCS surveys as presented in column (1); second, for those who moved out of poverty relative to staying poor in column (2); third, for those who moved into poverty relative to staying out of poverty over

Table 2.10: Persistent poverty across three MCS surveys (%)

	Income poor	Subjectively poor	Income poor and/or subjectively poor	Income poor and subjectively poor
In no MCS survey	61.3	42.5	35.1	72.1
In at least one survey	38.7	57.5	64.9	27.9
In at least two surveys	24.4	34.7	45.6	14.1
In all three surveys	13.8	15.8	27.4	4.9
n	10,705	10,705	10,705	10,705

Notes: Sample = All MCS 3 main respondents with interviews at MCS 2 and MCS 1.

Analysis restricted to respondents in all three MCS surveys who gave income and subjective poverty data in all three MCS 3 surveys.

Table 2.11: Movements into and out of poverty between MCS 1 and MCS 3 (%)

	Poor in both waves	Left poverty	Moved into poverty	Not poor in either wave	Total % (n)
Income poverty	19.3	9.6	9.7	61.4	100.0 (12,951)
Subjective poverty	22.4	14.9	15.3	47.3	100.0 (13,968)
Poor on one measure	35.3	13.5	13.4	37.8	100.0 (12,889)
Poor on two measures	8.8	8.6	9.2	73.4	100.0 (12,889)

Notes: Sample = All MCS 3 main respondents with valid data at both MCS 3 and MCS 1.
Weighted percentages (by MCS 2 overall weight); (unweighted numbers).

Table 2.12: Multivariate regression of the odds of staying, leaving and moving into poverty

Independent variables	(1) Consistently reliably poor across MCS 1, MCS 2 and MCS 3	(2) Moved out of poverty relative to stayed poor between MCS 1 and MCS 3	(3) Moved into poverty relative to stayed out of poverty between sweeps MCS 1 and MCS 3
Number of children in family at MCS 1			
1	1.00	1.00	1.00
2	1.39**	0.97	0.99
3	1.98**	0.76	1.28**
4+	2.10**	0.61**	1.96**
Family type and earners at MCS 1			
Married natural parents – 2 earners	1.00	1.00	1.00
Married natural parents – 1 earner	6.17**	0.72	2.25**
Married natural parents – 0 earners	25.23**	0.37**	4.01**
Cohabiting natural parents – 2 earners	1.82	1.13	2.09**
Cohabiting natural parents – 1 earner	7.43**	0.70	3.19**
Cohabiting natural parents – 0 earners	33.52**	0.45**	5.46**
Natural mother & stepfather – 2 earners	Cases	Cases	Cases
Natural mother & stepfather – 1 earner	11.96**	Cases	3.44**
Natural mother & stepfather – 0 earners	45.37**	0.33	7.64**
Lone natural mother – 1 earner	17.71**	0.69	2.90**
Lone natural mother – 0 earners	34.65**	0.41**	5.48**
Mother's age at birth			
35+	1.00	1.00	1.00
30-34	1.03	Cases	1.17
25-29	0.93	1.12	1.32**
20-24	0.77	1.17	1.90**
Under 20	0.81	1.09	1.72**
Mother's ethnicity			
White	1.00	1.00	1.00
Mixed	0.56	0.90	1.81
Indian	1.66	0.62	1.18
Pakistani and Bangladeshi	3.83**	0.56**	2.54**
Black or Black British	0.82	1.04	1.86**
Other ethnic groups	2.21	0.63	2.51**
Mother's highest qualification at MCS 1 [a]			
NVQ Level 5	1.00	1.00	1.00
NVQ Level 4	1.23	0.77	2.28
NVQ Level 3	2.20	0.57	3.75**
NVQ Level 2	2.81	0.41	8.48**
NVQ Level 1	2.84	0.40	6.42**
No recognised qualifications	3.20	0.39	7.97**
Housing tenure at MCS 1			
Owner-occupier	1.00	1.00	1.00
Social housing	3.76**	0.49**	2.49**
Private rented/other	2.25**	0.66**	1.74**
Sample size	9,809[b]	2,331[c]	10,158[d]

Notes: [a] Those with only overseas qualifications are classed as missing as we have no means of identifying or ranking these qualifications. [b] Sample = all cases with valid data present at MCS 1, MCS 2 and MCS 3. [c] Sample = all cases with valid data present at MCS 1 and MCS 3 who were poor on two dimensions at MCS 1. [d] Sample = all cases with valid data present at MCS 1 and MCS 3 who were not poor on two dimensions at MCS 1.
Cases = insufficient sample size. Significance ** $p < 0.05$

the three surveys in column (3). Significant characteristics predicting persistently being in poverty or making transitions were as follows:

- lone parents all had higher odds of staying in poverty and moving into poverty than married parents;
- larger families (two or more children) had higher odds of staying in poverty. Families with three or more children had higher odds of moving into poverty. Families with four or more children had lower odds of moving out of poverty;
- cohabiting parents were more likely to remain in poverty than married parents (unless both were earning) and were also more likely to move into poverty, regardless of whether or not they were earners;
- stepfamilies with one earner were more likely to stay in or move into poverty;
- families with no earners at MCS 1 were more likely to remain in poverty, were less likely to move out of poverty and were more likely to move into poverty than those with two earners;
- families with one earner at MCS 1 were more likely to be poor in all three MCS surveys and to move into poverty at MCS 3;
- younger mothers were more likely to move into poverty than those who were over 30 at the cohort birth, although after controls for other factors there was no significant difference between age groups in staying poor or moving out of poverty;
- families where the mother was of Pakistani and Bangladeshi ethnicity were more likely to remain in poverty in all three MCS surveys and also were more likely to move into poverty (as were mixed and other ethnic groups) than families where the mother was of white ethnicity;
- mothers whose highest qualification was NVQ Level 3 or lower were more likely to move into poverty than mothers with higher qualifications;
- families who were renting their home, either as social housing or as private renters, were more likely to remain in poverty and to move into poverty, and were less likely to leave poverty than those in other housing tenures.

In Table 2.13 we observe changes in employment and marital status and their association with changes in poverty between the MCS 1 and MCS 3 surveys. From MCS 1 to MCS 3 the most common single occasion for moving out of poverty was entering employment: 29% of those who moved out of poverty did so as one or both parents entered employment and another 10% went from being a household with one earner to a household with two earners. Forming partnerships, in the case of lone parents, was also a way out of poverty over this period; 18% of those who moved out of poverty did so in this way, nearly half of who formed a cohabiting relationship. Of course moves out of poverty were commonly associated with changes in partnerships and in the number of earners. Thus, of those who moved out of poverty by having an increase in the number of earners, 44% of them also moved from lone parent status to couple status. And 83% of the lone parents who moved out of poverty as a result of increasing the

Table 2.13: Changes in employment and marital status by changes in poverty status,[a] MCS 1 to MCS 3

	Remained out of poverty	Moved into poverty	Moved out of poverty	Remained in poverty	Total
Change in marital status from MCS 1 to MCS 3					
No change	82.0	58.7	65.0	71.5	77.5
Married natural parents to lone parent	3.6	11.0	3.0	4.7	4.3
Cohabiting parents to married parents	5.8	3.9	3.7	1.8	5.1
Lone parent to married parents	0.5	0.8	4.2	1.7	0.9
Lone parent to cohabiting parents	1.1	3.0	7.3	2.7	1.9
Lone parent to stepfamily	1.3	2.9	6.2	5.0	2.2
Cohabiting to lone parent	2.9	15.6	5.4	10.0	4.9
Stepfamily to lone parent	0.0	0.2	0.0	0.4	0.1
Total %	100.0	100.0	100.0	100.0	100.0
n	9,136	1,247	1,187	1,253	12,283
Change in family employment status from MCS 1 to MCS 3					
No change	63.9	51.6	48.3	66.1	61.6
0 workers to 1	2.0	6.6	20.2	12.2	4.9
0 workers to 2	0.7	0.4	8.5	1.6	1.4
1 worker to 2	13.9	3.8	10.3	3.3	11.7
1 worker to 0	3.7	20.9	7.6	14.6	6.6
2 workers to 1	14.7	10.5	4.3	1.2	12.3
2 workers to 0	1.1	6.3	0.7	1.0	1.5
Total %	100.0	100.0	100.0	100.0	100.0
n	9,159	1,248	1,198	1,273	12,878

Notes: Sample = All cases with valid data present at MCS 1 and MCS 3.

[a] Poverty defined as poor on both income and subjective criteria (see last column of Table 2.10).

number of earners also moved into couple households, although not necessarily into employment themselves. Transitions between employment and partnership states are also displayed later, in Chapter 6 of this volume.

The most common single association with moving into poverty between MCS 1 and MCS 3 was becoming a workless family: 27% of those who moved into poverty were families who became workless and another 11% lost one earner (out of two). The other main change associated with moving into poverty was having a relationship breakdown: 27% of those moving into poverty did so on becoming a lone parent, and over half of these, 16%, were breakdowns of cohabiting partnerships. However, changes in employment and family status go together. Two thirds of those who became workless between the surveys had become lone parents and 82% of those who had become lone parents had also become workless.

Moving into employment is not a guarantee of moving out of poverty: 17% of those who remained in poverty did so despite one or two parents becoming employed, and 11% of those who moved into poverty had one or two parents becoming employed. Partnering or re-partnering is also not a guarantee of moving out of poverty: 7% of those who remained in poverty and 3% of those who moved into poverty had re-partnered.

Conclusions

This chapter summarises the results of an analysis of poverty in MCS 3 when the cohort child was about 5 years old. Child poverty rates were produced using several different measures: income poverty, material deprivation, subjective poverty and benefit receipt. Around 30% of the MCS families when the child was aged 5 were in income poverty, but nearly 38% were 'reliably poor' in the sense that they were poor on three or more of four poverty dimensions. We also identified 28% of MCS families poor at age 5 using our latent classification, with a further 16% showing some level of hardship on latent income or subjective classifications of poverty. The odds of being poor on the various definitions show broadly similar patterns of association with social and demographic covariates, such as mother's education, ethnicity and housing, but above all, with the structure of the family and the number of adult earners. The latter are more closely related to income poverty than to subjective poverty.

Changes in poverty over the MCS surveys and the factors associated with changes between MCS 1 and 3, in particular, display the impacts of employment and family change. There is relatively more change in the number of earners in a family than the number of partners. The movement of mothers into and out of paid work, described later in Chapter 6 in this volume, helps to generate a good deal of the rotation among the families in poverty. While the extent of poverty on each of the various definitions stayed at around the same level, on average, over the cohort's first five years, there was considerable turnover among the families who experienced it. Alongside a 'core' group in persistent poverty, a much wider group reported at least one type of poverty at any one of the MCS surveys: more than half of all families and around twice the proportion of families in income poverty at any one time. A similar finding was seen in the LCA for MCS 3 where only 40% of families were classed as not poor. The dynamics as well as the dimensions of child poverty should be borne in mind when looking at its consequences, as is done in Chapter 14 later in this volume.

Notes

[1] Although measures have been announced that should lead to a further reduction.

[2] See Ward et al (2007) and Ketende and Joshi (2008) for details on the limits to comparability between the MCS and Family Resources Survey (FRS) as sources.

[3] The MCS deprivation questions have been changed in each MCS survey but they still do not match the deprivation questions now being used in the FRS to create the new combined deprivation and income measure that has been incorporated into the Households Below Average Income (HBAI) series (equivalent income

less than 70% of the median with a prevalence weighted deprivation score of less than 25).

[4] These exclusions apply to relatively few families for whom the analysis would be more complicated.

[5] Note that the sampling errors around these estimates mean that a constant level of income poverty across the surveys cannot be ruled out (Ketende and Joshi, 2008, Table 10.9).

[6] On near comparable items, MCS 2 suggests slightly less deprivation than at MCS 3. In MCS 2, 0.5% of the respondents lacked a warm waterproof coat for the 3-year-old child, 0.9% lacked new properly fitted shoes for the child, 26% did not go on a holiday once a year not staying with relatives and 19% lacked a small amount to spend on themselves weekly.

[7] The large odds ratios seen for lone natural mothers with no earners should be treated as 'infinite maximum likelihood estimates' and should therefore not be regarded as accurately estimated parameters. However, it has been noted that this is not necessarily problematic and indicates a near-perfect predictor as might be expected in this instance (see Rindskopf, 2002).

[8] Unfortunately it was not possible at the time of writing to include mother's age at first birth, which might be a better indicator.

[9] In MCS 1 and 2 we included families receiving Working Families' Tax Credit (WFTC) if they were also receiving Housing Benefit or CTB. By MCS 3 WTC and Child Tax Credit (CTC) had been introduced and so we included families receiving WTC. So these are not comparable over time.

Appendix

Table A2.1: Bivariate logistic regression of the family being poor at MCS 3

	Income <60%	Deprivation	Benefit	Subjective	Reliably poor (2 or more)	LC poor/Not poor
Number of adults in household	n = 13,192	n = 13,178	n = 13,174	n = 13,177	n = 13,158	n = 13,158
1	1.00	1.00	1.00	1.00	1.00	1.00
2	0.11**	0.20**	0.06**	0.31**	0.08**	0.09**
3	0.23**	0.29**	0.10**	0.40**	0.16**	0.16**
4+	0.41**	0.36**	0.11**	0.51**	0.21**	0.21**
Number of children in household	n = 13,227	n = 13,178	n = 13,174	n = 13,177	n = 13,158	n = 13,158
1	1.00	1.00	1.00	1.00	1.00	1.00
2	0.71**	0.74**	0.50**	0.75**	0.62**	0.89**
3	1.31**	1.00 NS	0.74**	0.84**	1.00 NS	0.88 NS
4+	3.35**	1.77**	1.59**	1.18 NS	2.39**	1.99**
Family type	n = 13,197	n = 13,175	n = 13,171	n = 13,174	n = 13,155	n = 13,155
Married natural parents	1.00	1.00	1.00	1.00	1.00	1.00
Cohabiting natural parents	2.12**	2.29**	3.86**	1.25**	2.43**	3.49**
Natural mother and stepfather	4.06**	3.17**	7.20**	2.21**	4.62**	5.45**
Lone natural mother	12.06**	6.19**	34.43**	3.75**	16.37**	22.01**
Mother's age at birth	n = 13,226	n = 13,177	n = 13,173	n = 13,176	n = 13,157	n = 13,157
35+	1.00	1.00	1.00	1.00	1.00	1.00
30-34	1.02 NS	0.94 NS	1.01 NS	0.81**	0.94 NS	1.06 NS
25-30	1.69**	1.47**	1.82**	0.94 NS	1.59**	1.46**
20-24	4.42**	2.86**	4.83**	1.51**	4.08**	4.02**
Under 20	8.73**	4.74**	10.84**	1.83**	8.61**	8.03**

(continued)

Table A2.1: Bivariate logistic regression of the family being poor at MCS3 (continued)

	Income <60%	Deprivation	Benefit	Subjective	Reliably poor (2 or more)	LC poor/Not poor
Mother's ethnicity	n = 13,220	n = 13,173	n = 13,169	n = 13,172	n = 13,153	n = 13,153
White	1.00	1.00	1.00	1.00	1.00	1.00
Mixed	3.26**	2.67**	4.17**	2.18**	3.32**	4.21**
Indian	1.17 NS	0.80 NS	0.32**	1.04 NS	0.89 NS	0.52**
Pakistani and Bangladeshi	8.07**	2.53**	1.58**	1.84**	4.13**	2.16**
Black or Black British	2.90**	2.96**	2.52**	2.82**	3.25**	3.01**
Other ethnic groups	1.52**	1.51**	1.23 NS	2.02**	1.51**	1.41 NS
Number of parent earners in family	n = 13,212	n = 13,169	n = 13,165	n = 13,168	n = 13,149	n = 13,149
2	1.00	1.00	1.00	1.00	1.00	1.00
1	5.56**	2.31**	16.75**	1.93**	5.02**	14.02**
0	72.73**	9.99**	334.0**	5.53**	67.88**	271.9**
Mother's highest qualification[1]	n = 13,841	n = 12,793	n = 12,787	n = 12,792	n = 12,778	n = 12,778
NVQ Level 5	1.00	1.00	1.00	1.00	1.00	1.00
NVQ Level 4	0.93 NS	1.08 NS	0.95 NS	1.12 NS	1.06 NS	0.83 NS
NVQ Level 3	2.62**	2.09**	2.82**	1.69**	2.40**	2.43**
NVQ Level 2	4.14**	2.91**	4.52**	1.97**	3.93**	4.66**
NVQ Level 1	7.90**	4.44**	9.05**	2.09**	7.56**	8.11**
No recognised qualifications	18.66**	7.23**	15.56**	3.49**	14.59**	16.52**
Housing tenure	n = 13,174	n = 13,173	n = 13,168	n = 13,170	n = 13,153	n = 13,153
Owner-occupier	1.00	1.00	1.00	1.00	1.00	1.00
Social housing	14.98**	7.01**	45.46**	3.93**	18.44**	30.86**
Private rented/other	6.91**	3.51**	19.86**	2.75**	7.75**	14.39**

Notes: [a] Those with only overseas qualifications are classed as missing as we have no means of identifying or ranking these qualifications.
Significance ** *p* <0.05. NS = not significant.

THREE

Ethnicity, community and social capital

Alice Sullivan

Introduction

This chapter focuses on indicators of social capital in the lives of the mothers of the Millennium Cohort Study (MCS) children. The mothers' social networks, social support and experiences of their local areas will be relevant to their children as they grow up. The concept of social capital has been influential in policy circles, but is contested, and has been used for varying purposes by social theorists. For Coleman, social capital refers to 'the set of resources that inhere in family relations and in community social organisation and that are useful for the cognitive or social development of a child or young person' (Coleman, 1994, p 300). Social capital in the family consists of the time and attention given to the child by family members, while social capital within the school and the community consists of social networks that allow social norms to be established and enforced (Coleman, 1988). For Putnam, social capital describes 'features of social organisation, such as trust, norms and networks' (Putnam, 1993, p 167). Putnam is particularly concerned with a perceived decline in sociability, associational life and political participation. He uses a wide range of measures of social capital, including measures of community organisational life, engagement in public affairs, community voluntarism, informal sociability and social trust (Schuller et al, 2000). As such, he has been criticised for overstretching the concept of social capital (Portes, 1998).

Social capital has been seen as particularly important for minority ethnic groups, because economic disadvantages, and even a lack of education, may be counterbalanced by high levels of social capital within the home and community (Lauglo, 2000). It may be possible, therefore, for minority ethnic communities who are economically disadvantaged still to promote high educational aspirations and educational success within their community (Gibson, 2000; Portes and Rumbaut, 2001). Conversely, the ability of strongly bonded social groups to enforce social norms can have negative consequences if anti-achievement norms prevail within such groups. Portes and Rumbaut put forward a model of 'segmented assimilation', suggesting that assimilation of immigrant groups into the norms of the native community is not always positive. Strong minority ethnic communities and families can act together to protect children against 'downward assimilation' into the under-class norms of gangs, crime, teen pregnancy and resistance or indifference to schooling. Some South Asian communities, in particular, are often perceived as maintaining norms of parental authority, and of good behaviour and discipline (Portes and Rumbaut, 2001). The gendered nature of such norms has been noted. In contrast to individuals from other ethnic groups, there have tended to be more Pakistani and Bangladeshi men than women in higher education in Britain (Bhattacharyya et al, 2003; Dwyer et al, 2006).

Putnam draws a distinction between bonding and bridging social capital. Bonding social capital implies strong ties within a group, while bridging social capital implies weak ties between heterogeneous groups. Bonding and bridging social capital can be seen as conflicting, since strongly bonded groups may have fewer links to the wider society. Wider social networks may be particularly important in gaining access to information and resources, such as labour market opportunities (Granovetter, 1973). Thus, a lack of 'bridging' ties to other ethnic groups may reinforce labour market disadvantage among minority ethnic groups.

Spatial and social patterns of segregation are linked (Peach, 2006). Concerns regarding the ethnic segregation of neighbourhoods and schools may reflect a liberal concern to promote tolerance and to remove barriers to social inclusion, but recently the issue has been presented in terms of immigrant groups' failure to integrate. Since 9/11 and the London tube bombings in July 2005, this anxiety has focused on Muslims. Following the 2001 so-called race riots in Oldham, Burnley and Bradford, concerns were raised (notably by Trevor Phillips, now Chair of the Equality and Human Rights Commission) that residential ethnic segregation was increasing in Britain, and that this was leading to a deeply divided society. However, researchers have challenged this view. Peach (cited in Norris, 2005) pointed out that segregation was actually declining across the country as a whole, while Simpson (2007) suggested that increasing segregation was a myth. It was argued that Britain should not be characterised as having US-style ghettoes, even though Pakistani and Bangladeshi populations show quite high rates of 'encapsulation' (that is, residential isolation from other ethnic groups) (Peach, 1996). It is recognised that minority ethnic groups may have positive reasons for clustering together, such as benefiting from social support. Family and friendship ties within neighbourhoods can be seen as indicators of social capital, which may lead to greater feelings of trust and safety. It has also been suggested that women rely more on local social networks than men, because of their multiple roles as mothers and workers. The social networks of mothers are often centred on their children (McCulloch, 2003). However, negative push factors, such as economic necessity and racial discrimination, may also contribute to minority ethnic groups being spatially concentrated.

This chapter examines a number of indicators of social capital that were available in the MCS data at age 5. These measures cover aspects of families' social ties and trust within the neighbourhood; experiences of racism, which can be argued to indicate both economic and social exclusion from the majority group; and parents' attitudes towards mixed-ethnic education. The idea that children should mix with those from different social groups is very pervasive in the schooling system in

Britain and an ideal underpinning comprehensive education. Ethnically mixed schools can be seen as a potentially important source of 'bridging' social capital, allowing young people to form connections across groups.

This chapter examines the links between ethnicity, nationality and religion, and then considers the ethnic composition of the areas in which MCS families lived at the age 5 interview using 2001 Census data, followed by mothers' perceptions of that area and the extent of their family and friendships in these local areas. Experiences of racism and attitudes towards schooling are then examined.

Ethnicity, nationality, language and religion

Because ethnicity is bound up with nationality, religion and language, it is important to consider the intersection between these variables. An eight-category breakdown of ethnicity was used. Although this sometimes led to small cell sizes, the alternative was less satisfactory; that is, to group together ethnic categories with very different migration histories and cultures. Nevertheless, we could not avoid a residual 'Other' category, including Chinese, and other groups with very small numbers.[1] Eighty per cent of black Caribbean mothers were born in the UK, compared to 27% of black African mothers (see Table 3.1). Bangladeshi mothers were the least likely to be born in the UK (9%), substantially less than Pakistani (41%) and Indian mothers (49%). This reflects the dates of the main migration streams into the UK, and also the practice of transnational marriage by the South Asian groups. Ninety per cent of Bangladeshi mothers and 72% of Pakistani mothers had partners who were not UK born.

Nearly all white MCS mothers (98%) spoke entirely in English, followed closely by black Caribbean mothers (95%) (see Table 3.2). Black African mothers were substantially less likely to use English exclusively (41%). Of the Asian mothers,

Table 3.1: Country of birth and mother's ethnicity

Country of birth				Mother's ethnic group					
	White	Mixed	Indian	Pakistani	Bangladeshi	Black Caribbean	Black African	Other	Total
UK born	95.5	69.7	48.6	40.5	8.5	80.0	27.3	2.0	90.6
Not UK born	4.5	30.3	51.4	59.5	91.5	20.0	72.7	80.0	9.4
Total %	100	100	100	100	100	100	100	100	100
Unweighted observation	11,552	111	328	535	204	154	237	222	13,343

F = 451.04, P>F = 0.000

Notes: Sample = all MCS 3 mothers (natural, adoptive, foster and step) who completed the main interview and for whom ethnicity was classified. This and other tables in this chapter exclude any mothers who were eligible but not interviewed, any fathers or grandparents who completed the main interview and cases without valid data on variables of interest. Percentages are weighted.

Table 3.2: English spoken within the home

English spoken	Mother's ethnic group								
	White	Mixed	Indian	Pakis-tani	Bangla-deshi	Black Caribbean	Black African	Other	Total
Entirely	97.7	77.8	30	13.9	(6.1)	94.8	41.3	38.7	91.9
Mostly	1.3	(13.5)	31.4	25.3	13.7	(4.5)	28	17.1	3.2
Half and half	0.6	(2.2)	23.3	34.2	36.8	(0)	17.3	18.3	2.6
Mostly other language	0.4	(5.5)	14.4	24.7	41.5	(0.7)	11.5	21.0	2.0
No English	(0.1)	(1.1)	(0.9)	(1.9)	(1.9)	(0)	(1.9)	(5.0)	0.3
Total	12,685	138	366	619	244	189	301	252	14,794

F = 256.68, P>F = 0.000

Notes: Sample: see Table 3.1. Table displays unweighted observations and weighted percentages (using *weight2* for All UK). Small cells (<30) in parentheses.

Indians (30%) were most likely to speak entirely in English, followed by Pakistani (14%) and Bangladeshi (6%) mothers. Forty-three per cent of Bangladeshi mothers spoke either mostly or exclusively in a language other than English. To the extent that this reflects a lack of English fluency, it may well restrict their interactions with the wider society, including their children's schools. It is also crucial to note that these mothers are relatively likely to have no educational qualifications: 44% of Pakistani and 41% of Bangladeshi mothers had no qualifications, compared to 8% of white and 10% of black Caribbean mothers.

Religion is strongly tied up with ethnicity, as shown in Table 3.3. White mothers were by far the most likely to report that they had no religion (43%), with the majority of the remainder divided between Protestants (35%), Catholics (12%), and Christians who did not specify a denomination, or whose denomination was categorised as 'Other' (10%). Black African and black Caribbean mothers were the most likely to identify themselves as Christian without specifying a denomination, or specifying a denomination outside the categories provided (39% and 36% respectively). There was also a substantial Muslim minority (26%) among the black African mothers. The Pakistani and Bangladeshi mothers were almost exclusively Muslim, whereas Indian mothers were more diverse, being mainly divided between Hinduism (41%), Sikhism (35%) and Muslim (13%).

Many of the mothers who indicated they had a religious attachment did not attend religious services; overall half of all such mothers said they rarely or never attended services (see Figure 3.1). Weekly religious attendance was most common among 'Other' (38%), Sikh (32%) and Catholic mothers (31%), whereas only 13% of Protestant mothers attended weekly religious services, and 61% did so rarely or never. Muslim women were the most likely to attend religious services rarely or never (65%). In contrast, Muslim partners were substantially more likely than partners from other religious groups to attend services weekly (57% compared

Table 3.3: Mother's religion and ethnicity

| Religion | Mother's ethnic group | | | | | | | | |
	White	Mixed	Indian	Pakis-tani	Bangla-deshi	Black Caribbean	Black African	Other	Total
None	42.5	34.2	(6.4)	(0.6)	(0.2)	16.4	(3.4)	20.7	39.3
Protestant	34.6	(14)	(0.8)	(0)	(0)	23.8	(16.2)	6.2	31.9
Catholic	12.1	(16.2)	(2.2)	(0)	(0)	19.6	14.1	13.0	11.7
Christian (denomination unspecified or other)	10.0	(15.8)	(0.4)	(0)	(0.5)	35.7	39.4	8.0	10.2
Hindu	(0)	(3.8)	40.7	(0.7)	(3)	(0)	(0)	18.9	1.1
Jew	0.3	(0)	(0.3)	(0.3)	(0.3)	(0)	(0.3)	(0)	0.3
Muslim	0.3	11.6	13.2	98.4	96.0	(3.5)	26.1	26.0	4.5
Sikh	(0)	(1.8)	35.1	(0)	(0)	(0)	(0)	(1.7)	0.7
Buddhist	(0.1)	(2.3)	(0)	(0)	(0)	(0)	(0)	(5.5)	(0.2)
Other	(0.2)	(0.3)	(1.1)	(0)	(0)	(1)	(0.5)	(0)	0.2
Total %	100	100	100	100	100	100	100	100	100
Unweighted *n*	12,686	138	366	619	244	189	301	252	14,795

F = 201.30, P>F = 0.000

Note: Sample: see Table 3.1.

Figure 3.1: Religious participation of MCS 3 mothers

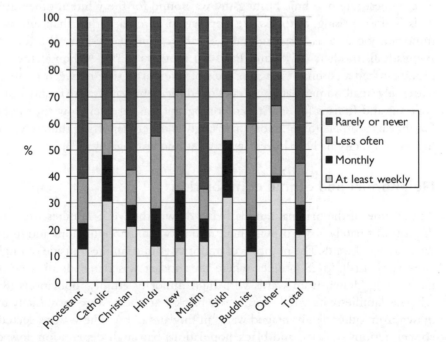

Note: Sample: all MCS 3 mothers with religious affiliation

to 20% of Catholic partners). Islam traditionally encourages women to remain within the home, and not to attend the mosque, and many British mosques still do not permit entry to women. This implies that religious attendance is likely to be a poor measure of religiosity for Muslim women. To the extent that mosques form focal points for Muslim communities, exclusion from the mosque may contribute to social exclusion for women.

Family and partnerships

Family structures vary considerably between ethnic groups. We classify mothers as lone parents if they do not have a partner living with them. Half of the black Caribbean mothers and 40% of the black African mothers were lone parents. The Bangladeshi (93%), Indian (90%) and Pakistani (86%) mothers were most likely to be married. White mothers were the most likely to be cohabiting (18%). The number of children in the household (including stepchildren) also varied considerably by ethnic group. Around two thirds of Bangladeshi and Pakistani respondents had three or more children, compared to around a third of white mothers. This overlaps with the low levels of labour market participation among Bangladeshi and Pakistani mothers (see also Table 6.1 in Chapter 6 of this volume). The prevalence of extended rather than nuclear family units also varied by ethnic group. Indian (24%), Bangladeshi (15%) and Pakistani (16%) mothers were all more likely to live with a grandparent than white mothers (2%).

Ethnic groups vary in the extent to which they partner within the same group. The highest rate of ethnic homogamy was found for the white mothers (98%). This is unsurprising, as the white population is much larger than any of the minority populations. Very high rates of ethnic homogamy were also found for Bangladeshi mothers (95%) and Pakistani mothers (93%). Although these two groups shared a common religion, rates of interpartnering between them were extremely small. Somewhat lower rates of ethnic homogamy were found for black Africans and Indians (85%). Ethnic homogamy was relatively low for the black Caribbean mothers (57%). Not surprisingly, mothers reporting themselves as of 'mixed' ethnicity had the lowest levels of ethnic homogamy (8%).

Neighbourhood ethnic composition

At the time of the original sample being drawn, the MCS families were living disproportionately in wards with high minority ethnic populations and in other disadvantaged wards. The numbers of minority ethnic families outside of England were very small. MCS families where the mother was Bangladeshi were most likely to be drawn from wards with high minority ethnic populations (85%), whereas families where the mother was black Caribbean were most likely to be drawn from other disadvantaged wards in England (34%). The wards selected for concentrations of Asian and black populations had high deprivation, low out-mobility and poorly rated conditions (see Chapter 7 later in this volume).

The MCS data provide us with a number of ways of looking at the characteristics of the neighbourhoods in which the MCS families live, and the social networks and experiences of the respondents. As a very simple measure of ethnic residential segregation at MCS 3, Table 3.4 shows the average proportion of people living in the ward of the MCS mother who were from the same ethnic group as the mother (this information is derived from 2001 Census data).[2]

Table 3.4: Ethnic composition of wards families were resident in at MCS 3, based on ethnic composition at 2001 Census

Mother's ethnicity	% of ward residents with same ethnicity as mother	95% Confidence Interval		% of ward residents who are white	95% Confidence Interval		Observation
White	95.5	94.8	96.2	95.5	94.8	96.2	12 686
Mixed	2.2	1.7	2.6	83.4	79.4	87.5	138
Indian	15.0	9.4	20.5	69.5	63.6	76.4	366
Pakistani	20.8	12.1	29.6	62.0	52.0	72.0	619
Bangladeshi	13.4	5.2	21.7	50.6	19.7	67.5	244
Black Caribbean	7.7	5.1	10.4	66.9	61.6	72.3	189
Black African	8.5	6.0	11.0	65.7	61.3	70.1	301
Other	4.3	3.4	5.2	76.6	71.4	81.8	252

Total Observation =14,795

Note: Sample: see Table 3.1.

White mothers lived in electoral wards where, on average, 96% of the other residents were white. In contrast, the average proportion of residents of the same ethnic group was less than a quarter for parents in each of the other ethnic groups. Pakistani (21%), Indian (15%) and Bangladeshi (13%) mothers lived in areas with a higher average proportion from their own ethnic group than black Caribbean (8%) and black African mothers (9%). Mothers from all ethnic groups lived in areas where, on average, the majority of the residents were white.

Neighbourhood ties and trust

At MCS 3 mothers were asked four questions about the neighbourhood they lived in which indicated something about their social ties and levels of trust. Of course, the area the mothers thought of as their neighbourhood would not necessarily correspond to the boundaries of the electoral ward they were located in:

- Is this a good area for raising children?
- How safe do you feel in the area?

• Are you friends with other parents in the area?
• Do you have other friends and family in the area?

Responses to the question regarding whether they thought they lived in a good area for raising children varied substantially by mother's ethnic group (see Figure 3.2). White mothers were most likely to believe that their area was excellent for bringing up children (35%), followed by Indian mothers (30%). Mothers from other ethnic groups were considerably less likely than white and Indian mothers to consider their area to be either excellent or very good for bringing up children.

When asked how safe they felt in their area, responses varied by ethnicity, with black Caribbean, mixed and black African mothers being substantially less likely than other groups to feel very safe (see Figure 3.3). (See also Chapter 7, this volume, for other characteristics of respondents giving adverse ratings to their MCS 3 neighbourhood.)

When asked about their social networks of friends and family in the local area, 90% of white mothers said they were friends with other local parents; the figure was lower for other ethnic groups. Black African mothers were the least likely to be friends with local parents (see Table 3.5).

Figure 3.2: Mothers' views about whether their area was good for raising children at MCS 3, by mother's ethnicity

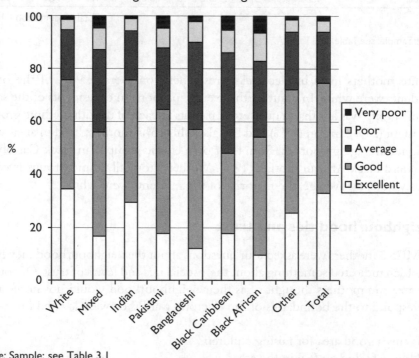

Note: Sample: see Table 3.1

Figure 3.3: Mothers' views about the safety of their area at MCS 3, by mother's ethnicity

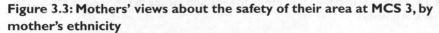

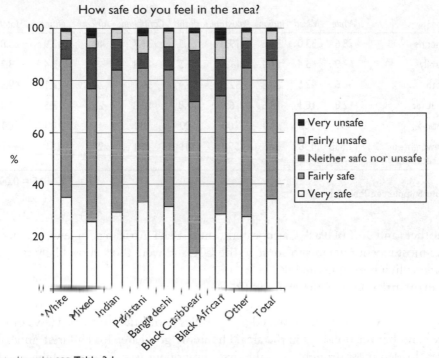

Note: Sample: see Table 3.1.

Table 3.5: Whether mothers were friends with other parents in the area at MCS 3, by mother's ethnicity

	White	Mixed	Indian	Pakis-tani	Bangla-deshi	Black Caribbean	Black African	Other	Total
Yes	90.2	79.5	81.8	85.3	86.4	84.2	73.6	78.9	89.4
No	9.8	20.5	18.2	14.7	13.6	15.8	26.4	21.1	10.6
Total %	100	100	100	100	100	100	100	100	100
Unweighted observation	12,637	138	366	598	241	188	295	251	14,714

$F = 7.32, P>F = 0.000$

Note: Sample: see Table 3.1.

A follow-up question asked whether the mothers had other friends and family in the area (see Table 3.6). The extent and type of these social ties varied greatly according to ethnicity. Bangladeshi (56%) and Pakistani (53%) mothers were the most likely to have both friends and family in the local community. This may show the positive side of residential concentration. Just over half of white mothers had both friends and family nearby, compared to only a quarter of black African

Table 3.6: Whether mothers had other friends and family in the area at MCS 3, by mother's ethnicity

	White	Mixed	Indian	Pakistani	Bangla-deshi	Black Caribbean	Black African	Other	Total
Friends	28.6	33.0	31.2	19.0	21.5	33.7	40.6	42.9	28.8
Family	7.9	5.4	11.4	11.5	12.3	11.3	9.2	12.4	8.2
Both	50.6	43.5	38.8	52.6	56.4	36.1	24.5	27.1	49.6
Neither	12.8	18.1	18.6	16.9	9.8	18.8	25.6	17.5	13.4
Total %	100	100	100	100	100	100	100	100	100
Unweighted observation	12,638	138	366	598	241	188	295	251	14,715

$F = 7.32, P>F = 0.000$

Note: Sample: see Table 3.1.

mothers and 36% of black Caribbean mothers. Black African people were among the most recent migrants to come to the UK, and were those most likely to have parents living outside the UK.

Principal components analysis (PCA) is a technique that can be used to combine several variables into a single factor reflecting neighbourhood social capital. PCA used the four preceding variables about the mothers' views of the area and her relationships in the area. The items 'good area for children' and 'safe area' loaded most strongly onto the first component (see Appendix Table A3.1). This PCA social capital scale was then used as the dependent variable in a series of regression models. The results, showing only the ethnic group parameters, are displayed in Table 3.7.

Model 1 shows that all minorities scored lower than whites on this measure of neighbourhood social capital. Model 2 introduced equivalised (log) family income, family structure and mother's work status and educational level, as well as stratum, and whether the respondent had a religious affiliation as additional independent variables (see full results in Appendix Table A3.2). Higher levels of education and income were associated with higher neighbourhood social capital. Marriage and cohabitation were also positive, compared to single status, as was being employed compared with no employment. Compared to non-disadvantaged wards in England, wards of high minority ethnic populations and disadvantaged wards in England, Wales and Scotland were negatively associated with social capital. Non-disadvantaged wards in Scotland and Northern Ireland were positively associated with social capital. Once the other factors in Model 2 are controlled, the Indian, Pakistani and Bangladeshi coefficients became non-significant, but the mixed, black Caribbean, black African, and 'Other' coefficients remained significant and negative. Thus, when other social background characteristics are similar, black mothers still scored lower than white mothers in terms of the measure of neighbourhood social capital used here. Perhaps surprisingly, having a religious affiliation was not significant after controlling for mother's ethnicity.

Table 3.7: Neighbourhood social capital, linear regression results

Mother's ethnicity	Model 1			Model 2			Model 3		
	B	Sig	SE	B	Sig	SE	B	Sig	SE
Mixed	-0.68	**	0.16	-0.34	**	0.14	2.24	**	0.38
Indian	-0.27	**	0.10	-0.15		0.10	1.85	**	0.33
Pakistani	-0.40	**	0.09	0.17		0.10	2.19	**	0.32
Bangladeshi	-0.39	**	0.11	0.20		0.11	2.20	**	0.33
Black Caribbean	-0.84	**	0.13	-0.37	**	0.11	2.01	**	0.31
Black African	-1.00	**	0.14	-0.52	**	0.10	1.83	**	0.31
Other	-0.42	**	0.09	-0.19	**	0.09	1.95	**	0.33
R^2	0.0193	**		0.1566	**		0.1739	**	
Observations	14,699			14,693			14,682		

Notes: Sample: see Table 3.1. Significance: ** $p<0.05$

Model 1: ethnicity only

Model 2: controls added for education, marital status, employment status, income, stratum, religious affiliation

Model 3: controls added for percentage of white people in ward, interacted with ethnicity of respondent.

Turning to the question of the ethnic composition of the local area, model 3 introduced a variable reflecting the proportion of white people in the ward (this variable is derived from the census small area statistics). This variable was interacted with the ethnic group of the mother, as we cannot assume that the proportion of white people in the area has the same impact on all ethnic groups. The main effect of this variable was positive, indicating that a high proportion of white people in the area was associated with high neighbourhood social capital for white MCS mothers. However, a high proportion of white people in the area was also significantly associated with a reduction in the extent of neighbourhood social capital for mothers in all other ethnic groups. Once we control for the proportion of white people in the ward, and the interaction between this variable and the mother's own ethnicity, all the minority ethnic coefficients become significantly positive (see Appendix Table A3.2). This suggests that a high proportion of white people living in the ward was linked to reduced social capital among minority ethnic MCS mothers.

Experiences of racism

Mothers were asked at MCS 3, in a self-completion questionnaire, whether they had received verbal racist insults within the last 12 months, whether they thought they had received racist treatment from shop staff within the previous 12 months and how often they thought they had been treated unfairly because of their race or ethnicity. These questions were not asked of mothers of white-British, white-Irish, white-Welsh or white-Scottish ethnicity. The possible response codes were: 'never', 'once or twice', 'several times', 'many times' or 'can't say'. The most common response across all ethnic groups was that they had never experienced any racist insults or treatment (see Figure 3.4). Seventy-seven per cent of mothers reported no verbal racist insults in the previous 12 months compared to 89% of white mothers who were asked this question. A substantial minority of mothers from non-white groups reported racist treatment from shop staff. Black Caribbean (70%) and black African (68%) mothers were the least likely to report that they had experienced no unfair treatment because of their 'race'.

Table 3.8 shows the results from a logistic regression analysis, where the dependent variable is a binary variable, coded 1 if the mother indicated she had experienced any racist treatment, and zero for all other responses. A range of covariates was included in model 2 that captured a range of background factors. The full model results are shown in Appendix Table A3.3.

Figure 3.4: Mothers' experiences of racism at MCS 3, by mother's ethnicity

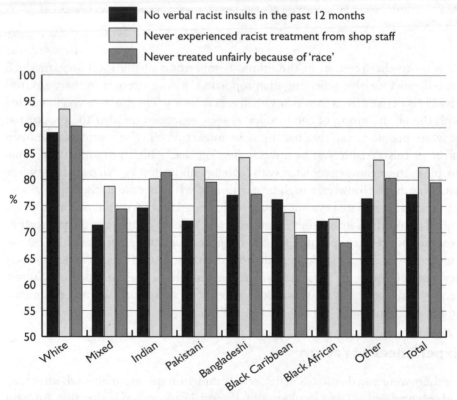

Notes: Sample = all MCS 3 mothers (natural, adoptive, foster and step) who completed the main interview and for whom ethnicity was classified. This figure excludes mothers identifying themselves as white British, white Irish, white Scots or white Welsh.

Table 3.8: Results of analysis of experience of racism from binary logistic regression

	Model 1			Model 2		
Mother's ethnicity	*Odds ratio*	*Sig*	*SE*	*Odds ratio*	*Sig*	*SE*
Mixed	3.30	**	0.92	0.12		0.17
Indian	2.43	**	0.56	0.48		0.39
Pakistani	2.35	**	0.47	0.34		0.28
Bangladeshi	2.01	**	0.60	0.29		0.31
Black Caribbean	3.69	**	0.86	0.23		0.22
Black African	4.29	**	0.81	0.14	**	0.12
Other	2.13	**	0.50	0.57		0.48
F	11.77	**		4.12	**	
Observations	1,796			1,792		

** $p<0.05$.

Notes: Model 1: ethnicity only. Model 2: controls added for education, marital status, employment status, income, stratum, religious affiliation, percentage of white people in ward interacted with ethnicity of respondent, neighbourhood social capital and religious affiliation.

Model 1 shows that black African and black Caribbean mothers were the most likely to report experiencing racism. In model 2 estimates allow for further controls (not shown in Table 3.8). These show that mothers with educational qualifications were more likely to report experiencing racism. Family income, partnership status and being in employment were not significant. Mothers living in disadvantaged wards in England were significantly more likely to report experiencing racism than mothers living in advantaged English wards. The proportion of white people resident in the ward was negatively associated with experiencing racism for white MCS mothers from outside the British Isles, but positively associated with experiencing racism for MCS mothers in other ethnic groups: that is, the higher the proportion of white people in the ward, the higher the chances of experiencing racism for MCS mothers from minority ethnic groups. This association was significant for the black African, black Caribbean, mixed and Pakistani groups of mothers. The proportion of white people resident in the ward appeared to drive the variability between ethnic groups in the chance of mothers reporting an experience of racism. Once this factor was controlled, the only significant minority ethnic parameter was a *lower* odds of experiencing racism for black African mothers, as shown in Table 3.8.

However, the measure of neighbourhood social capital was negatively linked to the chance of experiencing racism. The higher the neighbourhood social capital, the lower the chance of experiencing racism. Neighbourhood social capital appeared, therefore, to work as a protective factor. Religious affiliation was not significant.

Attitudes to ethnically integrated schooling

Mothers in Britain (excluding those in Northern Ireland, who were not asked this question) were asked whether they would mind their child attending a school where half the children were of another ethnicity (see Figure 3.5). Of course, we have to bear in mind that some mothers may have felt that saying they minded in answer to this question would be frowned upon, and this may have affected their responses. Overall, 25% of mothers strongly agreed and 30% agreed with the statement that that they would not mind their child attending a mixed-ethnic school. White mothers were least likely to agree (24% agreed strongly, 12% disagreed, 5% disagreed strongly). Mothers from minority ethnic groups were much more likely to agree that they would not mind; mixed (47%) and black African (43%) mothers were most likely of non-white mothers to agree strongly with this statement. In Northern Ireland, an equivalent question was asked regarding religion. Those with no religion were most likely (56%) to strongly agree that they would not mind their child attending a school where half the children were from a different religious background. Protestants and Catholics had similar levels of agreement, with 63% of Protestants and 65% of

Figure 3.5: Mother's attitudes towards cohort child attending a mixed-ethnic school at MCS 3, by mother's ethnicity

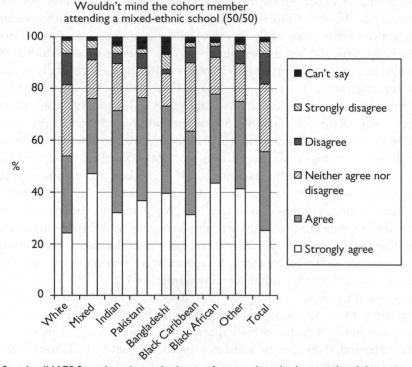

Note: Sample: all MCS 3 mothers (natural, adoptive, foster and step) who completed the main interview and for whom ethnicity was classified.

Catholics either agreeing or strongly agreeing with the statement that they would not mind their child attending a school where half the children were from a different religious background.

The correlates of agreeing with the statement that mothers did not mind their child attending an ethnically mixed school were examined through a multivariate logistic regression model. As well as ethnic dummies, other covariates included in the model captured background demographics as in previous regressions (see Appendix Table A3.4 for the full set of results).

Table 3.9 shows the results from the binary logistic regression analysis. The dependent variable is coded as 1 = agree or agree strongly that the mother would not mind the child going to a mixed-ethnic school, and 0 = any other response.

With the exception of black Caribbean mothers, all minority ethnic mothers were significantly more likely than white mothers to agree that they would not mind sending their child to an ethnically mixed school where their child would not be in the ethnic majority.

Mothers who had degrees were more likely to give a tolerant response regarding ethnically mixed schooling, but income was negatively linked to this response, as was being in work and being married. All of the ward-type 'strata' (neighbourhoods were classified into areas as part of the design of the survey) were positive compared to the non-disadvantaged English wards, but the coefficient for English wards with high minority ethnic populations was not statistically significant. Disadvantaged wards were more ethnically diverse than non-disadvantaged wards, which might have been expected to lead to more parental concern about ethnically

Table 3.9: Attitudes towards racially mixed schooling, logistic regression results

Mother's ethnicity	Model 1			Model 2		
	Odds ratio	Sig	SE	Odds ratio	Sig	SE
Mixed	2.71	**	0.63	2.44	**	0.58
Indian	2.12	**	0.33	2.48	**	0.45
Pakistani	2.72	**	0.38	2.46	**	0.40
Bangladeshi	2.30	**	0.52	2.24	**	0.57
Black Caribbean	1.48		0.43	1.23		0.39
Black African	2.99	**	0.55	2.67	**	0.55
Other	2.54	**	0.46	2.47	**	0.47
F	17.80	**		16.32	**	
Observations	12,522			12,517		

** $p < 0.05$.

Notes: Sample: all MCS 3 families living in England, Wales and Scotland.

Model 1: ethnicity only. Model 2: controls added for mother's education, marital status, religious affiliation, employment status, family income, and design stratum.

mixed schools. However, this is clearly not the case. It may be that this association between ethnic diversity and economic disadvantage is a factor that makes mothers from non-disadvantaged wards in England less positive about ethnically mixed schooling. Scotland and Wales have relatively small minority ethnic populations. This makes the question of their attitudes towards schools with 50% of children from another 'race' a purely hypothetical one for most white mothers from these countries. It may be easier to give a positive response where this is not a sensitive issue. Mothers with a religious affiliation were less likely to agree that they would not mind sending their child to a mixed school.

In an additional model, not shown here, the proportion of white people living in the area and the social capital scale were added to the regression. These variables were not significant predictors of the outcome variable, despite the significance of the ward-type strata.

Conclusions

Social capital has been linked to a whole range of social outcomes, including crime, education and health (Kawachi et al, 1999; Sampson et al, 1999; Halpern, 2005). Concerns have been raised that ethnic diversity is linked to lower levels of neighbourhood social capital, in terms of both social ties and trust (Putnam, 2007). This chapter has provided some evidence that the proportion of white people in the local ward is a negative predictor of some elements of neighbourhood social capital for minority ethnic mothers. The proportion of white people in the ward area was also linked to a higher chance of these MCS mothers stating they had experienced racism.

Mothers' expressions of willingness or unwillingness to send their child to a school where half of the children were from another ethnic group reflects attitudes towards diversity and integration. White mothers were the least likely to report that they would not mind their child attending a school where they were not part of an ethnic majority, although the majority of them would not mind. 'Contact theory' suggests that contact between different groups fosters trust, while 'conflict theory' suggests the opposite hypothesis, that proximity fosters distrust of out-groups (Putnam, 2007). The findings presented here regarding the effect of ethnic residential segregation on attitudes to mixed schooling are not entirely clear-cut. Mothers in non-disadvantaged wards in England were less likely to accept mixed-ethnic schooling than either mothers in disadvantaged wards (where mixed-ethnic schools are more common) or mothers in Scotland and Wales (which have small minority ethnic populations). Nevertheless, within strata (areas classified according to whether or not they are minority ethnic or disadvantaged wards) the proportion of white people living in the ward had no impact on this outcome, either for white MCS families or for MCS families from any of the minority ethnic groups. These findings do not seem to offer clear support for either contact or conflict theory.

The debate on ethnic residential segregation in Britain has focused on the supposed reluctance of certain groups to integrate. This chapter has sought to highlight some of the reasons that minority ethnic mothers may have for clustering in particular areas. Avoiding racism may be seen as a 'push factor', while social ties and trust within the neighbourhood can be seen as a 'pull factor'. From a policy perspective, the results presented here question the idea that ethnic residential clustering is an unequivocally 'bad thing'. Social capital has been seen as having both tremendous potential benefits and pitfalls for young people. On the one hand, informal networks among parents and other adults in the community are said to allow social norms regarding young people's behaviour to be enforced (Coleman, 1988). On the other hand, local social ties can be said to have negative consequences for education, social mobility and even mental health (O'Brien-Caughy et al, 2003).

As the MCS children grow older, we will be able to track the impacts of some of these forms of social capital on their lives. Future research questions could investigate: the impact of mothers' perception of neighbourhood safety on children's freedom of movement and health; the impact of mothers' social networks on mothers' and children's well-being; mothers' experiences of racism and children's well-being. Further down the line we will be able to examine issues such as mothers' attitudes to racially mixed schooling and children's political attitudes; and mothers' social capital and children's educational and occupational attainment through the life course.

Notes

[1] The clustered sampling strategy used by MCS was not appropriate to locate ethnic groups such as Chinese people, whose settlement patterns are dispersed.

[2] The 2001 Census data is superior to the binary indicator of 'minority ethnic wards' used in the stratification of the sample, since the sample was drawn before 2001 Census results were available, and relied solely on 1991 evidence.

Appendix

Table A3.1: Results from the principal components analysis

Principal components (eigenvectors)

	Component 1	Component 2	Component 3	Component 4	Unexplained
Good area for children	0.63	-0.32	0.03	-0.71	0
Safe area	0.62	0.34	0.12	0.70	0
Friends with parents	0.39	0.57	-0.73	0.06	0
Friends with others	0.28	0.68	0.69	-0.04	0

Obs=14,708. Eigenvalue for principal component 1 = 1.74

Table A3.2: Neighbourhood social capital, linear regression results: full regression to accompany Table 3.7

	Model 1			Model 2			Model 3		
	B	Sig	SE	B	Sig	SE	B	Sig	SE
Mixed	-0.68	**	0.16	-0.34	**	0.14	2.24	**	0.38
Indian	-0.27	**	0.10	-0.15		0.10	1.85	**	0.33
Pakistani	-0.40	**	0.09	0.17		0.10	2.19	**	0.32
Bangladeshi	-0.39	**	0.11	0.20		0.11	2.20	**	0.33
Black Caribbean	-0.84	**	0.13	-0.37	**	0.11	2.01	**	0.31
Black African	-1.00	**	0.14	-0.52	**	0.10	1.83	**	0.31
Other	-0.42	**	0.09	-0.19	*	0.09	1.95	**	0.33
NVQ Level 1				0.20	**	0.06	0.18	**	0.06
NVQ Level 2				0.24	**	0.05	0.22	**	0.05
NVQ Level 3				0.25	**	0.06	0.23	**	0.06
NVQ Level 4				0.38	**	0.05	0.36	**	0.05
NVQ Level 5				0.31	**	0.06	0.31	**	0.06
NVQ missing				0.02		0.08	0.03		0.08
Married couple				0.39	**	0.04	0.37	**	0.04
Cohabiting couple				0.19	**	0.05	0.18	**	0.05
Family missing				1.08	**	0.06	1.03	**	0.06
Mother not in work				-0.10	**	0.03	-0.08	**	0.02
Income				0.19	**	0.03	0.20	**	0.03
England disadvantaged				-0.53	**	0.05	-0.45	**	0.05
England ethnic				-0.63	**	0.08	-0.29	**	0.08
Wales non-disadvantaged				0.14		0.09	0.10		0.08
Wales disadvantaged				-0.17	**	0.06	-0.21	**	0.06
Scotland non-disadvantaged				0.27	**	0.07	0.22	**	0.07
Scotland disadvantaged				-0.37	**	0.06	-0.42	**	0.06
NI non-disadvantaged				0.33	**	0.06	0.26	**	0.06
NI disadvantaged				0.13		0.08	0.06		0.07
Religious affiliation				0.04		0.02	0.05	**	0.02
% White area							0.02	**	0.00
% White area * Mixed							-0.26	**	0.09
% White area * Indian							-0.02	**	0.01
% White area * Pakistani							-0.03	**	0.00
% White area * Bangladeshi							-0.03	**	0.01
% White area * Black Caribbean							-0.07	**	0.02
% White area * Black African							-0.06	**	0.01
% White area * Other							-0.05	**	0.02
Constant	0.14	**	0.03	-1.36	**	0.16	-3.56	**	0.36
Observations	14,699			14,693			14,682		

** *p*<0.05

Table A3.3: Racism, binary logistic regression results: full regression to accompany Table 3.8

	Model 1			Model 2		
	B	Sig	SE	B	Sig	SE
Mixed	3.30	**	0.92	0.12		0.17
Indian	2.43	**	0.56	0.48		0.39
Pakistani	2.35	**	0.47	0.34		0.28
Bangladeshi	2.01	**	0.60	0.29		0.31
Black Caribbean	3.69	**	0.86	0.23		0.22
Black African	4.29	**	0.81	0.14	**	0.12
Other	2.13	**	0.50	0.57		0.48
NVQ Level 1				1.80	**	0.49
NVQ Level 2				1.85	**	0.40
NVQ Level 3				1.54		0.34
NVQ Level 4				2.58	**	0.48
NVQ Level 5				1.59	**	0.34
NVQ missing				1.71		0.57
Married couple				0.96		0.20
Cohabiting couple				1.15		0.34
Mother not in work				0.94		0.14
Income				1.01		0.13
England disadvantaged				1.84	**	0.41
England ethnic				1.55		0.42
Wales non-disadvantaged				0.60		0.29
Wales disadvantaged				1.11		0.40
Scotland non-disadvantaged				0.68		0.39
Scotland disadvantaged				1.42		0.69
NI non-disadvantaged				2.40		2.96
NI disadvantaged				0.89		1.21
% White area				0.99		0.01
% White area *Mixed				1.04	*	0.02
% White area *Indian				1.02		0.01
% White area *Pakistani				1.02	**	0.01
% White area *Bangladeshi				1.02		0.02
% White area *Black Caribbean				1.03	**	0.01
% White area *Black African				1.04	**	0.01
% White area *Other				1.01		0.01
Neighbourhood social capital				0.78	**	0.04
Religious affiliation				1.17		0.26
Constant	-1.34	**	-0.15	-0.84		-0.91
Observations	1,796			1,792		

** *p*<0.05

Table A3.4: Racially mixed schooling, binary logistic regression results: full regression to accompany Table 3.9

	Model 1			Model 2		
	OR	Sig	SE	OR	Sig	SE
Mixed	2.71	**	0.63	2.44	**	0.58
Indian	2.12	**	0.33	2.48	**	0.45
Pakistani	2.72	**	0.38	2.46	**	0.40
Bangladeshi	2.30	**	0.52	2.24	**	0.57
Black Caribbean	1.48		0.43	1.23		0.39
Black African	2.99	**	0.55	2.67	**	0.55
Other	2.54	**	0.46	2.47	**	0.47
NVQ Level 1				0.94		0.10
NVQ Level 2				0.91		0.08
NVQ Level 3				1.07		0.10
NVQ Level 4				1.21		0.12
NVQ Level 5				1.58	**	0.19
NVQ missing				0.99		0.16
Married couple				0.77	**	0.05
Cohabiting couple				0.95		0.07
Mother not in work				1.12	**	0.05
Income				0.75	**	0.03
England disadvantaged				1.36	**	0.10
England ethnic				1.23		0.14
Wales non-disadvantaged				1.38	**	0.12
Wales disadvantaged				1.72	**	0.14
Scotland non-disadvantaged				1.76	**	0.18
Scotland disadvantaged				2.04	**	0.19
Religious affiliation				0.78	**	0.04
Constant	0.16	**	-0.034	0.45	**	-0.12
Observations	12,522			12,517		

** $p<0.05$

FOUR

Parental relationships and parenting

Elizabeth Jones

Introduction

A large body of research suggests that the quality of the relationship between parents is related to parenting behaviours, the interactions between parent and child and child behavioural and cognitive outcomes. The quality of a relationship may affect child outcomes directly or may have an effect through parenting behaviours – that is, relationship quality may affect parenting behaviours that in turn affect child outcomes. Theoretical models have been proposed to explain both direct and indirect pathways for such effects.

This chapter uses data from the Millennium Cohort Study (MCS) to examine the self-reported perceptions of parents about their relationships, how well they predict later break-up of relationships and whether they are related to parenting behaviours and to child outcomes at age 5.

Literature review

Conflict in the relationship between parents has been found to have an effect on parenting behaviours. Brody et al (1997) asked parents to give their perceptions of the level of conflict in their relationships with their spouses. Higher levels of perceived conflict were related to lower involvement with children and harsher parenting. Interparental conflict has also been found to be related to lower acceptance of children, less consistency in discipline and greater hostility in the parent–child relationship (Gonzales et al, 2000).

In a meta-analysis of research on the relationship between parents and its relation to parenting behaviours, Erel and Burman (1995) found that parents who reported lower levels of conflict and higher levels of satisfaction with the marital relationship were less likely to use emotional forms of control and less likely to use harsh discipline practices. Marital conflict was also found to have a moderate relationship with parents' use of harsh discipline and lower acceptance of their children in a meta-analysis carried out by Krishnakumar and Buehler (2006).

In turn, parenting behaviours have an effect on child outcomes. An authoritarian parenting style, characterised by expectations that children unquestioningly obey parents, was found to be associated with overt aggression in children, while a permissive style was found to be associated with children's higher levels of relational aggression (Sandstrom, 2007). Having at least one authoritative parent was found to be related to lower levels of delinquency and depression and higher levels of school commitment in children (Simons and Conger, 2007).

Given that marital conflict is related to negative parenting behaviours and negative parenting behaviours are related to poorer child outcomes, one might expect that marital conflict has an effect on child outcomes. A meta-analysis by Buehler et al (1997) found a moderate relationship between marital conflict and child externalising and internalising behaviours. This association was found regardless of the age, gender or ethnic composition of the research samples. Zimet and Jacob (2001) reviewed the literature on marital conflict and child outcomes and found that the effect of marital conflict on child outcomes was stronger when the conflict was more frequent or more intense.

All of this implies that one of the mechanisms through which marital conflict affects child outcomes is through parenting behaviours, but direct tests are needed to provide evidence that parenting behaviour acts as a mediator. Buehler and Gerard (2002) found that marital conflict was related to children's maladjustment and that this relationship was partially explained by parents' use of harsh discipline and lower involvement with their children. Gerard et al (2006) found that the relationship between marital conflict and child externalising behaviours was mediated through harsh discipline and parent–child conflict.

Theoretical models of how marital conflict affects child outcomes include a number of theoretical elements. Four theories are of relevance. First, *modelling theory* states that children observe the conflict and hostility between their parents and model those behaviours in their interactions with others. Second, in the *cognitive-contextual model*, children are thought to observe the conflict and interpret it. They make conclusions about the meaning of the conflict, its cause, its threat to them and their ability to cope with it. The effects of the conflict on children, therefore, are likely to depend both on the characteristics of the conflict and how children interpret it. A third theory is the *emotional security model*. Here marital conflict causes children to experience negative emotional arousal and feel insecure about family stability and attachment to caregivers. This lack of secure attachment then leads children to have interpersonal problems and greater emotional problems such as anxiety and depression. These three theories are alike in that they rely on children observing the conflict and being directly affected by it.

A fourth theory is the *spillover model*. Unlike the other three, this theory does not require that children observe or be aware of the conflict. In the spillover model, marital conflict affects parents' own parenting behaviour, which then affects children. Parents may become absorbed in their marital difficulties and become less involved with their children and less consistent in their approach to discipline (Zimet and Jacob, 2001). It is the spillover model that is supported by research that found parenting behaviours mediated the relationship between marital conflict and child outcomes.

The focus of past research has largely been on how martial conflict affects parenting and child outcomes. The meta-analysis by Erel and Burman (1995) included both conflict and marital satisfaction and found that both were related to parenting behaviours, although the magnitude of the effect was lower for satisfaction than for conflict. The spillover model of marital conflict also applies to marital satisfaction. An alternate model for the effect of marital satisfaction on parenting behaviour is the *compensatory model*, which stipulates that poor marital relationships would lead to more positive parenting behaviours as parents try to use their relationship with the child to compensate for their unsatisfactory marital relationship.

This chapter examines parents' perceptions of the quality of their relationships and whether they are related to parenting behaviours and child outcomes. The correspondence of mothers' and partners' perceptions of their relationship is also examined using MCS data, as is the correspondence between partner' perceptions of the likelihood of a future separation and actual later break-up.

It is hypothesised that people in relationships which later break up will report lower earlier levels of marital satisfaction than people in relationships that do not break up. Theoretical models predict one of two things: either that parents who are happier with their marital relationships will be less likely to use harsh discipline practices and be more involved with their children, the spillover model. Or they predict the reverse: that parents who are dissatisfied with their relationship will be more involved and use less harsh discipline, the compensatory model. Past research has lent more support to the spillover model than the compensatory model, and it is therefore hypothesised that the current data will also support the spillover model. Finally, it is hypothesised that parents who are less satisfied with their marital relationship will have children who experience poorer behavioural and cognitive outcomes.

Data

This chapter uses data from the first three surveys of the MCS, when the MCS children were approximately aged 9 months, 3 years and 5 years. The sample consists of families who participated in all three surveys, in which the main respondent was the same person at each survey, 12,828 families. We excluded 1,227 two-parent families in which the partner respondent was not the same at each survey, so as to ensure that data were obtained for couples where partners were the same people. As over 99% of the main respondents were mothers, the six main respondents who were not mothers were dropped from the analysis. This left 11,595 families.

All analyses used MCS mothers and their partners' ratings of their relationships at MCS 1. Those who were not in relationships at the time would not be able to complete this rating. Analyses were limited to the 10,506 mothers plus partners who were in co-resident relationships at MCS 1. Chapter 5 (this volume) shows all of the partnership trajectories followed by cohort families including the initial lone parents and those forming stepfamilies, not covered in this chapter. In MCS families with twins or triplets, the data for only the first-born child were used.

Relationship status

There were several indicators of relationship status available at each MCS survey. The main variables used were an indicator of the relationship of parents or carers in the household to each other and the number and type of parents or carers in the household. Through these two variables, mothers were classified as married, cohabiting or lone at each sweep.

These relationship status variables were then used to create an indicator of whether mothers had broken up with their partners between MCS 1 and 2, or between MCS 2 and 3. The break-up indicator was set to zero if the mother was in a relationship at both sweeps and the partner respondent was the same person at both MCS surveys. The break-up indicator was set to 1 if she was in a relationship at the earlier survey but not at the later survey. At MCS 2, there was also a question about the reason the partner was no longer in the household: if the answer was separated/divorced, the MCS 2 break-up indicator was set to 1. Figure 4.1 shows the number of mothers in or not in relationships at each of the surveys. The majority of respondents in a relationship at MCS 1 were also in a relationship at MCS 2 (95%) and at MCS 3 (90%).

Figure 4.1: Changes in MCS parents' relationships across three MCS surveys

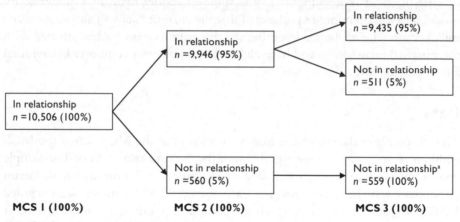

MCS 1 (100%)	**MCS 2 (100%)**	**MCS 3 (100%)**

Notes: Couples with a new partner are not included.
[a] One case was missing information on relationship status at MCS 3.

Partners' relationship quality

A measure of the quality of partners' relationship with each other was generated from the MCS data to investigate relationship quality and to use it as a predictor variable for other behaviour and outcomes. Both mothers and partners answered five questions about the quality of their relationship with each other, administering the same questions to each partner across the three surveys. The relationship quality items were part of the self-completion section of the interview, so the answers were not audible by anyone else in the room. In one of these items, both partners were asked to comment on the statement: 'I suspect we may be on the brink of separation'. The response to this item was examined across both partners to assess the consistency of partners' predictions about imminent break-up.

A relationship quality scale was created for each partner by summing the five items on relationship quality, common to all three surveys (see Appendix Table A4.1). This provided a measure of relationship quality for each partner in up to three surveys. A higher score on the scale indicated a higher perceived quality of relationship.

Harsh discipline

It was possible to generate one measure of parenting behaviour based on questions about discipline contained in the MCS surveys. The intention was to analyse this as a potential outcome variable arising from poor quality partnership relationships. Main respondents, almost all mothers, were also asked about their parental discipline practices at MCS 2 and 3. A scale was created from five items that were common at the two surveys. The items assessed the frequency of the use of shouting, smacking, ignoring, bribing and telling off as disciplinary actions. The specific items are shown in Appendix Table A4.1.

Parent involvement with the MCS child

It was possible to generate another measure of parenting behaviour based on questions about parents' involvement with the child contained in the MCS surveys. The intention was to use this as both a dependent and a predictor variable in analyses. MCS mothers and their partners were asked about their parenting behaviours and activities. Mothers were asked how often 'someone' did a range of activities with the cohort child at MCS 2. It is assumed that in the vast majority of cases the 'someone' would be one of the child's parents. The responses to these items were summed to create a scale of parental involvement. Higher scores indicate higher levels of involvement. The items included are shown in Appendix Table A4.1.

British Ability Scales (BAS): naming vocabulary

The child cognitive outcome used is the naming vocabulary scale of the British Ability Scales (BAS), individually administered to MCS 3 children around age 5 (details are given in Box 1.1 of Chapter 1, this volume). The computation of the t-score that was used in analyses is based on the item set administered and is normed to the BAS sample and adjusted for the cohort member's age.

Strengths and Difficulties Questionnaire (SDQ)

The total difficulties scale from the Strengths and Difficulties Questionnaire (SDQ) was used as a behavioural child outcome measure. Further details of the scale can be found in Box 1.2 (Chapter 1, this volume). The total difficulties scale contains all items except for the pro-social ones, and is a combination of internalising and externalising behaviours.

Parents' relationships

The correspondence between mothers' and partners' answers to the item 'I suspect we are on the brink of separation' is shown in Table 4.1. Most people, whether mother or partner, indicated that they did not agree with the statement, with few respondents agreeing or strongly agreeing. Mothers and partners tended to agree about their relationship and there was a statistically significant association between their answers, at all MCS surveys. However, there was a notable level of disagreement. In cases in which the mother strongly agreed that the relationship was on the brink of separation, the majority of partners still disagreed or strongly disagreed, 85% at MCS 1, 54% at MCS 2 and 52% at MCS 3. Agreement between the two partners was higher at MCS 2 and 3 than at MCS 1.

Table 4.2 shows there is a statistically significant association between mothers' and their partners' ratings of the likelihood of separation and whether the relationship actually broke up over the next two years. Both mothers and partners who agreed or strongly agreed that they were on the brink of separation were significantly more likely to break up later than those who disagreed. However, among those who strongly agreed a break-up was likely, the rate of actual break up after two years was no higher than 35%. Most people who suspected they were close to separating were still together two years later. These results indicate that people's perceptions of their relationships are complex, partners do not necessarily have the same opinion of their shared relationships and self-predictions about separation are often inaccurate over this timescale.

Parents' relationships and parenting behaviour

Regression analyses were used to examine whether the quality of partners' relationship was related to parenting behaviour. First, regressions were run to test whether harsh discipline was an outcome of poor relationship quality between the mother and her partner.

All regression models included a number of other covariates, to control for the effect of other family, parent and child characteristics. The independent variables included were mother's and partner's ages at MCS 1, mother's and partner's ethnicities, whether the mother was in employment, whether the partner was in employment, the highest parental qualification level in the family, the highest parental occupational status in the family, whether the family income was below

Table 4.1: Mother and partner levels of agreement on likelihood of separation MCS 1, MCS 2 and MCS 3

Mother's response	Partner's response									
	Strongly agree		Agree		Neither agree nor disagree		Disagree		Strongly disagree	
	%	Obs	%	Obs	%	Obs	%	Obs	%	Obs
MCS 1										
Strongly agree	6.2	7	7.7	8		1	23.6	21	61.3	49
Agree	5.0	3	24.2	12		9	26.6	12	25.2	13
Neither agree nor disagree	2.6	5	7.0	11		47	35.3	88	36.3	79
Disagree	0.8	13	1.6	26		95	32.6	523	58.8	929
Strongly disagree	1.1	76	0.3	33		105	16.4	1,175	80.5	5,444
MCS 2										
Strongly agree	15.0	11	18.5	14		12	9.1	10	44.4	33
Agree	5.8	6	14.0	12		18	37.1	38	21.6	20
Neither agree nor disagree	2.8	9	4.7	13		47	38.4	106	37.3	111
Disagree	0.8	16	2.1	16		88	29.8	468	61.3	989
Strongly disagree	0.5	30	0.3	12		83	14.7	778	82.8	4,325
MCS 3										
Strongly agree	18.7	14	14.7	12		8	13.6	10	38.5	30
Agree	15.3	14	12.8	13		38	22.6	26	13.9	24
Neither agree nor disagree	1.7	6	9.4	28		55	36.6	129	35.9	135
Disagree	0.8	12	2.2	33		108	31.1	498	59.2	939
Strongly disagree	0.5	30	0.4	17		109	15.7	926	81.5	4,589

Notes: Percentages weighted with covwt2. Observations are unweighted.

Table 4.2: Parents' predictions about separation and whether accurate

	Broke up by next survey, two years later		
Suspect we are on the brink of separation	*Percentage*	*Observation*	*Total count*
MCS 1, mother			
Strongly agree	20.4	22	106.4
Agree	20.1	17	72.7
Neither agree nor disagree	23.3	61	298.3
Disagree	7.9	146	1,909.0
Strongly disagree	2.8	216	7,821.0
MCS 1, partner			
Strongly agree	4.9	6	104.8
Agree	29.9	26	87.9
Neither agree nor disagree	17.1	46	282.8
Disagree	7.0	125	1,842.0
Strongly disagree	2.5	168	6,784.0
MCS 2, mother			
Strongly agree	34.8	38	118.9
Agree	29.4	33	132.4
Neither agree nor disagree	18.0	64	416.0
Disagree	6.3	123	2,113.0
Strongly disagree	2.5	189	6,649.0
MCS 2, partner			
Strongly agree	28.6	20	78.0
Agree	21.0	18	108.5
Neither agree nor disagree	14.1	36	312.0
Disagree	9.4	126	1,623.0
Strongly disagree	3.0	173	6,344.0

Notes: Percentages and Total Count weighted with covwt2. Observations are unweighted.

the (income) poverty level (as defined in Chapter 2, this volume), the child's age and the child's gender. The highest parental qualification level was the higher of the mother's or partner's education, combining academic and vocational qualifications. Highest parental occupational status was derived from the higher of mother's or partner's occupation status, summarised in one dummy variable, as professional or managerial, or not. With the exception of age, the covariates were from the same MCS survey as the dependent variables representing parenting behaviours, in this case, whether there was harsh discipline or not. In cases of break-up, where the partner from MCS 1 was no longer in the family or participating in later MCS surveys, the partner information from the latest survey available was used. For example, if a mother broke up with her partner between MCS 2 and MCS 3 and there was no partner information for MCS 3 therefore, partner information from MCS 2 was used for the covariates.

The first analysis, shown in Table 4.3, focused on the dependent variable harsh discipline at MCS 2 and its potential link to relationship quality at MCS 1

Table 4.3: Regression results for harsh discipline at MCS 2, mother-reported relationship quality at MCS 1

Independent variable (reference category)	Parent and family model (1)	Child model (2)	Full model (3)
Child age in months at MCS 2		-0.02 (0.03)	-0.04 (0.03)
Child sex (male)			
Female		-0.52 (0.08)**	-0.59 (0.08)**
Mother-reported relationship quality at MCS 1			-0.13 (0.01)**
Mother's age group at MCS 1 (19 and younger)			
Age 20-29	-0.07 (0.35)		0.03 (0.37)
Age 30-39	-0.59 (0.35)*		-0.51 (0.37)
Age 40 plus	-1.22 (0.41)**		-1.10 (0.44)**
Partner's age group at MCS 1 (29 and younger)			
Age 30-39	-0.06 (0.14)		-0.04 (0.14)
Age 40 plus	-0.35 (0.19)*		-0.36 (0.19)*
Mother's ethnicity (White)			
Mixed	0.59 (0.56)		0.57 (0.54)
Indian	1.10 (0.75)		0.94 (0.79)
Pakistani or Bangladeshi	-1.22 (0.78)		-0.96 (0.76)
Black	-0.30 (0.52)		-0.37 (0.55)
Partner's ethnicity (White)			
Mixed	0.05 (0.55)		-0.06 (0.58)
Indian	-0.73 (0.62)		-0.78 (0.62)
Pakistani or Bangladeshi	1.03 (0.71)		0.78 (0.70)
Black	-0.64 (0.45)		-0.76 (0.49)
Mother's work status at MCS 2 (not employed)			
Employed	-0.21 (0.10)**		-0.17 (0.10)*
Partner's work status at MCS 2 (not employed)			
Employed	0.38 (0.20)*		0.47 (0.21)**
Mother's highest qualification at MCS 2 (no qualifications)			
NVQ Level 1	0.10 (0.30)		0.14 (0.31)
NVQ Level 2	0.17 (0.22)		0.28 (0.22)
NVQ Level 3	0.34 (0.24)		0.46 (0.24)*
NVQ Level 4	0.27 (0.23)		0.42 (0.23)*
NVQ Level 5	0.18 (0.27)		0.30 (0.27)
Partner's highest qualification at MCS 2 (no qualifications)			
NVQ Level 1	-0.12 (0.25)		-0.05 (0.25)
NVQ Level 2	-0.10 (0.20)		-0.01 (0.20)
NVQ Level 3	-0.22 (0.21)		-0.14 (0.21)
NVQ Level 4	-0.08 (0.21)		0.03 (0.20)
NVQ Level 5	-0.49 (0.26)		-0.35 (0.26)

(continued)

Table 4.3: Regression results for harsh discipline at MCS 2, mother-reported relationship quality at MCS 1 *(continued)*

Independent variable (reference category)	Parent and family model (1)	Child model (2)	Full model (3)
Highest parental NS-SEC at MCS 2 (below professional and managerial)			
Professional and managerial	0.07 (0.10)		0.12 (0.10)
Income poverty status at MCS 2 (above poverty level)			
Below poverty level	-0.42 (0.14)**		-0.54 (0.14)**
Observation	8183	9467	7971
F, p	F=4.01, p=0.000	F=21.38, p=0.000	F=8.94, p=0.000
R^2	0.01	0.01	0.04

* $p<0.10$, ** $p<0.05$

Notes: Analysis uses weight covwt2. Mother-reported relationship quality at MCS 1 without covariates was -0.12 (0.01)** F=100.41, $p=0.000$. NS-SEC is the National Statistics Socio-Economic Classification based on occupation.

according to the mother. Relationship quality was significantly associated with harsh discipline, both on its own and after the other covariates were entered into the model. This means that mothers who were more satisfied with their relationships used fewer harsh discipline practices, even after other family and parent characteristics were taken into account. Other variables that were also significantly related to mother's lower use of harsh discipline included the mother being older, the partner not being employed, the family having an income below poverty level and the child being a girl. Estimates of the effect on harsh discipline of the partner's ratings of relationship quality were also modelled separately from those of the mother's ratings. The estimated size of association between harsh child discipline and partner's reporting of relationship quality was lower than that of mother's reports, but still statistically significant (results not shown).

The second analysis examined parental involvement to see whether partners' relationship quality was associated with this parenting behaviour outcome. The quality of the parental relationship, according to the mother, was found to be significantly related to parental involvement, both before and after other covariates were included (results not shown). It would appear that mothers who were happier with their relationships also did more activities with their children. Higher parental involvement was also related to being a younger mother, the partner not being in employment, parents having higher qualification levels and the child being a girl. Similar findings emerged when partner's rating of relationship quality was substituted for mother's reports of quality (see Table 4.4).

Table 4.4: Regression results for MCS 2 parental involvement,[a] partner's reports on relationship quality at MCS 1

Independent variable (reference category)	Parent and family model (1)	Child model (2)	Full model (3)
Child age in months at MCS 2		-0.05 (0.03)	-0.03 (0.04)
Child sex (male)			
Female		1.42 (0.14)**	1.44 (0.16)**
Partner reported relationship quality at MCS 1			0.06 (0.02)**
Mother's age group at MCS 1 (19 and younger)			
Age 20-29	-1.03 (0.56)*		-1.44 (0.56)**
Age 30-39	-1.21 (0.57)**		-1.61 (0.58)**
Age 40 plus	-1.16 (0.70)*		-1.51 (0.70)**
Partner's age group at MCS 1 (29 and younger)			
Age 30-39	-0.22 (0.21)		-0.29 (0.22)
Age 40 plus	-0.38 (0.32)		-0.42 (0.33)
Mother's ethnicity (White)			
Mixed	-1.33 (1.00)		-1.51 (0.96)
Indian	1.60 (1.01)		1.89 (1.02)*
Pakistani or Bangladeshi	-3.45 (1.44)**		-3.22 (1.64)*
Black	0.68 (0.91)		0.28 (0.99)
Partner's ethnicity (White)			
Mixed	-1.72 (0.90)*		-1.66 (0.93)*
Indian	-0.90 (1.04)		-0.86 (1.05)
Pakistani or Bangladeshi	2.13 (1.55)		2.23 (1.80)
Black	-1.88 (0.64)**		-2.02 (0.78)**
Mother's work status at MCS 2 (not employed)			
Employed	-0.16 (0.17)		-0.17 (0.17)
Partner's work status at MCS 2 (not employed)			
Employed	-0.57 (0.39)		-0.73 (0.40)*
Mother's highest qualification at MCS 2 (no qualifications)			
NVQ Level 1	0.54 (0.40)		0.52 (0.44)
NVQ Level 2	0.44 (0.33)		0.40 (0.34)

(continued)

Table 4.4: Regression results for MCS 2 parental Involvement,[a] partner's reports on relationship quality at MCS 1 (continued)

Independent variable (reference category)	Parent and family model (1)	Child model (2)	Full model (3)
Mother's highest qualification at MCS 2 (no qualifications) (continued)			
NVQ Level 3	1.38 (0.36)**		1.50 (0.37)**
NVQ Level 4	1.36 (0.35)**		1.30 (0.36)**
NVQ Level 5	1.17 (0.49)**		1.14 (0.51)**
Partner's highest qualification at MCS 2 (no qualifications)			
NVQ Level 1	0.59 (0.42)		0.75 (0.45)*
NVQ Level 2	0.59 (0.31)*		0.60 (0.33)*
NVQ Level 3	0.65 (0.35)*		0.64 (0.36)*
NVQ Level 4	0.97 (0.34)**		0.95 (0.35)**
NVQ Level 5	0.39 (0.47)		0.47 (0.47)
Highest parental NS-SEC at MCS 2 (below professional and managerial)			
Professional and managerial	0.09 (0.23)		0.03 (0.24)
Income poverty status at MCS 2 (above poverty level)			
Below poverty level	-0.19 (0.25)		-0.25 (0.26)
Observation	6810	7961	6501
F, p	F=3.99, p=0.000	F=53.53, p=0.000	F=6.99, p=0.000
R^2	0.02	0.01	0.03

*$p<0.10$, **$p<0.05$

Notes: [a] activities by anyone at home as reported by mother. Analysis uses weight covwt2.

Partner-reported relationship quality at MCS 1 without covariates was 0.06 (0.02)** F=7.10, p=0.008. NS-SEC is the National Statistics Socio-Economic Classification based on occupation.

Examining child cognitive outcomes – BAS naming vocabulary

Regression analyses were also used to look at whether the quality of the partner's relationship was a predictor of child outcomes both before and after including other predictors of child outcomes. As we have seen earlier parenting behaviours were themselves related to the quality of parents' relationship, so it is possible for there to be direct effects on child outcomes from parents' relationships as well as indirect effects through the influence of partner's relationship quality on parenting behaviour.

The results from a regression analysing child BAS naming vocabulary scores are shown in Table 4.5. As in previous regression analyses, the relationship quality sets

Table 4.5: Regression results for models of BAS naming vocabulary at MCS 3

Independent variable (reference category)	Parent and family model (1)	Child model (2)	Parenting model (3)	Full model (4)	Parenting mediation model (5)
Child age in months at MCS 3		-0.13 (0.05)**		-0.13 (0.04)**	-0.17 (0.05)**
Child sex (male)					
Female		0.57 (0.28)**		0.66 (0.27)**	0.46 (0.28)
Harsh discipline at MCS 2			0.05 (0.04)		0.03 (0.04)
Parental involvement at MCS 2			0.14 (0.02)**		0.10 (0.02)**
Breakup between MCS 1 and MCS 3			-3.21 (0.49)**		-0.81 (0.51)
Relationship quality at MCS 1, mother				0.10 (0.04)**	0.08 (0.04)*
Relationship quality at MCS 1, partner				0.02 (0.04)	-0.02 (0.04)
Mother's age group at MCS 1 (19 and younger)					
Age 20-29	1.06 (1.05)			0.95 (1.04)	1.07 (1.02)
Age 30-39	1.45 (1.09)			1.35 (1.08)	1.43 (1.05)
Age 40+	1.17 (1.34)			1.04 (1.32)	1.25 (1.37)
Partner's age group at MCS 1 (29 and younger)					
Age 30-39	0.67 (0.34)*			0.68 (0.34)**	0.30 (0.38)
Age 40+	0.82 (0.46)*			0.84 (0.46)*	0.60 (0.55)
Mother's ethnicity (White)					
Mixed	-1.62 (1.61)			-1.55 (1.56)	-1.32 (1.61)
Indian	-2.09 (1.29)			-1.98 (1.32)	-2.21 (1.20)*
Pakistani or Bangladeshi	-4.94 (2.03)**			-5.00 (2.02)**	-1.25 (2.87)
Black	-5.04 (1.44)**			-5.25 (1.46)**	-4.99 (1.81)**

(continued)

Table 4.5: Regression results for models of BAS naming vocabulary at MCS 3 (continued)

Independent variable (reference category)	Parent and family model (1)	Child model (2)	Parenting model (3)	Full model (4)	Parenting mediation model (5)
Partner's ethnicity (White)					
Mixed	-0.21 (1.56)			-0.11 (1.55)	-2.34 (1.52)
Indian	-2.67 (1.38)*			-2.68 (1.40)*	-2.68 (1.52)*
Pakistani or Bangladeshi	-5.04 (1.97)**			-4.91 (1.95)**	-6.99 (2.81)**
Black	-4.00 (1.21)**			-3.76 (1.24)**	-2.71 (1.39)*
Mother's work status at MCS 2 (employed)					
In work	-0.05 (0.27)			-0.04 (0.27)	0.12 (0.30)
Partner's work status at MCS 2 (employed)					
In work	1.74 (0.51)**			1.70 (0.51)**	1.67 (0.62)**
Mother's highest qualification at MCS 2 (no qualifications)					
NVQ Level 1	3.37 (0.67)**			3.40 (0.67)**	2.14 (0.82)**
NVQ Level 2	4.19 (0.60)**			4.23 (0.60)**	3.02 (0.69)**
NVQ Level 3	5.04 (0.64)**			5.08 (0.64)**	3.83 (0.76)**
NVQ Level 4	6.80 (0.64)**			6.83 (0.64)**	5.61 (0.77)**
NVQ Level 5	6.63 (0.72)**			6.65 (0.72)**	5.54 (0.85)**
Partner's highest qualification at MCS 2 (no qualifications)					
NVQ Level 1	1.50 (0.74)**			1.48 (0.74)**	0.54 (0.84)
NVQ Level 2	1.40 (0.53)**			1.35 (0.52)**	1.24 (0.57)**
NVQ Level 3	2.40 (0.53)**			2.34 (0.52)**	2.28 (0.55)**
NVQ Level 4	3.42 (0.57)**			3.31 (0.56)**	2.97 (0.59)**
NVQ Level 5	3.36 (0.64)**			3.27 (0.64)**	2.95 (0.68)**

(continued)

Table 4.5: Regression results for models of BAS naming vocabulary at MCS 2 (continued)

Independent variable (reference category)	Parent and family model (1)	Child model (2)	Parenting model (3)	Full model (4)	Parenting mediation model (5)
Highest parental NS-SEC at MCS 2 (below professional and managerial)					
Professional and managerial	1.44 (0.31)**			1.42 (0.31)**	1.45 (0.34)**
Income poverty status at MCS 2 (above poverty level)					
Below poverty level	-0.71 (0.40)*			-0.66 (0.40)	-0.59 (0.50)
Observation	8,277	8,667	6,192	8,277	5,963
F,p	F=31.3, p=0.000	F=4.8, p=0.000	F=28.6, p=0.000	F=30.5, p=0.000	F=17.6, p=0.000
R^2	14.45	0.00	0.02	0.15	0.12

$*p<0.10$, $**p<0.05$.

Notes: Analysis uses weight covwt2. Regression results for mother-reported relationship quality at MCS 1, without covariates -0.21 (0.04)** and for partner-reported relationship quality at MCS 1, without covariates 0.10 (0.04)**. NS-SEC is the National Statistics Socio-Economic Classification based on occupation.

of variables were entered first on their own and then in combination. In this case, a parental model was tested that also included the parenting behaviour variables and an indicator of whether the relationship had broken up between MCS 1 and MCS 2. This was to examine whether the addition of these variables affected or mediated the association between relationship quality and child outcome.

Mothers who reported being happier with their relationships had children with significantly higher vocabulary scores. This relationship was reduced, although it remained statistically significant, by the addition of the other covariates, suggesting that it is partly explained by the parent, family and child variables. The inclusion of the parenting behaviour variables weakened the relationship only slightly.

Partner's rating of relationship quality was significantly associated with child outcomes when entered with only mother's reports of relationship quality (results in the notes to Table 4.5), but this was not statistically significant once the covariates were added (column 1). The addition of the parenting variables did not reduce the size of association between partner's relationship quality and child vocabulary scores. These results do not, therefore, lend support to the spillover model, which suggests that marital relationship affects parenting behaviours, which in turn affect child outcomes. Of the parenting behaviour variables, parental involvement and break-up between surveys were associated significantly with child outcomes. However, only parental involvement remained statistically significant once other covariates were included.

Other variables that were related to higher vocabulary scores (at $p<0.05$) were partners being employed, parents having higher qualification levels, parents having a professional or managerial occupation, children being younger at interview and children being girls. Although it seems counterintuitive that younger children had higher vocabulary scores, it should be remembered that the BAS vocabulary scores were normed by age. This association does not mean, therefore, that older children received lower raw scores, but that they scored lower relative to children of their own age in the reference population.

Examining child behaviour outcomes – total difficulties

Table 4.6 shows the regression results for analyses of SDQ total difficulties in terms of its associations with other variables. Mothers' ratings of relationship quality were significantly associated with total difficulties scores in all models. However, the magnitude of the association was reduced by the inclusion of the family, parent and child covariates and further by the inclusion of the parenting behaviour variables. Mothers who reported being happier with their relationships had children with fewer behaviour problems. Partners' reports of relationship quality were not significantly related to total difficulties scores once other covariates were entered. All of the parenting behaviour variables were related to total difficulties scores; parents who used more harsh discipline, or were less involved with their children, or whose relationships broke up, all had children who had more behaviour problems. When the other covariates were entered, all

Table 4.6: Regression results for models of SDQ total difficulties at MCS 3

Independent variable (reference category)	Parent and family model (1)	Child model (2)	Parenting model (3)	Full model (4)	Parenting mediation model (5)
Child age in months at MCS 3		−.05 (0.02)**		−0.04 (0.02)**	−0.04 (0.02)
Child sex (male)					
Female		−.98 (0.11)**		−0.97 (0.11)**	−0.72 (0.12)**
Harsh discipline at MCS 2			0.26 (0.02)**		0.24 (0.02)**
Parental involvement at MCS 2			−0.06 (0.01)**		−0.04 (0.01)**
Breakup between MCS 1 and MCS 3			1.60 (0.25)**		0.59 (0.27)**
Relationship quality at MCS 1, mother				−0.22 (0.02)*	−0.18 (0.02)**
Relationship quality at MCS 1, partner				−0.01 (0.02)	−0.01 (0.02)
Mother's age group at MCS 1 (19 and younger)					
Age 20-29	0.24 (0.58)			0.32 (0.57)	0.19 (0.62)
Age 30-39	−0. 9 (0.60)			−0.12 (0.59)	−0.21 (0.65)
Age 40+	1.17 (0.67)			−0.13 (0.65)	−0.14 (0.74)
Partner's age group at MCS 1 (29 and younger)					
Age 30-39	−0.55 (0.17)**			−0.54 (0.16)**	−0.31 (0.18)*
Age 40+	−0.65 (0.25)**			−0.71 (0.24)**	−0.30 (0.28)
Mother's ethnicity (White)					
Mixed	0.98 (0.66)			0.74 (0.68)	1.05 (0.87)
Indian	1.28 (0.79)			1.22 (0.78)	0.64 (0.64)
Pakistani or Bangladeshi	1.12 (1.03)			1.48 (0.87)*	1.54 (0.82)*

(continued)

Table 4.6: Regression results for models of SDQ total difficulties at MCS 3 (continued)

Independent variable (reference category)	Parent and family model (1)	Child model (2)	Parenting model (3)	Full model (4)	Parenting mediation model (5)
Mother's ethnicity (White) (continued)					
Black	-0.26 (0.57)				0.58 (0.74)
Partner's ethnicity (White)					
Mixed	0.66 (0.63)			0.62 (0.66)	0.09 (0.57)
Indian	-0.89 (0.68)			-0.93 (0.63)	-0.39 (0.53)
Pakistani or Bangladeshi	-0.26 (1.05)			-0.48 (0.87)	-0.86 (0.74)
Black	0.24 (0.54)			-0.20 (0.52)	0.00 (0.74)
Mother's work status at MCS 2 (not working)					
In work	-0.12 (0.14)			-0.14 (0.14)	-0.14 (0.15)
Partner's work status at MCS 2 (not working)					
In work	-0.56 (0.32)*			-0.47 (0.30)	-0.54 (0.30)*
Mother's highest qualification at MCS 2 (no qualifications)					
NVQ Level 1	-0.55 (0.40)			-0.64 (0.38)*	-0.43 (0.43)
NVQ Level 2	-1.08 (0.31)**			-1.12 (0.31)**	-0.75 (0.34)**
NVQ Level 3	-1.28 (0.35)**			-1.30 (0.35)**	-0.81 (0.37)**
NVQ Level 4	-1.77 (0.33)**			-1.78 (0.32)**	-1.44 (0.36)**
NVQ Level 5	-1.67 (0.37)**			-1.65 (0.36)**	-1.21 (0.39)**
Partner's highest qualification at MCS 2 (no qualifications)					
NVQ Level 1	-0.31 (0.31)			-0.40 (0.31)	-0.34 (0.33)
NVQ Level 2	-0.50 (0.25)**			-0.48 (0.24)**	-0.54 (0.27)**
NVQ Level 3	-0.48 (0.27)*			-0.48 (0.27)*	-0.41 (0.29)

(continued)

Table 4.6: Regression results for models of **SDQ total difficulties at MCS 3** (continued)

Independent variable (reference category)	Parent and family model (1)	Child model (2)	Parenting model (3)	Full model (4)	Parenting mediation model (5)
Partner's highest qualification at MCS 2 (no qualifications) (continued)					
NVQ Level 4	-0.74 (0.26)**			-0.63 (0.26)**	-0.69 (0.26)**
NVQ Level 5	-1.05 (0.28)**			-0.97 (0.28)**	-0.89 (0.29)**
Highest parental NS-SEC at MCS 2 (below professional and managerial)					
Professional and managerial	-0.34 (0.15)**			-0.23 (0.14)	-0.13 (0.17)
Income poverty status at MCS 2 (above poverty level)					
Below poverty level	0.27 (0.22)			0.13 (0.21)	0.28 (0.25)
Observation	6,820	7,087	5,161	6,820	4,988
F, p	F=11.6, p=0.000	F=13.6, p=0.000	F=93.9, p=0.00C	F=20.9, p=0.000	F=24.4, p=0.000
R^2	0.05	0.01	0.07	0.10	0.14

*$p<0.10$, **$p<0.05$.

Notes: Analyses use weight covwt2. Regression results for mother-reported relationship quality at MCS 1, with covariates -0.24 (0.02)** and for partner-reported relationship quality at MCS 1, without covariates -0.03 (0.02)*. NS-SEC is the National Statistics Socio-Economic Classification based on occupation.

of the parenting behaviour variables remained statistically significant. Parents with higher qualifications had children with fewer problem behaviours, and girls were reported to have fewer behaviour problems.

Conclusions

Although prediction of separation and rating of relationship quality between parents were associated with actual break-up, there are many cases in which the relationship was highly rated and separation was not predicted, but break-up happened. There were also cases in which the perceived quality of a relationship was low, or separation as was predicted, but the couple stayed together. This finding is similar to that of Karney and Bradbury (1995) in their review of research on the predictors of marital stability over time – they found that while marital satisfaction was significantly related to marital stability, dissatisfaction with the relationship was not a strong predictor of relationship or partnership break-up.

Mothers' and their partners' perceptions of the quality of their relationships were significantly related to parenting behaviours, both to levels of parental involvement with their children and to parents' approach to disciplining their children. Both mothers and their partners who rated their marital relationship more poorly were less involved with their children and used harsher discipline with them. These findings support the spillover model of marital dissatisfaction rather than the compensatory model.

Mothers' ratings of their relationships were also found to be significantly associated with child cognitive and behavioural outcomes. Mothers who rated their relationships highly had children who scored higher on naming vocabulary and lower on total behavioural difficulties. Partners' ratings of their relationships were not related to child outcomes when other factors were taken into account. Parental involvement with the child was related to both of the child outcomes considered, with children who had more involved parents having more positive outcomes on vocabulary and total difficulties. Harsh discipline was not significantly related to naming vocabulary scores, but was significantly associated with total difficulties scores. This may signal that children who have fewer problem behaviours receive less harsh discipline from their parents.

It should be noted that the models reported here explained relatively little of the overall variance in the dependent variables. Partners' relationship quality and the covariates explained only a very small portion of parenting behaviour, leaving a large portion unexplained. Similarly, although relationship quality was significantly related to child outcomes, it, along with the covariates and parenting variables, explained little of the variation in the two child outcome measures examined.

Although both parents' relationship quality and parenting behaviours were related to child outcomes, there was no evidence that the parenting behaviours mediated the pathways from partners' relationship quality to measures of child outcomes. Overall, the research presented here lends support to that element of the spillover model that suggests partners' relationship quality influences their parenting behaviour. However, the results do not support the idea that relationship quality affects child outcomes indirectly via parenting behaviours.

Appendix

Table A4.1: Items in scales

Relationship quality
Partner sensitive and aware of needs
Partner doesn't listen
Sometimes lonely even when with partner
Suspect on brink of separation
How happy with relationship?

Parental involvement
How often does someone help CM learn the alphabet?
How often does someone try to teach CM counting?
How often does someone teach CM songs/poems/rhymes?
How often does CM paint/draw at home?
How often do you read with CM?

Harsh discipline
How often do you ignore CM when he/she is naughty?
How often do you smack CM when he/she is naughty?
How often do you shout at CM when he/she is naughty?
How often do you tell off CM when he/she is naughty?
How often do you bribe CM when he/she is naughty?

Note: CM = cohort member or the cohort child

Table A4.2: Characteristics of sample families and main respondents at MCS 3, unless otherwise stated

	%	Observation	Count
Country at MCS 3			
England	59.5	6,652	6,470
Wales	14.9	1,496	1,624
Scotland	13.1	1,310	1,425
Northern Ireland	12.5	1,043	1,358
Relationship to cohort child			
Mother	100.0	10,505	10,952
Marital status			
Married	74.0	7,859	8,101
Cohabiting	15.4	1,554	1,687
Lone	10.5	1,070	1,144
Employment status			
Not in employment	36.6	3,928	4,006
Employed	63.4	6,571	6,941
Age group at MCS1			
14 to 19	2.2	229	240
20 to 29	37.4	3,993	4,093
30 to 39	56.4	5,855	6,175
40+	4.0	424	440
Mother's ethnicity			
White	90.5	9,181	9,883
Mixed	0.6	62	70
Indian	2.0	279	215
Pakistani or Bangladeshi	3.9	607	425
Black	1.7	191	181
Other	1.3	159	146
Highest qualification			
No qualifications	7.9	938	844
NVQ Level 1	6.5	658	695
NVQ Level 2	28.1	2,764	3,006
NVQ Level 3	15.4	1,616	1,643
NVQ Level 4	34.1	3,392	3,642
NVQ Level 5	8.1	859	865

Notes: Percentages and counts weighted with covwt2, except for country, which is weighted with covwt1. Observations are unweighted.

Table A4.3: Characteristics of partner respondents at MCS 3 or most recent survey, unless otherwise stated

	%	Observation	Count
Relationship to cohort child			
Father	97.9	8,372	8,803
Other	2.1	176	189
Age group			
Under 29	25.5	2,774	2,778
30 to 39	61.5	6,331	6,714
40+	13.1	1,363	1,424
Employment status			
Not in employment	7.7	922	848
Employed	92.3	9,583	10,104
Father's ethnicity			
White	91.0	8,303	8,891
Mixed	0.7	62	73
Indian	2.0	246	195
Pakistani or Bangladeshi	3.1	459	304
Black	1.8	184	176
Other	1.4	136	133
Highest qualification			
No qualifications	9.9	1,146	1,008
NVQ Level 1	6.3	608	641
NVQ Level 2	26.9	2,618	2,730
NVQ Level 3	15.7	1,513	1,596
NVQ Level 4	30.2	2,761	3,064
NVQ Level 5	10.9	1,038	1,105

Notes: Percentages and counts weighted with covwt2. Observations are unweighted.

Table A4.4: Means for relationship quality, parental involvement and harsh discipline scales

MCS survey	Respondent	Mean	Standard error	Observation
Relationship quality				
MCS 1	Mother	22.37	0.05	9,996
	Partner	22.33	0.04	8,889
Parental involvement				
MCS 2	Mother	24.99	0.14	7,961
Harsh discipline				
MCS 2	Mother	14.91	0.05	9,467

Notes: Means and standard errors weighted with covwt2. Observations are unweighted.

FIVE

Partnership trajectories, parent and child well-being

Kathleen Kiernan and Fiona Mensah

Introduction

The structure of British family life has undergone substantial changes over recent decades. Rises in extra-marital childbearing, cohabitation and parental separation coupled with declines in marriage have translated into more diverse, complex, transient and often inequitable family settings for children. Very large movements in financial circumstances of families can often be associated with these family changes and family changes can also affect the emotional well-being of family members. Consequently, there has been growing concern about the instability of family life and the impact on the well-being of children which has led to a plethora of inquiries, reports and initiatives around children, for example, *A good childhood* (Layard and Dunn, 2009), Social Justice Policy Group (2006), *Every Child Matters* (HM Treasury, 2003), and *The Children's Plan* (DCSF, 2007).

A substantial body of research already exists on the consequences of divorce and remarriage for British children both in the short and the long term (see Kiernan, 1997; Rogers and Pryor, 1998) but much less is known about the potential consequences for children of being born into different family settings and whether subsequent family trajectories matter. This chapter explores these issues. We start by looking at changes over the first five years of the children's lives and map the family trajectories of children born into four different settings: to married parents, cohabiting parents, to solo mothers who were in a relationship with the father at the time of the birth and those who were not in a relationship at that time. By following the partnership behaviour of these parents over the first five years of the child's life we can assess the extent to which there is stability or change in the lives of the Millennium Cohort Study (MCS) children. Given there is a good deal of ethnic diversity in the parental context within which children are born, we also examine the trajectories for mothers from different ethnic groups. Frequent accompaniments to family transitions are changes in the economic circumstances of families and in the emotional well-being of the parents and children; the second half of the chapter is devoted to these issues.

Family context at birth and age 5

At the first interview, carried out when their baby was around 9 months old, a parent of the child, usually the child's natural mother, reported the family setting in which the child had been born (see Table 5.1). Fifty-nine per cent of children were born to parents who were married to one another, 25% were born to parents who were cohabiting and 16% were born to solo mothers. Among these solo mothers, 7% reported they were closely involved with the father (that is, intimate) and 8% were not, including those who were just friends, not in any relationship or were separated or divorced. These different types of relations between the parents could be deemed to represent a hierarchy of bonding or commitment between parents at the outset of the child's life. Earlier work showed there were marked differences across these groups with respect to socioeconomic characteristics (Kiernan and Smith, 2003), the extent of father involvement in the children's lives (Kiernan, 2006) and health behaviours (Kiernan and Pickett, 2006). For example, compared with unmarried mothers those who were married were more likely to have planned their pregnancies, given up smoking, breastfed and were less likely to suffer post-natal depression. They were also on average more educated, much less likely to become mothers at a young age and also had higher family incomes than unmarried mothers. There were also marked differences across ethnic groups in the extent to which they had babies in different partnership contexts, which we discuss later.

For those children followed up, a cross-sectional snapshot of the family situation at age 5 (see Table 5.1) showed that slightly more were now living in married parent families (60% compared with 59%); fewer were living with cohabiting parents (15% compared with 25%); and more were living in a lone-parent family (19% compared with 16%). The remaining 5% were living in stepfamilies formed through remarriage or cohabitation. However, this simple comparison of the situation at the time of the birth and the situation when the children were 5 years old only provides a partial picture of the family dynamics occurring over the first five years of the child's life.

Family trajectories

The story was more complex when we analysed the more detailed information collected on family situations and changes. At each of the three surveys, at 9 months, age 3 and age 5, information was collected on whether natural or social parents were resident in the household and the type of relationship between the co-resident parents. This information, together with that derived from reports on periods of partnerships and lone parenthood, provided the basis for our trajectories. Given that a full partnership history was not collected in the surveys, our family trajectories are derived from the relationship between the natural parents at the time of the child's birth, the living arrangements and relationship of parents at the age 5 survey, and any reported intervening family transitions.

Table 5.1: Relationship between natural parents at the time of birth, and family structure at MCS 3

Relationship between natural parents at birth (%)	
Married	59.1
Cohabiting	25.2
Closely involved	7.4
Not in a relationship	8.2
Total %	100
Unweighted sample size	18,474[a]
Family structure at age 5 (%)	
Married	60.3
Cohabiting	15.1
Lone natural mother	18.7
Lone natural father	0.5
Natural mother and other parent	5.0
Natural father and other parent	0.2
Neither natural parent	0.2
Total %	100
Unweighted sample size	14,678[b]

Notes: [a] Sample: all MCS 1 main respondents; not reported for 78 families, sample percentages weighted to correct for sampling design and non-response to MCS 1 survey.

[b] Sample: all MCS 3 main respondents; including families in MCS 3 from the original sampling frame, sample percentages weighted to correct for sampling design, non-response and sample attrition up to MCS 3.

For those who were married at the time of the birth we have identified four trajectories shown in Table 5.2: stably married, currently married but had periods of separation, and two types of separated families – those headed by a lone parent, typically the natural mother, and those where a parent has re-partnered and the child has a social parent, typically the natural mother and a social father. For those who were cohabiting at the birth of their child we have an additional category of families, namely those who had subsequently married and continued to live together until the child was 5 years old. Identifying periods of separation for subsequently reconciled married and cohabiting parents indicates another dimension in the instability of family life not normally captured in cross-sectional surveys. For the group of mothers who had a child outside of a co-residential union we identified five trajectories from birth to when the child was 5 years old: stable lone motherhood; marrying the natural father and currently living with him; starting to cohabit with the natural father and currently living with him; living with a partner who was not the natural father; and currently a lone mother but has had periods living with a partner over the five years since the baby was born. Among the children born to solo mothers a very small proportion were living with a lone natural father, or the natural father and other social parent by age 5; these families are also shown in the table.

Table 5.2: Relationship between natural parents at the time of birth and subsequent family trajectories to MCS 3

Family trajectory	Relationship between natural parents at child's birth (%)					
	Married	Cohabiting	Closely involved	Not in a relationship	Total	(Parents resident at age 5 if not both natural parents)
Married at birth						
Stable	88.1				52.3	
Periods of separation	2.1				1.3	
To lone parenthood	7.6				4.5	(4.3% lone mother, 0.2% lone father)
To re-partnered	2.1				1.2	(1.1% natural mother and social parent, 0.1% natural father and social parent)
Total %	100					
Cohabiting at birth						
Stable		43.4			10.9	
To married		23.2			5.8	
Periods of separation		5.7			1.4	
To lone parenthood		20.5			5.1	(4.9% lone mother, 0.3% lone father)
To re-partnered		7.3			1.8	(1.7% natural mother and social parent, 0.1% natural father and social parent)
Total %		100				
Solo at birth						
Stable			30.6	52.8	6.6	(6.6% lone mother, 0.02% lone father)
To married			12.0	5.3	1.3	
To cohabiting			24.8	10.6	2.7	
To new partner			10.0	16.2	2.1	(2.1% natural mother and social parent, 0.01% natural father and social parent)
Periods of partnership			22.6	15.1	2.9	(2.9% lone mother, 0.04% lone father)
Total %			100	100	100	
Total sample %	59.3	25.0	7.6	8.1	100	
Unweighted sample size	8,706	3,407	1,241	1,240	14,594[a]	

Notes: [a] Sample: all MCS 3 main respondents also interviewed at MCS 1; including families in MCS 3 from the original sampling frame, sample percentages weighted to correct for sampling design, non-response and sample attrition up to MCS 3; 54 families excluded where relationship at birth was not reported and 30 families excluded where child was not living with either parent at age 5.

It is clear from Table 5.2 that parents who were married at the time of the child's birth were more likely to remain living together than those who were cohabiting at the child's birth. Cohabiting parents were more likely to have separated and to have re-partnered than married parents. Eighty-eight per cent of the married parents were still married and living together when their child was age 5 whereas, among parents who were cohabiting at the child's birth 67% were still living with each other five years later, with 43% continuing to cohabit and 23% having married. A greater fragility of cohabiting unions compared with marital ones has been observed across most developed nations (Andersson, 2002; Kiernan, 2004). In the MCS sample, children born to cohabiting parents were almost three times as likely as those born to married parents to be no longer living with both these parents when they were 5 years old (28% compared with 10% respectively).

Among the mothers who were neither married nor cohabiting at the time of the child's birth, not surprisingly those who were closely involved with the father of their child were more likely to marry or cohabit following the birth than those who were not in a relationship with the father. Mothers who were not in a relationship at the birth of their child were more likely to continue to live as a lone-parent family or to live with another partner than those in a closely involved relationship. Among mothers who were in a close relationship with the other natural parent at the child's birth, just over a third were living with the father when their child was 5 years old, with more cohabiting (25%) than married (12%); just under a third lived as a stable lone-parent family over the five years (31%); and 23% had lived in a partnership with the father or another partner for a period of time but were living as a lone parent at the age 5 interview; and 10% were living with another partner at this time. Among the lone mothers who were not in a close relationship with the father at the child's birth: just over one half (53%) continued to live as a lone mother, 16% were living with the father when the child was 5 years old, with more cohabiting (11%) than married (5%); 16% were living with another partner; and 15% had lived in a partnership at some time since the birth of the baby, but were lone mothers at the time of the interview. Given sample size constraints for the analyses that follow we have combined the two sets of mothers who were solo at the time of the birth.

We have described these family trajectories in some detail as this is the first time that we have such detailed information on family changes for a nationally representative sample of children. These trajectories clearly highlight how cross-sectional snapshots of children's living arrangements can disguise the dynamics of family living arrangements and some of the complexities of family situations experienced by these children even over this relatively short timespan.

Ethnic diversity in family trajectories

The UK is a culturally and ethnically diverse society and there were some noteworthy differences across ethnic groups in the context within which their children were born and the types of family trajectories that followed. For this study we used the reported ethnic status of the mother. The great majority of mothers in the MCS were white (89%), the next largest ethnic group were those of South Asian – Indian, Pakistani or Bangladeshi – origin (6%), 3% of the mothers were of black Caribbean or African ethnic origin, 1% were of mixed ethnicity and 2% other ethnic origins. Across the ethnic groups there was much variation with respect to the partnership context within which the baby was born (see the top section of Table 5.3). South Asian mothers were much more likely to be married at the time of the birth (and the great majority were married) than either the white or black mothers. Having a child within a cohabiting union was rare among the South Asian groups and was less common among black mothers than among white mothers. The groups who were the least likely to have been in a partnership at the time the baby was born were the black and mixed origin mothers; among these groups non-partnered parenthood was more common than or almost as common as marital childbearing. Among the set of black and mixed ethnic origin mothers, those of Caribbean origin had the highest proportion of non-partnered births; one in two of these mothers were not in a co-residential partnership when they had their baby.

Given that the family contexts within which children were born varied substantially across ethnic groups we looked at the trajectories separately for the married, cohabiting and solo motherhood groups so that we were better placed to compare families with the same starting point. These are shown in the lower three parts of Table 5.3.

Among all the children born into married families 88% were still living with both parents at age 5; high rates of continuity were to be seen among the white, South Asian and mixed ethnic origin mothers. Fewer, but still the great majority, of the black Caribbean and black African married mothers were still married. Becoming a lone mother following the break-up of the marriage was most common among black mothers, with 20% of mothers with black Caribbean origins and 17% with black African origins having become lone mothers as compared with 8% of the white mothers. Periods of separation were much less common among the white and black Caribbean families than among the other sets of families. Very few of the initially married mothers had re-partnered, but where they did it was more common among the white and Bangladeshi families than among mothers in other ethnic groups.

Cohabiting at the time of the birth was very rare among the South Asian mothers so we confine our comparisons to the white, black and mixed origin mothers. Stable cohabitation was most frequent among the white, mixed origin and black African mothers and was less frequent among the black Caribbean mothers. A transition from cohabiting into a lone-mother family was most frequent among the black Caribbean mothers and periods of parental separation were more prevalent among black African and black Caribbean mothers than among white and mixed origin mothers.

Fifteen per cent of the babies in the MCS were born to parents not living together at the time of the birth. It is clear from Table 5.3 that South Asian

Table 5.3: Relationship between natural parents at the time of birth and subsequent family trajectories to MCS 3 according to mother's ethnicity

Mother's Ethnicity	White	Mixed	Indian	Pakistani	Bangladeshi	Black Caribbean	Black African	Other	Total
Sample %	(88.5)	(1.0)	(1.9)	(3.1)	(1.1)	(1.1)	(1.5)	(1.7)	(100)
Relationship between natural parents at the time of birth									
Married	57.4	42.2	90.7	91.7	93.7	30.8	45.9	74.3	59.2
Cohabiting	27.6	19.3	1.8	1.3	0.7	16.5	13.4	9.1	25.2
Close	7.2	20.8	4.9	1.9	0.6	30.2	14.8	10.1	7.4
Not in a relationship	7.9	17.7	2.6	5.2	5.0	22.6	25.9	6.6	8.2
Total %	100	100	100	100	100	100	100	100	100
Unweighted sample size	15,477	190	475	891	370	263	376	382	18,424[a]
Family trajectories up to age 5 among parents who were married at birth									
Stable	88.4	87.2	92.5	85.8	88.9	78.4	75.5	88.6	88.2
Periods of separation	1.8	5.9	2.5	4.5	5.7	1.9	7.3	4.8	2.1
To lone parenthood	7.5	6.9	4.7	8.8	4.0	19.7	17.2	6.7	7.6
To re-partnered	2.4	0.0	0.3	0.9	1.4	0.0	0.0	0.0	2.1
Total %	100	100	100	100	100	100	100	100	100
Unweighted sample size	7,111	47	321	589	252	58	124	182	8,684[b]
Family trajectories up to age 5 among parents who were cohabiting at birth									
Stable	43.9	29.5	29.1	48.4	50.1	18.7	30.2	32.8	43.4
To married	23.4	5.3	13.2	0.0	49.9	17.5	26.4	33.2	23.2
Periods of separation	5.4	7.4	0.0	0.0	0.0	19.9	26.8	10.9	5.7
To lone parenthood	20.0	51.5	16.9	51.6	0.0	42.6	16.6	15.3	20.4
To re-partnered	7.3	6.3	40.9	0.0	0.0	1.4	0.0	7.8	7.2
Total %	100	100	100	100	100	100	100	100	100
Unweighted sample size	3,266	23	6	4	2	33	35	27	3,396[b]

(continued)

Table 5.3: Relationship between natural parents at the time of birth and subsequent family trajectories to MCS 3 according to mother's ethnicity *(continued)*

Mother's ethnicity	White	Mixed	Indian	Pakistani	Bangladeshi	Black Caribbean	Black African	Other	Total
Family trajectories up to age 5 among solo parents at birth									
Stable	40.7	50.5	33.4	43.4	23.3	52.4	62.1	36.3	42.0
To married	6.6	4.7	55.7	41.2	44.0	2.9	15.6	41.2	8.5
To cohabiting	18.8	13.7	0.0	1.4	27.9	18.4	4.4	6.6	17.5
To new partner	14.9	9.0	0.0	2.0	4.9	2.3	0.4	4.3	13.2
Periods of partnership	19.0	22.2	10.9	11.9	0.0	24.0	17.5	11.5	18.8
Total %	100	100	100	100	100	100	100	100	100
Unweighted sample size	2,050	60	34	52	15	84	118	60	2,473[b]

Notes: [a] Sample: all MCS 3 main respondents also interviewed at MCS1 and MCS 2; not reported for 128 families, sample percentages weighted to correct for sampling design and non-response to survey 1.

[b] Sample percentages weighted to correct for sampling design, non-response and sample attrition up to MCS 3.

mothers in this situation were the most likely to be married to the natural father at age 5 and it may be that there were particular geographical constraints that had prevented the parents being together when the baby was born. Black Caribbean mothers were the least likely to marry the natural father and black African mothers were the most likely to continue to live as a lone mother compared with other ethnic groups. There is also an interesting contrast in the behaviours of the black Caribbean and black African mothers with respect to moving in with the father. Black African mothers were more likely to marry whereas the black Caribbean mothers were more likely to cohabit with the father of their child. From our trajectories we also identified a sub-set of mothers who, although lone mothers at the time of the birth and at the age 5 survey, had had periods of living with a partner since the baby was born. Around one in five of these mothers of white, black and mixed origin had had periods of partnership since the birth of their baby. Most data sources fail to capture this added instability in family life.

In sum, it is clear that there are marked differences in the partnership behaviours of mothers from different ethnic groups. Overall the most unstable family lives are found among black mother families, particularly those of Caribbean origin, regardless of whether they were married or not when they had their baby. Marriage is central to South Asian family life but these families are no more stable than white married families, at least over the first five years of the children's lives. Stable cohabiting unions are most frequently found among white and mixed origin families, rare among South Asian families and such unions are the most prone to breakdown among black mothers.

Family environment at age 5

The next question addressed was whether families with differing trajectories varied in their circumstances five years after the birth of their child. Our focus was on two aspects that were well known to be related to changing family circumstances, namely levels of family income and the psychological well-being of parents and children. It is well established that family transitions are associated with declines in income when parents split and increases when parents re-partner (Jenkins, 2008). Here our focus is on the bottom end of the income distribution and an examination of the extent of poverty in families with different family histories. Changes in mental well-being of parents and children also occur with family changes. There is evidence that separations lower the mental well-being of mothers and re-partnering can enhance it (Acock and Demo, 1994; Pevalin and Goldberg, 2003). Here we examine whether the mothers with different partnership histories varied in the extent to which they exhibited depressive symptoms. Poverty and maternal depression are two aspects of family life that have also been found to be very important in accounting for variation in children's cognitive and emotional development (Downey and Coyne, 1990; Shonkoff and Phillips, 2000; Petterson and Albers, 2001) and this was the case for the MCS children at age 3 (Kiernan and Huerta, 2008; Kiernan and Mensah, 2009). Moreover, there is ample evidence from the extant literature, including our earlier work using the MCS, that poverty and maternal depression are interrelated and this needs to be borne in mind as it is not directly addressed here. Income poverty was examined further in Chapter 2 of this volume.

Poverty

From Table 5.4 we see that at the time of the age 5 interview 30% of the MCS sample of children were estimated to be living in income poverty, with poverty defined as living below 60% of equivalised median income (Ketende and Joshi, 2008); we note these figures are based on the data which include imputed income data where this was not reported. Families with two natural parents were the least likely to be living in poverty; where the two parents were continuously married to each other 15% were living in poverty, and where the two parents were initially cohabiting but then married, 16% were living in poverty. The next most advantaged group were families with continuously cohabiting parents – 23% of these families were in poverty. Compared with married families with children, cohabiting families were found to be more likely to be economically disadvantaged since the early 1990s when comparisons were first made and cohabitation was less frequent (Kiernan and Estaugh, 1993). Living in a lone–mother family raises the chances of living in poverty but we also observed a significant gradient with previously married lone mothers being less likely to be in poverty than their cohabiting contemporaries (52% compared to 67%) who in turn were less likely to be in poverty than families where the mother had been a lone mother since the birth of the cohort child (79%). Interestingly, solo mothers who subsequently married or cohabited with the natural father, although their circumstances improved relative to other women who started out as lone mothers, were not in as advantaged circumstances as married or cohabiting natural families or cohabitants who had made the transition into marriage. All the mentioned differences were statistically significant from one another. There was also some evidence that solo mothers who married the natural father were somewhat less likely to be poor than those who were cohabiting with the natural father (35% as compared with 43% respectively). In sum, it appears from this analysis that the chances of a family living in poverty are associated with both the partnership context at the time of the birth as well as with subsequent partnership.

Maternal depression

The story was somewhat different with respect to whether the mothers were exhibiting depressive symptoms when their child was 5 years old. Depression was assessed from the mother's responses to the Kessler 6 item screening scale for psychological distress (Kessler et al, 2002), which was fully completed by mothers in 92% of the families. In an evaluation on a general population of US adults, scores of 13 or more have been taken as denoting serious mental illness

Table 5.4: Family trajectories: poverty and mother's psychological well-being at MCS 3

Family trajectory	Family experiencing income poverty[a]	Mother experiencing psychological distress[b]
	%	%
Married at birth		
Stable	15.4	9.5
Periods of separation	31.1	15.4
To lone parenthood	52.1	24.1
To re-partnered	36.1	15.6
Cohabiting at birth		
Stable	23.2	14.5
To married	16.4	11.6
Periods of separation	42.2	11.9
To lone parenthood	66.5	20.1
To re-partnered	38.5	22.1
Solo at birth		
Stable	79.3	25.4
To married	35.0	12.1
To cohabiting	47.2	21.6
To new partner	50.0	21.1
Periods of partnership	82.0	33.0
Total	29.7	14.0
Unweighted sample size	14,579[c]	13,115[c]

Notes: [a] Income poverty, less than 60% of the median equivalised household income.

[b] Psychological distress, mother reporting 7–24 points on the Kessler scale.

[c] Sample percentages weighted to correct for sampling design, non-response and sample attrition up to MCS 3.

Sample: all MCS 3 main respondents also interviewed at MCS 2 and MCS 1.

(Kessler et al, 2003). On this basis 3% of the responding mothers in the MCS 3 survey reported serious mental illness. On a less stringent definition of seven or more points, 14% of the responding mothers could be deemed have high levels of psychological distress. It is this latter categorisation that we use here.

From Table 5.4 we see that all the married mothers regardless of whether they were married, cohabiting or solo at the time of the birth had similar levels of depression that were also the lowest rates. Marriage, it seems, is associated with lower reported levels of depression, but we cannot say from this analysis whether this arises from selection of the less depressed into marriage or that being married lessens the chances of depression. Cohabitation, on the other hand, does not appear to bestow the same level of benefit. It is also apparent that women who became lone mothers after the break-up of a marriage or a cohabiting union or at the birth of their baby had relatively high and similar rates of reported depression when their child was 5 years old. The highest levels of reported depression occurred among the solo mothers who had periods of time living with a partner but had reverted to being a lone parent at the time of the 5-year-olds survey. These mothers and their children will have had among the most unstable family lives; 33% of these mothers had high levels of distress compared with 25% of the stable solo lone mothers.

Children's emotional well-being

We now turn our attention to the emotional well-being of the children in these families. In particular we examine whether children with different family experiences are more or less prone to emotional and behavioural problems. Our measures come from assessments derived from the Strengths and Difficulties Questionnaire (SDQ) (see Box 1.2 in Chapter 1, this volume). Responses were summed to provide a total score for each dimension. In this study we examine the externalising (behavioural problems) and internalising dimensions (emotional problems) of the children's behaviour; the former includes the responses to the sections on conduct problems and inattention/hyperactivity, and the latter responses to the section on emotional symptoms. We divided the children according to whether or not they were in the top quintile of the internalising and externalising scales. It may be the case that depressed mothers are more likely than non-depressed mothers to report more negatively on their children's behaviour and consequently the association between maternal depression and child behaviour problems may be not clear-cut or uni-directional (see Smith, 2004, for a clear exposition of these issues).

Logistic regression was used to compare the odds that children with different family histories would be in the upper quintiles of the distributions for externalising and internalising difficulties. The results are shown in Table 5.5. In all models the reference category was families where the parents had been continuously married since the child was born. In model 1 the estimated odds ratios were adjusted for the child's gender and age; in model 2 experience of poverty and maternal depression were also taken into account; and in model 3 a number of further controls were added including: mother's educational attainment, age at first birth, parity and ethnicity, whether English was spoken in the home, number of children in the household, parents' work history, housing tenure and type of pre-school care and education experienced by the child.

Compared with children living in stable married families, virtually all the children with different family histories were more likely to be reported to have externalising behavioural problems at age 5 (Table 5.5). The most marked differences were to be seen for children born into cohabiting families where the parents had separated and solo mothers who had not married the natural father, where the odds of exhibiting behavioural problems for these children were around threefold compared to children in stable married families. Taking account of the mental well-being of mothers and family poverty attenuated the differences and the introduction of additional controls attenuated them still further. However, there are still indications that children born to cohabiting parents who separate and children of solo mothers who cohabit with the natural father or partner another man are more likely to be exhibiting behaviour problems.

The story was somewhat different with respect to internalising emotional problems. From Table 5.5 we see that children born to lone mothers who subsequently married or cohabited with the father and were still living with him at the time of the age 5 survey were not significantly different in their emotional well-being from those who had lived with their married parents from the outset. But compared with children living in stable married families, those who were living in lone-parent families were more likely to be exhibiting emotional problems as were children of separated cohabiting parents and solo mothers who had re-partnered.

Table 5.5: Family trajectories and children's emotional well-being at MCS 3

		Child experiencing externalising difficulties[a]					
		(Model 1)		(Model 2)		(Model 3)	
Family trajectory	%	OR[c]	95% CI	OR[d]	95% CI	OR[e]	95% CI
Married at birth							
Stable	12.8	1 (ref)		1 (ref)		1 (ref)	
Periods of separation	15.9	1.35	[0.85, 2.16]	1.14	[0.69, 1.89]	1.00	[0.59, 1.70]
To lone parenthood	22.1	2.01**	[1.56, 2.59]	1.46**	[1.13, 1.89]	1.33**	[1.01, 1.76]
To re-partnered	19.6	1.77**	[1.14, 2.74]	1.48	[0.94, 2.33]	1.30	[0.83, 2.05]
Cohabiting at birth							
Stable	18.8	1.58**	[1.30, 1.91]	1.44**	[1.20, 1.73]	1.21**	[1.00, 1.46]
To married	17.7	1.45**	[1.13, 1.87]	1.44**	[1.13, 1.85]	1.28	[0.98, 1.68]
Periods of separation	26.5	2.50**	[1.67, 3.72]	2.28**	[1.49, 3.47]	1.67**	[1.07, 2.61]
To lone parenthood	29.0	2.82**	[2.26, 3.52]	2.11**	[1.67, 2.66]	1.66**	[1.28, 2.15]
To re-partnered	32.9	3.41**	[2.30, 5.06]	2.68**	[1.79, 4.02]	2.02**	[1.30, 3.15]
Solo at birth							
Stable	28.7	2.79**	[2.34, 3.32]	1.85**	[1.50, 2.27]	1.22	[0.92, 1.63]
To married	20.7	1.79**	[1.23, 2.59]	1.55**	[1.06, 2.27]	1.21	[0.80, 1.84]
To cohabiting	31.3	3.24**	[2.49, 4.22]	2.68**	[2.05, 3.50]	1.81**	[1.35, 2.43]
To new partner	33.0	3.42**	[2.53, 4.62]	2.70**	[1.99, 3.68]	1.89**	[1.30, 2.76]
Periods of partnership	34.0	3.65**	[2.76, 4.82]	2.21**	[1.62, 3.01]	1.53**	[1.10, 2.14]
Total	18.2						
Unweighted sample size	12,762[f]						
Other covariates added		Child gender and age		Plus income poverty and maternal depression		Full set	

(continued)

Table 5.5: Family trajectories and children's emotional well-being at MCS 3 (continued)

Family trajectory	%	OR[c]	95% CI	OR[d]	95% CI	OR[e]	95% CI
		Child experiencing internalising difficulties[b]					
		(Model 1)		(Model 2)		(Model 3)	
Married at birth							
Stable	15.6	1 (ref)		1 (ref)		1 (ref)	
Periods of separation	19.9	1.35	[0.86, 2.10]	1.17	[0.74, 1.85]	1.05	[0.66, 1.68]
To lone parenthood	22.3	1.56**	[1.22, 1.99]	1.15	[0.88, 1.49]	1.14	[0.87, 1.51]
To re-partnered	17.8	1.17	[0.76, 1.81]	0.95	[0.59, 1.51]	0.94	[0.58, 1.52]
Cohabiting at birth							
Stable	17.7	1.17	[0.96, 1.43]	1.09	[0.89, 1.33]	1.04	[0.84, 1.28]
To married	17.4	1.14	[0.89, 1.47]	1.14	[0.88, 1.48]	1.09	[0.83, 1.41]
Periods of separation	23.1	1.63**	[1.08, 2.47]	1.49	[0.97, 2.27]	1.26	[0.83, 1.92]
To lone parenthood	20.4	1.39**	[1.13, 1.72]	1.03	[0.82, 1.28]	0.93	[0.73, 1.20]
To re-partnered	21.5	1.50**	[1.02, 2.20]	1.17	[0.80, 1.72]	1.09	[0.74, 1.62]
Solo at birth							
Stable	23.1	1.63**	[1.31, 2.02]	1.10	[0.86, 1.41]	0.94	[0.70, 1.25]
To married	20.5	1.40	[0.92, 2.14]	1.19	[0.76, 1.84]	1.00	[0.63, 1.58]
To cohabiting	17.1	1.11	[0.81, 1.54]	0.88	[0.63, 1.25]	0.71	[0.49, 1.02]
To new partner	21.7	1.52**	[1.07, 2.17]	1.19	[0.81, 1.74]	0.97	[0.65, 1.44]
Periods of partnership	27.2	2.03**	[1.54, 2.66]	1.26	[0.95, 1.68]	1.06	[0.78, 1.44]
Total	17.8						
Unweighted sample size	13,416[f]						
Other covariates added		Child gender and age		Plus income poverty and maternal depression		Full set	

Notes: [a] Highest quintile in distribution of externalising scores from parent-reported SDQ, 8 to 20 points.

[b] Highest quintile in distribution of internalising scores from parent-reported SDQ, 3 to 10 points.

[c] Odds ratio including controls for child's gender and age.

[d] Odds ratio including controls for child's gender and age, income poverty and mother's psychological distress.

[e] Odds ratio including controls for child's gender and age, income poverty (MCS 3), mother's psychological distress (MCS 3), mother's level of educational qualification (MCS 1), mother's age at first birth (MCS 1), mother's ethnicity (MCS 1), language spoken in the home (MCS 1), whether the child was the mother's first born (MCS 1), total number of children in the household (MCS 3), history of parental unemployment (MCS 1, 2, 3), housing tenure (MCS 3) and use of early education or childcare facilities prior to primary school (MCS 3).

[f] Sample percentages and regression models weighted to correct for sampling design, non-response and sample attrition up to MCS 3.

Sample: all MCS 3 main respondents also interviewed at MCS 2 and MCS 1 (** $p<0.05$).

However, after taking into account whether the family was living in poverty or the mother was exhibiting depressive symptoms then no significant differences were to be seen between the children with differing family trajectories and children living in stably married families. This suggests that the association between the family trajectories and the child's emotional well-being may be mediated via parental socioeconomic circumstance and mother's mental well-being.

Family status at age 5 and children's well-being

Family trajectories provide a detailed picture on family transitions that children experience and the settings that they have lived through. Generally speaking most studies in this field tend to examine current marital status rather than family histories. So the question posed is whether we would get similar insights on the well-being of children if we just considered the family structure in which they were living at age 5. Table 5.6 shows the extent of emotional and behavioural problems among children in four types of families: married parents, cohabiting parents, lone-parent families and stepfamilies formed through either cohabitation or marriage. This is a simpler classification and, as a consequence, the numbers in the different groups are larger, which gives more statistical power so that an odds ratio of, for example, 1.2 on a smaller sample may not reach statistical significance but may on a larger sample. From these analyses we see that compared to children in married couple families children in the other three types of families were more likely to exhibit emotional problems, but after taking into account whether the family was living in poverty or whether the mother was depressed there was no significant differences across the different families. With regard to behavioural problems we see that compared with children in married couple families children in the other types of families exhibited more behavioural problems, with children living in lone mother and stepfamilies having somewhat higher odds than those living in cohabiting families. Again, after the introduction of the background factors, the odds of children experiencing behaviour problems are much attenuated but remain statistically significantly different from the children living in married couple families and children living in stepfamilies exhibit the highest odds. The higher odds of behaviour problems seen for children in stepfamilies accords with findings from other research studies (see, for example, Dunn et al, 1998).

The additional insights derived from the trajectories are that the greater emotional distress observed among children in stepfamilies who were born to unmarried parents occurs regardless of the route taken to this family form; that children in lone-mother families where the mother has had a prior cohabiting relationship exhibit lower emotional well-being than children in lone-mother families without this experience; and there is lower well-being among children whose parents are cohabiting but who have been reunited after a period of separation. Table 5.5 (model 3) also shows that children in stepfamilies formed after cohabitation have elevated risks of behaviour problems, as do children in lone-mother families following the break-up of a cohabiting union, and children in

Table 5.6: Family status and children's emotional well-being at MCS 3

		Child experiencing externalising difficulties[a]						
		(Model 1)		*(Model 2)*		*(Model 3)*	
Family status at age 5	%	OR[c]	95% CI	OR[d]	95% CI	OR[e]	95% CI
Married	13.5	1 (ref)		1 (ref)		1 (ref)	
Cohabiting	21.4	1.75**	[1.50, 2.03]	1.57**	[1.35, 1.82]	1.24**	[1.06, 1.44]
Lone parent	28.0	2.54**	[2.24, 2.88]	1.71**	[1.47, 2.00]	1.29**	[1.07, 1.55]
Stepfamily	29.6	2.76**	[2.21, 3.45]	2.19**	[1.74, 2.75]	1.60**	[1.23, 2.09]
Total	18.2						
Unweighted sample size	12,802[f]						
Other covariates added		Child gender and age		Plus income poverty and maternal depression		Full set	

		Child experiencing internalising difficulties[b]						
		(Model 1)		*(Model 2)*		*(Model 3)*	
Family status at age 5	%	OR[c]	95% CI	OR[d]	95% CI	OR[e]	95% CI
Married	15.9	1 (ref)		1 (ref)		1 (ref)	
Cohabiting	18.2	1.18**	[1.00, 1.38]	1.07	[0.90, 1.26]	1.00	[0.84, 1.19]
Lone parent	22.8	1.56**	[1.38, 1.77]	1.09	[0.95, 1.26]	1.02	[0.86, 1.21]
Stepfamily	20.5	1.37**	[1.10, 1.72]	1.08	[0.87, 1.36]	1.01	[0.80, 1.29]
Total	17.8						
Unweighted sample size	13,456[f]						
Other covariates added		Child gender and age		Plus income poverty and maternal depression		Full set	

Notes: [a] Highest quintile in distribution of externalising scores from parent-reported SDQ, 8 to 20 points.

[b] Highest quintile in distribution of internalising scores from parent-reported SDQ, 3 to 10 points.

[c] Odds ratio including controls for child's gender and age.

[d] Odds ratio including controls for child's gender and age, income poverty and mother's psychological distress.

[e] Odds ratio including controls for child's gender and age, income poverty (MCS 3), mother's psychological distress (MCS 3), mother's level of educational qualification (MCS 1), mother's age at first birth (MCS 1), mother's ethnicity (MCS 1), language spoken in the home (MCS 1), whether the child was the mother's first born (MCS 1), total number of children in the household (MCS 3), history of parental unemployment (MCS 1, 2, 3), housing tenure (MCS 3) and use of early education or childcare facilities prior to primary school (MCS 3).

[f] Sample percentages and regression models weighted to correct for sampling design, non-response and sample attrition up to MCS 3.

Sample: all MCS 3 main respondents also interviewed at MCS 2 and MCS 1 (** *p*<0.05).

families where cohabiting parents have temporarily separated also have heightened odds of behaviour problems.

Conclusions

The MCS children have experienced a diversity of family forms in their short lives, which are more complex and unstable than was the case among earlier generations of children. By the time they were 5 years old 75% of the children were living with both natural parents compared with around 90% of children born in 1970 who approximate the parental generation of the MCS children (Kiernan, 2004). Furthermore, 41% of the MCS children were born to unmarried parents as compared with 8% of children born in 1970 (OPCS, 1997).

Our array of family trajectories portrays some of the complexity of family life that we encounter in the 21st century and how it varies across ethnic groups and economic circumstances. Here we highlight some of the key findings. It is clear that children born to married parents are much less likely to see their parents separate compared with those born to cohabiting parents. On the other hand, mothers and children in stable cohabiting partnerships (whether they convert into marriages or not) are similar to mothers and children in marital unions in terms of their emotional well-being.

Continuing cohabiting families tend to be more economically disadvantaged than married families. Mothers who had a baby on their own but subsequently cohabited with or married the father of their child are the most disadvantaged of the two-parent families. Undoubtedly, the most economically disadvantaged families are those headed by a lone mother. However, within this set there is also a gradient of disadvantage with the erstwhile married mothers being less likely to be poor than erstwhile cohabiting mothers who in turn are better off than the never-partnered lone mothers. These gradients are likely to be due to the initial selection of the more advantaged women into these different family situations at the outset (Kiernan, 2002) and these legacies continue into the early years of their children's lives.

Mothers living with the father of their child tended to have better mental health than those living with other partners and lone mothers were the most likely to have poor mental health. Poorer mental health is associated with less engaged parenting, which in turn can affect the psychological/emotional well-being of children (Shonkoff and Phillips, 2000; Smith, 2004) and this was shown to be the case among the 3-year-olds in the MCS (Kiernan and Huerta, 2008).

Children who had experienced different family trajectories varied in the extent to which they displayed emotional and behaviour problems. It was clear that, without allowance for other attributes of the families, that children who had not lived with stably married parents over their first five years of life exhibited more behavioural problems at age 5. However, after taking into account other characteristics, the differences were attenuated but not eliminated. Children from cohabiting families that had broken down still exhibited relatively high levels of behaviour problems and similarly children born to solo mothers who cohabited with the natural father or who had re-partnered had higher levels of reported behaviour problems. Family instability and change seem to be an important element in young children's behaviour problems. The most common explanation for these findings from the divorce literature (Coleman et al, 2000) is that partnership changes increase stress among the parents, partners and the children involved as the families adjust to new routines, as the mother focuses attention on the new partner and children compete for the attention of the mother. It may be that such increased stress causes children to have more behavioural problems.

In conclusion, the partnership context in which children are born is associated with a range of disadvantages but post-birth partnership behaviour of parents can also temper or enhance the disadvantage experienced by these families and their children. This is not to say that a parent's partnership situation, either at the time of the birth or subsequently, affects children directly, but rather it reflects parental situations and inputs, which in turn affect outcomes for these families.

SIX

Employment trajectories and ethnic diversity

Shirley Dex and Kelly Ward

An important part of the content of children's early years is their parents' employment, which influences the time children spend with their parents and the level of income in the family. Hours of employment and the quality of working conditions will also influence the extent to which parents are satisfied, tired, exhausted or stressed when they come home. Over time we have seen changes to family economies in Western societies. Mothers have taken up paid work in greater numbers and the predominant family model is no longer that of the traditional male breadwinner with the father employed full time and the mother staying at home to look after the children. What has replaced this in the UK as the dominant arrangement is the 1.5 earner family where fathers work full time and mothers work part time. Dominant patterns may hide diverse experiences. Families from UK minority ethnic groups show variations from the patterns among white families (Dale et al, 2008).

A raft of new policies, statutory provisions and entitlements have been launched in the UK since 1997 to ameliorate some of the pressures on families, their time and their financial circumstances. Attempts to help no-earner families enter the labour market and low-income families to stay employed led to the introduction of the Working Families' Tax Credit (WFTC) system in 1999 and its successor in 2003, the Working Tax Credit (WTC) system, accompanied by the Childcare Tax Credits (CCTC) and the 2003 Child Tax Credits (CTC). Attempts to help families with childcare were also adopted through the 1998 National Childcare Strategy and the 1998 Sure Start programme. These initiatives were the backbone of policies aimed at giving parents a financial incentive to be employed in order to prevent their children from growing up in poverty. Lone parents were a particular target group for such measures. There have even been UK government interventions, in the form of a randomised controlled trial, to test whether a package of new measures could help get lone parents into paid work, the Employment Retention and Advancement (ERA) initiative (see Dorsett et al, 2007; Riccio et al, 2008).

On the workplace side, there have been initiatives focused on getting more employers to offer more flexible working arrangements by, for example, paying for consultants to help them introduce such arrangements (the 2000 Work–Life Balance Challenge Fund). Employed parents with young children (under 6) have been given the right to ask for flexible arrangements of their choice (2003), with the employer given a duty to give their request serious consideration. In addition, parents have been given statutory parental leave entitlements (1999), enhanced statutory maternity leave entitlements (2003), and statutory (paid) paternity leave entitlements (2003), which have all extended the time employed parents can spend out of work to care for new babies without losing their jobs and, in some cases, have offered partial income replacement. The Millennium Cohort Study (MCS) children have been growing up within the context of prolific government activity and interventions to promote, encourage and assist working families. The policy context has been changing substantially, therefore, while we are observing these cohort children's early years.

In this chapter we consider diversity arising from the parents' varied employment hours and care combinations, which we call family economies for both couples and lone parents. We are also interested in diversity linked to ethnicity and diversity linked to partnership status as these are important policy issues. Since we have most data about MCS mothers' employment patterns over this five-year period, we examine more of the detailed employment trajectories that MCS mothers followed over these five early years and their correlates with mothers' characteristics and use of childcare. Mothers' use of flexible working arrangements is also documented and its relationship to their work–life balance. All analyses that follow were weighted using a product of the original sampling weights and an allowance for attrition.[1]

Family economies

The single largest family economy over these years, at approximately one third of MCS families, was one where the father worked full time and the mother worked part time (1.5 earner family). The traditional breadwinner family (father only working) was still evident in these patterns and was practised by almost one third of MCS families when the cohort child was age 9–10 months. This dropped to one quarter by the time the cohort child was 5 years old. Around 11% of MCS families were dual full-time earner families at each of the three MCS surveys, but not necessarily the same couples. The less traditional family economies where women worked more than men were very infrequent across the UK (2%). Lone parents (mainly lone mothers) who were employed constituted 9% of families at age 5, 6% at age 3. Five to six per cent were no-earner couples and a further 11-13% were non-earning lone-parent families, depending on the interview date.

MCS family economies when the cohort child was aged 5 varied according to mother's ethnicity (see Table 6.1). Families where the mother was Indian stood out as having higher percentages of dual full-time earners, 18% compared with the average of 10%, which was also the rate for white families. For families where the mother was white, the predominant type was the neo-traditional type with father employed full time and mother employed part time (37%). This type was also high in frequency among families where the mother was Indian (36%), but fairly uncommon among where she was Pakistani, Bangladeshi (8%) or black (12%). Families where the mother was Indian also had the lowest rates of lone-parent

Table 6.1: Parents' partnership and economic status at age 5 by mother's ethnicity

	Mother's ethnicity					
Parents' partnership and economic status	*White*	*Indian*	*Pakistani/ Bangladeshi*	*Black Caribbean/ Black African*	*Other*	*All UK total*
Both employed full time	10.2	17.5	1.8	12.3	12.8	10.2
Both employed, father full time and mother part time	37.0	36.2	8.4	12.1	18.5	34.9
Both employed, father part time and mother full time	2.3	3.8	2.5	3.8	2.4	2.4
Mother employed, father not employed	1.9	2.2	2.8	0.6	2.2	1.9
Father employed, mother not employed	23.1	26.3	55.6	10.4	26.0	23.9
Both not employed	4.4	2.9	13.1	4.1	5.9	4.7
Lone parent employed	9.1	5.5	2.1	19.5	9.1	9.1
Lone parent not employed	12.0	5.7	13.8	37.3	23.2	12.9
Total	100	100	100	100	100	100
Unweighted sample sizes	11,090	289	611	374	321	12,685

F=2.45, *p*=0.001

Notes: Sample: all MCS 3 lone and couple mothers and lone and couple fathers (natural, adoptive, foster and step) who completed the main or partner interview.

This table excludes any mothers or fathers who were eligible but not interviewed (approximately 50 mothers and 1,225 fathers). The table displays unweighted observations, and weighted percentages.

families. The old traditional family economy of father employed full time and a stay-at-home mother was the predominant type for families where the mother was Pakistani and Bangladeshi (56%), but was much less common among families where the mother was black (10%). Families where the mother was Pakistani or Bangladeshi had higher rates of no-earner couple families (13%), more than double the rates for other ethnic groups. Among MCS families where the mother was black, the most common model was workless lone parenthood (37%) followed by employed lone parenthood (20%). These patterns reflect some of the ethnic differences in mothers' employment patterns described in earlier studies (Dale et al, 2002, 2008; Lindley et al, 2006), and in family trajectories described in Chapter 5 (this volume).

Family economy transitions

We can examine how family economies changed from MCS 1 to MCS 2, a gap of just over two years from approximately 2001/02 to 2004, and between MCS 2 and MCS 3, another two-year gap from 2004 to 2006. Examining the transitions in family types between MCS surveys shows that substantial and complex changes took place in mothers' employment statuses, working hours and in fewer cases, family partnership statuses.

Dual earners were the most stable group in terms of their family economy and partnership status. Among mothers in couples, out of those who were employed at MCS 1 (or MCS 2) approximately four fifths stayed employed and partnered at the next interview (see Figure 6.1). Of the lone parents, it was those starting out as not employed at either MCS 1 (or MCS 2) who were most likely to stay in the same partnership and employment statuses at the next interview; approximately two thirds retained their status as a non-employed lone parent at two successive interviews.

For lone mothers who were not employed, between 13% and 15% moved into employment while remaining lone parents over the two-year gaps between interviews; a further 4-6% moved into a couple and gained employment. A further flow took place from being a lone mother (not employed) into being partnered but not employed; this was 16% between MCS 1 and MCS 2 and 12% between MCS 2 and MCS 3 of the lone but not-employed mothers. However, in the reverse direction, between 20% and 13% of employed lone mothers were not employed by the next interview, two years later. There was also a small percentage flow out of being a partnered but not employed mother into being a

Figure 6.1: Wave-on-wave transitions in mothers' employment and partnership statuses from MCS 1 to MCS 2 and MCS 2 to MCS 3 (% of base in origin interview)

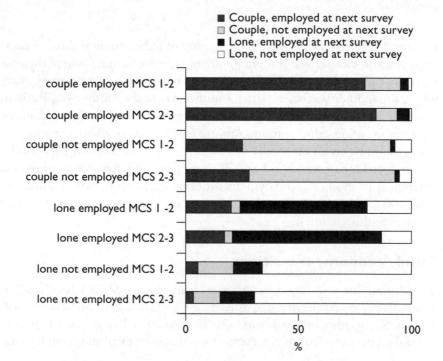

lone mother and not employed by the next interview two years later, of between 7% and 5% of such families. The net effect of all of these flows, given the relative sizes of these sample populations, was an overall reduction in the stock of non-employed lone mothers at MCS 2 and MCS 3 interviews. This is still a positive result from the government's policy perspective. It should be remembered that this five-year period was one of economic growth in the UK economy when jobs were relatively plentiful and expanding. This is likely to have helped the flow into employment. Chapter 2 of this volume contains estimates of the impact of work and family transitions on poverty.

Mothers' employment trajectories

In earlier generations up to 1980, the most common working pattern was for women to work full time after they left school until their first child and then have a period out of employment (Dex, 1984). Over successive generations, this period out of work for childbirth got progressively shorter (Macran et al, 1996). We also know from earlier studies that mothers' employment rates gradually increase as their children grow older. Studies have shown that around the time when a child first enters compulsory schooling is a critical point in mothers' decisions about employment (Paull, 2008), although one that varies across UK countries. This is particularly the case when there are no younger children in the family.

Approximately half of MCS mothers had entered work by the time the baby was 9 months, a figure reached only after five years for mothers born in 1970 (Hansen et al, 2006). Most of these MCS mothers had taken maternity leave (Dex and Joshi, 2005). Mothers who were returning very quickly to their paid work, even returning before the end of the statutory maternity leave entitlement, were most likely using formal childcare. The MCS generation of mothers were also returning to paid work between successive births to a greater extent than used to be the case, having taken up the opportunities of maternity leave (see Martin and Roberts, 1984; and Dex, 1984 for behaviour of earlier generations). It is also the case that far higher proportions of MCS children than in earlier generations attended some form of pre-school childcare whether or not mothers were employed (Hansen et al, 2006), as seen in Chapter 8 later in this volume.

In Figure 6.2 we display the employment trajectories of these mothers from the point when they were pregnant with the MCS cohort child. For some this was their first child, but for others it was a later child. At this point they were in one of three statuses: either 'employed', 'never employed', or a category called 'not employed', although this latter group did have some earlier employment experience before the time they were expecting the MCS child.

Our earlier analysis of the period around pregnancy noted that approximately 80% of those who were employed during pregnancy went on maternity leave and the majority of these (84%) were back at work by the time the baby was 9-10 months old (Dex and Ward, 2007). Clearly, working while pregnant is a good predictor of early (re)entries to work. The later 2008 Maternity Rights

Figure 6.2: Mothers' employment trajectories over first three years (all % on base of status at pregnancy)

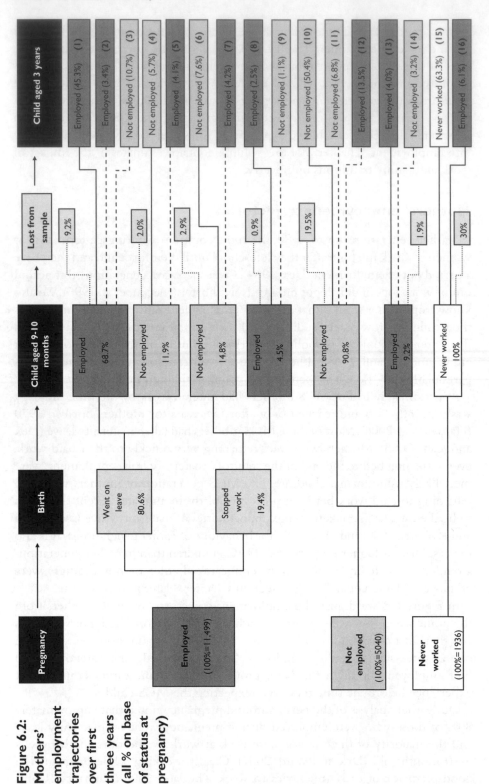

Survey supports this finding (La Valle et al, 2008). Of the 16% who were not employed when the MCS baby was 9–10 months old, 27% had taken some form of maternity leave (and were no longer on leave) but described themselves as no longer working. Of those mothers employed while pregnant, 19.4% finished their job and did not go on maternity leave, but we do not know whether they stopped work in preference, or because they were ineligible for maternity leave with their current employer. Over three quarters of those who took this route were not working when their child was aged 9–10 months, although approximately one in five had returned to work. The vast majority of the women who were not employed during pregnancy were not employed when the baby was 9–10 months old. It is noteworthy that where mothers were employed in pregnancy, the vast majority took up the opportunity of statutory maternity leave, whereas in earlier generations it was a small minority who were eligible, and an even smaller group who took it (Martin and Roberts, 1984). This represents a gradual but now enormous change from past generations.

Starting by looking up to the time their child was aged 3, substantial proportions of mothers had changed their employment status and further changes took place by age 5. The main trajectories up to age three are summarised in Figure 6.2. Because there is attrition in the MCS sample between the first and second surveys, we have shown this group of non-responders in a box of the trajectories. The largest single group was a continuously employed core group of mothers who worked in pregnancy, went on maternity leave, returned by 9–10 months after childbirth and continued in employment without interruptions until the child was 3. This group constituted approximately 45% of those who were employed at pregnancy, and 56% of those who went on maternity leave. Approximately 12% of mothers who went on leave had not returned by 9–10 months after the birth, and only a minority (trajectory 5 = 4.1%) were known to be employed when the child was age 3. Of those who stopped work before the birth, as opposed to going on leave, approximately two thirds were not employed by 9–10 months after the birth. By age 3, approximately 3% had been continuously employed (trajectory 8) and 8% (trajectory 6) had been continuously non-employed since age 9-10 months, on the base of those who were employed at pregnancy; the rest have intermittent spells of employment and non-employment (trajectories 7 and 9 = 4% + 1%). Of those who were not employed during pregnancy, the majority were also not employed at age 3 (trajectories 10, 11, 14 = 50% + 7% + 3%). However, a small proportion did have some, mainly intermittent, employment experience (trajectories 11, 12, 13, 14 = 7% + 14% + 4% + 3%). Approximately 6% of those who had never been employed by age 9–10 months also had some employment experience by age 3.

The characteristics associated with the diverse set of trajectories are displayed in Table 6.2, where there were sufficient sample sizes to carry out an analysis. Mothers who were in employment during pregnancy were more likely to be having their first child. Twenty-three per cent of mothers had another new baby by the time the MCS child was aged 3. These mothers reported the highest rates

Table 6.2: Characteristics associated with mothers' employment trajectories

	Status at MCS 1	Gap between MCS 1 and MCS 2	MCS 2	First birth = CM	New birth since cohort child	SOC^a 1,2,3 at MCS 1	SOC^a 1,2,3 at MCS 2*	Partner at MCS 1	Poverty income at MCS 2	Used part time flexible working at MCS 1^a	Any other flexible working used at MCS 1^a	Unweighted sample size
1	Employed	Continuous	Employed	49.3	21.3	77.1	78.4	95.1	7.2	88.2	75.2	5,178
2	Employed	Intermittent	Employed	46.3	14.2	60.6	62.8	91.3	16.0	83.5	64.8	368
3	Employed	Intermittent	Non-employed	53.2	36.9	58.4	0.0	91.8	26.5	81.7	69.4	1,187
4	Non-employed	Continuous	Non-employed	51.6	19.1	57.6	0.0	89.1	15.8	0.0	0.0	442
5	Non-employed	Intermittent	Employed	64.1	37.3	61.8	58.1	88.9	28.7	0.0	0.0	579
6	Non-employed	Continuous	Non-employed	58.4	33.9	41.1	0.0	77.9	41.9	0.0	0.0	884
7	Non-employed	Intermittent	Employed	45.1	13.8	47.1	49.0	84.8	17.9	0.0	0.0	470
8	Employed	Continuous	Employed	46.1	18.6	54.1	62.8	92.9	14.9	81.7	65.1	287
9	Employed	Intermittent	Non-employed	56.3	39.2	35.2	0.0	87.9	40.2	82.3	60.9	117
10	Non-employed	Continuous	Non-employed	15.8	20.0	38.3	0.0	80.9	47.7	0.0	0.0	2,549
11	Non-employed	Intermittent	Non-employed	23.7	27.3	21.2	0.0	70.8	68.0	0.0	0.0	338
12	Non-employed	Intermittent	Employed	14.6	8.5	43.3	45.1	84.1	26.1	0.0	0.0	636
13	Employed	Continuous	Employed	22.6	13.1	44.3	51.5	84.9	29.0	80.4	54.4	191
14	Employed	Intermittent	Non-employed	20.0	30.0	30.9	0.0	89.3	45.9	81.2	54.4	134
15	Never worked	Continuous	Never worked	31.1	28.1	0.0	0.0	68.5	80.6	0.0	0.0	1243
16	Never worked	Intermittent	Employed	50.4	10.6	0.0	38.5	77.5	44.5	0.0	0.0	122
	All UK total			**41.7**	**23.4**	**55.0**	**38.4**	**87.6**	**26.0**	**86.4**	**72.3**	**14,725**

Notes: Statistics weighted by sweep weight and based only on cases who responded to each item at the sweep. ^{a} = based on employed at sweep. Poverty income of family as defined in Chapter 2. SOC = Standard Occupational Classification 2000.

of intermittent employment and were less likely to be employed when the child was 3.

Over 70% of women in the continuously employed trajectory were in the highest occupational groups. Similarly, over half the mothers who were employed during pregnancy and when their child was 9–10 months, but then went on to be employed intermittently, also belonged to these higher occupational groups.

A large majority of mothers across all trajectories had a partner when their child was 9–10 months of age. Mothers who had never worked were least likely to report having a partner – only two thirds had a partner – whereas mothers who had worked continuously were the most likely to have one, approximately 95%.

Mothers who had never worked by the time the child was 3 were the most likely to be in a household with a low income at age 3 (81%). Those who were not in employment when their child was 9–10 months, nor when the child was 3 years old, regardless of whether or not they had worked between those ages, were also more likely to be below the family income poverty line. Clearly, where the mother was employed, families were far less likely to be below the poverty line.

For further analysis related to these trajectories it was necessary to amalgamate some groups into a smaller set of categories that then allowed us to examine, in a few cases, how ethnic groups varied. Six main categories were produced by taking the two extremes of continuous employment and never employed, and combining other groups largely on the basis of whether mothers had been mainly employed or not employed. These are described in Appendix Table A6.1.

There were interesting variations in mothers' employment trajectories up to age 3 depending on their qualifications, as shown in an earlier investigation (Dex and Ward, 2007, Table 5.10). Just over half of mothers with degrees had been continuously employed up to their child reaching 3. In contrast, over 50% of those with no qualifications had never been employed. Similar proportions of mothers with NVQ Levels 1 and 2 and degree-level qualifications (NVQ Levels 4 and 5) had been employed intermittently since the birth of the cohort child. Clearly, higher educational qualifications are associated with a trajectory of continuous employment or near continuous employment up to age 3. This is consistent with economic theories that suggest the opportunity cost of not working is greater for these highly qualified mothers.

Pakistani and Bangladeshi mothers were the least likely to report continuous employment patterns up to MCS 2 (trajectory 1, 7%), and instead were more likely to have never worked (trajectories 15 and 16, Pakistani 49% and Bangladeshi 64%). In contrast, nearly 2 in 5 black Caribbean, white and Indian mothers had worked continuously (trajectory 1) (trajectories shown in Figure 6.2).

While approximately a third of mothers who reported at MCS 2 that they had breaks from employment since the cohort child was 9–10 months old had had another birth; this proportion was one fifth for the continuously employed group. Mothers who had spent more time working tended to have fewer children. Around 3 in 10 Indian and black Caribbean mothers had only one child by age 3, compared with 2 in 10 black African and Pakistani mothers. Just over 65% of

Bangladeshi mothers had previous children in the household as well as the cohort child, compared to 49% of white mothers.

A multivariate analysis of the characteristics associated with each of the main six trajectories (shown in Appendix Table A6.1) was carried out using multinomial logistic regression analysis. Multinomial regression examines the characteristics associated with mothers having one or other of these six trajectories by MCS 2, although one trajectory ((3), namely an intermittent pattern of working and not working) is omitted and used as a reference group for the rest. The characteristics we examined included ethnicity of the mother, her highest educational qualification, age at birth, whether the cohort child was the first child, whether the mother had an employed partner or was a lone parent, whether the cohort child experienced childcare of some kind, and whether the mother had had another baby since the cohort child. All but the last of these were measured at MCS 1. However, this analysis should not be considered to be examining causal relationships.[3] It was carried out to help describe some of the characteristics that were associated with each broad trajectory up to age 3, with ethnicity being a particular interest. A summary of the findings is displayed in Table 6.3. (See Appendix Table A6.2 for the full results.)

Mothers' ethnicity was significantly associated with some, but not all of these trajectories.[4] This was the case when ethnicity was entered, as a set of dummy variables, into the multivariate analysis as the first step. But the results of adding further independent controls did not eliminate the significant associations of some trajectories with particular ethnic groups of mothers. Pakistani plus Bangladeshi and mothers from Other ethnic groups were more likely to have trajectories that involved the least amounts of paid work up to age 3. Black African, black Caribbean and Indian mothers joined Pakistani plus Bangladeshi mothers in being significantly more likely than white mothers to never have worked up to age 3. However, black Caribbean mothers were also significantly less likely to be associated with the other mainly not working trajectory. This may point to a polarisation within black Caribbean mothers, with some being more likely to be in paid work, and others being more likely to be completely out of the labour market.

On the relationships between trajectories and other characteristics, there were expected results. Being continuously employed up to age 3 was significantly associated with having higher qualifications, having a first child in the MCS and using childcare, although not necessarily only formal care but also care by partners and the child's grandparents. Correspondingly, being more highly qualified made it less likely that mothers would follow one of the trajectories that involved spending longer periods out of work; using formal childcare at MCS 1, similarly, was less associated with these trajectories. This is largely the human capital mechanism at work, where the highly qualified have a greater opportunity cost of not being in paid work and so are more continuous participants in employment, and need to make some sort of childcare arrangements. Having an employed partner was associated with trajectories containing more employment and made it less likely that one of the non-employed trajectories would be followed. Being a young mother, especially a teenage mother, made it more likely that one of the trajectories with relatively little or no employment would be followed, even after allowing for qualifications, and these trajectories were also associated with having another baby in quick succession after the cohort child (by age 3). Spending more time employed over this three to four year period since pregnancy was more likely to be associated with having only one child.[5]

Overall, this set of characteristics by no means fully distinguished between the trajectories mothers followed up to age 3. At the extremes of being in continuous employment, or never employed, the characteristics of these two groups of mothers were distinctive. It may be the case that a wider set of characteristics would help to distinguish more fully between the others. However, it may also be the case that some of these trajectories are not very distinguishable from each other; that mothers who were employed a bit more, or a bit less, over the first three years of the cohort child's life, were not very different from each other.

By age 5 further changes occurred to mothers' employment status and we capture these only in summary form in Figure 6.3. These patterns show much continuity. Mothers who already had strong continuous commitment to employment by the age 3 interview were highly likely, at least 70%, to be employed again when their child was 5. This group of mothers was similar to Hakim's work-centred mothers (Hakim, 2000). However, there was a small group of such mothers who did not keep up this employment continuity. Another group of mothers had a high proportion, 59%, who were employed when their children were 5; these were employed during pregnancy, but stopped work rather than going on leave, but were back in work by the time the cohort child was 9–10 months old. This group is likely to be those who were not eligible for maternity leave at the time, but who had a strong necessity to be earning. This fits the picture of mothers in low-paid jobs with poor conditions. Where earlier participation had been intermittent, the proportions who were employed when their children were 5 were lower. These mothers are more akin to Hakim's description of adaptive mothers, that is, mothers who tend to fit paid work around their family commitments, the latter being given higher priority. Those who had considerable amounts of non-employment in their trajectory up to age 9–10 months were far less likely to be employed when their children were 5. These are more like Hakim's home-centred mothers (Hakim, 2000). However, there were some surprises from these generalisations. A small proportion (at least 8%) of the hard core non-employed group were employed when their children were 5.

If we compare MCS mothers' experiences up to age 5 with those from earlier generations, it is clear that MCS mothers have been returning to employment considerably faster than earlier generations. By the time their first child was 5 years old, 29% of National Child Development Study (NCDS) mothers who had a child born in 1958 had worked at some point over the five years, compared with 48% of mothers of children born in 1970[6] (Hansen et al, 2006) and 78% of mothers of the MCS children. The figure for MCS mothers varied by their qualification

Table 6.3: Characteristics significantly associated with mothers' employment trajectories up to age 3

Trajectory up to MCS 2, age 3	More likely if:	Less likely if:
Always employed	• Higher qualifications • Cohort child is first born • Used formal childcare at MCS 1 • Used partner childcare at MCS 1 • Used grandparent childcare at MCS 1	• Lone mother • Age of mother at birth 14-19 or 20-29
Stopped work after pregnancy and no return made by time child aged 3	• Age of mother at birth 14-19 • Cohort child is first born • Additional child born since cohort child	• Employed partner • Used formal childcare at MCS 1 • Used partner childcare at MCS 1 • Used grandparent childcare at MCS 1
Employed during pregnancy, intermittent spells in and out of employment following pregnancy, not employed when child aged 3	• Cohort child is first born • Additional child born since cohort child • Used formal childcare at MCS 1 • Used partner childcare at MCS 1 • Used grandparent childcare at MCS 1	• Lone parent • Indian
Not employed at MCS 3 (intermittent spells of employment, but overall more out than in)	• Age of mother at birth either 14-19, 20-29 or 30-39 compared with 40+ • Additional child born since cohort child • Pakistani/Bangladeshi or Other ethnicity	• More highly qualified • Employed partner • Lone parent • Cohort child is first born • Used formal childcare at MCS 1 • Used partner childcare at MCS 1 • Used grandparent childcare at MCS 1 • Black Caribbean ethnicity
Never worked	• Age of mother at birth either 14-19 or 20-29 compared with 40+ • Additional child born since cohort child • Indian, Pakistani/Bangladeshi, Black African or Other ethnicity	• More highly qualified • Employed partner • Lone parent • Cohort child is first born • Used formal childcare at MCS 1 • Used partner childcare at MCS 1 • Used grandparent childcare at MCS 1

Notes: Results from multinomial logistic regression where omitted trajectory = intermittent employment and employed at MCS 2.

Sample: All MCS mothers in both MCS 1 and MCS 2. See Table A6.2.

Figure 6.3: All MCS mothers' summary employment trajectories up to age 5 (MCS 3), by employment status at pregnancy

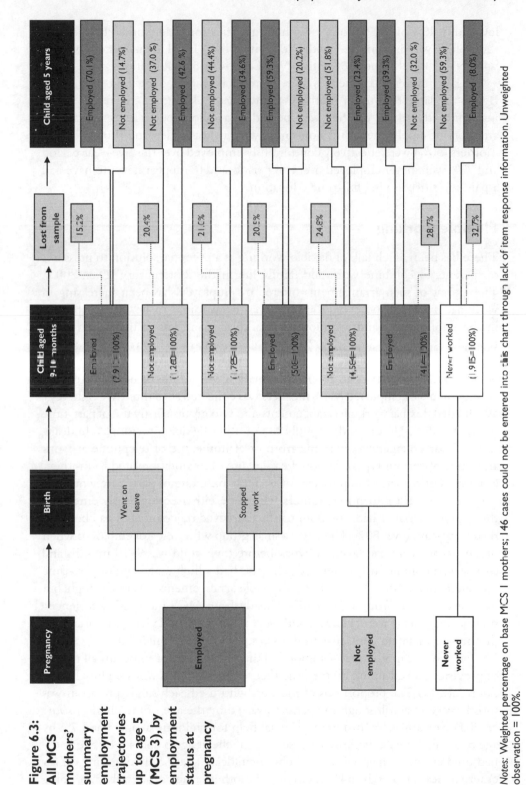

Notes: Weighted percentage on base MCS 1 mothers; 146 cases could not be entered into this chart through lack of item response information. Unweighted observation = 100%.

level: only 45% of MCS mothers with no qualifications had worked by the time their child was 5, compared with 76% with NVQ Level 1 qualifications, 86% with NVQ Level 3 and 90% with NVQ Level 4 or 5 qualifications.

Clearly, mothers' experiences were extremely varied over these five years. By far the largest group of mothers, approximately half (53%), were employed intermittently taking the five-year period as a whole, but with very varying amounts of employment and non-employment. Just under one third of MCS mothers (30%) were effectively continuously employed over this five-year period and 22% were never employed over this period, and 6% appear never to have had a paid job since leaving full-time education.

Flexible working

There has been much talk of flexible working as a potential solution to pressures on parents to combine work and family life in the 21st century (Dex, 2003). The extent of such arrangements offered by employers has been increasing in workplaces (Woodland et al, 2003) and has been found to be more extensive in the public sector and in unionised workplaces and less in male-dominated workplaces (Dex and Smith, 2002). However, there has also been recognition that it has been mainly mothers who have accessed employers' provisions (Hogarth et al, 2000; Woodland et al, 2003). Information on the use of flexible working arrangements by employed MCS mothers was collected at all three MCS surveys. We divided flexible working arrangements into two groups: firstly use of part-time work or reduced hours, and secondly use of other flexible provisions (childcare, time off for emergencies, working from or at home, use of telephone at work and leave of various types). As noted earlier, use of flexibility related to mothers' employment trajectories up to age 3 (see Table 6.2). Use of part-time work was very high on first return for mothers who were either continuously employed throughout (88%) or had a predominantly employed trajectory and had been on maternity leave (over 80%). There was a small group who were not employed when pregnant, but who had taken up work before their child was 9–10 months and then stayed continuously employed who also had a high usage rate of part-time arrangements (80-81%). Use of other flexible arrangements was not as high, but extensive, ranging from 54% to 75%. Clearly from MCS mothers' experiences, such arrangements are, in general, both very widespread and vitally important for mothers to maintain contact with the workplace around childbirth.

Of all MCS 2 mothers, 24% responded that they were not using any of the list of provisions asked about. By the time their child was 5 this was a slightly higher figure, at 31%. The proportions of mothers who used each single provision was mostly very small, although the patterns varied by the age of the child in some cases. For example, 9% had used financial help for childcare at age 3 and 7% by age 5; 3% had used a workplace nursery or crèche at age 3 and 4% by age 5; 6% had used employer help with after-school childcare at age 5. Taking time off for emergencies was used by 54% of employed mothers at age 3, but only 39% going up to age 5. Time off for family emergencies, which became an employee right in 2000, declined in use as children got older.

The public sector has commonly been thought to provide better working conditions for its employees. Use of employers' family-friendly provision by MCS employee mothers at age 3 supported the idea that the public sector was a better provider than the private sector, albeit by a fairly small margin (see Table 6.4). The provision of allowing employees the use of a telephone at work was an exception. By age 5, employee mothers' usage of employers' family-friendly provisions was mostly but not significantly different between public and private sectors. This may be because provisions in the public sector have been deteriorating since budget cuts in 2006.

The use of family-friendly provisions by employed mothers varied considerably by mother's NS-SEC occupational classification at every age of the child. With few exceptions, mothers in managerial and professional occupations had the highest usage of this set of family-friendly provisions (with the exception of term-time-only working). The size of the difference was large in the case of financial help with childcare vouchers, use of maternity leave and working at, or from, home occasionally. It was not uncommon for the frequency of using one of these provisions by professional and managerial employees to be more than double the size of the use by semi-routine and routine employees, and somewhere between the extremes for the other intermediate NS-SEC occupations. Semi-routine and routine occupations tended, therefore, to have the lowest percentages of mothers using such arrangements. This difference in use across occupations is likely to have arisen in part from employers being less likely to offer family-friendly provisions to lower-paid employees. Also, where they were offered, employees on low earnings could not always afford to take up unpaid provisions. There appears to be a virtuous (or vicious) circle therefore. Mothers in better jobs, who may need these less, appeared to get access to better working conditions tailored to

Table 6.4: Extent to which mothers used flexible working arrangements, by type of organisation (%)

Used employer provisions for:	Age 3 Private	Age 3 Public	Age 5 Private	Age 5 Public
Financial help with childcare	7.7[a]	9.6[a]	7.6	7.6
Care for child after school	5.0[a]	7.2[a]	6.5	5.2
Time off for emergencies	52.0[a]	57.3[a]	37.8[a]	42.3[a]
Use of telephone at work	44.7	45.6	26.1[a]	23.9[a]
Working at or from home occasionally	– [b]	– [b]	15.4	14.4
Unweighted sample size	4,313	2,703	4,415	3,023

Notes: [a] Significantly different by type of organisation at 95% confidence level. [b] Question asked on this topic at MCS 2 not comparable with question asked at MCS 3.

Sample: MCS 2/MCS 3 employee mothers reporting the type of organisation they worked in and multiple responses on employer's provisions. Weighted percentages.

their needs of combining work and care, whereas those with greater pressures for income appeared to have access to less favourable conditions.

Work–life balance

Lastly we examine the work–life balance of MCS mothers who were asked about this when the child was aged 5. Approximately two thirds of all employed mothers said they were very or fairly satisfied with their work–life balance at this age (see Table 6.5). Mothers who worked full time and had not used any part-time options were the least likely to be very or fairly satisfied with their work–life balance (38%), and those who had used part-time working arrangements were the most likely (75%) to be very or fairly satisfied with their work–life balance. Satisfaction with work–life balance was highest among those working as small employers or self-employed (74%), and semi-routine or routine workers (71%) and lowest among low supervisory and technical (60%) or managerial and professional workers (61%). There were also differing rates of satisfaction with work–life balance associated with the various employment trajectories. To be included in this analysis mothers had to be employed at MCS 3, otherwise they were not asked about their work–life balance. Given this, rates of satisfaction with work–life balance were lower among mothers who had spent more time at work over the last five years and higher among those who had spent less time, although the differences were not large. So, for example, 63% of those who were continuously employed up to age 3 and employed at age 5 were very or fairly satisfied with their work–life balance. In comparison, 78% of mothers who had been intermittently employed from the birth up to age 3, not-employed at MCS 2 but employed again at age 5 were very or fairly satisfied with their work–life balance. There are pointers here suggesting that continuous attachments to the labour force over the first five years of a child's life may prove challenging for some mothers and a drain on their energy. It is not possible to go into detail about mothers' mental health in this chapter, but other descriptive analyses of MCS mothers (Roberts and Ketende, 2008) suggest that the mental health of mothers who are in paid work at age 5 is reasonably good, and that it is those who are out of work who are more likely to have problems. Chapter 5 (this volume) shows that mother's mental health is also related to partnership instability.

Conclusions

This examination of parents' employment has shown that this generation of children is growing up in a wider range of family economies with a very varying set of mothers' employment trajectories. These differences signal differences in family incomes (discussed more in Chapter 2, this volume), but also varying year-to-year amounts of time spent in the home as opposed to the workplace at least by mothers. While further family formation is responsible for some of mothers' year-to-year transitions in and out of employment, by no means all of it can be attributed to having new

Table 6.5: Mothers' views on their work–life balance at MCS 3 by use of flexible working arrangements up to MCS 3

	Work–life balance at MCS 3				
	Very/fairly satisfied	Neither	Very/fairly dissatisfied	Total	Unweighted n
MCS 3 – Types of flexible working used					
Uses flexible working options (ie either has financial help with childcare, workplace nursery or care for child after school)	62.1	13.3	24.6	100	7,362
Does not have use of these flexible working options	66.1	13.7	20.2	100	7,362
Uses time off for emergencies	61.4	15.0	23.6	100	7,362
Works part time or has job share or has term-time contracts	75.0	11.3	13.7	100	8,030
Works full time and does not have job share or term-time contracts	37.6	20.1	42.4	100	8,030
Employment trajectory up to MCS 2					
Always employed	63.4	13.7	22.8	100	4,394
Employed at pregnancy and not employed at MCS 2	77.8	8.4	13.8	100	245
Intermittently employed and employed at MCS 2	65.6	14.7	19.6	100	1,675
Intermittently employed and not employed at MCS 2	78.0	9.0	13.0	100	561
Mainly not employed	76.1	11.5	12.4	100	524
All UK total	66.5	13.4	20.1	100	7,574

Note: Sample: MCS 3 employed mothers. Weighted percentages.

babies who need greater amounts of parental care. Ethnic cultural differences and other general preferences of parents play a part in decisions about paid work and care. But also the plain economic incentives are evident among highly qualified mothers. Their higher amounts of human capital swing the balance of decision making towards keeping in continuous contact with the labour market over the period of family formation, assisted by their being able to access flexible working arrangements, in order to secure the benefits of their earlier investments in education.

On the other hand there is a group, mainly lone mothers, who are persistently out of the labour market, not only over the five-year period we have examined, but dating back to leaving full-time education. While there was some evidence of lone parents moving into paid work over this period, in an era of buoyant job opportunities and government interventions to assist them, the majority of this non-employed group stayed out of paid work and locked into low income and, in the majority of cases, were bringing up their children in poverty, as shown in Chapter 2 (this volume).

There are a few warning signs that all is not well in the work–life balance for some mothers who have been keeping up a continuous employment profile over this five-year period. However, the majority of employed mothers appear content with their work–life balance. This suggests that the majority of MCS children are growing up with mothers who are reasonably content with their allocation of working and caring time, although as many as one third of these families and their children may not be so fortunate. Compared with earlier generations of children, it is no longer unusual for MCS children to have a working mother when they are pre-school age, even though many mothers may be in and out of paid work over this period. Even children whose mothers are not employed over this five-year period are likely to have seen other children's mothers in jobs. So MCS children are growing up thinking that working mothers are the norm.

Since the point in time at which our data stop for these mothers, around 2006, policies and statutory entitlements have moved on, yet again. Statutory Maternity Pay was increased from 26 weeks of paid leave to 39 weeks in 2007; the National Childcare Strategy was refreshed in 2009; and the New Deal for Lone Parents has announced obligations for lone parents with respect to benefit receipts and employment. These will form some of the background for the next phase of these MCS parents' lives and decision making, and because of that, provide further context for children growing up.

Notes

[1] The attrition weights used were derived from an analysis of MCS 2, which have been demonstrated to be very similar to those later produced on the basis of MCS 3 non-response.

[2] The age 3 weighted percentages in the final column were calculated on the weighted base of status at the time of pregnancy, although it is the unweighted sample size base shown in the Figure 6.2. A few mothers returned to work before MCS 1 and were not working by MCS 1. They are classified by their status at MCS 1.

[3] Given the trajectories covered a period of time, it was not possible to have strict time sequences between the employment and non-employment spells making up the trajectory and other timed measures. Also, given some trajectories represented having no or very little employment over the period, up to age 3, it was not possible to include as independent variables, characteristics that were only available if mothers had been employed.

[4] It is possible that the lack of significance may be due to the small sample sizes of minority ethnic groups in comparison with whites.

[5] At a last stage, we included the use of any flexible working arrangements at age 9-10 months into the multivariate analysis. This could never be a wholly satisfactory procedure, since mothers would only be using flexible working arrangements if they were employed, and some trajectories could be bound to have few, if any, cases because they represented being predominantly out of paid work. The results suggested that having used any of a set of employers' flexible working arrangements, or having worked part time, both made it significantly more likely that the mother would have had one of the two trajectories containing more employment experience. This confirmed findings noted earlier in this chapter, that mothers who were managing to do more paid work over this period did so with the support of employers' flexible working arrangements, including working part time.

[6] NCDS reports mothers having any paid work before the child went to school; the British Cohort Study of 1970 (BCS 70) statistic refers to mothers having any paid work at or up to the age 5 interview who held a job that started more than a year earlier; the MCS statistic refers to weighted statistics of any paid work experience recorded up to and including the age 5 interview.

Appendix

Table A6.1: Mothers' amalgamated employment trajectories to when child aged 3

Mother's employment trajectory from pregnancy to child aged 3	%	Groups covered in Figure 6.2
Continuously employed from pregnancy to when child aged 3	35.2	(1)
Stopped work after pregnancy and no return made by time child aged 3	9.8	(6, 9)
Employed during pregnancy, intermittent spells in and out of employment following pregnancy, employed when child aged 3	17.2	(2, 5, 7, 8, 12, 13)
Employed during pregnancy, intermittent spells in and out of employment following pregnancy, not employed when child aged 3	8.1	(3, 4)
Not employed (intermittent spells of employment, but overall remained not employed)	20.5	(10, 11, 14)
Never worked	9.3	(15, 16)
n	14,725	

Note: Sample: MCS 2 mothers. Weighted percentages.

Table A6.2: Results of the multivariate multinomial regression analysis on mothers' employment trajectories up to age 3

	Always employed	Stopped work after pregnancy and no return made when child aged 3	Employed during pregnancy, intermittent spells in and out of employment following pregnancy, not employed when child aged 3	Not employed (intermittent spells of employment, but overall remained not employed)	Never worked
Ethnic group (ref = white)					
Indian	0.230	-0.448	-0.608**	0.047	2.089**
Black Caribbean	0.263	-0.446	-0.080	-0.577*	-0.100
Black African	0.404	-0.130	0.406	-0.528*	1.966**
Pakistani/Bangladeshi	0.001	-0.178	0.139	1.382**	3.489**
Other	-0.254	-0.042	-0.224	0.651**	2.277**
Qualifications (ref = none + overseas)					
Degree education	0.847**	-0.135	-0.038	-0.749**	-2.493**
NVQ Level 3	0.820**	0.103	0.070	-0.585**	-2.506**
NVQ Levels 1 or 2	0.542**	-0.042	-0.006	-0.363**	-1.874**
Age of mother at birth (ref = age 40+)					
13-19	-1.586**	0.553**	-0.378	1.216**	2.785**
20-29	-0.528**	0.006	-0.340	0.373*	1.002**
30-39	0.122	0.090	-0.127	0.485**	0.395
Partnership					
Employed partner	0.612	-0.381**	-0.169	-1.339**	-1.930**
Lone mother	-0.428**	-0.153	-0.452*	-0.611**	-0.649**
Children					
Child first born	0.267**	0.429**	0.258**	-1.573**	-1.245**
Another child since	-0.048	0.490**	0.805**	0.537**	0.415**
Childcare at MCS 1					
Formal	2.223**	-1.872**	0.881**	-2.461**	-1.544**
Partner	1.293**	-1.239**	0.673**	-1.886**	-3.971**
Grandparent	2.170**	-1.246**	0.931**	-1.853**	-1.781**
Constant	-1.313**	-0.334	-1.045	1.681**	0.657**
Observations, F=69.91 p=0.000	14,686				

**/* significant at 5%/10% level of confidence

Notes: Sample: All MCS mothers in both MCS 1 and MCS 2 sweeps. Weighted analyses. Omitted trajectory = intermittent employment and employed at MCS 2.

SEVEN

Neighbourhoods and residential mobility

Sosthenes Ketende, John McDonald and Heather Joshi

Introduction

In the Millennium Cohort Study (MCS) children's early years, many families had not settled permanently in the home and place in which they would spend most of their childhood. Nearly half had moved home at least once between the interviews at 9 months and age 5. This chapter is concerned with the families' satisfaction with the area they were living in at age 5 and the moves that had been made to get there, from diverse social and spatial starting points.

It is relatively common for families with young children to move home (Plewis et al, 2008). Such mobility often benefits both adults and children, for example when it is related to changes of job. The unemployed may move to improve their employment prospects (Boheim and Taylor, 2002). Residential mobility may be motivated by consideration of school choice, with families relocating close to 'good' schools (Gibbons and Machin, 2006). After a(nother) child is born, some families will move to larger/better accommodation or to a better/safer area. Others move in less favourable circumstances, for example, because they have been evicted, or because a couple splits up. Whatever the circumstances, moving home, and possibly moving job or school as well, can be very stressful for both adults and children. Moving can result in the loss of a supportive social network of friends and neighbours and this loosening of the 'ties that bind', as discussed in Chapter 3 (this volume), may have untoward consequences. Frequently moving couples have been found to have a high risk of union break up (Boyle et al, 2008).

Is there evidence that moving home disrupts children's lives? Cullis (2008) found no difference in cognitive and behavioural scores of MCS children at age 3 according to whether the families had moved home between the first two surveys. Verropoulou et al (2002) examined the relationship between moving home, family structure and children's well-being, using data collected on the school-aged children of one third of the British 1958 cohort members (National Child Development Study, NCDS). They found little to no association between moving residence and children's well-being measured by attainment in mathematics and reading and on assessments of aggression and anxiety. However, moving residence can potentially disrupt the relationships with healthcare professionals and providers. Using MCS data, Pearce et al (2008) found that moving residence was negatively associated with the uptake of childhood immunisations in MCS cohort children. Hence, the effects of moving home are mixed and might be positive, negative or neutral depending on the outcome measures used, the reason for the move and the circumstances and characteristics of the people making the move or staying put.

The relationship between child well-being and the characteristics of a neighbourhood is also not straightforward. While a 'better' environment should, by definition, promote child well-being, such environments tend to attract parents better equipped to give their child a good start in life. Researchers are not always able to distinguish the effects of the characteristics of the setting from those of the people selected into it. Cullis (2008) had difficulty identifying many independent 'neighbourhood effects' on MCS children's development at age 3 when the family's individual characteristics were also taken into account. Contextual variables included mothers' subjective ratings of the area at MCS 1 and interviewer rating of the street at MCS 2. However, if the ward was classified as disadvantaged in the MCS sample design, this did appear to intensify family-level disadvantages detected in Cullis's analysis. Chapter 13 (this volume) reports similar findings, of few independent neighbourhood influences on children being overweight. Families' private circumstances tend to match the qualities of the place where they live, so they should be treated as parallel, if not interacting, dimensions of living standards. This chapter makes no attempt to assess its impact on children, but treats the quality of the area as an object of interest in itself.

This chapter focuses on the place the cohort family has been living, and changes in it if they move home. It relates residential mobility to factors such as type of housing and neighbourhood. How much mobility has there been over the three surveys since MCS 1? Do family circumstances, for example, type of accommodation and housing tenure at MCS 2, predict subsequent mobility? We also look at families' perception of their neighbourhood in terms of whether the respondent feels the family lives in a good area for raising children and how safe they feel the area is. We investigate whether these perceptions are related to subsequent mobility and whether neighbourhood ratings at age 5 are related to disadvantaged family circumstances including housing tenure at younger ages.

Housing tenure, neighbourhood and mobility

There is particular interest in housing tenure, since the location of homes in the UK is tied up with their ownership status. Socially subsidised tenancies from councils or housing associations are generally concentrated in areas with few owner-occupiers. There has been a great deal of interest in the consequences, or at least outcomes, of growing up in social housing. Although it is not necessarily the intention of housing policy, on average the homes in this sector are of poorer quality in terms of size and many features of the neighbourhood. It has also been found that for the cohorts born in 1958 and 1970, the social housing sector was not an auspicious place to be brought up (Feinstein et al, 2008; Lupton et al,

2009). This was not always the case. Children brought up in council housing in the 1946 cohort did not appear to have been at any extra disadvantage in later life. This fits with the changing nature of the social housing sector, reflecting changing allocation policies, the 'Right to Buy' and changes in the structure of families and the labour market. The resulting residualisation of the clientele to which it catered was summed up as shifting from the 'neat and tidy' in the post-war generation, to providing for the 'tight and needy' by the turn of the century (Lupton et al, 2009; quoting Donnison and Ungerson, 1982). Like other welfare benefits, public housing may constitute both a safety net and a trap. There are some reasons to think that social housing constitutes a disadvantage in itself – through the stigmatisation of neighbourhoods, such as 'problem estates', or through obstacles to job mobility. People may become immobilised by the non-transferability of their low rent (Hills, 2007). However, there are advantages to a young family from having a secure tenancy. Parents effectively outside the labour market, such as lone mothers, might not be seeking work anyway. There is again a problem of identifying consequences and the effects of selection. The sorts of people for whom social housing is provided may bring their own economic or health disadvantages with them, so the reasons for the poorer long-term prospects for their children are not clear, nor are the policy implications straightforward (Feinstein et al, 2008; Lupton et al, 2009). The MCS cannot yet provide evidence of the outcomes for the children currently growing up in this less favoured tenure, but there is already evidence of a greater social divide between those families in social housing and other tenures than there was in previous cohorts at similar ages.

At the age 5 survey 22% of the families (who had been in all three surveys) lived in social housing, 68% in owner-occupation, 8% in private renting and 3% in other arrangements, such as living with their parents. This represents a small shift towards owner-occupation, which was 64% at MCS 1, coming mainly from other arrangements, and a net drop of around 1% in social housing. When their children were 5, the social renters were most likely among the tenure groups to have low income (see also Chapter 2, this volume), low education, low rates of employment for mothers and to be lone parents. Black, but not Asian, ethnic groups were also over-represented in the sector. One contrast, for example, is that 54% of lone parents lived in social housing at MCS 3 compared with 14% of couples. Children living in social housing were generally rated less well by their teachers even after allowing for other characteristics, as Chapter 12 notes later in this volume.

Mobility and follow-up surveys

The movers are by definition no longer at the address at which they were first interviewed. Keeping up with them has been one of the challenges of the survey fieldwork, as it is for all longitudinal surveys. There are nevertheless lower rates of successful follow-up for the mobile than for those who do not move (Plewis et al, 2008). Loss of families with different characteristics to those who remain poses a challenge for analysis. In this chapter, in order to study longitudinal patterns in mobility we restrict our analysis to what is called the balanced panel, where each family provides information at every survey, and apply attrition weighting in an attempt to minimise bias.

Residential mobility over three surveys

Over a third of MCS families (38%) moved home between the cohort child being 9 months to age 3 (Hughes et al, 2007). When the child grew from age 3 to 5, residential mobility was substantially lower (24%). Among the 2,477 families who reported a move over the second period, the most common reasons mentioned were a larger home (42%), a better area (22%), a better home (21%) and for children's education (13%). Less common responses included more negative reasons for moving like partnership break-up (10%), trouble with neighbours (4%) and eviction (3%) (Ketende and McDonald, 2008). The pattern of reasons given for moving between MCS 1 and 2 was very similar, with even more emphasis on wanting a larger home (47%) (Hughes et al, 2007).

Among those families participating at all three surveys, around half reported at least one change of address, with 40% reporting one move and 9% two or more moves. There was more stability in the type of housing reported (90% were in the same type of dwelling at all three surveys, usually a house or bungalow) and the tenure of that housing (79% were the same throughout). Even those who moved mostly stayed in their original tenure (66%). There was a small net increase in owner-occupation from the child being 9 months to age 5, which arose from an excess of shifts into owner-occupation (23% of non-owners at MCS 1) over shifts in the other direction (6% of owners ceased to own). One way to summarise the direction of these moves is offered in Figure 7.1. Here we classify the three addresses by a small geographical unit, the lower super output area (LSOA), used in the census. It is smaller than the ward, used in the sample design, and is available for all three surveys, classified into deciles of the Index of Multiple Deprivation (IMD). LSOAs have a minimum population of 1,000, whereas wards vary more in size, but with an average population around 5,000. This index has been combined from those published in each of the four countries of the UK (Scottish Government, 2004; NISRA, 2005; WAG, 2005; CLG, 2007). The index for England uses some 37 indicators of local conditions and service provision, mainly as obtaining at the 2001 Census. We dichotomised the index at the 30th percentile, which roughly approximates the line used to separate non-disadvantaged and disadvantaged wards in the MCS sample design, as shown in Figure 7.1.

Wards were originally classified as 'disadvantaged' on the basis of one indicator, the child poverty index. Addresses in these wards were classified here as 'deprived' on the basis of the usually smaller LSOA. The discrepancies reflect varying conditions within wards, changing ward boundaries and the wider criteria used in the IMD. There are very few families living in 'deprived' LSOAs within the

Figure 7.1: IMD of areas of residence (LSOA) at MCS 1–MCS 3, by original ward (unweighted percentages, balanced panel)

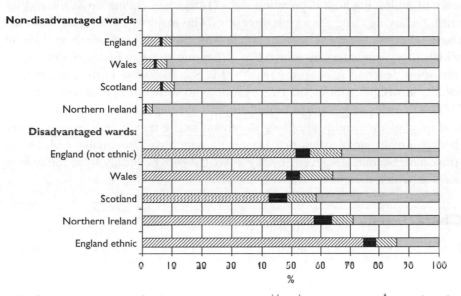

non-disadvantaged wards at even one survey. On the contrary, only a minority originally sampled in 'disadvantaged wards' have ever been interviewed outside a 'deprived' LSOA, particularly few from the 19 minority ethnic wards.

The two left-hand bars of Figure 7.2 divide the sample into the 42% with at least one house move taking them over a LSOA boundary and the 58% whose interviews all took place in the same small locality. This excludes approximately 7% of the sample whose moves were confined to the immediate locality.

Figure 7.2: Stability of residence by locality (LSOA) and the level of its deprivation index at three surveys

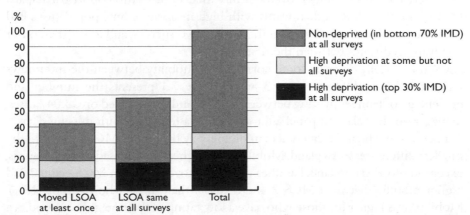

The total bar on the right of Figure 7.2 shows that 64% of the (weighted) sample had been interviewed in low deprivation areas at all three surveys, and that 25% had been in high deprivation localities on all occasions; 11% had a mixed experience or 26% of those with changes in locality. Among these changers there were more leaving high deprivation areas (14%), than ending up in them (9%), with 2% having changes in both directions. The majority of families, including those who did not move, remain at age 5 in the type of deprivation zone in which they were interviewed at MCS 1. Among those in places classed in the 30% most deprived areas on the IMD at MCS 1, 81% were in the same type of locality at MCS 3. Among the larger group who were not in a high deprivation IMD originally, only 6% had moved into a high deprivation area. This implies that most of the families are likely to remain in the type of area in which they were originally sampled, but that a minority, which will presumably continue to grow, have become distanced, socially as well as geographically, from the type of ward in which they were originally sampled.

Characteristics of movers

Residential mobility is related to many factors. There were substantial differences in the extent of residential mobility in recent years of MCS families by UK country (Ketende and McDonald, 2008, Table 13.2). The highest rate of mobility between MCS 2 and 3 was in Northern Ireland (30%) and the lowest in Wales (19%). However, almost all these moves were within country (99% of our whole sample were interviewed at MCS 3 in the same country as at MCS 1). Wales had also shown relatively low mobility when the children were under 3, but at that stage Northern Ireland had the lowest rate (Hughes et al, 2007). An examination of another aspect of moves between MCS 1 and 2 by rural–urban residence (for England) found most moves were within the original zone, with slightly more of those who changed going towards rather than away from rural destinations (Joshi et al, 2008). The highest incomes were found in villages and those moving towards them, suggesting that 'flight' from the cities, for those that can afford it, is one of the positive flows of family movement in which some of this cohort participate. In contrast, the wholly urban wards with high minority ethnic populations had the lowest mobility of all between the second two surveys, and lower than other disadvantaged wards between the first two.

We now briefly describe some correlates of mobility between the interviews when the MCS child was aged 3 and 5. Table 7.1 presents the number and percentage of families moving between MCS 2 and 3. It is based on 13,047 cases, drawn from the balanced panel after discarding a few cases with missing data.

There were substantial differences in mobility by the type of MCS ward with the smallest differences in England. Mobility was highest in the disadvantaged wards, except in Northern Ireland. Families who had moved between MCS 1 and 2 had higher mobility between MCS 2 and 3 (24%) than those who had not (18%). Mobility was higher for those who gave a low rating of their neighbourhood as a

Table 7.1: Whether the cohort family moved address between MCS 2 and MCS 3: frequencies of predictor variables and logistic regression estimates[1]

Predictor variables		Moved address between MCS 2 and MCS 3		Model estimates moved = 1 versus not moved = 0	
		Moved %	Unweighted observed base (n)	Odds ratio	95% CI
Ward type at MCS 1	**England:**				
	Non-disadvantaged	19.2	3,661	1	
	Disadvantaged	21.1	3,088	0.83**	[0.71, 0.98]
	Ethnic minority	18.6	1,435	0.57**	[0.47, 0.68]
	Wales:				
	Non-disadvantaged	14.6	618	0.75**	[0.56, 0.99]
	Disadvantaged	18.3	1,364	0.75**	[0.64, 0.88]
	Scotland:				
	Non-disadvantaged	20.4	835	1.05	[0.86, 1.27]
	Disadvantaged	26.6	748	1.04	[0.85, 1.26]
	Northern Ireland:				
	Non-disadvantaged	29.7	532	2.05	[0.91, 4.62]
	Disadvantaged	23.1	766	1.07	[0.83, 1.37]
Address at MCS 1 and MCS 2	Did not move	18.4	8,309	1	
	Moved	24.0	4,738	1.13**	[1.04, 1.24]
Whether MCS 2 location is good to bring up children	Excellent	16.5	3,987	1	
	Good	19.0	5,155	1.25**	[1.12, 1.40]
	Average	23.9	2,725	1.67**	[1.46, 1.92]
	Poor	29.8	752	2.38**	[1.94, 2.92]
	Very poor	36.4	428	3.02**	[2.35, 3.87]
Family income at MCS 2	Not low	19.0	9,319	1	
	Low[a]	23.9	3,728	0.91	[0.82, 1.02]
Housing tenure at MCS 2	Own including mortgage	16.3	8,703	1	
	Private renting	44.3	943	3.29**	[2.81, 3.84]
	Social renting	22.2	2,962	0.90	[0.78, 1.04]
	Other	38.0	439	2.74**	[2.21, 3.41]

(continued)

Table 7.1: Whether the cohort family moved address between MCS 2 and MCS 3: frequencies of predictor variables and logistic regression estimates[1] *(continued)*

Predictor variables		Moved address between MCS 2 and MCS 3		Model estimates moved = 1 versus not moved = 0	
		Moved %	Unweighted observed base (n)	Odds ratio	95% CI
Type of accommodation at MCS 2	House or bungalow	18.6	11,798	1	
	Flat or maisonette	37.1	1,196	2.29**	[1.96, 2.68]
	Room, bedsit, etc	39.6	53	2.26**	[1.27, 4.03]
Highest academic qualification of mother[b]	Graduate level	20.0	3,587	1	
	Other qualifications	20.0	7,371	0.79**	[0.71, 0.88]
	No qualifications	22.6	2,089	0.86**	[0.74, 0.98]
Parental informants, MCS 1 and MCS 2	No change	19.1	11,488	1	
	At least one person different at MCS 2	30.1	1,559	1.36**	[1.19, 1.55]
Mother's age at MCS 2[b]	Under 30 years	27.2	4,151	1	
	30 years and above	17.2	8,896	0.68**	[0.62, 0.75]

Notes: Analysis sample n=13,047 **p < 0.05

[a] Low income is defined as either family net weekly income (adjusted for family size on OECD scale) below 60% of national median, or receiving Income Support.

[b] Mother or other main respondent, at MCS 2.

good area to bring up children (36% mobility for a very poor rating, 17% mobility for an excellent rating). Low-income families, defined here as those with an income below 60% of the national median income adjusted for the number of children and adults in the family or those receiving Income Support at MCS 2, were more likely to move (24%) than those with higher incomes (19%). Homeowners (16%) were less likely to move between MCS 2 and 3 than those in social housing (22%) and those renting privately were most likely to move (44%). Families in houses or bungalows were much less likely to move (19%) than those in a flat or maisonette (37%) or other types of accommodation (40%). Mobility went down slightly as level of education went up, from no qualification to some. We also look at the stability of parental informant figures over these surveys, where changes would usually be due to partnership break-up or re-formation (see also Chapter 5, this volume). If there was no change between MCS 1 and 2, mobility was lower (19%) than if at least one informant was different at MCS 2 (30%). If the mother figure was under 30 years old at MCS 2, mobility was higher (27%) than if older (17%). There was a similar pattern of characteristics associated with moving between the first two surveys (Hughes et al, 2007). In addition, the analysis of earlier transitions showed particularly low mobility among South Asian families, and higher mobility among couples where the father was not employed and also for families in the highest as well as the lowest income groups. Although these differentials are not explicitly tested in the model for moves after age 3, they are also likely to persist.

The likelihood of moving between MCS 2 and 3 was investigated using logistic regression. Table 7.1 presents the results as odds ratios along with their 95% confidence interval (CI). The (odds ratio − 1) × 100 may be interpreted as the percentage change in the odds relative to the reference category for each categorical variable, holding other things constant.

Once the other characteristics about individual circumstances were controlled, the odds of moving between MCS 2 and 3 were significantly lower for those originally living in the England disadvantaged, England ethnic, both Welsh disadvantaged and non-disadvantaged wards, all relative to the England non-disadvantaged wards. The odds of moving for people originally living in English wards with a high minority ethnic population were 43% lower. This multivariate analysis gives a different pattern from the bivariate analysis. Those originally living in Scotland have the same propensity to move, adjusting for other factors such as the family's level of disadvantage/poverty as those in non-disadvantaged England wards. While in England, those originally living in disadvantaged wards become significantly less likely to move than those living in non-disadvantaged wards, when other things were taken into account.

The odds of moving between MCS 2 and 3 were 13% higher for those who moved between MCS 1 and 2. If at least one informant was different at MCS 2 than at MCS 1, which may be due to a change in partnership/union, the odds of moving were 36% higher than if there was no change in informant. Families were more likely to move the worse they rated their area at MCS 2, with odds of moving doubling for those stating the area was very poor for raising children compared to those who felt their area was excellent. There were also independent associations with low income, privately rented housing tenure and types of housing other than houses or bungalows. Holding other factors constant, the odds of moving increased for main respondents with high qualifications, but decreased with their age. Tenants of social housing are less mobile than private renters and others in least stable tenures. Their small excess mobility over owners is accounted for by other characteristics, but it does not seem exceptionally low. This is not strong support for the concern that the tenure itself inhibits job mobility.

Perceptions about the neighbourhood

As one reason for moving house/address/home is to reach a better or safer area, the perception of the current neighbourhood is important for predicting future mobility. The mother's (or alternative main respondent's) perceptions are recorded in MCS 2 and 3 with reference to a neighbourhood as 'the area within 20 minutes' walk' of the home, not necessarily the ward area. Five-point scales were used to measure whether the neighbourhood was thought to be 'a good area to bring up children' (very poor, poor, average, good, excellent) or how safe the area was (very unsafe, fairly unsafe, neither safe nor unsafe, fairly safe and very safe).

Movers between MCS 2 and 3 gave a more favourable account of the area into which they had moved than stayers did at MCS 3. Movers were more likely to report their MCS 3 area as excellent for raising children (37% for movers, 32% for stayers) or a very safe area (40% for movers, 33% for stayers). They were less likely to report their area of residence at MCS 3 was a poor or very poor area for raising children (5% for movers, 6% for stayers) or a fairly unsafe or very unsafe area (4% for movers, 5% for stayers).

Area ratings are reasonably stable, but change in opinion is common and ratings go up as well as down. 'Good area for raising children' ratings from MCS 2 to 3 were reasonably stable (53%): they went up for 22% of respondents and went down for 25% of respondents. 'How safe an area' ratings from MCS 2 to 3 were more stable (57%): they went up for 23% of respondents and went down for 20% of respondents.

Now we focus on 'bad' neighbourhood ratings, that is, whether the area of residence at MCS 3 was reported to be a poor or very poor area for raising children or a fairly unsafe or very unsafe area (henceforth 'poor' and 'unsafe' for short). At both MCS 2 and 3, using the balanced panel, we also look at families' perception of their neighbourhood in terms of whether the respondent felt it was a good area for raising children and how safe they felt the area was. We also investigate whether rating the neighbourhood as an unsafe area or a poor area to live at MCS 3 was related to family disadvantaged circumstances at previous surveys.

Few respondents at MCS 3 in any of the UK countries reported their current area was a poor one for raising children (from 4% to 7% across the countries), or an unsafe one (from 3% to 6%) (Ketende and McDonald, 2008). Earlier analyses of MCS 2 suggest area satisfaction was likely to be related to living in rural as opposed to urban areas, with those living in urban areas more likely to perceive their current area as unsafe (Dex, 2007). Northern Ireland was perceived as the best place and safest place to bring up children, with views perhaps reflecting the context of relief after the earlier Troubles.

Table 7.2 presents the number and percentage of respondents commenting unfavourably on their neighbourhood at MCS 3. It is based on 13,022 cases, drawn from the balanced panel after discarding a few cases with missing data.

Around 7% in total thought that the area was a poor area for raising children, that is, a 'poor' or 'very poor' opinion. There were substantial differences in opinion by MCS type of ward. For non-disadvantaged wards, from 1% to 3% thought their area poor for raising children, and for disadvantaged wards, from 5% to 11% did so. The percentages are lowest for Northern Ireland and highest for England, in particular for areas of high minority ethnic population (17%). Only 2% of those who thought their area was very safe thought their area was poor, while 45% of those who thought their area was very unsafe thought their area was poor. Those with low incomes at MCS 2 were more likely to think their MCS 3 area as poor (14%) than those with higher incomes (4%). Families renting

Table 7.2: Whether living in a poor area to bring up children, main respondent's views at MCS 3: frequencies of predictor variables and logistic regression estimates

Predictor variables		Area rating as 'poor'		Model estimates	
		Poor or very poor	Unweighted observed	Poor/very poor = 1 versus excellent, good or average = 0	
		%	base (n)	Odds ratio	95% CI
Ward type at MCS 1	**England:**				
	Non-disadvantaged	2.3	3,658	1	
	Disadvantaged	10.8	3,080	2.62**	[1.95, 3.50]
	Ethnic minority	16.6	1,428	3.95**	[2.77, 5.65]
	Wales:				
	Non-disadvantaged	2.4	617	1.19	[0.63, 2.23]
	Disadvantaged	7.7	1,359	1.84**	[1.31, 2.57]
	Scotland:				
	Non-disadvantaged	2.6	835	1.35	[0.82, 2.23]
	Disadvantaged	7.8	746	1.97**	[1.20, 3.21]
	Northern Ireland:				
	Non-disadvantaged	1.1	532	0.71	[0.26, 1.98]
	Disadvantaged	4.6	763	1.38	[0.86, 2.22]
Whether MCS 2 area felt to be safe	Very safe	2.2	4,839	1	
	Fairly safe	5.4	6,506	1.97**	[1.55, 2.50]
	Neither safe nor unsafe	16.6	850	5.13**	[3.88, 6.78]
	Fairly unsafe	33.1	598	10.4**	[7.83, 13.9]
	Very unsafe	44.9	225	13.7**	[9.59, 19.5]
Family income at MCS 2	Not low	4.0	9,299	1	
	Low [a]	14.1	3,719	1.34**	[1.12, 1.61]
Housing tenure at MCS 2	Own outright or mortgage	3.0	8,688	1	
	Private renting	8.9	930	1.67**	[1.25, 2.23]
	Social renting	17.5	2,961	2.38**	[1.92, 2.94]
	Other	7.5	439	1.45	[0.99, 2.14]
Mother's highest academic qualification[b]	Graduate level	2.5	3585	1	
	Other qualifications	6.9	7361	1.39**	[1.10, 1.75]
	No qualifications	14.4	2072	1.77**	[1.32, 2.36]

(continued)

Table 7.2: Whether living in a poor area to bring up children, main respondent's views at MCS 3: frequencies of predictor variables and logistic regression estimates *(continued)*

Predictor variables		Area rating as 'poor'		Model estimates	
		Poor or very poor	Unweighted observed	Poor/very poor = 1 versus excellent, good or average = 0	
		%	base (n)	Odds ratio	95% CI
Informants, MCS 1 and 2	No change	6.0	11,467	1	
	At least one person different	13.1	1551	1.26**	[1.05, 1.51]
Age of mother at MCS 2[b]	Under 30 years	11.5	4,132	1	
	30 years and above	4.7	8,886	0.75**	[0.65, 0.87]

Notes: Analysis sample *n*=13,022, ** *p*<0.05

[a] Low income is defined as either family net weekly income (adjusted for family size on OECD scale) below 60% of national median, or receiving Income Support.

[b] Mother or other main respondent, at MCS 2.

from a local authority or housing association were most likely to think their area as poor (18%) ahead of private renters (9%) and homeowners. For those with graduate-level qualifications only 3% thought it a poor area, in contrast to 14% at the other extreme among those with no qualifications. If there was no change in parental informants between MCS 1 and 2, the percentage was lower (6%) than if at least one informant was different at MCS 2 (13%). For younger mothers/main respondents, the percentage was higher (12%) than older respondents (5%). Having moved home between MCS 2 and 3 was not significantly associated with a poor area rating.

The likelihood of 'mothers' rating their area poor for raising children at MCS 3 in terms of various characteristics was investigated using logistic regression (see Table 7.2, where the estimates are odds ratios along with their 95% CI). Other things being equal, the odds of a poor rating at MCS 3 were significantly higher for those originally living in the disadvantaged wards of England (162%), Wales (84%) and Scotland (97%) and the England minority ethnic wards (295%). The multivariate analysis gives the same patterns as the bivariate. Within country, those originally living in disadvantaged wards have higher odds of a poor area rating than those originally living in non–disadvantaged wards, adjusting for other factors such as the family's level of disadvantage/poverty. Those sampled in England ethnic wards have the highest odds of rating their area poor at MCS 3. The odds of a poor area rating at MCS 3 increased the less safe they thought their MCS 2 area to be, the odds of a poor rating increased 14-fold for those rating their area very unsafe, compared to a very safe rating. The odds of a poor area rating were 34% higher for families with a low income at MCS 2. Relative to homeowners, the odds of a poor area rating were 67% higher for those renting privately, 138%

higher for those in social housing and 45% higher for those in other tenures. Relative to those with higher qualifications, the odds of a poor area rating at the other extreme for those with no qualifications were 77% higher. If at least one informant was different at MCS 2 than at MCS 1, the odds of a poor area rating were 26% higher than if there was no change in informant. Older main respondents had lower odds of a poor area rating by 25% relative to the younger ones. There was no significant difference found in the ratings of MCS 3 areas by those who had moved since MCS 2, and families who had been in the same place at both surveys. However, among the movers, movement across this extreme divide was more often favourable than not: 11% had moved out of areas rated poorly at MCS 2 while only 3% had moved from better areas into the places rated poor, and 2% were in them at both surveys.

Overall around 5% of informants thought their neighbourhood at MCS 3 was an unsafe area to live, that is, rating it 'fairly unsafe' or 'very unsafe'. Table 7.3 investigates these ratings based on 12,992 cases, again drawn from the balanced panel logistic regression, and showing the logistic regression results.

Table 7.3: Whether area feels unsafe, main respondent's views at MCS 3: frequencies of predictor variables and logistic regression estimates

Predictor variables		Area rating as unsafe		Model estimates Fairly unsafe, very unsafe = 1 versus very safe, fairly safe, neutral = 0	
		Fairly/very unsafe	Unweighted observed base (n)	Odds ratio	95% CI
		%			
Address change between MCS 2 and MCS 3	Did not move	5.6	10,338	1	
	Moved	4.5	2,654	0.49**	[0.40, 0.60]
Ward type at MCS 1	**England:**				
	Non-disadvantaged	2.1	3,656	1	
	Disadvantaged	8.8	3,069	2.01**	[1.54, 2.63]
	Ethnic minority	11.8	1,418	2.15**	[1.57, 2.95]
	Wales:				
	Non-disadvantaged	2.6	615	1.38	[0.70, 2.73]
	Disadvantaged	6.2	1,359	1.42**	[1.03, 1.94]
	Scotland:				
	Non-disadvantaged	1.2	835	0.66	[0.37, 1.19]
	Disadvantaged	5.8	745	1.40	[0.98, 2.00]
	Northern Ireland:				
	Non-disadvantaged	1.1	532	0.84	[0.38, 1.88]
	Disadvantaged	3.4	763	1.04	[0.60, 1.79]

(continued)

Table 7.3: Whether area feels unsafe, main respondent's views at MCS 3: frequencies of predictor variables and logistic regression estimates *(continued)*

Predictor variables		Area rating as unsafe		Model estimates Fairly unsafe, very unsafe = I versus very safe, fairly safe, neutral = 0	
		Fairly/very unsafe	*Unweighted observed base (n)*		
		%		*Odds ratio*	*95% CI*
Whether MCS 2 location is good area to bring up children	Excellent	1.0	3,977	I	
	Good	2.8	5,137	2.19**	[1.55, 3.11]
	Average	8.3	2,708	5.29**	[3.74, 7.48]
	Poor	21.9	743	14.2**	[9.33, 21.7]
	Very poor	30.0	427	20.1**	[13.0, 31.0]
Family income at MCS 2	Not low	3.1	9,285	I	
	Low [a]	11.0	3,707	1.49**	[1.23, 1.81]
Housing tenure at MCS 2	Own outright or mortgage	2.6	8,673	I	
	Private renting	7.0	930	1.81**	[1.34, 2.44]
	Social renting	12.8	2,953	1.65**	[1.31, 2.08]
	Other	6.4	436	1.91**	[1.30, 2.80]
Type of accommodation at MCS 2	House or bungalow	4.7	11,749	I	
	Flat or maisonette	12.0	1,190	1.29**	[1.04, 1.60]
	Room, bedsit, etc	7.5	53	2.27	[0.84, 6.13]
Mother's highest academic qualification[b]	Graduate level	2.2	3,577	I	
	Other qualifications	5.3	7,347	1.34**	[1.05, 1.70]
	No qualifications	11.2	2,068	1.70**	[1.28, 2.26]

Notes: Analysis sample *n*=12,992, ** *p*<0.05

[a] Low income is defined as either family net weekly income (adjusted for family size on OECD scale) below 60% of national median, or receiving Income Support.

[b] Mother or other main respondent, at MCS 2.

Families who moved between MCS 2 and 3 were significantly less likely to rate their area as unsafe at MCS 3 (odds for movers were 51% lower relative to stayers). This partly reflects moves to a different, safer area. Compared to the area they had been in before, 5.2% of the movers had left an unsafe area and 2.9% had arrived in one, and 1.1% had moved from one area perceived as unsafe to another. Just over 90% thought that their area was not unsafe at both surveys. There were significant odds of an unsafe rating for those originally living in the England disadvantaged, England ethnic and Wales disadvantaged wards. Those originally living in areas of high minority ethnic population in England had the highest odds of an unsafe rating at MCS 3. Whether their neighbourhood was reported at MCS 3 to be an unsafe area went down the better the rating of the MCS 2 area as a good area to bring up children. The odds of rating their area unsafe were 20-times bigger for those who at MCS 2 rated their area very poor than for those who rated their area very good. The odds of an unsafe rating at MCS 3 were 49% higher for those with low income at MCS 2. Relative to homeowners, the odds of an unsafe rating were 65% higher for those in social housing and 81% higher for private renting. Relative to families in houses or bungalows, the odds of an unsafe rating were more than double for those living in miscellaneous types of accommodation including, for example, studio flats, rooms or bedsits. Relative to those with higher qualifications, the odds of an unsafe rating at MCS 3 were 70% higher for those with no qualifications, other things equal.

In general, the odds of an unsafe rating at MCS 3 were significantly higher for those originally living in the England disadvantaged areas and areas of high minority ethnic population in England as well as the Wales disadvantaged wards. Those originally living in disadvantaged areas have higher odds of an unsafe rating at MCS 3 than those sampled in non-disadvantaged areas. Those originally living in areas of high minority ethnic population in England have the highest odds of reporting an unsafe rating at MCS 3. The odds of an unsafe rating at MCS 3 go down as their rating at MCS 2 of whether the area they live in is a good area to bring up children goes up, as the quality or tenure of their current accommodation goes up and the main respondent's level of education goes up.

Mobility between age 3 and 5 does not predict being observed at age 5 in a good area, but it does reduce the chances of being observed in one rated unsafe. Those living in public housing reported somewhat lower levels of satisfaction with their neighbourhoods than average. Social housing tenants were most likely to live in areas identified as particularly bad for bringing up children, or unsafe. These were significant differences from owners (around half as likely again), but not from the other non-owning tenures. (For an analysis of mothers' satisfaction with their neighbourhood according to their ethnic origin see Chapter 3, this volume, where the results overlap with the poorer ratings presented in this chapter for people living in wards with high minority ethnic populations.)

Conclusions

MCS families recorded considerable geographical movement over the children's first five years, with around half of all MCS families reporting at least one change of address, but mostly within the same housing tenure and within the original side of an area deprivation divide. Moving home may have been the outcome of having another child and wanting more space or better accommodation, or it may have been the outcome of other changes and events in their families' lives. Often there was little change in their type of housing, with 90% reporting living in the same sort of dwelling and 79% the same tenure. One quarter of the cohort lived in high deprivation localities at all three surveys and another 11% had done so at one or two surveys. Disadvantaged wards appear to have more movers than other locations in three of the four UK countries, but these differences are accounted for (or reversed) once the other individual factors are taken into account. Families originally living in wards of high minority ethnic population, mostly from minority groups, had a consistently low rate of mobility.

The overall aggregate improvement in the quality of the local environment inhabited by the MCS families is small and slow. Objective and subjective accounts of moves are generally more positive than negative on balance, but everything did not move in the same direction over time. The perceived safety of their neighbourhoods deteriorated slightly as the children reached age 5. Mobility can be a route out of poverty for some and a characteristic of disadvantaged circumstances and insecurity for others.

The amenities of neighbourhoods in which people prefer to stay and into which they choose to move to are an important dimension of family well-being. A small minority of families have explicitly mentioned moving at this pre-school stage to enhance educational opportunities, given parents' preferences for good schools to be close to home, as reported in Chapter 11 later in this volume. The dis-amenities of a few areas are also important to bear in mind when considering the well-being of every child and the various aspects of social inequalities, particularly ethnic, encountered by this new generation of children.

If the patterns observed in families with older children in the 2001 Census are replicated, the next five years of the cohort will see less movement geographically (Plewis et al, 2008). This will give the children a better chance of establishing themselves at a school and with friends. It may also reinforce an emerging polarisation between owner-occupied and other housing tenures, and a closing off of 'escape' from the places rated the worst for bringing up children.

Note

[1] In Tables 7.1, 7.2 and 7.3, unweighted observed sample, percentages were weighted using longitudinal weights to adjust for sample design and attrition. Longitudinal weights were used to adjust for sample attrition; see Chapter 11 of Hansen (2008) for the details on longitudinal weights and the treatment of the MCS clustered sample design. In all analyses, we take the MCS clustered design into account in estimating corrected standard errors allowing for the observations within a ward being correlated. In order to account for the MCS stratified design with nine strata (that is, type of electoral ward within UK country), we include the MCS stratum identifier in all our logistic models as a set of eight dummy variables. For further details, see Reiter et al (2005). Apart from the terms identifying the stratum of ward type sampled, the logistic models presented in Tables 7.1, 7.2 and 7.3 otherwise only include variables significantly associated with our outcome of interest, based on the adjusted Wald test at the 5% level.

EIGHT

Childcare in the pre-school years

*Fiona Roberts, Sandra Mathers, Heather Joshi, Kathy Sylva
and Elizabeth Jones*

Introduction

For the children born around the turn of the millennium pre-school care and education became a near universal experience. This reflects the spread of education to younger children and the increasing 'normality' of mothers taking paid work outside the home. This chapter is concerned with the Millennium Cohort Study (MCS) children's experience of care from people other than the mother, with an emphasis on those children who attended group childcare settings at some point during their pre-school years. It begins by outlining the evolving experience of non-maternal care for all the children in the MCS, across the UK, from infancy to primary school. It goes on to put a microscope on 301 childcare settings attended by a sub-group of children in England in 2005, providing a detailed picture of the services that children received in an unprecedented era of public and private provision. We compare the families who did, and did not, use centre-based care, then describe the quality of centre-based care experienced by the children who did attend, and explore differential access to high-quality services. We also describe the characteristics of centres that were providing high-quality care because they may provide guidance for good practice. Finally, we discuss the results in terms of government policy, ending with recommendations that could improve the quality of childcare provision.

Four questions are addressed in this chapter:

1) What are the childcare experiences of children in the MCS?
2) Is social class related to patterns of childcare use?
3) What is the quality of the group childcare experienced by the MCS, and does it vary according to family and child characteristics?
4) Which characteristics of childcare centres are related to high-quality provision?

What is childcare?

The term 'childcare' has various, overlapping, definitions. It refers to services that provide custody and nurture to children whose parents are not present, for a variety of reasons, and a variety of timespans. The parents may be unable to take direct care of their children, because a mother is working outside the home, because the parents are incapable of looking after their children or because they choose to delegate at least some of the care to others, particularly specialists. Instead of viewing childcare merely as a service to *parents*, one can also consider the ways in which such arrangements aim to enhance the well-being and development of *children*, regardless of whether their mothers have jobs outside the home or are competent to take care of them.

For most of the last decades of the 20th century, childcare in the UK was viewed mainly as something related to (and constraining) mothers' employment. It received little attention in public debate, data gathering, or indeed, public expenditure (Paull and Taylor, 2002; Hansen et al, 2006). Public day nurseries sprang up during the Second World War to facilitate female employment, but services dwindled in the following decades to provisions by local authority social services primarily for 'children at risk', whose parents had many problems. The increasing band of mothers in the labour force during the 1980s and 1990s had to make private arrangements for childcare, which made their employment possible. These arrangements were predominantly informal ones with neighbours or family members, especially the child's father or grandparents. Other arrangements, instead of, or alongside, informal ones, involved remuneration for the carer: nannies and others working in the child's home, childminders working in their own homes and group settings such as day nurseries, playgroups and nursery schools. These group settings could be run by private companies, voluntary organisations or the state sector. The cash-nexus arrangements are sometimes classified as formal care although the dividing line is blurred – some types of paid in-home caregivers are unlikely to have any professional training or to be subject to state regulation, and some clients of professional, regulated settings may not themselves pay for the service, for example in a state nursery school.

There were some concessions toward recognising the role for public promotion of childcare under the Conservative governments of the 1990s. Despite tax relief for employers offering workplace nurseries, and a disregard for childcare expenditure as part of the in-work benefit Family Credit, there was a paucity of affordable childcare places as well as information on how to find them. However, it was not until New Labour's National Childcare Strategy in 1998 that the UK government dedicated resources to childcare as 'Early Years services', no longer focusing exclusively on the objective of promoting mothers' employment but also on enhancing the experiences of all young children, and eventually 'every child' (see HM Treasury, 2003).

Why childcare is important in the English policy context

Educational policy is devolved across England, Scotland, Wales and Northern Ireland, but most of our discussion of childcare policies concentrates on England, where a supplementary study was funded.

Along with the National Childcare Strategy came substantial new funding and the reorganisation of services to become better coordinated and inspected. The National Childcare Strategy set out through the Green Paper *Meeting the childcare challenge* (DfEE/QCA, 1998) to deliver *quality, affordable* and *accessible* childcare in every neighbourhood. Since the 2006 Childcare Act (UK Parliament, 2006) there has been substantial expansion in childcare provision with a large increase in the number of new childcare places in the public, private and voluntary sectors, and also a wider variety of provision offered, for example, day nurseries, playgroups, out-of-school clubs and childminders. A major part of this expansion has been free nursery education places for all 4-year-olds across all sectors of provision, first introduced in late 2002 and extended in April 2004 to include all 3-year-olds. This was during the time that the second survey of the MCS (MCS 2) at age 3 was in the field, from September 2003 to December 2004.

Another feature of the government's strategy was to implement new national standards with minimum quality levels for childcare, and a strengthened regulatory regime for early education and care with more consistent inspection of providers. In 2000 the government introduced a new curriculum framework, the Foundation Stage (DfEE/QCA, 2000), for children from the age of 3 to the end of their reception year (see Chapter 12 of this volume). It became statutory in 2002. This was followed in 2003 by *Birth to three matters* (DfES/Sure Start, 2003), which extended the framework to provision for children under the age of 3.

In 2008, the Early Years Foundation Stage (EYFS; DCSF, 2008) replaced the curriculum guidance for the Foundation Stage and the *Birth to three matters* framework. It incorporates both previous frameworks into one set of guidance for the care, learning and development of all children attending registered Early Years settings from birth to age 5 years.

The largest initiative for disadvantaged children has been Sure Start (Belsky et al, 2007), which, from 1999 to 2005, set up over 500 local programmes catering for children up to the age of 4 and their families. These programmes, phased in during the early years of the new century, are run by local partnerships and deliver a range of services including childcare, adult training and basic skills education to disadvantaged communities. Another key programme for disadvantaged children is the Neighbourhood Nurseries Initiative (NNI Research Team, 2007), which was targeted at the most disadvantaged areas of England and provided funding as pump priming to kick-start childcare in places where suitable care could be scarcer. The children's centre programme was launched in 2003 to build on the Sure Start and neighbourhood nurseries programmes already established in disadvantaged areas. In the 10-year strategy for Early Years and childcare (HM Treasury, 2004), the government further committed to invest in childcare and education, promising a children's centre in every community by 2010.

The MCS cohort experienced many of these policy initiatives. When they attended childcare as 3- and 4-year-olds, the moves to better integration of early education and care were already well advanced with early excellence centres, neighbourhood nurseries and others providing Early Years education, childcare and parent/family support services all on one site. However, only a small minority were born early enough and in the right places to reap the full benefit of Sure Start programmes from birth. Just under one quarter (24%) of the childcare settings observed in the current study in England in 2005 were linked to Sure Start.

MCS experience of childcare from 1st to 5th year

Another reflection of the new policy era for the MCS families was the participation of mothers in paid work. When the children were 9 months old nearly half the mothers had a job, mostly part time. All mothers were asked about the arrangements they made for childcare both when at work and when not working. Around two thirds of the arrangements reported for these babies were linked to mothers' working, and most of them were exclusively informal (Dex and Ward, 2004 and Chapter 6 in this volume). Table 8.1 considers nearly 13,400 families who were present at all three surveys up to age 5. It summarises the sort of non-maternal childcare arrangements the cohort child encountered before attending primary school, refining the reconstruction of childcare histories presented by

Table 8.1: Rates of childcare use in the pre-school period

	% making any use			
Care type	At 9 months	At age 3 survey	Between ages 3 and 4	All up to starting school
Partner	24.8	10.6	18.2	55.3
Grandparents	30.4	16.0	20.4	44.0
Other relative	7.8	2.8	4.5	15.2
Non-relative (including paid in home)	4.3	1.4	2.8	11.1
Any informal care	49.3	27.3	37.4	76.6
Childminder	9.6	6.8	10.0	17.5
Day nursery	11.7	18.7	22.4	25.1
Nursery school/class	na	31.1	62.2	62.3
Playgroup	na	24.7	32.8	35.2
Pre-school	na	15.4	25.0	24.9
Other	0.7	0.8	1.0	1.8
Any formal care	20.3	76.3	96.2	96.1
Informal only	39.3	5.2	1.1	2.3
Formal only	10.2	54.2	59.9	22.4
Both formal and informal	10.0	22.1	36.3	74.3
Any non-maternal care	59.8	81.5	97.3	99.1
Observations =100%	13,392	13,372	13,391	13,391

Notes: Sample based on respondents who were present at all of the first three surveys and of all the childcare episodes, possibly multiple, reported at any of them (also excludes missing data, of which 26 cases are on housing tenure). Weighted percentages use sampling and MCS 3 attrition weighting. Observations unweighted.

na = not applicable. (Nursery schools, playgroups and pre-schools which do not cater for infants were not included in the 9 months questionnaire.)

Jones (2008). As there may be more than one arrangement at any one time, the entries in the table sum to more than 100%. The type of care used may also vary over time, as is shown by the increasing share of combinations as the time window expands. The earliest spells recorded are, on the whole, those reported at 9 months. The latest spells considered are those that ended before primary school started. Therefore the table does not count any out-of-school arrangements reported at age 5 if they had not also existed earlier. The age 5 replies on childcare history at MCS 3 not only fill in the gaps at ages 3 and 4, but they also 'repair' the under-reporting of some arrangements at MCS 2. It is thought that the wording of the MCS 2 question did not elicit a full report of early education as it was too closely identified with care arrangements to support mothers' employment. Table 8.1 distils the results of three sets of complex questions about childcare arrangements in the MCS. However, parents use a variety of terms to describe their children's early education and care. What many parents call a nursery school may not align with government classifications.

At 9 months, 60% of the children were receiving some non-maternal care: 10% of families were using formal care exclusively with a further 10% using a mixture of formal and informal care, so 20% in total accessed formal childcare. In addition, 39% were using exclusively one or more types of informal care. Within the latter category, 30% involved at least some care from grandparents and 25% from partners.

Grandparents (often maternal grandmothers) were a particularly common source of care while the mother was not at work, but they were also the most

Figure 8.1: Combinations of any childcare used in the pre-school period

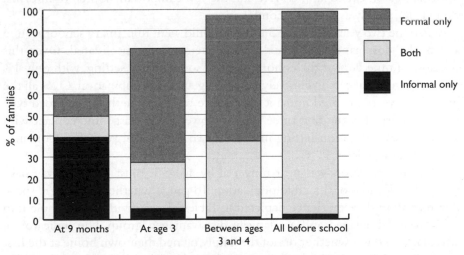

Notes: Sample based on respondents who were present at all of the first three surveys and all of the childcare episodes, possibly multiple, reported at any of them (also excludes missing data, of which 26 cases are on housing tenure). Weighted percentages use sampling and MCS 3 attrition.

frequent type of cover while she was (Dex and Ward, 2004). The arrangements made by these working mothers in 2001–02 did not presage a break from the past, although the number of mothers employed while their children were so young had increased in relation to previous decades. The formal arrangements reported, namely day nurseries and childminders, were virtually all paid for by parents, although some may have been subsidised. Only 5% of employed mothers paying for childcare reported receiving the Childcare Tax Credit (CCTC) within Working Families' Tax Credit (WFTC) in Hansen et al (2006).

By the time the children were 3 years old and no longer infants, they had grown into the age and era when they could benefit from the new Early Years policies. Our reconstruction of the childcare arrangements being used when the child was 3 shows a shift from predominantly informal arrangements at 9 months to predominantly formal and educational arrangements at and after age 3. Some type of non-maternal childcare arrangement was reported for 82% of 3-year-olds, compared with 60% at the first survey. Nearly all 3-year-olds (76%) had some formal arrangement: 54% received such care exclusively, 22% received it in combination with informal care and only 5% received informal care only. The formal arrangements were mainly group care settings with an educational curriculum. Thirty-one per cent of children were reported as attending a nursery school or nursery class in a primary school (mostly but not exclusively in the state sector), almost as many (25%) attended playgroups and 15% attended pre-schools. A further 19% attended day nurseries and 7% attended childminders. The 'early educational establishments' would not usually have taken charge of 3-year-old children for a full working day, so mothers with full-time jobs, who accounted for 13% of all mothers, relied on a portfolio of arrangements, often involving the informal sector. Grandparents were still the most important source of informal care (16%), usually as part of a combination.

Across the two years from age 3 until the child went to primary school around age 5, the dominance of formal arrangements was consolidated. Over this window of time, 96% of the cohort attended some formal setting, with only 1% receiving informal care exclusively, and 36% getting a combination. Over all the pre-school years, the predominant experience was of more than one broad type of care, informal in the first three years, followed by at least some contact with a formal early education setting in the last two pre-school years, in accordance with the new policies.

As formal provision was near universal by age 5 it must in some way have reached all sections of the child population. To gauge whether there were social differentials in the experience depicted in Table 8.1, we divided the sample into a relatively advantaged and a relatively disadvantaged group. The indicator of advantage used was whether or not the family owned their own home at the first survey. This dichotomy is chosen for simplicity, but is just one of many possible markers of social inequalities. Housing tenure is a more stable indicator over these five years than, say, income, as shown in the transitions into and out of poverty in Chapter 2 (this volume); very few of the owners ceased to own their own homes over the period, and not many of the renters became homeowners (see also Chapter 7, this volume). The 8,547 owners at MCS 1 represent 65% of the weighted sample. Figure 8.2 shows that both groups display the same major trend towards formal care arrangements as the child grows older, but the disadvantaged group was less likely to use any care for infants (reflecting their lower maternal employment rates) and more likely to use informal arrangements at all stages than the more advantaged group. Among formal arrangements, those not owning their own homes were more likely to report nursery schools than other types of group setting. Given differential access, it is all the more important to know about the standard of care offered in diverse settings.

Figure 8.2: Use of non-maternal childcare arrangements in the pre-school period, by social advantage at MCS 1

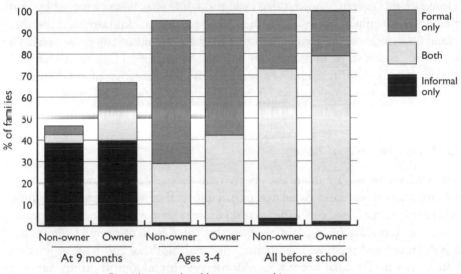

Notes: Sample: see Figure 8.1.
Owner = in owner-occupied housing; Non-owner = in other type of housing than owner occupied.

Use of centre-based care in a sub-sample of the MCS

The childcare experiences of a sub-sample of the MCS children living in England were investigated through systematic observation in childcare settings. These settings were identified at the age 3 parental interview and are described in Mathers et al (2007).

The Department for Children, Schools and Families (DCSF) funded this sub-study in England because they realised that the design and data of the MCS provided a rare opportunity to take a snapshot of centre-based early education and care in England at the start of the 21st century. The MCS data is a rich resource that makes it possible to investigate 'typical' centre-based childcare. Research programmes such as the MCS are well placed to make policy recommendations because of its large scale, and its national sample includes children from diverse backgrounds.

Sample

A sub-sample of MCS electoral wards in England was selected in which 1,217 families reported the use of group childcare at age 3, their children attending 825 settings. This sub-sample of families was further reduced to produce a cost-constrained target of 301 childcare settings, attended by 632 MCS 2 children. It had been hoped that there would be more cohort children per setting on average, since the original sample was based on addresses clustered by electoral ward. However, this exercise showed that even though homes were clustered by ward, this does not imply clustering in the use of particular childcare settings; there could be a number of settings patronised by the residents of any given ward. The selection, at this stage, over-sampled settings attended by more than one MCS child. The sample of 632 children was broadly representative of children across England using the sampling procedure and weightings described in the technical appendix of Mathers et al (2007).

Differential use of care

Table 8.2 compares families in the selected sub-set of electoral wards according to whether they used centre-based care or had informal or no arrangements. Families who used centre-based care differed from those who did not in several important ways: they tended to be from more advantaged families, as measured by household employment and income; have better educated mothers; and have at least one parent in a professional occupation. Mothers with children in group care were more likely to have jobs than other mothers, but not exclusively. Families with only one child were more likely to be using some form of care than not, while large families (those with two or more siblings) were less likely to be using any form of childcare. The most disadvantaged families, indicated here by worklessness and low income, were less likely to have any childcare arrangement at all.

Information collected in the centres

Childcare settings were visited between March and October 2005. Observations lasting up to a day were carried out in one of the rooms catering for children between the ages of 3 and 5 years. These observations were made using two instruments measuring various aspects of the quality of provision. These instruments included measures of the social interactions, the physical environment, the learning activities and the sensitivity of staff, as described later in this chapter.

Table 8.2: Characteristics of MCS 2 families in selected wards in England by broad childcare arrangements at age 3 and selection for observation

Characteristics at MCS 2	Families using observed group care settings	Families using non-observed group care settings	Families using informal childcare only	Families reporting no childcare arrangement
Mother's mean age	30.8	30.0	27.4	28.6
% of mothers with degree	47.7**	45.7**	22.3	14.8**
% of mothers with less than 5 A-C GCSEs	13.6**	15.6**	34.1	43.9**
% in two-parent two-worker families	64.4**	59.3**	42.2	6.7**
% in two-parent, one-worker families	27.6**	27.8**	36.9	58.5**
% in two-parent, workless families	1.4**	2.8	5.1	13.5**
% in single-parent worker families	1.2	3.0	3.2	0.4
% in single-parent workless families	5.3**	7.2	12.6	20.9**
% with at least one professional parent	34.3**	38.8**	14.9**	12.8**
% of families with incomes of £52,000+ pa	13.9	15.0**	2.0**	4.1**
% of families with incomes < £10,400+ pa	9.3**	12.9**	25.6	35.0**
% of cohort members without siblings	27.1	31.8**	26.3**	15.7**
% of cohort members with 2+ siblings	23.1	20.1**	21.6**	43.6**
% of White cohort members	92.9	90.6	87.6	82.7
%of Black cohort members	1.2	2.3	2.0	1.7
% of Indian, Bangladeshi or Pakistani cohort members	2.2**	3.3	6.7	10.7**
n (unweighted)	632	835	542	1,215

Source: From Mathers et al (2007, Table A3.2)

Notes: ** indicates results differing significantly from others in their group ($p<0.05$). Survey and nursery weights applied to percentages.

Information was also collected about each centre visited (and its staff) through an interview with the centre manager. This covered a variety of centre characteristics, particularly those which may relate to quality of provision, including:

- sector (local authority-maintained, private, voluntary)
- programme participation (links with Sure Start local programmes [SSLPs], children's centre status, neighbourhood nursery status)
- centre size (total children enrolled)
- staff–child ratios in the room observed
- qualifications of the centre manager
- qualifications of staff working in the room observed.

General characteristics of the settings

The parental interview at age 3 identified various sorts of group setting families were using – day nurseries, nursery schools/classes, playschools and playgroups – although parents were not asked to identify the sector of the provider. During the observation visits to selected nurseries, researchers were careful, therefore, to clarify the type of provider according to government classifications. It is likely that most of the 'maintained' providers were state nursery schools. As seen in Table 8.3, more than three quarters of the observed settings were found to be in the private or voluntary sectors.

For each room observed, information was gathered on childcare qualifications for centre managers and all staff members who worked at least 10 hours per week with the children (including working managers). Table 8.4 shows that on the whole, centre managers and staff in the rooms were adequately qualified, with a mean qualification level of NVQ Level 3 or equivalent (for example, a National Nursery Examination Board [NNEB] diploma). On average, 14% of staff members working in the rooms observed were unqualified, while 70% were qualified to Level 3 or above. Of the 301 sample settings, 106 (35%) had a staff member with a qualification at Level 4 or 5 (for example a degree or higher degree) working with the children in the room observed, while 78 (26%) had a qualified teacher either working within the room or as the centre manager (note that these figures do not appear in the table).

Table 8.3: Childcare group settings in observation sample by sector

	Frequency	% (unweighted)
Local authority-maintained	60	20
Private	167	55
Voluntary	68	23
Other	6	2
Total *n* and %	301	100

Note: Sample: childcare settings observation sample.

Table 8.4: Qualifications of centre managers and staff in room observed

	N	Minimum	Maximum	Mean
Manager qualification (standard qualification Levels 1-5)	298	0	4	3
Mean qualification level of all staff in room observed (standard qualification Levels 1-5)	300	1	4	3
% of staff in room qualified to Level 3 or above	300	0	100	70
% of unqualified staff in room	300	0	67	14

Note: Sample: childcare settings observation sample.

Quality of childcare in settings attended by MCS children

It has long been known that quality of childcare influences child development (for example, Whitebook et al, 1990; Phillipsen et al, 1997; Sylva et al, 2004, 2008). There have been many studies on the effects of quality of childcare in large samples, for example, the Cost, Quality and Outcomes Study (Peisner-Feinberg and Burchinal, 1997) and the National Institute for Child Health and Human Development (NICHD) Study of Early Child Care and Youth Development (NICHD, 2003) in the US, and the Effective Provision of Pre-school Education project in England, (EPPE; Sylva et al, 2004). However, most of these studies are on quality effects in non-representative samples. Their main focus was not to investigate quality of the child's experience per se, but to study the effects of different levels of quality on children's development, and their respective designs reflect this.

The Quality of Childcare Settings in the MCS was the first study on quality of provision *for its own sake* in a broadly representative sample – rather than focusing only on disadvantaged areas or deliberately oversampling certain provision. Since we were able to compare the MCS data with previous data from the EPPE study, it was also one of the first to be able to assess the impact of ongoing development of government childcare policy since the 1997 General Election.

An overview of data collection and methods used in the study

Staff interviews, as described earlier, established the 'structural' characteristics of the care settings, for example, centre size, staff qualifications and age range of children. In order to assess the 'process' characteristics (see Melhuish, 2002) systematic observations were made of the daily activities that took place over a full day at the setting. Settings were assessed using ratings on two internationally recognised observation instruments: the Early Childhood Environment Rating Scales (ECERS). The ECERS-R (Revised) is a 'global' measure of quality, incorporating both process and structural aspects of quality, focusing equally on 'care' and 'education' (Harms et al, 1998). The ECERS-E (Extension) is concerned with pre-school curriculum and aims to measure 'pedagogical' quality related to children's learning (Sylva et al, 2003).

Quality rating scales used

ECERS-R is a measure of quality that has been developed in the US and is used widely in research and professional development. Early Years practitioners and researchers devised it to create a numerical profile for rating the 'quality' of a setting across a broad set of seven sub-scales, each dedicated to a different aspect of practice. This measure describes the characteristics of the physical environment but, as important, it also rates the quality of the social and pedagogical environment which children experience. ECERS-R has 43 items divided into seven sub-scales;

however, the quality of childcare settings in the MCS used only the three sub-scales thought to be most related to child development: personal care routines, language and reasoning, and interaction. Each item is rated on a seven-point scale with explicit indicators for scores of 1 (inadequate), 3 (minimal/adequate), 5 (good) and 7 (excellent). There are clear rules for giving even-number scores between the 'anchored' criteria for the odd numbers. The scores are usually averaged to provide an overall ECERS-R mean. However, in this study the three sub-scales used were usually treated separately.

ECERS-R has been widely used in research assessing the quality of early childhood settings, and has been shown to have good psychometric properties and good predictive validity in being significantly related to children's developmental outcomes (see for example, Peisner-Feinberg and Burchinal, 1997; Burchinal et al, 2002).

The emphasis in the instrument is very much on a balanced and 'whole child' programme. The word 'environment' in the ECERS-R is taken in its broadest sense to include the quality of social interactions, strategies to promote all-round learning, and relationships between children as well as between adults and children. For example, the interaction sub-scale has an item called 'interactions among children', which gives high-quality ratings when staff actively promote opportunities for children to work or play together. To score 3 (minimal/adequate) the staff must 'stop negative peer interaction', while to score 5 (good) the staff must 'model good social skills' and a score of 7 (excellent) requires staff to 'provide some opportunities for children to work together to complete a task'.

The importance in ECERS-R of high-quality interaction is illustrated by the many observational indicators that give high scores to the way staff engage with children, even when that is not the explicit focus of a particular item. For example, in the item 'supervision of gross motor activities' (again in the interaction sub-scale), a score of 7 requires that 'staff help children develop positive social interactions (for example, help children to take turns on popular equipment; provide equipment that encourages cooperation such as a two-person rocking boat, walkie-talkie communication devices)'. On items throughout the scale there are criteria for scoring that take into account the role of the staff. So, despite its title of 'Environment Rating Scale', ECERS-R describes the social processes of the educational and care environment even more than the physical space and materials on offer (Sylva and Roberts, 2009).

There are four sub-scales of the curriculum-oriented ECERS-E (literacy, mathematics, science and environment, and diversity) based on the curriculum guidance for the Foundation Stage (DfEE/QCA, 2000). These are compatible with the national 'learning goals' (statutory curriculum objectives) and some 'stepping stones' (developmental steps children take before reaching each statutory goal) in the EYFS (DCSF, 2008). ECERS-E was designed because ECERS-R was thought to be insufficiently detailed in its assessment of curricular provision for literacy, numeracy and science. These are important curricular areas for children's intellectual and linguistic progress in the run-up to school. The fourth sub-scale, diversity, assesses the extent to which the curriculum is tailored to children of different genders, cultures/ethnicity and ability levels.

ECERS-E is specifically designed to tap the dimensions of quality that should support children in achieving many of the learning goals in the published guidance. For example, consider the ECERS-E literacy sub-scale item 'sounds in words'. High scores are obtained in it by settings where members of staff explicitly highlight rhyme, alliteration and syllabification in everyday activities such as nursery rhymes and clapping games. This relates closely to the early learning goals (in the EYFS curriculum) related to children's 'linking sounds and letters'. Other examples include the ECERS-E mathematics sub-scale item 'shape and space' which assesses the capacity of the setting to nurture children's development in the area that is part of the statutory learning goals. Finally, the diversity item 'multicultural education' is closely linked to the early learning goals specified under 'confidence and self-esteem' in the EYFS document.

ECERS-E is scored in the same way as ECERS-R with each item rated on a seven-point scale. For example, in the item 'book and literacy areas', a minimal/adequate score of 3 requires that there are 'some books available', while to achieve an excellent score of 7 a setting must have a 'comfortable book area filled with a wide range of books of varied style, content and complexity'. The scores on all the items are averaged to give an overall mean.

In the following sections we report on the overall quality of the 301 settings in the sub-study, as measured by the observational rating scales, and describe how certain characteristics of the cohort families were related to quality of provision. We then explore the various characteristics of settings that scored significantly higher or lower on the rating scales in order to examine predictors of quality.

Findings on the quality of group care experienced

There was huge diversity across the sample in terms of the quality of provision on offer. Figure 8.3 shows that the scores on each of the dimensions measured by the rating scales varied widely, with some settings offering provision of substantially higher quality than others, and some offering less than adequate quality provision. In general, the scores on ECERS-R, the social and interactional processes of the environment and physical space and materials the children use, tended to be higher than those on ECERS-E; the latter represents the quality of the curricular provision in the setting. However, there was considerable variation in all sub-scales. The finding that scores on ECERS-E are relatively low is one mirrored in similar studies (for example, EPPE, see Sylva et al, 1999), but is also a worrying one.

Most of the scores were in the range 3-4, rated 'minimal' (or just above), where 5-7 is the 'good' to 'excellent' range. Across all the dimensions measured, scores

Figure 8.3: Box plot to show spread of ECERS-R and ECERS-E scores achieved by the MCS sample (*n* = 301)[a]

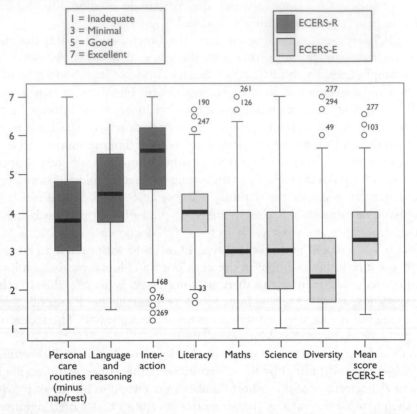

| 1 = Inadequate |
| 3 = Minimal |
| 5 = Good |
| 7 = Excellent |

■ ECERS-R
□ ECERS-E

Personal care routines (minus nap/rest) · Language and reasoning · Inter-action · Literacy · Maths · Science · Diversity · Mean score ECERS-E

Note: [a] The band near the middle of the box is the median, while the bottom and top of the box represent the 25th and 75th percentiles respectively. The lines extending from the top and bottom of the box represent the highest and lowest values that are not outliers. Outliers, values that are markedly smaller or larger than the other values in the dataset between 1.5 and 3 times the interquartile range, are represented by circles. The numbers next to the outliers merely represent the case number in the database.

were highest for the interaction sub-scale, which had a mean of 5.3. This indicates that, on average, MCS children experienced good quality interactions in their childcare settings. The relatively high mean score tells us that the interactions among children, as well as between staff and children, were generally positive. This score also reflects a good level of supervision of the various activities and the positive way in which discipline is practised.

The language and reasoning sub-scale had a mean score of 4.6, which is lower than interaction and shows that the verbal communication between staff and children (including development of the children's verbal reasoning skills) fell short of 'good'. The books and pictures (and how they are used) in the room also fell short.

The mean score of 4.0 for personal care routines was the lowest of the ECERS-R sub-scales. This reflects the settings' management of children's arrivals and departures as well as health and safety issues; the items concerning health and hygiene were particularly low scoring.

Turning to the quality of educational provision, MCS settings scored highest on the literacy sub-scale, although the mean score of 4.0 is well below the 'good' range. This reflects only moderate quality of environmental print, adults reading with children, and the talking, listening and emergent writing that occurs in the settings.

Both the mathematics and science and environment sub-scales had overall lower scores, with means of 3.2, just above minimal. This indicates that the development of children's counting skills and early understanding of shape and space, for example, was not of particularly good quality in terms of the curricular provision on offer. Similarly, the range of natural materials and science resources available to children, as well as the opportunities children have for developing an understanding of scientific processes, were only of minimal quality.

The diversity sub-scale was the weakest of all, with quality measured as 'below minimal' (mean − 2.6). This shows that planning for individual learning needs (for example, SEN, or special educational needs) and awareness and equality of gender and 'race' is of particularly low quality in settings generally. This includes, for example, the provision of books and other materials with non-stereotyped images.

Differential experiences of children attending group childcare settings

Information collected on the quality of settings was linked with data on child and family characteristics. Table 8.5 shows the results from an exploratory analysis of ECERS-R and ECERS-E scores observed in settings attended by 626 children according to some characteristics of the child and the home; it shows the relationship between characteristics of children/families and observed quality in their childcare centres. Only characteristics demonstrating statistically significant differences are reported.

Although disadvantaged families were less likely to *use* centre-based care, those disadvantaged families who did experience centre-based care receiving higher-quality provision (see Table 8.5). First, children with 'social' disadvantage (for example children from lone-parent households, non-working households and families living in rented rather than owned accommodation) received better quality provision (measured by ECERS-E) than their more advantaged peers. Second, children with 'individual' disadvantage (for example child health problems) received higher-quality provision in terms of ECERS-R scores. Finally, children from families who reported no home learning activities at the interview were more likely to attend group care settings of higher quality. However, children from families who encouraged many types of learning at home were also more likely to attend settings of higher quality.

Table 8.5: Selected child and family characteristics significantly related to quality of provision

	Mean ECERS-R (environment)	Mean ECERS-E (curriculum)
Child characteristics		
Child has longstanding health condition at 3 years	-0.36 (2.33)	
Child's ethnic group (reference category = White): Pakistani/Bangladeshi		0.86 (3.2)
Family characteristics at first survey		
Mother older than 40 at birth	0.75 (2.5)	
Lone natural parent family		0.34 (2.0)
Mother at home (versus working) at 9 months		0.26 (2.2)
Mother's SES at 9 months NS-SEC (reference category = 1: managerial and professional):		
• Lower supervisory and technical		-0.45 (2.4)
• Semi-routine and routine		0.26 (1.98)
Mother's highest qualification Postgraduate versus no qualification	0.49 (2.1)	
Partner's SES at 9 months NS-SEC 5 class categorisation (reference category = 1: managerial and professional):		
• Small employers and self-employed		-0.34 (2.2)
Housing tenure at MCS 1 (in comparison to owning home outright):		
• Renting from local authority		0.53 (2.5)
• Renting from private landlord/housing association		0.46 (2.5)
• Living rent free or with parents		0.60 (2.2)

Notes: Sample: MCS 2 families who used childcare providers included in the childcare settings in the observation study.

Bivariate regression coefficients and T-statistics. n = 626.

The pattern of quality scores in childcare settings contrasts with US findings. A study using data from the Project on Human Development in Chicago Neighbourhoods found centre care quality being *lower* in disadvantaged neighbourhoods (Burchinal et al, 2008). Furthermore, neighbourhood structural disadvantage was more negatively related to quality when mothers had less education. However, quality was higher for publicly funded programmes, which is similar to the finding in the MCS data (described later) that maintained settings tended to be offering higher-quality provision.

A further point is that in the MCS sample a number of other sociodemographic characteristics, such as parental age, the presence of siblings or other adults in the household, father's education and notably family income were not related to the quality scores of the settings their children attended.

The positive relationship between disadvantage and higher quality of care may be a consequence of national policies that targeted resources to disadvantaged neighbourhoods. The fact that less privileged children who attended one of these care settings received higher-quality care than their more advantaged peers suggests that policies for 'narrowing the gap' may be reaching toward their target.

Which settings had higher quality scores?

We are interested in the predictors of quality, that is, which kinds of settings had higher quality scores? A strong relationship was found between certain 'structural' characteristics of a setting (for example, staff qualifications, centre size) and its quality as assessed through systematic observation. Exploring this relationship will lead to a better understanding of features of childcare that are associated with high quality of provision.

Centre characteristics related most to quality

Which kinds of centres were providing higher-quality care? Multiple regression analyses were carried out to investigate which setting characteristics were related to quality of provision, as measured by the three ECERS-R components, the four ECERS-E components and a combined ECERS-E score. The analyses predicting quality scores in 301 centres (see Table 8.6) showed that the following factors were associated with higher quality (in order):

- maintained (by the local authority) rather than private or voluntary status (apart from personal care routines)
- larger groups of children (with commensurate numbers of staff in the room observed)
- higher proportion of staff trained, especially with teacher qualifications (qualified teacher status or QTS)
- having children's centre status
- older children being present in the room alongside younger ones
- higher staff–child ratios
- *not* being one of the 72 settings linked with an SSLP
- smaller centres, that is, total enrolment
- higher-level nursery manager qualifications.

With regard to the advantage in maintained settings, in two of the sub-scales the effect of sector was only significant when staff qualifications were removed from the model. However, five of the sub-scales showed a significant effect of sector even when staff qualifications were taken into account.

The contrast between the positive impacts of children's centre status and a negative association with the Sure Start programme related specifically to provision for mathematics and for language and reasoning. A possible explanation is that

Table 8.6: Contributors to quality of provision[a]

Sub-scales of instruments Dependent variables	Personal care routines (ECERS-R)	Language and reasoning (ECERS-R)	Interaction (ECERS-R)	Literacy (ECERS-E)	Maths (ECERS-E)	Science (ECERS-E)	Diversity (ECERS-E)	Mean ECERS-E score
Independent variables								
Sector (maintained status)	− -0.15	+ 0.20	(+) (0.14)	+ 0.22	(+) (0.60)	+ 0.32	+ 0.26	+ 0.30
Children's Centre status	+ 0.20	(+) (0.14)	(+) (0.10)			+ 0.19	+ 0.22	+ 0.13
Link with Sure Start local programmes		− -0.12		− 0.11	− -0.22			− -0.14
Centre offers child/family health services	− -0.18	− -0.11	− -0.15	− -0.12	− -0.12			
Manager qualification (Levels 1-5)	+ 0.14	(+) (0.16)	(+) (0.12)	(+) (0.13)				(+) (0.03)
Mean qualification level of staff		+ 0.22	+ 0.16	+ 0.25	+ 0.15	(+) (0.18)	+ 0.13	+ 0.21
Any qualified teacher		(+) (0.17)	(+) (0.16)	+ 0.14	+ 0.15	+ 0.16	(+) (0.14)	+ 0.17
Staff member qualified to Level 4+		(+) (0.15)	+ 0.14	+ 0.23	(+) (0.14)	(+) (0.15)		+ 0.17
Proportion of staff in room observed qualified to NVQ Level 3 or above		+ 0.14	(+) (0.14)	+ 0.15	+ 0.13	(+) (0.11)	(+) (0.13)	+ 0.12

(continued)

Childcare in the pre-school years

Table 8.6: Contributors to quality of provision (continued)

Sub-scales of instruments Dependent variables Independent variables	Personal care routines (ECERS-R)	Language and reasoning (ECERS-R)	Interaction (ECERS-R)	Literacy (ECERS-E)	Maths (ECERS-E)	Science (ECERS-E)	Diversity (ECERS-E)	Mean ECERS-E score
Proportion of unqualified staff in room observed		0.23	-0.4	-0.21	-0.12	(-) (-0.14)	-0.17	-0.19
Age of oldest child in room observed (months)		+ 0.5	+ 0.16				+ 0.12	+ 0.12
Children under 3 present in room		-0.14		-0.13	-0.15	-0.13		-0.14
Group size (children present in room on day)		(+) (0.21)	+ 0.16	+ 0.16	+ 0.22	+ 0.18	+ 0.22	+ 0.23
Ratio in room observed (children to one adult)	-0.15	-0.13	-0.15				0.25	-0.12
Centre size (total enrolled – all ages up to 5)			-0.15					

Notes: Sample: childcare observation settings (beta values, only significant effects reported at $p<0.05$).
[a] + or - indicates the direction of an effect; (+) or (-) indicates an effect that was not independent of other variables (ie was only significant when one or more other variables were removed from the regression model).

those Sure Start programmes that were up and running at that time had a wider range of services, including child health and parenting, while the children's centres were more focused on services around children's learning.

The contribution of maintained sector and higher staff qualifications to centre quality was also found in the evaluation of the NNI study of toddler care in a large sample of settings (Mathers and Sylva, 2007). Using different measures of quality, a recent North American study found that staff training was related to quality scores (Vu et al, 2008).

The quality of provision offered by the sample settings varied widely, with some settings offering excellent provision and others less than adequate quality. Settings maintained by the local authority were providing the highest quality provision overall, particularly with regard to the 'learning' aspects of provision. Comparing the MCS and EPPE (2004; data collected 1997-99; see Sylva et al, 1999) revealed that quality scores on the full set of ECERS-R sub-scales in EPPE are slightly lower (mean ECERS-R = 4.3) than on those used in MCS (mean ECERS-R = 4.6). Further, mean scores on ECERS-E are also lower in EPPE (mean ECERS-E = 3.1) than in the MCS (mean ECERS-E = 3.4). This might be a consequence of a wealth of government funding and initiatives since 1997 (see Sylva and Pugh, 2005).

Conclusions

The study of group childcare in a sub-sample of MCS children has provided a snapshot of centre-based care across England in 2005. We found that less advantaged children were less likely to attend formal care than their more privileged peers, but those centres they did attend were of higher quality. The maintained sector offered the most stimulating learning experiences to young children, compared with the private sector. Finally, quality was higher in children's centres compared to other kinds of provision.

Taken together, these findings have important messages for policy makers: childcare, and its quality, is important in policy since substantial experience of childcare has become the norm for all children. The many initiatives to support the development of disadvantaged children appear to be at least hitting the target of their Early Years focus; less privileged children who attended centre-based care were experiencing significantly higher quality in their settings than their more advantaged peers. However, less advantaged children were less likely to attend centre-based care, and therefore steps might be taken to encourage its higher use.

If high-quality provision is the goal of government, centres in the maintained sector and those with highly qualified staff were more likely to be providing it in this 2005 sample. For children over the age of 3, larger centres tend to provide higher-quality care and education. The study is also noteworthy for finding very few centres with the highest quality of care – although most were in the 'adequate' range, there is much room for improvement. Since the Quality of Childcare survey the government has taken steps to improve quality and qualifications, for example, in introducing the Graduate Leader Fund to support the training and employment of graduates in private, voluntary and independent settings and supporting many professional development programmes for Early Years staff. The new century has seen a revolution in the range and quality of services supplementing the care of young children beyond the home. How far this investment has improved the prospects for both poor and priveleged children, time will tell.

NINE

Intergenerational inequality in Early Years assessments

Jo Blanden and Stephen Machin

Introduction[1]

One of the principal motivations for the launch of the new Millennium Cohort Study (MCS) was to gather up-to-date evidence on the extent to which family background impacts on child outcomes. In this chapter we use data from the MCS to provide some new empirical evidence on the extent to which one measure of parental background, family income, is correlated with two child outcomes, cognitive vocabulary ability and behavioural outcomes.[2] The analysis we undertake considers the magnitude of age 3 and 5 test score gaps and gaps in behavioural (or non-cognitive) outcomes by family income group. We also use these data to describe the dynamics of child achievement and behaviour between these ages. Much of the interest in early age outcomes is motivated by the link between early achievement gaps and the longer run relationship between the economic fortunes of parents and their adult children. Hence there is a natural connection between income gradients in early age child outcomes and the extent of intergenerational income mobility, and we also consider these connections.

We explore cross-cohort comparisons, comparing the MCS findings with those from earlier birth cohort studies. Using up-to-date empirical analysis assessing changes over time in the impact of family background on young children is particularly important in the light of the government's focus on improving children's outcomes since 1997. This policy agenda has gradually gathered pace since the New Labour government took office, so that the millennium cohort have experienced some, but not all, of the raft of policy initiatives in this direction. The MCS children would have experienced the beginnings of Sure Start, and free nursery provision for the neediest 3-year-olds (also discussed in Chapter 8, this volume). In addition, the rate of child poverty began to drop in 1997 (Brewer et al, 2003), which should equate to fewer disadvantages for those at the bottom. By exploring changes over cohorts born since the mid-1980s we can get a sense of the success of government policy since 1997. Our consideration of both formal tests of achievement and behaviour is also in line with the *Every Child Matters*[3] policy agenda launched in 2003, which sought to make more explicit the links between all the different aspects of children's lives, including achievement, enjoyment and 'making a positive contribution'.

The rest of the chapter is structured as follows. First, we offer a brief and necessarily highly selective description of relevant literature followed by a description of the data and the sample selections we adopt for our empirical analysis. We then present new evidence on the inequality of early age child cognitive and behavioural outcomes, with the inequality dimension studied being how these outcomes vary across the family income distribution. The relationships between these findings on inequality are then connected to aspects of intergenerational mobility in economic and social status. The early age dynamics of child achievement and behaviour are then examined. Finally we present our conclusions.

Brief literature review

The study of the economic determinants of children's development is a sizeable and growing field. In this chapter it is only possible to undertake a partial review. We focus here on earlier research that is relevant for our empirical analysis using MCS data. More extensive surveys of research in this area are included in Duncan and Brooks-Gunn (1997) and Mayer (1997).

In an influential study, Feinstein (2003) found that, among the British Cohort Study of children born in 1970 (BCS 70), gaps in child development by parental socioeconomic status emerged as early as 22 months. The gap also appeared to expand slightly as children aged, through 42 months and 60 months. Feinstein also showed his index of child development at early ages to be important for determining adult labour market performance age 26 years; it seemed, therefore, that inequalities in very early outcomes are, in part, responsible for long-lasting differences in life chances associated with family background. Feinstein also found important interactions between development trajectories and socioeconomic status. He identified children as high and low achieving at 22 months and found that those children in the highest achieving group with parents in the most disadvantaged socioeconomic group were overtaken, on average, around age 6 by those from advantaged backgrounds who were initially in the low-achieving group.

In the US context Carneiro and Heckman (2005) documented gaps in mathematics achievement and antisocial behaviour for children aged 6-10 for the children of the National Longitudinal Survey of Youth. They showed that substantial gaps by permanent income were found for both maths and antisocial behaviour, with those in the top income quartile fairing approximately 14 percentiles better than those at the bottom in mathematics, and 18 percentiles better in terms of the antisocial behaviour index at age 6. Gaps tend to widen slightly between ages 6 and 10. The implications of this are demonstrated by Heckman et al (2006), who show that gaps in cognitive ability and non-cognitive skills in early adulthood matter for wages at age 30, both because those with high ability get more education, and because even among those with the same education level, those with higher ability tend to earn more. These cognitive and non-cognitive characteristics were also shown to be related to the later outcomes of employment, smoking, crime and early motherhood.

Blanden et al (2008) explicitly make the link between differences in children's test scores and non-cognitive traits and later life chances, showing how the correlation between childhood ability, soft skills and family income mediate the connection between childhood parental income and the child's later adult earnings. When taken individually, the role of mathematics and reading ability at age 5 and 10 accounts for 19% of the intergenerational income elasticity in the 1970 cohort, and the role of non-cognitive skills at these ages accounts for 27%. However, cognitive and non-cognitive skills are closely correlated. When considered together they account for about one third of the intergenerational link.

Early age gaps in attainment are a forerunner or precursor of longer-term intergenerational immobility. Therefore, by examining the relationship between family income and intermediate outcomes such as age 3 and 5 vocabulary scores, we are able (under certain assumptions) to make predictions about the relationship between children's later earnings and family income. This provides predictions of trends in intergenerational mobility into the future. Blanden and Machin (2008) carried out this exercise using a variety of data. In this chapter we reproduce some of the results from this article which compare analysis from the MCS with analysis from other data sources. This will help us to judge, as far as we can, the likely extent of future intergenerational mobility facing the MCS children as they grow up.

This short literature review has emphasised that, on both sides of the Atlantic, gaps in achievement and behaviour emerge early and persist, and they also lead to inequalities in adult life chances. In this chapter we update our knowledge about the size of these gaps at ages 3 and 5 in the UK. Comparing information gained from the MCS with knowledge from the earlier data sources gives us a perspective on whether gaps are narrower for the MCS than for earlier cohorts of children, and the likely future implications for trends in intergenerational mobility. Feinstein's work from the BCS 70 cohort indicates that disadvantage in early childhood affects children's progression, with those from less advantaged backgrounds more likely to lose ground. Analyses in this chapter update this picture with information from the MCS.

Data

In this section we describe the MCS cognitive and behavioural test outcomes we study and how we measure family income, together with out sample selections and our use of MCS data to make comparisons with other cohorts.

Cognitive tests

At age 3, two cognitive assessments are made: the British Ability Scales (BAS) naming vocabulary and the Bracken School Readiness Assessment (BSRA). At age 5, the BAS vocabulary assessment was repeated and supplemented by BAS tests in picture similarities (to assess pictorial reasoning) and pattern construction (to obtain information on spatial abilities). The details of these cognitive assessments at ages 3 and 5 area set out in Box 1.1 (Chapter 1, this volume). Jones and Schoon (2008) show that if the three cognitive assessments administered at age 5 are combined to make a single factor, then all three components are correlated with this factor with a correlation coefficient of around 0.6. Ermisch (2008) reports that the two age 3 measures are also strongly positively correlated, with a correlation coefficient of 0.575. In this chapter we focus on the vocabulary scores, as these allow us to directly compare children's performance at ages 3 and 5. While we should remember that the vocabulary scores we use are designed to pick up the verbal dimension of children's skills, they appear to be closely related to more general measures of cognitive ability.

Measures of behaviour

The cognitive assessments were supplemented with a number of behavioural assessments. At both ages 3 and 5 the 'main' respondent (usually the MCS child's mother) was asked to complete a self-reported module, which included the 25 items of the Strengths and Difficulties Questionnaire (SDQ) across five sub-scales. The details of these assessments and sub-scales are provided in Box 1.2 (in Chapter 1, this volume). A composite difficulties scale was generated by adding together scores on all the sub-scales with the exception of the pro-social item.

Family income

Our family background measure for most of this chapter is 'permanent' income (that is, averaged over MCS 1, 2 and 3). In each survey the main respondent is asked to assess their net family income as falling into one of 18 or 19 bands, with the options varying depending on whether the child lives in a one- or two-parent family. We assign the family the midpoint of the stated category[4] then average these over all three surveys to give a measure of permanent income. The mean average weekly income in December 2007 prices is £567, with a median of £474. We supplement this income measure of status with a measure based on socioeconomic status to show figures that are as comparable as possible with Feinstein (2003), who did not have parental income data available to utilise.[5] For the analyses comparing MCS with other earlier cohorts we are careful to use measures of family income that are similar across all datasets, and we use income that is observed at the point when the age 5 outcomes are observed. We provide more information on comparability issues at the end of this section.

Sample selection

For the MCS-only analysis we limit the sample to those individuals who have scores available at both ages 3 and 5, and consider only singletons plus the first child listed for twins and triplets. We use weights made available by the MCS team in September 2008 to account for the sample design and attrition. The use of the new attrition weights makes little difference to the analysis.

Cross-cohort comparisons

One of the objectives of this chapter is to map the evolution of the relationship between test scores, behaviour and parental income over time. To do this we compare the MCS data with information from two other groups of children, the children of the National Child Development Study (NCDS) and the children of the BCS. In 1991, data were collected about natural or adopted co-resident children for one third of the NCDS (those born in a week in 1958). Three thousand children were included aged between 3 and 17. Tests administered were the Peabody Individual Attainment test (for mathematics and reading) and the Peabody Picture Vocabulary test. The mother also answered a questionnaire providing more information on the behaviour and home environment of the children.

In 2004 a similar exercise was conducted for the BCS 70 children. In this case, data on children were collected for half of the cohort. Age-appropriate assessments of word and number skills from the BAS were carried out to gauge children's cognitive skills and attainment. Similar child behavioural measures were taken from parents in both cohorts.

The offspring of these two cohorts can be matched with information from the main surveys, which provides details of their parental education, family income and earnings, among numerous other characteristics. Information on family income is formed from adding together information on all of the cohort members' and their partners' sources of income (careful cleaning has been carried out here).

To compare these datasets with the MCS we use NCDS/BCS children's (within-sample) percentiles in the word tests as our measure of cognitive ability, and compare this with the MCS children's performance in the vocabulary test at age 5. All three surveys have some identical questions on behaviour, and we combine these to create a behavioural index that is standardised to have a mean of zero and a unit standard deviation within each dataset.

It should be noted that the 'offspring of' datasets were not designed to be representative samples of all children in the age group and while we have tried our best to adapt the data in our youngest cohorts to be comparable, the issue of representativeness introduces a caveat on our results. One useful aspect of the data we use is that the samples of the 'offspring of' BCS and the MCS were born only about one year apart. Therefore if we find similar results on these datasets we can be less worried about issues of comparability.

Among the issues we must address to ensure comparability is the selection of age groups within the 'offspring of' data. We need to construct age samples of 'offspring of' data in the two cohorts as close as possible to those in the MCS sample. We also need to construct similarly appropriate family income measures to use, and select data of equivalent ethnic composition out of the three datasets. There is more detail on these issues in the Appendix to Blanden and Machin (2008). Most importantly, we select the younger 'offspring of' children in the NCDS/BCS (5- to 7-year-olds in the NCDS and 4- to 6-year-olds in the BCS) and limit the comparable MCS sample to those with mothers aged 33–35 at the age 5 survey so as to match with mothers in the NCDS and BCS.

Inequality of early age child cognitive and behavioural outcomes

We begin by documenting MCS children's vocabulary score adjusted for age[6] and converted into percentiles. Figure 9.1 plots these at ages 3 and 5. Figure 9.2 shows gaps in MCS children's problem behaviour as revealed by percentile performance in the total difficulties scale at these ages. The gaps at both ages in vocabulary performance are substantial, with those with parental income in the bottom quintile performing, on average, at the 35th percentile at age 3, and those in the top quintile scoring at the 56th percentile at this age. It seems that the penalty for coming from a low-income family is greater than the advantage of coming from a high-income family, when compared to the middle-income group.

Figure 9.1: Vocabulary scores by parental income quintile in the MCS

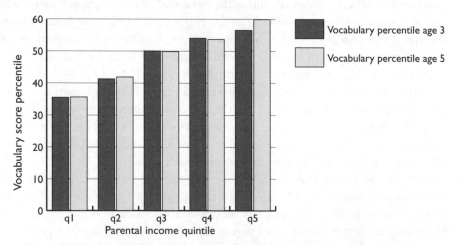

Notes: All figures and tables based on MCS data alone are derived using the weights provided by the Centre for Longitudinal Studies at the time of writing (covwt2, released in September 2008). The income measure used is net parental income averaged (as available) across MCS 1, MCS 2 and MCS 3.

Feinstein (2003) and Carneiro and Heckman (2005) showed that as children aged, the impact of family background appeared to increase. From MCS there is limited evidence of a widening gap from age 3 to 5 according to parental income (see Figure 9.1). The gaps across quintiles remained steady, with the exception of the very top income group, who move ahead by about 3 percentiles. This widens the overall gap between the richest and poorest children only slightly. The widening gaps documented by Carneiro and Heckman focused on older children, from ages 6–10, so it may be that our data are taken too early for us to observe gaps widening over the school years. The MCS 4 survey at age 7 will provide new evidence on this dimension. Feinstein (2003), using the BCS 70, found a marked (although not statistically significant) deterioration of performance in test scores among his most deprived group between ages 22 and 42 months, and a smaller decline between 42 and 60 months (closer to the age groups we observe here). There is no evidence of any decline at the bottom end among these MCS children, which could be cautiously greeted as a sign of a small improvement in their fortunes.

An alternative way to quantify the assessment gaps we observe is to think of them in terms of the amount of progress we would expect children to make in a month. Hansen (2008) includes estimates of expected monthly improvement from the BAS manual, revealing that children progress by 1.25 points per month on the vocabulary ability score[7] on average around their 3rd birthday and by around 0.83 points per month around their 5th birthday. The gap between the richest and poorest MCS children, in terms of vocabulary ability scores, is 11.9 points at age 3 and 12.4 points at age 5. Improvement is expected to be faster at younger ages and this translates to a gap in vocabulary development between the richest and poorest groups of children, of around 10 months at age 3 and 15 months at age 5.

Figure 9.2: Total difficulties behaviour scores by parental income quintile in the MCS

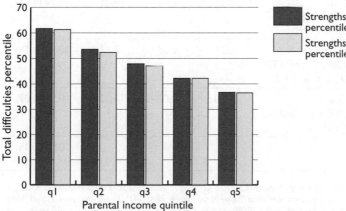
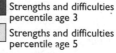
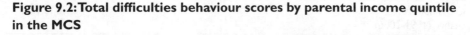

Figure 9.2 provides information on the average percentile performance on the total difficulties scale. Once again, the gaps are large, with those in the poorest quintile scoring 25 percentile points higher than those in the richest quintile on this measure (recall that a higher score here means worse behaviour). There is no evidence of any growth in gaps between ages 3 and 5.[8]

Cross-cohort changes concerning intergenerational mobility

One of the objectives of our examination of the MCS children is to make comparisons with earlier cohorts. In the previous section some loose comparisons were made between our findings from the MCS and Feinstein's results for the BCS 70. However, there are a number of differences between the data and the precise variables used in these two cohort comparisons. In this section we report

Table 9.1: Changes in gaps associated with parental income between cohorts

		Lowest 20% of parental income	Middle 60% of parental income	Highest 20% of parental income	Educational inequality (highest 20% minus lowest 20%)
	1991 ('Offspring of' 1958 Cohort aged 5-7)	38.39	52.84	52.74	14.35 (4.73)
Vocabulary scores	2004 ('Offspring of' 1970 Cohort aged 4-6)	40.76	50.86	56.00	15.24 (3.92)
	2006 (MCS comparable age 5)	38.96	48.75	55.61	16.65 (1.98)
Cross-cohort change (1991-2006)					2.30 (5.13)
	1991 ('Offspring of' 1958 Cohort aged 5-7)	0.29	0.06	-0.21	-0.50 (0.13)
Total difficulties behaviour (standardised)	2004 ('Offspring of' 1970 Cohort aged 4-6)	0.21	-0.09	-0.14	-0.34 (0.14)
	2006 (MCS comparable age 5)	0.20	-0.07	-0.32	-0.52 (0.07)
Cross-cohort change (1991-2006)					-0.01 (0.15)

Notes: Standard errors (SEs) are in parentheses. MCS sample is selected to be comparable with the samples from the second generation data. Sample sizes are 384; 541; 2,661 in panel 1, and 366: 545; 2,585 in panel 2. Blanden and Machin (2008), and in particular the appendix, provide more information on the samples and methods used.

some results based on a more precise comparison of the MCS with data from the offspring of the NCDS born around 1985 and BCS born around 1999.

Table 9.1 provides information on average scores in vocabulary ability and problem behaviour by quintile of family income at the point the test was taken. In all three samples the gaps from highest to lowest family income in vocabulary ability score percentiles are around 15 points, with no evidence of any significant change across the three groups of children. The gaps in the behaviour index (note that this is not the same as the total difficulties score mentioned earlier) are around 0.5 of a standard deviation, with again, no significant change across the three groups of children, spanning the 15-year period.

Intergenerational mobility is often measured in terms of a linear regression that relates parental earnings or income (income in our case) to adult earnings. It can be shown that this can be broken down to show how early age outcomes and their relationship with parental income can be mapped into future intergenerational mobility. In order to see this, consider two life cycle stages, one which looks at how early age factors relate to parental income, and the other which looks at how income as an adult relates to these early outcomes, or the 'returns' to early characteristics. Total intergenerational mobility will be influenced by both of these stages: if the strength of the relationship between early outcomes and parental income increases this will reduce subsequent intergenerational social mobility *ceteris paribus*. If the returns to childhood characteristics rise, then this will act to push intergenerational mobility in the same direction. There is also a third factor, the direct relationship between parental income and earnings that is not mediated through early characteristics. If we assume that the second and third dimensions are unchanging, then changes in the linear relationship between early outcomes and parent income will provide a guide to changes in mobility for young cohorts (for more on the plausibility of these assumptions see Blanden and Machin, 2008).

Table 9.2 shows the results for the association of vocabulary and problem behaviour scores to standardised parental income from Blanden and Machin (2008). This linear approach confirms the finding that the relationship with parental income is unchanged across these three cohorts of children and leads us to expect that total intergenerational income mobility will be similarly unchanged. Indeed, putting this result together with evidence from other data sources used

Table 9.2: Changes in associations of vocabulary and behaviour scores with parental income across cohorts

	'Offspring of' 1958 cohort (aged 5-7 in 1991)	'Offspring of' 1970 cohort (aged 4-6 in 2004)	MCS (aged 5 in 2006) comparable	Cross-cohort change in θ, 1991–2006
Vocabulary scores, OLS	5.17 (1.66)	5.63 (1.31)	5.66 (0.80)	0.49 (1.83)
Total difficulties behaviour, OLS	-0.21 (0.06)	-0.14 (0.04)	-0.18 (0.03)	0.03 (0.07)

Notes: Ordinary least squares (OLS) estimates condition on parental age and the sex of the child. Standard errors are in parentheses. Sample sizes from left to right: row 1: 384; 541; 2,661; row 2: 366; 545; 2,585.

in the same article (that concentrates on even older cohorts) indicates we would expect intergenerational mobility for the MCS children to be at a similar level to those children born in 1970. However, this is obviously a speculative assessment at this stage that will need to be reassessed as more data become available. As the MCS children age, we will have more and more information about how they compare with children growing up in earlier years. We also need to keep in mind the caveat that while we have made the datasets as comparable across time as possible, the necessary sample restrictions mean that the changes we observe are not representative of all children.

Early age dynamics of child achievement and behaviour

As well as documenting raw gaps by family background in young children's performance, Feinstein (2003) also considered the interaction between early years' ability and socioeconomic status (SES) in shaping development and achievement trajectories among the 1970 cohort members. Figure 9.3 reproduces Feinstein's influential finding from the BCS which shows that even those from lower SES who do well (top quartile) in test scores at 22 months have their relative performance bypassed between age 5 and 10 by those who are in the bottom quartile of test score achievement at 22 months but in the highest SES group. This result has been taken to imply that the interaction of schooling with SES has more influence on

Figure 9.3: Evolution of test scores by early ability and socioeconomic status (SES) in the 1970 cohort

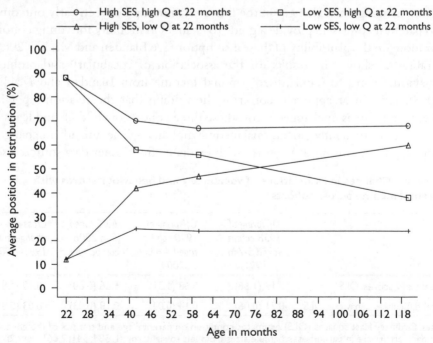

Source: Feinstein (2003). © Wiley-Blackwell, reproduced with permission.

later outcomes than early ability. For our purposes it should be noted that while the gap between high ability–low SES and high SES–low ability children narrowed between 42 and 60 months in the BCS cohort (close to the age range we can study in the MCS), the two trajectories do not cross until later ages.

Figures 9.4 and 9.5 use the data from the MCS to replicate Feinstein's analysis for children growing up in the 2000s. It is clear that Feinstein's basic finding is replicated – high vocabulary achievers at age 3 with low SES are losing ground between ages 3 and 5, while low achievers with high SES are improving their percentile scores more quickly than other children starting from a similar baseline (see Figure 9.4). The MCS results include two additional data series that were not included in the original BCS analysis. As well as looking at the extreme cases of high and low SES, we also consider the middle SES group. High achievers from the average socioeconomic group tend to lose ground at a similar rate to those from the low socioeconomic group; those from high SES backgrounds do markedly better. Among the lowest quartile of achievers there is more of a distinction between the three different types of family background, with the more advantaged by SES being ahead of the average group at age 5, and the average

Figure 9.4: Progression of MCS vocabulary scores by ability at age 3 and SES

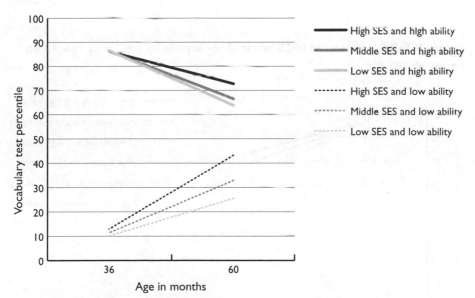

Notes: SES is defined by parental occupation/work status in MCS 1. The status of both parents is taken into account in two-parent households; for lone parent households, only the resident parent is used in the definition.
Low SES indicates that parents are workless or that all working parents have semi-routine or routine occupations.
High SES is defined as all working parents have a managerial or professional occupation.
The middle SES group is the remainder.
High ability children are those in the top quartile by vocabulary score at age 3; low ability are those in the bottom quartile.

group ahead of those from lower socioeconomic backgrounds. These results encourage us to speculate about the additional resources that advantaged parents offer high-achieving children at age 3.

Figure 9.5 shows results based on our permanent measure of family income, where the advantaged group is defined as those in the top quintile of permanent income (a smaller group than those in the top SES), the disadvantaged are the bottom quintile and the remainder make up the 'middle group'. While the overall pattern in the results is the same, the distinction between high achievers from the most advantaged group with high achievers from the middle-income group has disappeared, with those from the lower-income group appearing more distinctive in the way that they lose ground. Figures 9.6 and 9.7 reproduce the results for the total difficulties score with similar, but less pronounced, results.

As well as the interaction between social background and early ability we can also consider the relationship between behaviour at age 3 and progression in vocabulary scores between ages 3 and 5. These results are shown in Table 9.3. As we might expect, children with better behavioural traits at age 3 tend to make more progress than those with the greatest behaviour difficulties. For those in the bottom quartile of the vocabulary scores at age 3, those with the lowest difficulty score end up improving their position by 4 percentiles at age 5. For those in the higher performing vocabulary groups at age 3, lower difficulties scores

Figure 9.5: Progression in MCS vocabulary scores by ability at age 3 and parental income

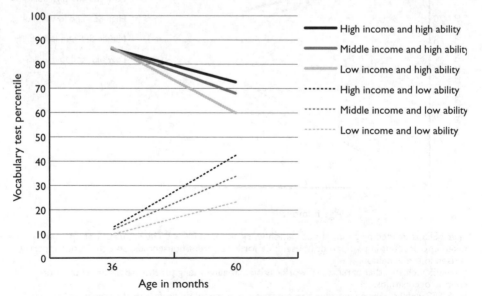

Notes: The income measure used is net parental income averaged (as available) across MCS 1, MCS 2 and MCS 3.
High income is defined as the top quintile by this measure. Low income is defined as the bottom quintile.

Figure 9.6: Progression in MCS behaviour outcomes at age 3 and SES

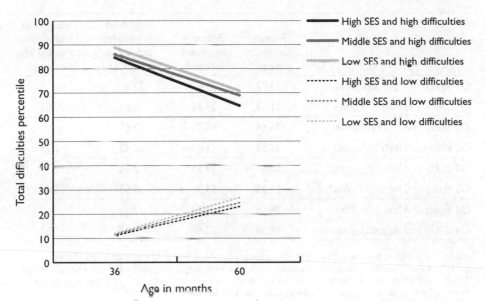

Notes: SES is defined as in Figure 9.4. 'Difficulties' are based on the sum of all the difficulties items in the Strengths and Difficulties Questionnaire (SDQ) at age 3. 'High' difficulties and 'low' difficulties refer to the top and bottom quartile of this scale respectively.

Figure 9.7: Progression in MCS behaviour outcomes at age 3 and parental income

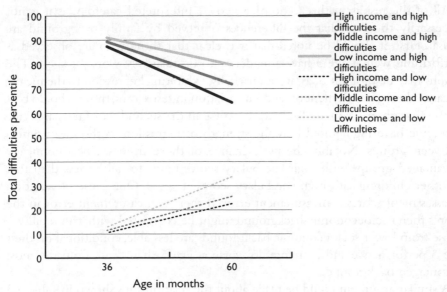

Notes: See previous figures.

Table 9.3: Interactions between vocabulary score progression and behaviour – MCS

	Percentile vocabulary at age 3	Percentile vocabulary at age 5	Progression (percentile at 5 minus percentile at 3)	Difference in progression associated with behaviour
Q1 ability and low difficulties	12.77	35.63	22.86	
Q1 ability and high difficulties	11.12	29.93	18.81	4.05
Q2 ability and low difficulties	36.64	49.31	12.67	
Q2 ability and high difficulties	35.64	41.06	5.42	7.25
Q3 ability and low difficulties	59.6	57.14	-2.46	
Q3 ability and high difficulties	59.25	53.30	-5.95	3.49
Q4 ability and low difficulties	86.58	69.43	-17.15	
Q4 ability and high difficulties	86.38	67.60	-18.78	1.63

Notes: Q1 ability is the lowest quartile of vocabulary score at age 3, Q4 indicates the highest quartile. Low difficulties indicates the child was in the lowest quartile of the difficulties scale at age 3, high difficulties means that the child was in the top quartile at the same age. These figures are derived from available sample with information on test scores at ages 3 and 5 and strengths and difficulties at age 3, the number of observations is 7,448.

are associated with a smaller decline in their position, although these effects are smaller than those for children with poorer vocabularies at age 3. Interestingly, the association between low difficulties and a better performance trajectory in vocabulary between ages 3 and 5 is greatest for children in the second quartiles of vocabulary performance at age 3.

All of the results in this section have to be interpreted carefully, as it is not necessarily the case that the differences observed by family background are causal. First, it should be noted that it is clear that those who are observed as performing well at age 3 have a tendency to do relatively worse at age 5. The graphs may be thought of as, at least partially, exhibiting 'regression to the mean'; because there is an element of random variation in test scores, those who do best in the first observation are likely to do worse in the second set of tests and vice versa. We have highlighted how the strength of regression to the mean differs between groups. Notably, the performance of those from socioeconomically advantaged groups with high vocabulary scores tends to fall by less than that of other children with high vocabulary scores at age 3. One cause of variation in assessment scores is measurement error. If there is measurement error in the scores then socioeconomic background might be correlated with 'true' ability – those from lower socioeconomic backgrounds are less able, conditional on their age 3 performance and therefore do worse at age 5 than those from the most advantaged background.

A similar argument could be made about the relationships shown in Table 9.3 where differences in progression by behaviour could be due to a correlation between age 3 behaviour and 'true' ability at ages 3 that feeds through to vocabulary performance at age 5. While we should bear this caveat in mind, the results in Table 9.3 indicate some likely complementarities between behaviour and vocabulary score performance. They are also useful from the perspective that it is instructive to compare results on the dynamics in the MCS with those from Feinstein's study of the earlier BCS cohort of children born in 1970, especially as this study has been so widely quoted both in academic and policy circles.

Conclusions

This chapter has shown that gaps in vocabulary scores and behaviour by family background are substantial for the MCS children, with those from the most advantaged groups performing over a year ahead in vocabulary compared to those from disadvantaged backgrounds at ages 3 and 5. There is only limited evidence of a widening of the gap in attainment as the MCS children age. However, it will be extremely interesting to observe the evolution of cognitive verbal scores in the next survey (at age 7), which will cover the first few years of school.

The relationship between family income and Early Years outcomes can be thought of as an early manifestation of the inequalities that can go on to impede social mobility in later life. A comparison of results from MCS on this dimension with evidence from data for earlier cohorts of children shows no substantive change. These early findings therefore show that the pre-school factors shaping the levels of mobility among children born around the millennium are not very different from children born in the mid-1980s or even for those born in 1970. Of course, drawing more definitive conclusions about mobility patterns for this cohort as compared to older cohorts will be an important research venture as they age through the childhood years and into adulthood.

Notes
[1] This work was in part financially supported by the Sutton Trust and we benefited from the comments of Lee Elliott Major during the research project.

[2] Economists have lately begun to explore the importance of 'non-cognitive' traits or skills (Heckman et al, 2006, inter alia). However, as this description is contentious, we do not describe our findings in this way, although we recognise there is a clear link with this literature.

[3] See www.everychildmatters.gov.uk. The Scottish Executive has a similar policy framework GIRFEC (Getting it Right for Every Child): www.scotland.gov. uk/Topics/People/Young-People/childrensservices.

[4] Ketende and Joshi (2008) find that the use of the midpoint is a reasonable approximation for the data compared with imputation using an underlying log normal distribution.

[5] In order to minimise the impact of missing values in income, we form the average of income from the surveys in which it is available. An additional advantage of complementing our income analysis with SES is to check the sensitivity of the results to the income variable used.

[6] We use the T-score test score measure provided in the data that uses external norms to take account of the age at which the test was taken.

[7] The vocabulary ability score ranges from 10 to 170.

[8] Notice that for both the difficulties and vocabulary score there are less than 100 unique values to base the percentile ranking on. We could instead standardise the scores and look at gaps in terms of standard deviations (as Ermisch, 2008, does). We have tried this alternative methodology and find that the patterns that emerge change very little compared to the results shown here.

TEN

Ethnic inequalities in child outcomes

Lorraine Dearden and Luke Sibieta

Introduction

This chapter reports some findings from the first three surveys of the Millennium Cohort Study (MCS) on the nature and extent of ethnic differences in early childhood environment and outcomes up to age 5.[1] Due to the lack of suitable data, it has not been possible to consider these issues in the UK before – the MCS is one of the first longitudinal surveys in the UK that has the ability to look at this important issue, particularly as the MCS design involved over-sampling individuals from minority ethnic groups and individuals living in disadvantaged areas of the country.

In this chapter we examine ethnic differences in child outcomes, together with background and mediating factors that are likely to have impacted on these outcomes. This draws on earlier work using the MCS looking at ethnic differences in birth outcomes (see Dearden et al, 2006). Our results suggest that in explaining ethnic differences in child outcomes, it is important not only to consider differences in socioeconomic and family characteristics, such as parental education and socioeconomic status (SES), but also family background, family structure and child demographics. It is also important to consider other mediating factors such as family interactions, family health and well-being, the early home learning environment (HLE) and parenting styles and rules. It turns out that these other mediating factors point to possible policy responses to reducing ethnic differences in child outcomes.

The rest of the chapter is organised as follows. First, we outline how we define our ethnic groups used in the rest of the chapter. We then show how our outcomes of interest vary by ethnic groups. This shows that ethnic gaps in childhood development start early in life. Following that, we examine how some possible explanatory factors of this gap vary by ethnic group, namely selected family background characteristics and selected measures of the early childhood environment. We present the multivariate analysis we carried out to see the extent to which family background characteristics and the early childhood environment can act as mediating factors – in some sense 'explaining' the ethnic divide in early child development. This analysis is purely descriptive, but provides some clues to policy makers where interventions may be fruitful to lessen the ethnic differences.

Defining our ethnic groups

Although minority ethnic groups have been over-sampled in the MCS survey, the data sample sizes only allow us to split ethnicity into eight groups: white, Indian, Pakistani, Bangladeshi, black African, black Caribbean, 'Other' ethnic origins and 'Mixed' ethnic origins. The same eight categories are applied to the cohort child's mother in Chapter 3 (this volume). In Table 10.1 we show the weighted means (using sampling weights) of our ethnic groups as well as the unweighted means. We have dropped observations for which we have missing outcome data at MCS 2 or 3, which is unfortunately more likely to occur for minority ethnic groups. Table 10.1 makes it clear that even with these sample selections, all ethnic groups are still over-sampled by MCS 3, with the exception of parents of children with 'Mixed' ethnic origins.

Table 10.1: Ethnic breakdown of MCS sample

Ethnic group of child	Weighted mean %	Unweighted mean %
White	90.7	88.9
Indian	1.6	2.2
Pakistani	2.0	2.9
Bangladeshi	0.4	0.7
Black African	0.9	1.0
Black Caribbean	0.8	0.9
Other ethnicity	0.8	0.9
Mixed ethnicity	2.8	2.5
Total %	100	100
Sample size	11,054	11,054

Ethnic differences in early childhood outcomes

In this chapter we focus on ethnic differences in two child outcomes that have been measured in the second and third surveys of the MCS: cognitive and non-cognitive development. Our measure of cognitive outcomes is the British Ability Scales (BAS) naming vocabulary administered in MCS 2 and 3 (see Box 1.1, Chapter 1, this volume). We then use the measure of total difficulties from the Strengths and Difficulties Questionnaire (SDQ) in MCS 2 and 3 as our measure of non-cognitive development (see Box 1.2, Chapter 1, this volume). We have combined the four sub-scales representing socioemotional difficulties (emotional, conduct, peers and hyperactivity) into a single score, but have rescaled it such that higher scores represent better outcomes in some sense. In contrast to the cognitive outcomes, the elements used in the SDQ measure are reported by the mother, such that ethnic differences in the measure could reflect ethnic differences in interpreting or reporting children's behaviour.

We have converted these scores into (weighted) percentile rankings within our selected sample and in Table 10.2 we look at the raw ethnic differences in mean percentile rankings for our two measures at ages 3 and 5.

We see from Table 10.2 that all minority ethnic groups perform significantly worse than their white counterparts in terms of cognitive outcomes (measured using the BAS verbal component) at ages 3 and 5. Pakistani and Bangladeshi children have the worst academic outcomes at ages 3 and 5, with Pakistani children being 32 percentile points behind white children at age 3 and Bangladeshi children 37 percentile points behind; both are just under 30 percentile points behind white children at age 5. Indian children are around 20 percentile points behind white children at age 3, although are only around 10 percentile points behind by age 5. Black African children are 17 percentile points below white children at age 3, as are black Caribbean children. By age 5, black African children are now about 20 percentile points behind at age 5, whereas black Caribbean children are 16 percentile points behind. Children from other ethnicities are around 20 percentile points behind white children at age 3, but closer to 15 percentile points behind by age 5. Children of mixed ethnicity are around 5 percentile points below white children at both ages.

The story for our non-cognitive measure, the SDQ, is very different to that for cognitive outcomes. At age 3, black African and children from other ethnic groups have significantly better outcomes than their white peers, while Pakistani children have significantly worse outcomes than white children. For the remaining ethnic groups, there are no significant differences from white children. By age 5, Pakistani, Bangladeshi and black Caribbean children have significantly worse

Table 10.2: Cognitive and non-cognitive percentile outcomes by ethnicity

Outcomes	White	Indian	Pakistani	Bangladeshi	Black African	Black Caribbean	Other	Mixed	All
BAS naming vocabulary:									
Age 3	48.3	28.9**	16.4**	11.4**	31.5**	31.2**	28.8**	43.2**	46.6
Age 5	46.2	35.2**	18.7**	17.8**	26.7**	30.5**	31.0**	42.4*	44.8
SDQ:									
Age 3	47.5	47.7	42.4**	48.8	55.4**	43.4	53.8**	47.7	47.5
Age 5	47.6	44.9	31.9**	39.3**	47.4	33.7**	42.8	44.5	46.9

Notes: Significant differences from white children, **p<0.05; *p<0.1. The SDQ percentile measure has been transformed so that a higher percentile score is a better outcome (as with the BAS naming vocabulary).

non-cognitive outcomes. All other groups have non-cognitive outcomes that are not significantly different from white children.

What can explain the large differences in early child cognitive development by ethnic group? It seems unlikely that these will be purely the result of ethnic differences. Instead, do these differences just reflect differences in the socioeconomic position and parents' education? How important are the other mediating factors we have defined? This will be the focus of the remainder of the chapter. We begin by looking at ethnic differences in groups of variables that might potentially act as mediating factors.

Ethnic differences in background and mediating factors

There are a number of factors that one would expect to mediate these ethnic differences in child outcomes. The factors we focus here on include family characteristics, SES, parental education and demographics (henceforth referred to just as family characteristics and demographics). We also focus on family interactions, family health and well-being, childcare, the home learning environment (HLE) and parenting style/rules. These factors have been found to have important roles in determining children's cognitive and non-cognitive outcomes in other UK and international work (see for example Wigfield and Eccles, 2000; Feinstein, 2003, 2004; and Dearden et al, 2006).

Later in the chapter we add these groups of factors individually to our baseline regressions, which show what proportion of the observed ethnic differences in cognitive and non-cognitive outcomes can be explained by these individual factors. We now list the individual elements of these different groups of factors before showing ethnic differences in a small selection of characteristics from each group.

Family characteristics and demographics consist of variables that have traditionally been controlled for in previous birth cohorts when looking at cognitive/educational outcomes. They include: parents' highest education level; the family's socioeconomic position;[2] the marital status and partnering of the parents at MCS surveys 1, 2 and 3; the sex of the child; whether they are a twin or triplet; the number of siblings and older siblings at MCS surveys 2 and 3; whether the child was in special care unit at birth; whether only English is spoken in the household at MCS 1; mother's age at MCS 1; parental employment at MCS 1, 2 and 3; and country of residence at MCS 1.

Family interactions are measured by: degree of parental harmony at sweeps 1 and 2; interviewer-assessed measure of mother–child closeness at MCS 2; mother–child relationship and conflict problems measured as the number of problems identified on 15-item sub-scales of the Pianta index (the parent–child relationship scale and the parent–child conflicts scale); and whether mothers and fathers felt that they spent plenty of time with their children at the second sweep.

Family health and well-being is measured by: the number of cigarettes smoked by the mother per day while pregnant; units of alcohol drank by mother while pregnant; length of gestation in days; birth weight (kg); did the mother try to breastfeed; age at which breastfeeding ceased (0–26 weeks); still breastfeeding after 26 weeks; whether the mother was suffering from depression during the child's infancy (defined as agreeing to four of the nine statements from a shortened version of the Malaise inventory, for example, do you often get into a violent rage?); infant temperament (mood, regularity and adaptability); the mother's height, weight and body mass index before birth; and the father's height, weight and body mass index at sweep 1.

Non-maternal childcare is measured as a series of dummy variables indicating whether or not children had attended the following settings by age 3 (MCS 2) and age 5 (MCS 3): nursery school/class; playgroup; pre-school; childminder.

Home learning environment (HLE) is constructed from the HLE index (frequency of reading to child, library visits, play with ABCs/letters, teaches numbers/shapes, songs/nursery rhymes, drawing/painting) and divided into quintiles in our sample. We also separately control for self-reported parenting competency and frequency of reading to child (which is also included in the HLE index). Including frequency of reading in addition to the overall HLE index allows us to see whether reading has a differential effect to the others elements. All measures are available at both MCS 2 and 3 (sweep).

Parenting styles/rules measure whether: the parents have lots of rules (at MCS 2), parents strictly enforce rules (MCS 2); children have regular bed times (MCS 2 and 3); children have regular meal times (MCS 2 and 3); the family eats breakfast together (MCS 3); children watch more than three hours of television a day (MCS 2 and 3); and children play on the computer for more than one hour a day (MCS 3).

In Table 10.3 we show differences in some of the characteristics from each of these groups by the child's ethnic group.

From the family characteristics and demographics group, we look at SES (being in the lowest quintile); mother's education (having no qualifications); whether only English is spoken in the home; and number of siblings. From Table 10.3 we see that over 60% of Bangladeshi children are in the in the lowest SES quintile, as are around 45% of our black African and black Caribbean children. The only ethnic groups to be under-represented in this quintile are white, Indian and children from other ethnic groups. In terms of having mothers with no qualifications, all minority ethnic groups are significantly more likely to have mothers in this group compared with white children. There are significant differences across almost all ethnic groups for whether only English is spoken in the home, the exception being black Caribbean children who are very similar to white children with most households only speaking English in the home. Pakistani, Bangladeshi and black African children have significantly more siblings than white children. For the remaining ethnic groups there are no significant differences compared with white children. A significantly greater proportion of black African and black Caribbean children live in lone-parent households at age 5 than do white children, while

Table 10.3: Differences in selected characteristics, by child's ethnic group

Selected characteristics	Child's ethnic group								
	White	Indian	Pakistani	Bangladeshi	Black African	Black Caribbean	Other	Mixed	All
Parents in lowest SES quintile (%)	18.6	12.6**	35.1**	62.0**	46.3**	45.9**	18.5	36.4**	20.0
Mother no qualifications (%)	10.0	24.1**	44.7**	37.3**	25.7**	17.7**	28.7**	16.0**	11.6
Only English spoken at home (%)	97.7	17.0**	7.7**	2.0**	47.4**	97.5	32.3**	83.6**	92.9
Number of siblings (age 5)	1.31	1.33	1.96**	2.06**	1.64**	1.62	1.41	1.24	1.33
Lone parent at MCS 3 (%)	16.4	5.0**	13.2	5.4**	37.4**	56.1**	12.1	30.3**	17.0
Mother–child relationship problems (0-7 scale)	0.11	0.06**	0.20**	0.23	0.18	0.12	0.05**	0.07*	0.11
Proportion who breastfed (%)	71.0	90.7**	78.3**	92.5**	97.4**	82.1**	93.9**	82.2**	72.4
Age stopped breastfeeding (weeks)	13.59	16.57**	11.75**	15.27	19.30**	15.98*	16.17**	16.64**	13.83
Birth-weight (kg)	3.39	3.02**	3.13**	3.13**	3.32*	3.06**	3.20**	3.22**	3.37
Mothers suffered post-natal depression MCS 1 (%)	12.3	18.9**	20.0**	16.9	7.6*	19.3	10.4	12.9	12.6
Went to nursery class/school by age 5 (%)	55.7	57.8	75.3**	73.7**	66.8**	61.2	61.1	59.8	56.5
Went to playgroup by age 5 (%)	24.8	18.8	17.3**	7.8**	9.4**	7.0**	15.8**	22.9	24.1
Read to every day at age 3 (%)	63.7	39.3**	39.8**	26.8**	23.7**	37.0**	52.1*	56.9**	61.8
Bottom fifth of HLE at age 3 (%)	22.6	31.0**	36.1**	59.4**	50.3**	32.4	30.8	23.0	23.6
Read to every day at age 5 (%)	52.8	42.8**	41.4**	39.9**	45.8**	35.6**	63.4	51.5	52.2
Bottom fifth of HLE at age 5 (%)	22.0	34.3**	36.5**	39.6**	42.5**	31.1	32.1*	23.5	22.9
Regular bed times at age 3 (%)	82.6	71.6**	66.2**	62.6**	50.5**	63.2**	73.9	77.4*	81.3
Regular meal times at age 5 (%)	94.5	95.7	85.6**	79.2**	82.0**	84.6**	89.6	92.4	94.0

Note: Significant differences from White children, $**p<0.05$; $*p<0.10$

significantly lower proportions of children from Indian and Bangladeshi family backgrounds do so.

In terms of the family interaction group of variables, we observe that children from Indian, mixed or other ethnic groups seem to experience significantly fewer relationship problems with their mother than their white counterparts, whereas Pakistani children seem to experience significantly more such problems with their mother than children from a white ethnic background.

In terms of health and well-being, children from minority ethnic groups are more likely to have been breastfed and generally for longer than white children – 97% of mothers of black African children breast-fed compared with 71% of mothers of white children. However, children from minority ethnic groups generally have significantly lower birth weights than children from the white ethnic group. This has been explored in more detail in Dearden et al (2006). There are also significant ethnic differences in mothers experiencing depression in the child's first year. In particular, mothers of Indian and Pakistani children are much more likely to suffer from depression during this time than mothers of white children (nearly 1 in 5), whereas mothers of black African children are much less likely to suffer from depression during their child's infancy.

In terms of child care, it actually seems as if children from minority ethnic backgrounds are more likely to have been to a nursery school by age 6. Although this difference is only significant for Pakistani, Bangladeshi and black African children. However, when we look at HLE, there are significant differences between ethnic groups. For instance parents of children from minority ethnic groups are much less likely to read to their children every day at age 3. While 64% of the parents of white children read to their child every day at the age of 3, only 24% of parents of black African children did the same. Children from minority ethnic backgrounds also seem to have less regular social routines. For instance, 83% of children from a white ethnic background had a regular bed time at age 3 compared with just over 50% of children from a black African background and 63% of children from a black Caribbean background.

We have shown that a number of factors, including those relating to HLE and health and well-being, seem to differ by ethnic background. However, to what extent can this observation be used to explain the ethnic differences in early child development? This will naturally depend on the extent of the ethnic differences in such factors, some of which were mentioned earlier. But it will also depend on how much these factors actually impact on early child cognitive and non-cognitive development. In the next section we show the extent to which the ethnic gradient changes after we control for these potentially mediating factors.

Multivariate analysis

Multivariate analyses were carried out to see how much of these observed ethnic differences in child cognitive and non-cognitive outcomes at the ages of 3 and 5 can be explained by differences in family characteristics and demographics and how much can be explained by the other mediating factors which we outlined in the previous section.

To do this we use multivariate regression techniques. We begin by showing the raw ethnic gaps in percentile point terms, which have already been show in Table 10.2. In column (1) of Tables 10.4 to 10.7 we see these raw ethnic gaps. In column (2) we then see how much of these gaps can be explained away by family background and demographics such as parental education and SES, family size, number of older siblings, parental age and so on (see earlier description of family characteristics and demographics). We then focus on the other mediating factors and see how each of these in turn affect the remaining estimated gap. In column (3) we look at how the estimates in column (2) change if we add family interactions (and no other mediating factors). In column (4) we look at how the estimates in column (2) change if we add family health and well-being (and no other mediating factors). In column (5) we look at the impact of childcare; in column (6), HLE; and in column (7), parenting style and rules. Finally, in column (8) we look at how much of the ethnic gap remains after we control for all family background characteristics and all mediating factors together.

It is important to note that the relationships we estimate cannot necessarily be interpreted as causal. For example, it is highly likely that parenting styles and the type of HLE are going to be influenced by the child's cognitive and non-cognitive attributes. We do not attempt to take into account this possible feedback/simultaneity. Furthermore, it is highly likely that there are other unobserved characteristics of the child or family mediating factors that influence these mediating factors such as HLE as well as the child outcomes we measure. If this is true, our estimates of impact are likely to be biased, although it is not clear in which direction a bias would operate.

Cognitive outcomes

Tables 10.4 and 10.5 show the results for cognitive outcomes at ages 3 and 5 respectively, always illustrating the gaps to white children in percentile point terms. We begin by focusing on the age 3 cognitive outcomes. Column (1) of Table 10.4 shows the raw ethnic gap in outcomes that we saw before in Table 10.2. As we saw earlier, the biggest raw gaps are between white children and Pakistani and Bangladeshi children (32 percentile points and 37 percentile points at age 3, respectively). For most groups there is some evidence of a slight narrowing of the raw ethnic gap between the ages of 3 and 5.

Looking at Table 10.4, when we control for family characteristics and other socioeconomic background variables, the gap to white children is significantly reduced for all minority ethnic groups at age 3. Therefore, differences in family background characteristics and demographics explain a large amount of the raw ethnic gap at this age. This is particularly true for the Pakistani and Bangladeshi groups, with the gaps reducing to around 40% of its raw value.

Table 10.4: Explaining the ethnic gradient in child's cognitive development at age 3

Child ethnic group	(1)	(2)	(3)	(4)	(5)	(6)	(7)	(8)
				BAS naming vocabulary at age 3				
Indian	-19.299**	-8.586**	-8.073**	-6.909**	-8.142**	-7.152**	-8.196**	-5.057*
Pakistani	-31.831**	-12.103**	-11.254**	-10.352**	-11.590**	-11.386**	-11.674**	-8.926**
Bangladeshi	-36.782**	-15.932**	-15.149**	-14.366**	-15.352**	-13.800**	-15.586**	-11.362**
Black African	-16.712**	-6.907**	-6.569*	-7.021**	-6.372*	-4.354	-5.994*	-3.423
Black Caribbean	-16.898**	-10.399**	-10.066**	-9.863**	-10.002**	-9.240**	-9.942**	-7.993**
Other ethnicity	-19.415**	-11.904**	-11.225**	-10.922**	-11.474**	-11.035**	-11.721**	-9.757**
Mixed ethnicity	-5.063**	-1.407	-1.548	-1.178	-1.217	-1.022	-1.198	-0.565
Controls:								
Family characteristics and demographics		✓	✓	✓	✓	✓	✓	✓
Family interactions			✓					✓
Family health and well-being				✓				✓
Childcare					✓			✓
HLE						✓		✓
Parenting style/rules							✓	✓
Constant	49.217**	-95.038**	-97.068**	-174.148**	-93.455**	-103.335**	-97.821**	-182.113**
Observations	11,054	11,054	11,054	11,054	11,054	11,054	11,054	11,054
R^2	0.05	0.22	0.23	0.22	0.22	0.24	0.22	0.25

Note: Significant differences from white children. **$p<0.05$; *$p<0.1$.

Columns (3) to (7) then show these estimated gaps after we control for other mediating factors. The addition of the family interaction variables in column (3) makes little impact on the remaining estimated gaps compared with column (2). However, the addition of the health and well-being factors in column (4) slightly reduces all of the estimated gaps by ethnicity, except for black African children for whom the gap increases very slightly. Childcare cuts the estimated gaps by only a small amount in column (5). On the other hand, the addition of HLE factors seems to make a noticeable impact on the remaining gaps, with the largest cuts for black African children. This is particularly driven by the impact of HLE at age 3 (for example reading to the child every day). Parenting styles or rules makes a small impact, similar to the effect of childcare, with most of the effect coming from having regular bed times.

Once all these potential mediating factors are controlled for together in column (8), most estimated gaps remain, but are much reduced compared with the raw gap in column (1), and slightly reduced compared with gaps left in column (2) after controlling for family background and characteristics. However, for two groups, black African children and children of a mixed ethnicity, the remaining gap with whites is no longer statistically significant (note that the gap to white children for children of a mixed ethnicity was no longer statistically significant in column [2]). Therefore, most of the raw ethnic differences in our age 3 cognitive outcomes can be explained by simple family demographics and characteristics, like SES, but some of the remaining gaps can also be explained by other mediating factors such as HLE, particularly for black African children.

Moving on to look at cognitive outcomes at age 5 in Table 10.5, we see a very similar pattern. Raw estimated gaps are much reduced after controlling for family characteristics and demographics, such as SES, with the gaps for Indian, Bangladeshi children and those of a mixed ethnicity no longer being statistically significant. For the most part, family interactions (column [3]), family health and well-being (column [4]) and childcare (column [5]) seems to make little difference to the remaining ethnic gaps. One exception to this rule is for Pakistani children whose estimated gaps to white children are noticeably reduced following the addition of family health and well-being factors. The addition of HLE and parenting style/rules in columns (6) and (7), respectively, make sizeable reductions in all the remaining ethnic gaps. Again, the reduction in the gap for black African is most stark following the addition of HLE factors, with the gap reduced by around 25% compared with column (2).

When we account for all of these factors in column (8) we see that the gap to whites for Indian, Bangladeshi and children of a mixed ethnicity remain insignificant. However, as compared with a statistically significant difference in column (2), the remaining gaps for Pakistani and children of other ethnic groups are now insignificant. The gaps for black African and black Caribbean children are still significant, although reduced compared with column (2), suggesting a mediating role for factors such as HLE and parenting style/rules. Nevertheless,

Table 10.5: Explaining the ethnic gradient in child's cognitive development at age 5

	BAS naming vocabulary at age 5								
Child ethnic group	(1)	(2)	(3)	(4)	(5)	(6)	(7)	(8)	(9)
Indian	-9.602**	-1.509	-0.958	-0.379	-1.261	-0.038	-0.776	1.742	2.935
Pakistani	-24.106**	-5.337**	-4.499**	-3.665	-4.976**	-4.879**	-4.497**	-2.072	0.934
Bangladeshi	-24.886**	-4.089	-3.268	-3.181	-3.65	-2.673	-3.311	-0.424	3.059
Black African	-17.092**	-8.658**	-8.039**	-8.690*	-8.475**	-6.439**	-7.215**	-5.035**	-5.349**
Black Caribbean	-13.787**	-8.249**	-7.796**	-8.111*	-7.954**	-6.854**	-7.584**	-5.734**	-2.825
Other ethnicity	-13.398**	-5.790**	-5.007*	-4.90	-5.399*	-5.107*	-5.090*	-3.139	-2.658
Mixed ethnicity	-3.360*	-0.732	-0.753	-0.92	-0.493	-0.479	-0.464	-0.186	-0.679
Controls:									
Family characteristics and demographics		✓	✓	✓	✓	✓	✓	✓	✓
Family interactions			✓					✓	✓
Family health and well-being				✓				✓	✓
Childcare					✓			✓	✓
HLE						✓		✓	✓
Parenting style/rules							✓		✓
Outcomes at 3									✓
Constant	40.207**	-98.217**	-98.473**	-151.149**	-96.655**	-100.516**	-105.246**	-149.267**	-119.606**
Observations	11,054	11,054	11,054	11,054	11,054	11,054	11,054	11,054	11,054
R²	0.03	0.21	0.21	0.21	0.21	0.22	0.21	0.23	0.38

** $p < 0.05$ * $p < 0.1$

the biggest reductions in the raw ethnic gaps do still take in place column (2) after the addition of family characteristics and demographics, such as SES.

Finally, in column (9) we control for child outcomes at age 3 to see if past performance can explain any of the gap that remains. It turns out that for all but one of the ethnicities with statistically significant gaps remaining in column (8), the estimated gap is much reduced when one accounts for previous cognitive and non-cognitive outcomes. The exception is black African children for whom there is no change in the remaining gap to white children. Indeed this is the only ethnic group for whom there is still a statistically significant gap after taking account of all the family characteristics, demographics, potential mediating factors and past child outcomes.

Therefore, to conclude this section on cognitive outcomes, we find that the large raw gaps in cognitive outcomes at ages 3 and 5 can mostly be explained by the family characteristics and demographics variables, for instance, the fact that minority ethnic groups are more likely to have a lower SES. In the case of Indian and Bangladeshi children at age 5 and children of a mixed ethnicity at both ages, the gaps become statistically insignificant.

Remaining (statistically significant) gaps are further reduced by family health and well-being, HLE and parenting style/rules at both ages. For black African children, the gap seems most reduced at age 3 by HLE. The gap after controlling for all factors is statistically insignificant at age 3 for this group and children of a mixed ethnicity. The gaps for Indian, Pakistani, Bangladeshi, black Caribbean and children from ethnic groups are all statistically significant after controlling for all factors at age 3. However, by age 5, the gap after controlling for all factors is now statistically significant for black African children and remains so for black Caribbean children (all others are insignificant). The gap for black Caribbean children can be explained by past outcomes, but the gap for black African children seems to indicate a falling behind given their previous outcomes.

Non-cognitive outcomes

Tables 10.6 and 10.7 repeat the previous exercise for our measure of non-cognitive ability, based on strengths and difficulties measured at ages 3 and 5. As was shown for the raw gaps in Table 10.2, the only minority ethnic group to have significantly worse outcomes at age 3 are Pakistani children. Indeed, black African children and children from other ethnic groups have significantly higher scores at age 3. These raw gaps are shown in column (1) of Table 10.6. After accounting for family characteristics and demographics in column (2), the gap is no longer statistically significant for Pakistani children. However, black African children now have even higher scores compared with white children. This pattern of results is largely unchanged as we add in other potential mediating factors in columns (3) to (7). After accounting for all variables in column (8), the gap remains positive and statistically significant for black African children, and of a similar magnitude to column (1). All the other gaps are statistically insignificant.

Table 10.6: Explaining ethnic differences in child's non-cognitive development at age 3

	SDQ at age 3							
	(1)	(2)	(3)	(4)	(5)	(6)	(7)	(8)
Child ethnic group								
Indian	0.199	-1.565	-4.479*	-0.506	-1.836	-1.062	-0.322	-3.387
Pakistani	-5.138**	-0.496	-0.695	0.619	-0.806	-0.334	0.976	0.083
Bangladeshi	1.3	6.711	5.966	5.576	6.343	5.99	8.357*	4.886
Black African	7.959**	10.110**	5.887~	8.877**	9.750**	9.994**	12.695**	6.437**
Black Caribbean	-4.099	0.595	-1.154	1.593	0.331	0.298	1.377	-0.657
Other ethnicity	6.213*	4.523	4.581	4.935	4.253	4.405	6.084*	4.598
Mixed ethnicity	0.216	2.41	1.126	2.659*	2.275	3.036*	2.59	1.529
Controls:								
Family characteristics and demographics		✓	✓	✓	✓	✓	✓	✓
Family interactions			✓	✓				✓
Family health and well-being				✓	✓			✓
Childcare					✓			✓
HLE						✓		✓
Parenting style/rules							✓	✓
Constant	48.302**	-2.935	10.164	-89.584**	-2.801	-10.708	-8.642	-69.284*
Observations	11,054	11,054	11,054	11,054	11,054	11,054	11,054	11,054
R^2	0	0.11	0.32	0.16	0.11	0.15	0.12	0.36

** $p<0.05$ * $p< 0.1$

Table 10.7: Explaining ethnic differences in child's non-cognitive development at age 5

	SDQ at age 5								
	(1)	(2)	(3)	(4)	(5)	(6)	(7)	(8)	(9)
Child ethnic group									
Indian	-2.281	-3.039	-3.392	-1.961	-3.243	-2.456	-1.863	-2.387	-1.102
Pakistani	-13.900**	-8.062**	-6.760**	-6.654**	-8.166**	-7.611**	-6.558**	-5.525**	-5.289**
Bangladeshi	-7.427**	-1.286	-0.679	-0.944	-1.297	-1.58	0.456	0.191	-1.287
Black African	-0.202	3.205	1.44	2.976	3.336	3.057	5.965*	3.187	0.306
Black Caribbean	-12.238**	-6.852**	-7.225**	-5.345**	-6.767**	-6.899**	-5.862**	-5.440**	-5.006**
Other ethnicity	-4.223	-3.877	-1.653	-3.58	-3.909	-4.103	-2.187	-1.832	-3.787
Mixed ethnicity	-2.752*	-0.325	-0.268	0.102	-0.444	0.304	-0.008	0.305	-0.488
Controls:									
Family characteristics and demographics		✓	✓	✓	✓	✓	✓	✓	✓
Family interactions			✓	✓	✓	✓	✓	✓	✓
Family health and well-being				✓	✓	✓	✓	✓	✓
Childcare					✓			✓	✓
HLE						✓		✓	✓
Parenting style/rules							✓	✓	✓
Outcomes at 3									✓
Constant	53.938**	13.744	17.908**	-44.229	13.994	2.441	-3.113	-44.717	-17.471
Observations	11,054	11,054	11,054	11,054	11,054	11,054	11,054	11,054	11,054
R²	0.01	0.12	0.25	0.17	0.13	0.17	0.15	0.29	0.41

** p<0.05 * p<0.1

Column (1) of Table 10.7 shows that at age 5, Pakistani, Bangladeshi and black Caribbean children now have significantly worse scores on our non-cognitive outcome, by nearly 14 percentile points for Pakistani children compared with their white counterparts. There is also a smaller, although statistically significant, gap for children of a mixed ethnicity. These negative gaps are much reduced in column (2) once we account for family characteristics and demographics, being nearly halved for Pakistani and black Caribbean children, although these gaps are still statistically significant. The gaps for Bangladeshi and children of a mixed ethnicity are now insignificant. The remaining statistically significant gaps are slightly reduced by family health and well-being in column (4) and by parenting rules/style in column (7). Therefore, after controlling for all factors, the gaps are further reduced for these two groups compared with column (2), although they are still statistically significant. But again the biggest impact on the gap was made by controlling for family characteristics and demographics in column (2).

Controlling for past outcomes in column (9) seems to make little difference to the pattern of significant results. This is not surprising given that there were statistically insignificant gaps between whites and Pakistani and black Caribbean children in non-cognitive ability at age 3 after controlling for other factors.

We find that there are fewer differences in non-cognitive than there were for cognitive outcomes. At age 3 children from minority ethnic groups have similar or better outcomes than white children, with this pattern little changed once one accounts for the set of other characteristics and mediating factors. By age 5, black Caribbean and Pakistani children have fallen behind in non-cognitive outcomes, most of which can be explained by family characteristics and demographics. A smaller amount of these gaps can be explained by family health and well-being factors and parenting style/rules.

Conclusions

We have shown that there are quite large ethnic gaps in early child cognitive development. The gap to white children is particularly large for Pakistani and Bangladeshi children. However, once we take account of differences in 'traditional' mediating factors, such as family background and individual demographics, these ethnic gaps in outcomes are much reduced. For example, children from minority ethnic backgrounds seem to live in poorer households and have parents that are less well educated and as a result have lower levels of cognitive development.

There are fewer gaps in terms of non-cognitive development – only Pakistani children are behind in raw terms at both ages 3 and 5, while black Caribbean, Pakistani and Bangladeshi children are behind at age 5. Again, however, a substantial amount of all these gaps can also be explained by family background and individual characteristics. This chapter also makes clear that there is still a role for other mediating factors in explaining some of the ethnic gaps in early child development. HLE seems to play a crucial role in both cognitive and non-cognitive development, but this only makes a difference if parents are able to provide a rich HLE at an early age (around age 3). This seems to particularly impact on black African children who have the worst measured HLE in our sample (at ages 3 and 5). This may point to a possible policy response to help black African children improve their early cognitive and non-cognitive outcomes. Health and well-being also seem to play a role in early child development, with early child health (for example birth weight and length of gestation) explaining some of the ethnic gaps in cognitive development and factors such as depression during early infancy explaining differences in non-cognitive development. Parenting styles and rules also seem to make a difference to both cognitive and non-cognitive development, with factors relating to the regularity of social routine activities, for example regular bed times, making the largest difference. Again minority ethnic children tend to have less regular bed times and this impacts on their early outcomes. This again may point to another possible policy response – for instance educating parents about the benefits of regular bed times and meal times could be part of the new children's centre agenda.

Notes

[1] This work draws heavily on earlier work using the MCS looking at socioeconomic gradient in early childhood outcomes: see Dearden et al (2010).

[2] For reasons of parsimony we construct a measure of socioeconomic position and divide our sample into quintiles of this measure. This measure aims to capture the longer-term material resources of the household and is constructed using principle components from the following variables: log equivalised household income (average across MCS 2 and 3), reported experience of financial difficulties at MCS 2 and 3, mother and father's occupational class and housing tenure. Full details are available from the authors, Lorraine Dearden (ldearden@ifs.org.uk); Luke Sibieta (luke_s@ifs.org.uk).

ELEVEN

School choice

Kirstine Hansen and Anna Vignoles

Introduction

In 1988, the Education Reform Act for England and Wales strengthened parents' rights to choose the school their child attended at primary and secondary school levels. Similar legislation was applied in Northern Ireland. The 1988 Act was introduced to encourage competition between schools, as they sought to attract pupils, with the idea that this would lead to higher standards of teaching and children's achievement. Despite obvious policy interest in the extent and consequences of school choice, there is remarkably little evidence on the process of school choice itself (at least from the parental perspective) and indeed there is only limited research into the factors that are uppermost in parents' minds when choosing their children's primary school. The introduction of a policy on school choice has also left the lingering concern that school choice will lead to social segregation or 'sorting' across different schools. Others argue that school choice is actually not a reality for most parents, particularly in rural areas, who have no choice but to send their child to their local school. School choice in the state sector may largely be, therefore, an issue for parents living in specific urban areas, such as London, where there may be a number of local schools potentially available to them and the schools may vary substantially in quality. This chapter provides new information from the Millennium Cohort Study (MCS) to examine the extent to which parents do actually choose the schools their children attend, as opposed to simply enrolling them in their local school. We also explore how successful parents are in securing their first choice of school and the reasons for their choice.

Existing evidence on the extent of school choice by parents contains mixed results that are difficult to interpret. Some quantitative evidence is available, based on examining the extent to which children attend their nearest school. The assumption here is that if a child does not attend his or her nearest school, this implies that either the parent has exercised their right to choose their child's school, or perhaps that the child was unable to get a place at his or her nearest school. Allen and Vignoles (2007) have suggested that only around 1 in 5 children in England and Wales are benefiting from parental school choice. Burgess et al (2006) estimated the proportion of children not attending their nearest local school at around one half. However, this does not necessarily mean that half of all parents are exercising school choice since many of these children may not have been accepted into their nearest school if it was over-subscribed. So it appears that while there is some real choice in the system, quantifying its extent is problematic. In any case, knowing where children actually go to school is insufficient to tell us whether their parents have exercised school choice. We really need to know in detail where their parents want the child to go to school and the reasons for this choice. We then need to know to what extent parents are able to secure their first choice of school. For this, we need to turn to richer data, such as from the MCS. However, there is still the possibility that some parents will have low expectations and not even apply for schools they consider to be out of their reach.

We start by examining the academic studies on school choice, before moving on to describe how the MCS data are particularly well suited to considering questions about school choice. We then describe the extent of school choice in the cohort, and describe the most common reasons why parents choose the schools they do.

Evidence on school choice

Although it is interesting to see how many parents get their first choice of school and indeed the reasons for their choices, there are also pressing policy reasons why we need to understand more about the extent of school choice in the English education system (see Burgess et al, 2004 for an overview of the issues). Initially, the motivation behind introducing a policy to allow parents to choose schools was to raise standards. The argument is that if parents can choose which school their child attends, they will try to get their children into the most effective schools. As schools compete for pupils, this is supposed to drive up standards of academic attainment. Studies on the possible impact of school choice systems on academic outcomes are now quite extensive, but the results remain contradictory and measuring competition between schools is extremely problematic. Some, although not all, evidence using school-level data seems to indicate that schools that are facing more competition from other schools do better, in terms of academic achievement (see Bradley et al, 2001 and Levacic, 2004, for a contrary view). Yet more recent work using pupil-level data finds very little significant impact from competition on pupils' academic progress (Burgess and Slater, 2006; Gibbons et al, 2006). Thus, the jury is out as to whether school choice is actually having an impact on school standards. Part of the reason for this may be that school choice is only being exercised by a very small minority of parents, an issue that we intend to shed more light on in this chapter.

While school choice may potentially improve children's educational outcomes, there have been ongoing concerns that school choice will lead to social segregation or 'sorting' across schools (Hoxby, 2000; Sandstrom and Bergstrom, 2005; Söderström and Uusitalo, 2005; Burgess et al, 2006; Lavy, 2006). In other words, it will be the more socioeconomically advantaged pupils who benefit from school choice, as their parents will manage to secure places for them in the more effective schools. In a choice system, there may also be situations where over-subscribed schools are able to select the more academically or socially advantaged pupils. Although schools publish their admissions criteria, it is not always obvious what the consequences of different criteria may be. Work by Allen and West (2008) and West et al (2004) on comprehensive secondary school admissions criteria suggests that some schools, for example some voluntary-aided faith schools, adopt criteria that may lead to greater levels of socioeconomic sorting. West et al (2004) also found that more than 1 in 10 foundation schools used ability or aptitude as their criteria for selecting pupils, as did more than 1 in 20 voluntary-aided schools. Covert selection of pupils by schools or rather targeting of particular types of student also occurs (Gewirtz et al, 1995). For instance, Gewirtz et al (1995) claim that efforts to promote the traditional image of schools and emphasise academic attainment increased post-1988 as schools tried more actively to attract middle-class pupils. The social consequences of school choice, therefore, are potentially very important and we need to understand better which types of parents are able to exercise school choice and the criteria on which different parents choose schools.

Much of the research on school choice has focused on secondary schools. A small number of qualitative studies have been carried out on how parents choose schools. Perhaps unsurprisingly a school's record on academic achievement appears to be of great importance to parents (for example Coldron and Boulton, 1991; West and Pennell, 1999). In response to surveys, it also appears that different types of parents choose schools on the basis of different criteria (West and Pennell, 1999; Hastings et al, 2005). Yet even here the evidence is partial and parents may report things that are not reflected in their actual school choice decisions. We need data that combine information on actual school choice and reasons for school choice to better understand this issue. This chapter provides a description of what parents say they are doing and their reasons when choosing their children's primary school. The data are provided by the age 5 survey of the MCS. The analyses are carried out using weighted data by country. Examining choices separately by UK country is important due to the different educational systems that exist across the four countries. For example, the 1988 Act introduced school choice into the state system in England, Wales and Northern Ireland but did not cover Scotland.

State versus fee-paying schools

One of the first choices parents who can afford it make about schools is whether to educate their child in the state sector or in a fee-paying school. Around 5% of MCS children in England were attending fee-paying schools at age 5. This percentage is much higher than in the other UK countries. In Northern Ireland it was around 3% and only 2% of children in Wales and Scotland. Cross-country differences in the proportion of children in private schooling are likely to be attributable to a range of factors, including wealth and cultural differences, as well as issues related to the quality of schooling available in the state system. It is also worth noting that the proportion of children attending fee-paying schools increases substantially during the secondary phase in all countries, but in the primary phase, at least, only a very small minority of parents choose private schooling.

These percentages are averages across the whole of each country and are likely to mask some variation across different regions. For instance, in England, if we look at London alone we get an extremely high rate of state opt out, with nearly 1 in 5 MCS children (18%) living in inner London attending fee-paying schools compared with 7% in outer London and 3% in non-city locations. It is important to note that our sample consists of children almost entirely born in the UK and is not inflated by temporary foreign resident families.

Whether the high proportion of parents opting out of the state school system in inner London is attributable to the poor quality of state schools in that area or simply the wealth of parents remains an open question, which merits further research. Here we can examine the extent to which the rate of opt-out from the state school system varies by family background. The data clearly show that attendance at a fee-paying school is largely the preserve of children with better-educated mothers (see Table 11.1). In England, nearly 1 in 10 pupils (9%), whose mother has a degree or higher, attended a fee-paying school in the primary phase. By contrast, children whose mothers have just GCSE level qualifications are very unlikely to attend a fee-paying school (1%). The differences by maternal education level are striking but do not diminish the differences across countries. So a child whose mother has at least a degree is twice as likely to attend a fee-paying school in England, than in Wales, Northern Ireland or Scotland.

Table 11.2 shows the rate of attendance at fee-paying schools by parental occupation across the four countries of the UK. In most countries, only children of professional or managerial parents attend a fee-paying school. In England, however, a small proportion of parents in other lower level occupations send their cohort child to a fee-paying school. This implies that some of the large differences across countries in opt-out rates from the state system may not necessarily be attributable simply to income differences between England and the other countries, although this issue needs to be explored in a multivariate analysis context. Some fee-paying schools offer bursaries to low-income families.

Table 11.1: Percentage of children attending fee-paying schools at age 5 by country and mother's education

| | Mother's highest qualification | | | | | |
	Less than 5 GCSEs grade A-C	5 GCSEs grade A-C	A-levels	Degree +	Total	p
England	–	1.4	1.7	8.7	4.8	0.000
Wales	–	–	1.1	3.5	1.7	0.007
Northern Ireland	–	2.0	–	4.1	3.1	0.039
Scotland	–	–	0.5	3.4	1.9	0.018

Notes: Table displays weighted percentages (using weight1).

– signifies too few observations.

Sample: children attending fee-paying schools with valid data on school choice.

Table 11.2: Percentage of children attending fee-paying schools by country and highest parental NS-SEC (National Statistics – Socio-Economic Classification) classification at MCS 3

	Parental occupation[a]						
	Professional and manager	Intermediate	Small employer	Low skill/ support	Semi-routine/ routine	Total	p
England	8.3	2.1	4.2	1.3	1.1	4.8	0.000
Wales	3.1	–	2.9	–	–	1.7	0.026
Northern Ireland	6.1	–	–	–	–	3.1	0.001
Scotland	2.9	–	–	–	–	1.9	0.014

Notes: Table displays weighted percentages (using weight1).

– signifies too few observations. [a] highest occupation of either parent using NS-SEC (5) categories.

Sample: children attending fee-paying schools with valid data on school choice and parental occupation.

Applying for a school place in the state sector

The data from the MCS 3 show that the vast majority of primary school pupils at age 5 are enrolled in state schools. The process of choosing a school is therefore largely about choosing a school within the state system. In this chapter we want to understand the extent to which parents express preferences about which school their child attends, as well as quantify the extent to which they are successful in securing their first choice of school. It is possible that most parents are happy to accept their local school as being appropriate for their child. However, if school choice is to have any impact on school competition and standards, it needs to be the case that a significant minority of parents express active preferences about their preferred schooling option and that a significant proportion are successful in securing their preferred choice.

In the state system, applying for a school place generally involves filling in an application form that gets sent to the local education authority (LEA), in England and Wales, or the education library boards (ELBs), in Northern Ireland. Parents can list one or more schools of their choice on these forms. Completing these forms can be seen, therefore, as an indication that parents are, at a minimum, expressing some kind of preference as to the school they want their child to attend. Even if a parent only fills in the form because they are 'told to' by their LEA, they have to put a school at the top of their preference list so some choice is being expressed, however weakly. In Scotland children are allocated a place in their local school but parents can ask for a place at a school other than this local school. If they wish to do this they make a request to their LEA. In Scotland, therefore, it is clearer that parents making such a request to their LEA are expressing a preference as to their child's schooling.

The extent to which MCS parents applied for a school place via an LEA/ELB form or requested a school place in Scotland was examined. In Northern Ireland 89% of parents and 75% of parents in England applied for a school place via an ELB or LEA form. This would imply that most parents in these countries were willing to express some kind of preference as to which school they wanted their child to attend. However, it is worth noting that some state primary schools in England and Wales have historically required a separate application form to be sent direct to the school; this is particularly the case for voluntary-aided faith schools. Where parents filled in both a direct application form to the school *and* an LEA form, it is not clear how they might respond to a question about how they applied to their child's school. Equally some parents may not fill in LEA forms at all and simply accept the allocation made by the LEA for their child. In Wales, fewer parents (58%) applied for a school place via their LEA, while in Scotland only 38% of parents requested a place at a particular school. In Scotland, this implies that the majority of parents accepted their allocated place at their local school.

As mentioned earlier, some parents chose to send their children to fee-paying schools and we may well think that parents who have made the decision to enroll their children in fee-paying schools would not also apply for a state school place via their LEA/ELB. In fact, relatively few parents who did not apply via their LEA/ELB or request a place at a particular school sent their child to a fee-paying school. Eighteen per cent of children in England, 15% in Northern Ireland, 3% in Wales and only 2% in Scotland went on to attend fee-paying schools (Figure 11.1). This is perhaps unsurprising as the decision to send a child to a fee-paying school may come after a parent has attempted to choose a state school. For instance, it is possible that choosing to send a child to a fee-paying school may be the result of failing to secure a place for a child in the state school of choice. However, as we will see later in this chapter, the majority of parents do appear to get their first choice school. The reverse may also be true of course. It could be that parents wishing to enroll their children in over-subscribed private schools are put on a

Figure 11.1: Percentage of children attending fee-paying school of parents who did not apply for, or request, a school place

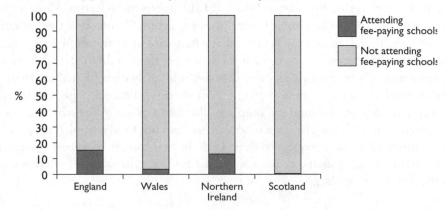

waiting list and apply to state primary schools as a reserve or interim solution. We also know that age 7 is a key entry point to the private system so some parents will only be enrolling their children in state schools for a few years. Nonetheless they are likely to make an active choice about where their child is educated in the meantime.

Opting out of the state sector into the private sector explains only a small fraction of those not applying for, or requesting, a place at a particular state school. This seems to confirm our view that the majority of those not completing an LEA/ELB form are in fact not expressing a preference about their child's schooling. Omitting those parents who sent their children to fee-paying schools, the data suggests that 21% of parents in England, 41% in Wales, 10% in Northern Ireland and a massive 62% of parents in Scotland made no application for their child to attend a particular school (see Table 11.3).

As has already been suggested, differences across countries in the extent to which parents express a preference as to which school they would like their child to attend may reflect a number of things. Firstly, in rural areas the local school may be the only practical option for many families, given the travelling distance to an alternative school. This may, for instance, explain the low proportion of parents expressing schooling preferences in Scotland. Secondly, if school quality is more similar in some of the UK countries than others, parents may accept their local school option simply because one school will be quite like any other. Also if information about schools is available to varying extents across countries, this could explain differences in parental behaviour. Only England currently produces school league tables. If parents do not have the information to be able to differentiate between schools then it will be harder for them to choose a school.

The MCS data also contain information on the number of schools parents applied to, which is a somewhat different expression of school choice. Figure 11.2 shows the distribution of parents who apply via an LEA/ELB form by the number of schools they apply to. The figure shows that among the MCS parents who actively express a school choice preference, not all name more than one school. In Scotland the majority (89%) of parents who request a particular

Table 11.3: School applications and fee-paying status

	England	Wales	Northern Ireland	Scotland
Applied for place using LEA/ELB form and goes to state school	73.9	57.3	87.2	36.6
Applied for place using LEA/ELB form and goes to fee-paying school.	1.0	0.5	1.6	1.6
Not applied and goes to fee-paying school	3.8	1.2	1.5	0.3
Not applied and goes to state school	21.3	41.0	9.7	61.5
Total observations	9,699	2,134	1,532	1,689

Notes: Table displays weighted percentages (using weight1) and unweighted observations.

Sample: children with valid data on school choice.

Figure 11.2 Number of schools applied for on LEA/ELB form, or requested

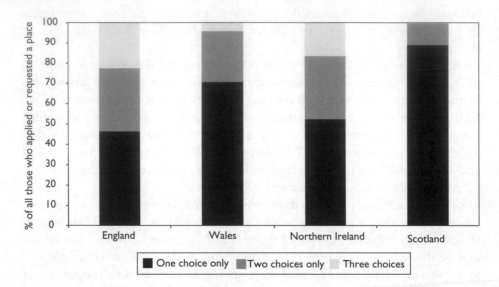

school choose only one school. In Wales the corresponding figure is 70%, 52% in Northern Ireland and 46% in England. Thus in England it is more common for parents to give a ranking of three possible school choices in order of preference.

Reasons for school choice

The MCS also asked parents why they made the choices they did. Table 11.4 shows the factors that parents claim are most important when choosing a school. Among fee-paying parents in England, around one quarter cited school performance as the crucial factor in determining their school choice. Friends or siblings attending the school are also important for 1 in 5 of these particular parents. Around one half of these parents also cited 'other' school characteristics as being important. These other factors included good impression of the school; good school (other than results); strong anti-bullying policy; small class sizes; caters for special needs; offers specialised curriculum; good facilities; offers childcare; religious grounds; ethnic mix of school; teaches in language other than English; and single-sex school.

Among state school pupils whose parents *did* express a preference on school choice, a far higher proportion (23%) gave proximity as being the most important factor (compared to just 4% in the private sector). Nineteen per cent of parents who expressed a school choice preference and whose child was in a state school cited school performance as being important, far less than those citing proximity or friends or siblings attending the school as prime motivators. Interestingly the motivating factors for parents whose child was in a state school but who did *not* express a school choice preference were very similar to those of parents who did express a preference.

Table 11.4: Most important factors for school choice by country and whether school was applied to/requested or not

| | England | | | Wales | | | Northern Ireland | | | Scotland | | |
| | State | | | State | | | State | | | | State | |
	Private	Applied	Did not apply	Private	Applied	Did not apply	Private	Applied	Did not apply	Private	Requested place	Did not request
Closest school	4.3	23.4	23.7	8.8	27.7	23.6	8.6	32.5	30.0	8.3	23.3	42.3
Friends or sibling attend the school	17.3	29.1	30.6	18.9	28.6	27.8	23.6	32.8	29.9	20.0	31.5	21.7
School performance	26.0	18.6	16.2	27.7	16.1	14.0	19.8	10.4	4.9	30.0	12.1	13.1
Other school characteristics	49.7	26.5	28.4	39.6	25.1	33.0	43.0	21.8	33.4	33.4	28.4	21.9
Other reason	2.7	2.2	1.0	5.1	2.4	1.6	5.0	2.4	1.8	8.3	4.8	1.0
Total observations	370	6,034	1,870	28	1,006	810	38	1,130	127	28	530	919

Notes: Table displays weighted percentages (using weight1) and unweighted observations.

Sample: children with valid data on school choice and reasons for school choice.

Broadly, a higher proportion of MCS parents using fee-paying schools cited school characteristics and school performance as being more important as compared to parents whose MCS child was at school in the state sector. Parents in the state sector were generally more likely to cite proximity and friends/siblings in the school as the most important factors. On the whole the factors identified by parents who applied/requested a place at a school as most important for school choice are the same factors identified by parents who did not apply for, or request, a school. Moreover, the pattern is similar across countries. However, in Scotland, those who did not request a particular school were far more likely to cite proximity as the most important factor in school choice.

Realising school choice

In addition to exploring the motivations behind parents' choice of primary school, there is also the question as to whether parents got their first choice of school. We have argued that filling in the LEA form represents an expression, if a weaker one, of school choice on the part of parents. We now examine the extent to which parents actually achieved their first choice of school.

The proportion of all children whose parents applied for a place in a state school and who attended a school that was their parents' first choice of school was 94% in England and 98% in each of Wales, Northern Ireland and Scotland. The results are remarkable: almost all parents who indicated having applied for a place stated that they achieved their first choice of school across all countries of the UK. If we take these data at face value, school choice appears to be working.

At first glance these figures suggest where parents of the MCS cohort members did make a choice they were, on the whole, successful in securing their first choice school. Of course, one explanation for the fact that the vast majority of pupils attend their first choice school is that their parents selected a school that they were very likely to get into. For instance, parents may have opted not to put a school that they preferred at the top of their choice list because they felt that their child had a low probability of getting into it due to over-subscription. If parents act fatalistically and do not make ambitious choices, this would explain why most do get their first choice.

MCS also asked parents who said they were successful in securing their first choice of school whether they would have liked to apply to a different school but did not. Between 4% and 7% of those who said they had been successful in getting their choice of school agreed that they had preferred a different school. If we consider these parents as unsuccessful in achieving their first choice school, this reduces the percentage of parents with children attending the first choice school from 94% to 88% in England, from 98% to 92% in Wales, from 98% to 95% in Northern Ireland and from 98% to 91% in Scotland.

Of course it might be the case that some parents are more likely to secure their first choice of school than others. The proportion achieving their first choice of school broken down by mother's education (see Table 11.5) shows little variation,

Table 11.5: Percentage of children attending first choice school by country and mother's education

| | Mother's highest qualification | | | | | |
	Less than 5 GCSEs grade A–C	5 GCSEs grade A–C	A-levels	Degree+	Total	p
England	93.7	90.6	91.4	87.2	88.8	0.001
Wales	96.6	94.6	88.3	91.7	91.8	0.254
Northern Ireland	96.2	95.5	95.0	94.3	94.9	0.635
Scotland	100.0	97.8	92.7	87.4	90.6	0.050

Notes: Table displays weighted percentages (using weight1).

Sample: children with valid data on school choice and mother's education.

with a high mean proportion of parents achieving their first choice. If anything, pupils in England whose mothers have at least a degree are marginally less likely to achieve their first choice of school. This could reflect the fact that these parents are more likely to choose a higher performing and therefore over-subscribed school. Results by parental occupation also show little variation in the likelihood of an MCS child achieving their first choice of school across occupation categories.

The mean child cognitive ability on entry into school by type of school choice is displayed in Table 11.6. Cognitive ability is measured using the total Foundation Stage Profile (FSP) scores as described in Chapter 12 (this volume). These are teacher assessed scores during the children's first year at school. We would expect that the mean entry ability of children in the private sector would be higher, given the socioeconomic advantage of these pupils. We might also expect that parents actively expressing a preference for a school in the state sector may place greater value on education, come from more advantaged backgrounds and that their children would consequently be more cognitively able on entry into school. However, while children who attend private schools in England, Wales and Scotland appear to have higher FSP scores than children in state schools, there is no difference in Northern Ireland and also no difference by whether their parents got their first choice of state school in any of the UK countries.

We may want to interpret these results cautiously. For England at least, the age 5 FSP scores come from official statistics and private schools are not obliged to submit them (we only have data on 120 of the 414 private pupils). It may be the case, therefore, that private schools who submit their results are a biased selection. The fact that the results are the same for Wales and Scotland where the results come not from official statistics but from a postal survey sent to teachers suggests this may not be a cause for concern.

Does school choice matter?

As noted earlier, the majority of parents who apply for, or request, a place secured their first choice school for their children. If parental choice is related to

Table 11.6: Mean FSP scores (or equivalent) by country, private/state sector and whether parents applied for/requested a school place

	England				Wales				Northern Ireland				Scotland			
	Private	State			Private	State			Private	State			Private	State		
		Applied – 1st choice	Applied – not 1st choice	Did not apply		Applied – 1st choice	Applied – not 1st choice	Did not apply		Applied – 1st choice	Applied – not 1st choice	Did not apply		Requested – 1st choice	Requested – not 1st choice	Did not request
Mean score	**95.0** (**1.81**)	88.6 (0.51)	87.2 (0.89)	84.5 (0.66)	**106.8** (**2.72**)	96.7 (1.78)	92.3 (5.38)	93.4 (1.55)	103.8 (4.43)	97.4 (1.02)	97.0 (3.71)	96.7 (2.15)	**110.9** (**2.11**)	102.2 (1.33)	102.2 (2.16)	103.3 (1.01)
Total observations	120	567	732	2132	17	440	39	377	23	603	30	60	15	242	19	368

Notes: Table displays weighted means (using weight1) and unweighted observations. Standard errors are in parentheses.

Bold means are significantly different from the others in that group at the 5% level.

Sample: children with valid data on school choice and FSP scores.

Table 11.7: Parents' reports of child school enjoyment and parental satisfaction with school by country, private/state sector and whether they applied for/requested a school place

	England				Wales				Northern Ireland				Scotland			
	Private	State Applied – 1st choice	State Applied – not 1st choice	Did not apply	Private	State Applied – 1st choice	State Applied – not 1st choice	Did not apply	Private	State Applied – 1st choice	State Applied – not 1st choice	Did not apply	Private	State Requested – 1st choice	State Requested – not 1st choice	Did not request
Parents report that the child always enjoys school	72.8	71.4	66.4	72.3	84.9	72.9	67.7	71.9	87.7	78.3	77.5	81.2	86.0	75.2	78.6	75.2
Total observations	414	6,103	800	2,381	30	1,059	93	952	44	1,262	71	177	30	575	55	1,029
Significance				$p=0.041$				$p=0.288$				$p=0.377$				$p=0.350$
Parents report of full satisfaction with the school their child attends	81.3	74.9	61.5	72.1	78.2	80.2	62.2	75.8	81.8	84.2	67.6	88.0	92.2	80.3	63.8	73.8
Total observations	414	6,103	800	2,381	30	1,059	93	952	44	1,262	71	161	30	575	55	1,029
Significance				$p=0.000$				$p=0.002$				$p=0.003$				$p=0.015$

Notes: Table displays unweighted observations and weighted percentages (using weight1).

Sample: children with valid data on school choice and child enjoyment and parental satisfaction with school.

competition, which is meant to raise standards (Bradley et al, 2001), we may well expect that schools which parents applied for, or requested, will be better than other schools. We may also hypothesise that children will gain more educational qualifications or higher grades in such schools or be happier. We would also expect parents to be more satisfied with these schools. Ideally, of course, we would want data on the child's achievement in the school, relative to his or her peers, and to the achievement of children in surrounding schools. While, as yet, the MCS data has not been linked to the pupil's administrative school record beyond age 5, we can examine parental satisfaction with the school and the extent to which the child enjoys school. Table 11.7 shows that there is very little difference in the child's enjoyment of school or in parental satisfaction with the school according to whether the parents applied for, or requested, a place at that school or not.

The test statistics show that there is no significant difference between the percentages of MCS parents in Scotland, Northern Ireland or Wales who say the child enjoys school at age 5 according to whether they applied/requested a school place, were successful in achieving their first choice or sent their child to private school. In England those parents who applied for a school but did not get their first choice are less likely than other parents to report their child always enjoys school.

With regard to parental satisfaction with the school the child attends at age 5, there are significant differences across all countries. Parents who applied for a school, but did not get their first choice, are less likely than other parents to report full satisfaction with the school.

Conclusions

This chapter has presented new information about school choices made by parents as the MCS children entered primary school at age 5. The information collected on school choice is important given the policy agenda, particularly in England, which has largely argued that increasing parental choice in schooling will encourage schools to raise achievement and standards.

The extent to which parents are exercising at least some level of primary school choice varies across countries. More parents in England, for example, are making school choices than in Scotland. Interestingly, however, it appears that the vast majority of parents do secure their first choice of school (whether or not they actively expressed a preference for a particular school). Further investigation of the data does, however, indicate that a small minority of parents did not express their true preference on their LEA/ELB form in that they did not name the option they genuinely preferred. Instead, they presumably opted for a safer alternative of naming a school that they had a higher probability of accessing. Therefore the extent of genuine school choice is being slightly overstated by these data. Equally, the responses to the MCS questions may partly reflect parents making an ex-post rationalisation of the situation they find themselves in, leading them to say the child's current school was their first choice and that the child is happy there when, in fact, this was not their first choice school. However, if the child turns out to be happy in the school, despite it not being the first choice, this too will sway parents to think this school, in the end, was the best choice. Clearly this is a complex set of issues.

There are, of course, other factors that may be influencing the likelihood that parents get their first choice school. For example, demographic factors such as birth rates and immigration mean that different cohorts of children (in different localities) face more or less pressure on school places. Therefore, even if the majority of parents from a particular cohort get their children into their first choice of school, it does not mean that this is likely to be the case for subsequent cohorts. In fact this point is particularly pertinent given the steady decline in primary school enrolments that has occurred since the middle of this decade. This fall in enrolment will potentially give these cohorts a greater chance of securing a place at their preferred school. Whether or not this happens in practice, of course, will depend on how any excess capacity in the system is taken out.

Whether parents applied to, or requested, a school appeared to matter little to the criteria they identified as most important for choosing a school. Moreover, this chapter suggests that school choice also matters little for child enjoyment and parental satisfaction with the school at this age. In the future, when the MCS data are linked to other administrative data sources containing children's test scores, we will be able to examine the consequences of parents' choice of school.

TWELVE

Teacher assessments in the first year of school

Kirstine Hansen

Introduction

Children's development in the early years has been shown to be related to their success in later life in a range of areas including: education, employment, and avoiding crime and early parenthood (see Carneiro and Heckman, 2003; Feinstein and Duckworth, 2006). Determining why some children do better than others in the early years is a key issue for policy and is crucial in attempts to reduce inequalities. This chapter examines differences in Millennium Cohort Study (MCS) children's achievements at age 5 as rated by teachers. These teachers' assessments provide another view of MCS children's development at age 5, complementary to the cognitive and behavioural development indicators described in Chapters 9, 10 and 14 in this volume. In some cases, the teachers' assessments provide information for children who did not do the cognitive assessments that were part of the MCS 3 instruments, so this is an additional benefit of Foundation Stage Profiles (FSPs).

FSP and devolved administration teacher surveys

In state schools in England, teachers record the performance of pupils during the first year of school to produce FSP scores. These scores were collected by the Department for Children, Schools and Families (DCSF) for cohort members in state schools in England and linked to the survey data. Of 9,084 MCS children, 8,671 were successfully matched to their FSP scores. This constitutes a success rate of around 95%. Data were linked by fuzzy matching on: first name; gender; date of birth; child's home postcode; school establishment number; and surname. However, for children in Northern Ireland, Scotland and Wales, where FSP data were not routinely available, the information was collected by asking the same questions to the teachers in a postal survey. The response rate to this teachers' survey was 68% but this rate varied by country, being highest in Northern Ireland, with a response rate of 73%, and lowest in Wales, with a response rate of 63%. For the rest of this chapter the data will be collectively referred to as FSP scores. There is only a low coverage of children attending private schools in England (around 5% of the sample in England) unless these schools voluntarily submit their scores to the local education authority (LEA).

The FSP reports on six areas of learning:

1) Personal, social and emotional development (disposition and attitudes; social development; and emotional development)
2) Communication, language and literacy (language for communicating and thinking; linking sounds and letters; reading; and writing)
3) Mathematical development (numbers as labels and for counting; calculating; and shape, space measures)
4) Knowledge and understanding of the world
5) Physical development
6) Creative development.

Teachers give a child a score of 1–9 for each of the categories. If a child gets 9 this means their achievement is beyond what is expected during the Foundation Stage. It has the level of challenge found in aspects of Key Stage 1 and sometimes aspects of Key Stage 2b of the National Curriculum.

Teachers in state schools in England are trained in grading FSP scores and also do it for an entire class. However, the grading done specifically for MCS children in countries outside of England was, in many cases, for only one cohort child. The familiarity with the grading system is, therefore, substantially less than for teachers in England. It may make it difficult to make comparisons across the different UK countries. It is crucial, therefore, to include controls for country in any regression models in order to capture any effects from systematic differences in country measurements.

The descriptive statistics for each of the FSP measures are provided in Table 12.1, which shows the minimum and maximum scores possible, along with the mean

Table 12.1: Mean and percentile scores of FSP components

	Min/max	Mean	Standard deviation	10th percentile	25th percentile	50th percentile	75th percentile	90th percentile
Personal, social and emotional	0/27	21.4	4.4	15.0	19.0	22.0	24.0	27.0
Communication, language and literacy	0/36	25.7	7.1	16.0	21.0	27.0	31.0	34.0
Mathematics	0/27	20.8	4.7	14.0	18.0	21.0	24.0	26.0
Knowledge and understanding of the world	0/9	6.8	1.7	4.0	6.0	7.0	8.0	9.0
Physical development	0/9	7.4	1.5	6.0	7.0	8.0	8.0	9.0
Creative development	0/9	6.8	1.6	5.0	6.0	7.0	8.0	9.0

Notes: Sample: MCS 3 children with matched FSP score. All UK countries.
Weighted to account for sample design using weight2.

and standard deviation, 10th, 25th, 50th, 75th and 90th percentile scores. Higher scores indicate more advanced stages of development. Results show that, taking into account the fact that some scores have a higher maximum than others, mean scores are highest for physical development (7.4); then personal social and emotional (7.1); followed next by mathematics (6.9), knowledge and understanding of the world (6.8) and creative development (6.8). Communication, language and literacy has the lowest mean score (6.4), 0.9 points lower than the mean for physical development.

Analysis and modelling

Having charted the basic descriptive details of the outcomes, we now turn to investigating variations in achievement in a set of multivariate models, to see how far they are related to various characteristics of children and their families. To do this we use regression analysis that allows us to look at the relationship between outcomes and a number of factors in combination, which theory and past empirical work inform us may be related to achievement.

There are a number of advantages of using longitudinal data such as the MCS to do this type of analysis. Firstly, they are rich in background information, providing data not only on the cohort members themselves, but also the families and the environments in which the children grow up. Secondly, because they follow the same people over time, this allows us to model the association of outcomes at later time periods with inputs at an earlier time, which helps us get closer to identifying results that may have causal interpretations.

The approach to the analysis is based on considering children's FSP scores as the outputs in a model where children's outcomes depend on inputs of child characteristics but also on other family characteristics. The dependent variables are the FSP scores that have been transformed into z-scores across our sample by dividing the score by the standard deviation and subtracting the mean. This means that the coefficients can be interpreted as standard deviation differences. The input variables include a set of independent variables that examine:

- Children's characteristics (age, birth weight and gender) that may vary by child and mother. The age term included here has the potential to capture effects on FSP scores of children being born in different seasons of the year. The assessment for FSP was made at the end of the school year rather than at MCS 3 interviews close to when the child was age 5, and falling, therefore, across a school year.
- A set of family characteristics (ethnicity of the mother, highest educational qualification held by either parent, highest parental occupation, family income, maternal depression, whether there is a father present, whether the family live in social housing). Some of these were fixed characteristics at MCS 1; others were measured at MCS 2.

- A set of parental decision variables. These include parenting variables (reading to the child, teaching the alphabet and counting, as well as watching television, all measured at MCS 2 when the children were 3 years old); and a number of dummy variables indicating whether at MCS 1 a mother strongly agreed with the statements (1) babies need to be stimulated if they are to develop well, and (2) talking, even to a young baby, is important; and experience of formal childcare (up to age 3).
- The final set of independent variables were value-added variables capturing the child's achievement at age 3 measured using vocabulary and school readiness scores from the MCS 2 survey.

As the outcome measures are essentially continuous we run ordinary least squares (OLS) regressions using 'survey' commands in Stata. Sets of independent variables are entered into the model, block by block, to produce a set of nested OLS regressions.

The results of these regressions are shown in Tables 12.2 to 12.7 covering the range of FSP assessments carried out. The first column (1) is a regression of the outcome scores on child characteristics. The second column (2) adds in family characteristics; the third (3) includes parental decisions; the fourth (4) controls additionally for previous achievement and behaviour at age 3. If the coefficients on any of the control variables remain significant in the full model then these factors are either positively or negatively associated with that particular outcome even after controlling for other factors that may influence the relationship.

Personal, social and emotional development

The basic model for the personal, social and emotional scores (see Table 12.2) shows that the child characteristics are all positively associated with these scores. In terms of magnitude, being a girl has the largest association with this FSP outcome, with girls achieving on average 0.31 of a standard deviation higher scores than boys at age 5. Children born earlier in the school year show consistently higher scores as do those born heavier. All child characteristics remain statistically significant once other factors are controlled for.

Of the family characteristics, having a black mother, parents educated to less than degree level, having a mother with a higher maternal depression score and living in social housing are all negatively associated with personal, social and emotional scores, while there is a positive association between this outcome and family income. All of these factors remain significant when parental decisions are added to the model in Table 12.2 column (3). In addition the coefficient on Pakistani or Bangladeshi mothers now attracts a positive statistically significant coefficient. Of the parental decision variables, reading to the child every day at age 3, experience of formal childcare up to age 3 and having a mother who thinks it is important to stimulate young children are all positively associated with personal, social and emotional development at age 5. Apart from stimulating young children and

Table 12.2: Personal, social and emotional FSP scores

Variables	(1) Child characteristics	(2) Family characteristics	(3) Parental decisions	(4) Previous ability
Girl	0.308**	0.297**	0.292**	0.233**
Age in months at end of school year	0.047**	0.050**	0.049**	0.0506**
Birth weight (kg)	0.134**	0.063**	0.064**	0.0436**
Mother's ethnicity:				
Indian		-0.077	-0.053	0.011
Pakistani or Bangladeshi		0.070	0.117**	0.186**
Black		-0.242**	-0.182**	-0.056
Highest parental qualification:				
Less than 5 GCSEs grade A-C		-0.357**	-0.304**	-0.230**
5 GCSEs grade A-C		-0.176**	-0.147**	-0.104**
A-levels		-0.0892**	-0.0738**	-0.0478*
Log (equivalised family income) (MCS 2)		0.114**	0.101**	0.0732**
At least one parent in a professional or managerial role (MCS 2)		0.0445	0.0379	0.0172
Social housing (MCS 2)		-0.245**	-0.119**	-0.101**
Kessler maternal depression score measured (MCS 2)		-0.0139**	-0.0129**	-0.0062**
Child read to every day (at age 3)			0.111**	0.0605**
Child taught counting every day (at age 3)			0.0132	0.0004
Child taught the alphabet every day (at age 3)			-0.029**	-0.019
Child watches TV for three or more hours every day (at age 3)			0.007	0.024
Important to talk to the child MCS 1			0.026	0.028
Important to stimulate child MCS 1			0.096*	0.075
Child experienced formal childcare up to the age of 3			0.109**	0.066**
Standardised Bracken School Readiness Assessment (BSRA) at age 3				0.004**
Standardised vocabulary age 3				0.006**
Standardised problem behaviour age 3				-0.0167**
Observations	10,641	10,619	10,619	10,619
R^2	0.100	0.183	0.189	0.234

Notes: Sample: MCS 3 children with matched FSP score.

** $p<0.05$, * $p<0.1$; regressions weighted to account for sample design using weight2; includes controls for country.

having a black mother all of these variables remain statistically significant in the full model. Previous cognitive ability measured at age 3 was positively associated with this outcome at age 5 while problem behaviour at age 3 was negatively associated with personal, social and emotional development. The variables most associated with these FSP scores in the full model in terms of magnitude are as follows: being a girl (0.23), or having a Pakistani or Bangladeshi mother (0.19), were associated with higher scores. Having paretns with fewer than 5 GCSEs grade A–C (–0.23) or living in social housing (–0.18) were associated with lower FSP scores.

Communication, language and literacy

The results for the communication, language and literacy score are displayed in Table 12.3. As with the previous outcome the child characteristics were again all positively associated with communication, language and literacy scores in all models. Of the family characteristics having a black mother was negatively associated with this score until previous ability was controlled for in the final model, when its coefficient is reduced to statistical insignificance. However, the coefficients on having an Indian, Pakistani or Bangladeshi mother attracted positive and statistically significant coefficients, given the allowance for parents' education, significant and positive across all models. Family income attracted a positive coefficient in all models and social housing and maternal depression both attracted a negative coefficient. Having a mother who thought it was important to stimulate young children and experience of formal childcare were both positively associated with communication, language and literacy scores. School readiness at age 3 was positively, and previous problem behaviour negatively, associated with these outcomes.

Mathematical development

The child's gender, age and birth weight were all positively associated with mathematical development scores, as shown in Table 12.4. Parental education was also important for this outcome, with children scoring higher if they have at least one parent who was educated to degree level. Children living in households with higher incomes also scored, on average, higher than those with lower household incomes. Children who were read to every day at age 3 by a parent and children who had experienced formal childcare by age 3 also had higher mathematics scores at age 5. But having been taught to count at home made little difference. However, living in social housing at age 3 or having a mother who had ever been depressed meant that, on average, a child had a lower mathematics score than other children. These results were all significant at a greater than 1% level. Prior cognitive achievement at age 3 was also positively associated, and previous problem behaviour at age 3 negatively associated, with mathematical development at age 5.

Table 12.3: Communication, language and literacy FSP scores

Variables	(1) Child characteristics	(2) Family characteristics	(3) Parental decisions	(4) Previous ability
Girl	0.314**	0.298**	0.289**	0.221**
Age in months at end of school year	0.066**	0.070**	0.069**	0.071**
Birth weight (kg)	0.180**	0.092**	0.095**	0.0725**
Mother's ethnicity:				
Indian		0.006	0.046	0.130**
Pakistani or Bangladeshi		0.025	0.097	0.184**
Black		-0.261**	-0.169**	-0.011
Highest parental qualification:				
Less than 5 GCSEs grade A-C		-0.543**	-0.457**	-0.366**
5 GCSEs grade A-C		-0.272**	-0.222**	-0.171**
A-levels		-0.137**	-0.110**	-0.076**
Log (equivalised family income) (MCS 2)		0.149**	0.127**	0.096**
At least one parent in a professional or managerial role (MCS 2)		0.075**	0.063**	0.041
Social housing (MCS 2)		0.271**	0.215**	-0.192**
Kessler maternal depression score (MCS 2)		-0.0148**	-0.013**	-0.009**
Child read to every day (at age 3)			0.195**	0.130**
Child taught counting every day (at age 3)			0.040*	0.023
Child taught the alphabet every day (at age 3)			-0.048**	-0.034**
Child watches TV for three or more hours every day (at age 3)			-0.028	-0.020
Important to talk to the child (at 9 months)			0.031	0.030
Important to stimulate child (at 9 months)			0.106**	0.089**
Child experienced formal childcare up to age 3			0.169**	0.109**
Standardised BSRA at age 3				0.006**
Standardised vocabulary score at age 3				0.008**
Standardised problem behaviour score at age 3				-0.008**
Observations	10,645	10,624	10,624	10,624
R^2	0.124	0.253	0.270	0.336

Notes: Sample: MCS 3 children with matched FSP score.

** $p<0.05$, * $p<0.1$; regressions weighted to account for sample design using weight2; includes controls for country.

Table 12.4: Mathematics FSP scores

Variables	(1) Child characteristics	(2) Family characteristics	(3) Parental decisions	(4) Previous ability
Girl	0.144**	0.130**	0.123**	0.0578**
Age in months at end of school year	0.0620**	0.0649**	0.064**	0.066**
Birth weight (kg)	0.187**	0.106**	0.109**	0.088**
Mother's ethnicity:				
Indian		-0.066	-0.030	0.051
Pakistani or Bangladeshi		-0.028	0.035	0.117*
Black		-0.314**	-0.230**	-0.083
Highest parental qualification:				
Less than 5 GCSEs grade A-C		-0.490**	-0.417**	-0.332**
5 GCSEs grade A-C		-0.238**	-0.197**	-0.148**
A-levels		-0.124**	-0.101**	-0.0700**
Log (equivalised family income) (MCS 2)		0.114**	0.095**	0.065**
At least one parent in a professional or managerial role (MCS 2)		0.079**	0.069**	0.0463*
Social housing (MCS 2)		-0.226**	-0.203**	-0.153**
Kessler maternal depression score measured (MCS 2)		-0.012**	-0.0106**	-0.007**
Child read to every day (at age 3)			0.151**	0.089**
Child taught counting every day (at age 3)			0.032*	0.017
Child taught the alphabet every day (at age 3)			-0.048**	-0.036**
Child watches TV for three or more hours every day (at age 3)			-0.024	-0.017
Important to talk to the child (at 9 months)			0.057	0.061
Important to stimulate child (at 9 months)			0.096**	0.0780*
Child experienced formal childcare by age of 3			0.155**	0.099**
Standardised BSRA at age 3				0.006**
Standardised vocabulary score age 3				0.008**
Standardised problem behaviour score age 3				-0.008**
Observations	10,868	10,846	10,846	10,846
R^2	0.112	0.215	0.228	0.289

Notes: Sample: MCS 3 children with matched FSP score.

** $p<0.05$, * $p<0.1$; regressions weighted to account for sample design using weight2; includes controls for country.

Knowledge and understanding of the world

The variables associated with a child's knowledge and understanding of the world are presented in Table 12.5. The difference between girls and boys in terms of this FSP measure was positive and significant in the first three model specifications but was reduced to statistical insignificance in the final model that controlled for previous ability and behaviour. However, other child characteristics, age and birth weight, remained positive and significant in all models. Children with black mothers, on average, achieved lower scores but in the final model this result was only significant at the 10% level. Children with more highly educated parents scored higher on knowledge and understanding of the world as did children in families with higher incomes, not living in social housing, children who were read to every day by a parent and those who had experienced formal childcare. As with all previous models, prior cognitive achievement at age 3 was positively associated, and previous problem behaviour at age 3 negatively associated, with the measure of knowledge and understanding the world.

Physical development

The basic model for the FSP physical development scores (see Table 12.6) shows that child characteristics are all positively associated with physical development. In terms of magnitude, being female was most associated with this outcome with girls achieving on average 0.30 of a standard deviation higher scores than boys. All child characteristics remained statistically significant once other factors were controlled, although the magnitude was slightly reduced. Of the family characteristics parental education, household income and social housing were significant in all models, also slightly reduced in strength. Having a black mother or a depressed mother was negatively related to physical development in the family characteristics model (2), but this was reduced to statistical insignificance when previous ability and behaviour were also controlled in model (4). In this final model having a mother who was Pakistani or Bangladeshi was positively associated with physical development. Of the parental decision variables only experience of formal childcare was statistically significant in the model that controlled for previous ability (which was positively associated with physical development) and prior problem behaviour (negatively associated with this outcome).

Creative development

The factors associated with the FSP creative development scores are displayed in Table 12.7. The child characteristics were all positively associated with creative development in the basic model and in all subsequent models. Of the family characteristics, having an Indian or black mother was negatively associated with this score but after controlling for other variables only the coefficient on black mothers remained statistically significant. Parental education was related to this

Table 12.5: Knowledge and understanding of the world FSP scores

Variables	(1) Child characteristics	(2) Family characteristics	(3) Parental decisions	(4) Previous ability
Girl	0.068**	0.056**	0.0494**	-0.005
Age in months at end of school year	0.0476**	0.0500**	0.049**	0.051**
Birth weight (kg)	0.144**	0.069**	0.071**	0.053**
Mother's ethnicity:				
Indian		-0.141*	-0.112	-0.040
Pakistani or Bangladeshi		-0.109*	-0.056	0.017
Black		-0.360**	-0.291**	-0.155*
Highest parental qualification:				
Less than 5 GCSEs grade A-C		-0.382**	-0.320**	-0.247**
5 GCSEs grade A-C		-0.206**	-0.170**	-0.131**
A-levels		-0.088**	-0.068**	-0.044*
Log (equivalised family income) (MCS 2)		0.093**	0.075**	0.051**
At least one parent in a professional or managerial role (MCS 2)		0.059**	0.049*	0.031
Social housing (MCS 2)		-0.223**	-0.201**	-0.160**
Kessler maternal depression score (MCS 2)		-0.006**	-0.005*	-0.002
Child read to every day (at age 3)			0.128**	0.079*
Child taught counting every day (at age 3)			0.017	0.004
Child taught the alphabet every day (at age 3)			-0.040**	-0.0290**
Child watches TV for three or more hours every day			-0.038	-0.031
Important to talk to the child (at 9 months)			0.016	0.008
Important to stimulate child (at 9 months)			0.077	0.064
Child experienced formal childcare to age of 3			0.145**	0.100**
Standardised BSRA at age 3				0.005**
Standardised vocabulary score at age 3				0.007**
Standardised problem behaviour score at age 3				-0.007**
Observations	10,881	10,860	10,860	10,860
R^2	0.053	0.141	0.151	0.194

Notes: Sample: MCS 3 children with matched FSP score.

** $p<0.05$, * $p<0.1$; regressions weighted to account for sample design using weight2; includes controls for country.

Table 12.6: Physical development FSP scores

Variables	(1) Child characteristics	(2) Family characteristics	(3) Parental decisions	(4) Previous ability
Girl	0.296**	0.286**	0.283**	0.231**
Age in months at end of school year	0.0452**	0.047**	0.047**	0.048**
Birth weight (kg)	0.133**	0.077**	0.0772**	0.060**
Mother's ethnicity:				
Indian		0.029	0.044	0.106
Pakistani or Bangladeshi		0.009	0.040	0.104**
Black		-0.206**	-0.165*	-0.042
Highest parental qualification:				
Less than 5 GCSEs grade A-C		-0.302**	-0.265**	-0.198**
5 GCSEs grade A-C		-0.141**	-0.121**	-0.085**
A-levels		-0.077**	-0.066**	-0.045*
Log (equivalised family income) (MCS 2)		0.082**	0.072**	0.048**
At least one parent in a professional or managerial role (MCS 2)		0.033	0.028	0.010
Social housing (MCS 2)		-0.188**	-0.175**	0.175**
Kessler maternal depression score (MCS 2)		-0.009**	-0.009**	-0.003
Child read to every day (at age 3)			0.063**	0.019
Child taught counting every day (at age 3)			0.011	0.001
Child taught the alphabet every day (at age 3)			-0.019	-0.010
Child watches TV for three or more hours every day (at age 5)			-0.016	-0.003
Important to talk to the child (at 9 months)			-0.025	-0.030
Important to stimulate child (at 9 months)			0.075	0.057
Child experienced formal childcare up to age 3			0.099**	0.062**
Standardised BSRA at age 3				0.002**
Standardised vocabulary score at age 3				0.006**
Standardised problem behaviour score at age 3				-0.013**
Observations	11,028	11,006	11,006	11,006
R^2	0.108	0.159	0.162	0.196

Notes: Sample: MCS3 children with matched FSP score.

** $p<0.05$, * $p<0.1$; regressions weighted to account for sample design using weight2; includes controls for country.

Table 12.7: Creative development FSP scores

Variables	(1) Child characteristics	(2) Family characteristics	(3) Parental decisions	(4) Previous ability
Girl	0.398**	0.388**	0.383**	0.331**
Age in months at end of school year	0.0401**	0.0430**	0.0428**	0.044**
Birth weight (kg)	0.124**	0.0610**	0.0620**	0.0462**
Mother's ethnicity:				
Indian		-0.131**	-0.109	-0.040
Pakistani or Bangladeshi		-0.065	-0.023	0.046
Black		-0.323**	-0.268**	-0.136*
Highest parental qualification:				
Less than 5 GCSEs grade A-C		-0.349**	-0.297**	-0.229**
5 GCSEs grade A-C		-0.188**	-0.157**	-0.122**
A-levels		-0.068**	-0.052*	-0.032
Log (equivalised family income) (MCS 2)		0.088**	0.072**	0.049**
At least one parent in a professional or managerial role (MCS 2)		0.052*	0.042	0.026
Social housing (MCS 2)		-0.188**	-0.168**	-0.129**
Kessler maternal depression score measured (MCS 2)		-0.005*	-0.004	-0.000
Child read to every day (at age 3)			0.092**	0.048**
Child taught counting every day (at age 3)			0.008	-0.003
Child taught the alphabet every day (at age 3)			-0.034**	-0.025*
Child watches TV for three or more hours every day (at age 5)			-0.053**	-0.042*
Important to talk to the child (at 9 months)			-0.032	-0.041
Important to stimulate child (at 9 months)			0.073	0.057
Child experienced formal childcare to age 3			0.140**	0.101**
Standardised BSRA at age 3				0.003**
Standardised vocabulary score at age 3				0.006**
Standardised problem behaviour score age 3				-0.0097**
Observations	10,913	10,891	10,891	10,891
R^2	0.114	0.177	0.185	0.222

Notes: Sample: MCS 3 children with matched FSP score.

** $p<0.05$, * $p<0.1$; regressions weighted to account for sample design using weight2; includes controls for country.

outcome, like the previous outcomes but not as strongly as to mathematics and language. However, in the final model there is no statistical difference between the creative scores of children who had at least one parent with A-levels or a degree. Children with less educated parents, however, had lower creative development scores, on average. Children living in households with higher incomes had higher creative development scores in all models, while children living in social housing had lower scores than other children. Reading to children every day and experience of formal childcare were positively associated with creative development, while watching three or more hours of television every day at age 3 was negatively associated with creative development scores. Prior achievement was positively associated, and previous problem behaviour negatively associated, with this measure of creativity.

Conclusions

Despite the fact that the FSP measures six outcomes that focus on children's development in a wide variety of areas it is interesting that, on the whole, the same set of factors are associated with all outcomes. The child's characteristics were significant across most of the models with girls, older children and heavier birth weight children, on average, scoring higher in the different aspects of development measured by the FSP.

Parental education was consistently associated with all outcomes, with children where a parent was educated to degree level outperforming other children; children where a parent had A-levels scoring higher than children whose parents had less education; and children where at least one parent had 5 GCSEs grade A–C scored higher than children whose parents failed to achieve qualifications at this level. Family income was positively associated with all FSP scores, with children living in households with higher incomes, on average, scoring higher. Similarly, children living in social housing had lower scores, on average, than other children in all the outcomes measured in this chapter. Perhaps this represents additional disadvantages to living in social housing over and above low income, through, for example, a poor neighbourhood, not otherwise accounted for here. Of the parental decision variables, reading to the child every day at age 3 and experience of formal childcare up to age 3 were positively associated with all FSP scores.

Previous ability as measured by performance in the BAS naming vocabulary and the BSRAs at age 3 were positively associated with all FSP outcomes. Children scoring higher at the age 3 assessments, on average, also had higher scores in the FSP at age 5. Behaviour at age 3, as measured by the Strengths and Difficulties Questionnaire (SDQ) problem behaviour score was negatively associated with performance in the FSP at age 5. Children with more problem behaviour at age 3, on average, had lower FSP scores than other children.

In terms of magnitude, girls and having a parent with fewer than 5 GCSE grades A–C produced the largest coefficients. However, there were variations across the different outcomes that the FSP measures. The gender gap was largest for creative development with girls scoring 0.33 of a standard deviation higher than boys in this outcome. For mathematical development the gender gap was only 0.06 standard deviations and, for knowledge and understanding of the world, the gap between girls and boys was reduced to statistical insignificance. The gap in average scores for children with parents who have the minimum level of education (fewer than 5 GCSE grades A–C) compared to those with a graduate parent also varied across the different FSP areas of learning. The gap in scores associated with parental education was largest for communication, language and literacy scores (–0.37 sd) and smallest for physical development scores (–0.20 sd).

The magnitude of the coefficients on other variables varied similarly. The social housing estimate ranged from –0.19 standard deviations for for communication, language and literacy, –0.18 for personal, social and emotional scores through –0.16 for knowledge and understanding of the world, –0.15 for mathematics, –0.14 for physical development, and –0.13 for creative development. Experience of formal childcare also produced the largest coefficient (0.11 sd) for communication, language and literacy but the lowest (0.06) for physical development. Previous ability and behaviour, while significant in all models, produced only small coefficients in comparison to other variables (around 0.01 to 0.02 sd, positive in the case of performance and negative for behaviour).

In addition to the variables associated with all FSP scores there are a range of variables that were related to some of the scores but not others. Both mother's ethnicity and maternal depression fall into this category. Children whose mothers were Pakistani or Bangladeshi had higher scores, other things equal, than children with white mothers for personal, social and emotional development; communication, language and literacy; mathematics; and physical development. In addition, children whose mothers were Indian scored higher than children of white mothers in communication, language and literacy development. Children with black mothers had lower scores than children with white mothers in knowledge and understanding of the world and creative development; however, these relationships were significant only at the 10% level. These complex patterns of ethnic differences before and after other controls can be compared with those found in Chapter 10. Higher maternal depression scores were associated with lower FSP scores in personal, social and emotional development; communication, literacy and language; and mathematics. But maternal depression was insignificant in the models which examined: knowledge and understanding of the world; physical development; and creative development scores.

The findings from these analyses of FSP scores have considerable overlaps with analyses of cognitive scores at age 5 for MCS children. They show that children from lower-income families with parents who are less highly educated were not as advanced in their development at age 5 as children with more advantaged starts to life, in terms of having higher family income, higher parental education and not living in social housing. At these ages girls were also doing better than boys. But clearly there are also important parental behaviours that can assist children to develop. Experience of formal childcare and being read to improves all aspects of development measured in FSP. It would be worth policy makers exploring how, and why, these practices help children to develop to see whether they offer any levers for assisting disadvantaged children's development.

THIRTEEN

Childhood overweight and obesity

Lucy Jane Griffiths, Summer Sherburne Hawkins, Tim Cole,
Catherine Law and Carol Dezateux

Introduction

The rising prevalence of being overweight and obese is well recognised. According to the World Health Organization (WHO), 1.2 billion people are overweight, 300 million of whom are obese (Government Office for Science, 2007). The most startling increases have taken place in the US and UK where the prevalence of overweight and obesity has almost doubled in the last 25 years (Wardle and Boniface, 2008). These increases are not just confined to adult populations. Data from the Health Survey for England, using the UK national body mass index (BMI) percentile classification, indicates that the prevalence of overweight (including obesity) among 2- to 10-year-olds rose from 23% in 1995, to 28% in 2003, with the prevalence of overweight and obesity, and the rate of increase, being similar for boys and girls (Jotangia et al, 2005). These secular changes appear to be accelerating (Stamatakis et al, 2005; Jackson–Leach and Lobstein, 2006), and the age at onset of obesity is occurring at ever younger ages.

The health problems associated with adult obesity are well described and include type 2 diabetes, hypertension and coronary artery disease, sleep apnoea, pulmonary hypertension, hepatobiliary disease, cancers and reproductive and musculoskeletal disorders (Kopelman, 2007). Childhood obesity also has major implications in the short term for child health, development and well-being, and in the longer term for health in young and later adult life. However, the consequences of an increasingly early onset of childhood obesity are less clear (Reilly et al, 2003). Kimm and Obarzanek (2002) have consequently emphasised the need for prospective studies to delineate the morbidities associated with childhood obesity. Data from the Millennium Cohort Study (MCS) provide the ideal opportunity to examine the development of obesity and its consequences from a very young age.

Tackling childhood obesity is a priority for the UK government, given the substantial rise in obesity and overweight among very young children. In 2007, a long-term public service agreement (PSA) target for addressing childhood obesity was set, with the aim to 'reduce the proportion of overweight and obese children to 2000 levels by 2020 in the context of tackling obesity across the population' (HM Government, 2007).

In this chapter we analyse the weight and height data obtained, at the second and third surveys respectively, when cohort members were 3 and 5. We report on the prevalence of obesity and overweight at each of these ages in the UK and examine stability and change between these ages. We also explore the variation in these measures by individual and familial risk factors.

Examining MCS children's overweight and obesity

Research into the determinants of childhood growth, overweight and obesity has been an agreed and consistent priority within the MCS since its inception. Anthropometric measurements have been made in the MCS using trained interviewers and standard protocols: child body weight and height were measured at ages 3 and 5 years and waist circumference at age 5.

Parental reports of birth weight and weight at 9 months were obtained at the first interview: the former showed good agreement with that recorded at birth registration (Tate et al, 2005), while maternal reports of the child's last measured weight elicited at the age 9 month survey was aided by the ability to refer to the weight recorded in the parent-held personal child health record at the time of interview (Walton et al, 2006). Maternal self-report of weight and height and, if available, that of her partner, were also obtained at MCS interviews. Several relevant analyses from the first and second MCS surveys have already been published, for example, with respect to breastfeeding and infant feeding practices (Griffiths et al, 2005, 2007a; Bartington et al, 2006; Hawkins et al, 2007) and birth weight, infant growth and obesity (Tate et al, 2006; Griffiths et al, 2007b; Hawkins et al, 2008a).

In this chapter we define overweight and obesity using the International Obesity Taskforce (IOTF) cut-offs for BMI, expressed as weight divided by the square of height (BMI: kg/m^2), which are age and gender-specific (Cole et al, 2000). These BMI cut-offs are linked to the internationally recognised adult cut-offs for overweight ($25 kg/m^2$) and obesity ($30 kg/m^2$). The value of the cut-offs used at age 3 for overweight are BMI = 17.9 and 17.6 for boys and girls respectively, and 19.6 and 19.4 for obesity. At age 5, the cut-offs for overweight are BMI = 17.4 and 17.1 for boys and girls respectively, and 19.3 and 19.2 for obesity. The IOTF cut-offs are now internationally accepted definitions of overweight and obesity for children aged 2-18 and can be used to monitor prevalence estimates between countries.

Two different MCS samples were used for the analyses in this chapter. The sample used to explore risk factors at age 3 comprised 14,630 singleton children whose parents were interviewed at ages 9 months and 3 years. After excluding children with incomplete and/or implausible height and weight measurements, from families where the main survey respondent was not female, the partner respondent not male, or where there was more than one cohort child member, or children whose parents were not their biological parents, a sample of 13,128 children was available for analysis. The sample used to explore risk factors at age

5 comprised 12,989 singleton children who were interviewed at the first, second and third contacts. We used the same exclusion criteria as in the first sample, and this resulted in a sample size of 12,354 children.

Bivariate logistic regression analyses were conducted to examine the associations between individual sociodemographic factors and early childhood overweight and obesity, while associations between dietary factors (including infant feeding), physical activity behaviours and early childhood overweight were examined in greater depth using separate multivariate logistic regression analyses for each factor. We tested for overall significance of variables using adjusted Wald tests. All analyses were conducted using Stata/SE 10 (Stata Corporation, 2007). Results were calculated using sample and non-response weights and 'survey' commands to allow for the cluster sampling design effect of the MCS and attrition between contacts (Plewis and Ketende, 2006).

Prevalence of overweight and obesity in 3- and 5-year-olds

At age 3, 18% of MCS children were overweight (not including obese) and 5% were obese (see Table 13.1). By age 5, 16% of children were overweight and 5% were obese. Overall 81% of children did not change their BMI category between the ages of 3 and 5. However, by age 5, 7% of 3-year-olds with a normal BMI became overweight or obese. Conversely, 11% of overweight or obese 3-year-olds had reduced their BMI by age 5, with 9% having a normal BMI and 2% being overweight. The reasons for these transitions merit further investigation, but in combination they result in the apparent slight reduction in the prevalence of overweight or obesity at age 5 compared to age 3.

The prevalence of obesity and overweight varied significantly by UK country at both ages, being lowest in England and highest in Northern Ireland, with Scotland and Wales in between (see Figure 13.1). Within England, there were regional differences, with over a quarter of 3- and 5-year-olds living in the North East of England obese or overweight (27% and 26% at 3 and 5 respectively) compared with 19% of 3-year-olds in the East of England and 18% of 5-year-olds in the

Table 13.1: Prevalence[a] of normal BMI[b], overweight and obesity at ages 3 and 5

		Age 5			
		Normal BMI	Overweight	Obese	Total
Age 3	Normal BMI	70.3	6.0	0.9	77.2
	Overweight	8.0	8.1	1.8	17.8
	Obese	0.8	1.7	2.5	5.0
	Total	79.0	15.8	5.2	100.0

Notes: Base: 12,354 children (see text for sample description).
[a] Weighted percentages. [b] Normal BMI: a BMI below the IOTF cut-off for overweight.

Figure 13.1: Prevalence[a] of overweight (including obesity) at ages 3 and 5, by UK country

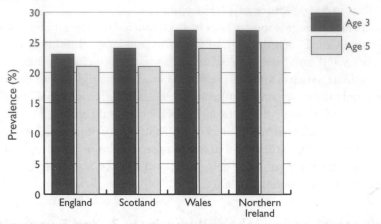

Note: [a] Weighted percentages.

South West. In the rest of the chapter, unless otherwise stated, we use the term 'overweight' to describe children of high BMI, including obese levels of BMI.

Overweight and obesity at age 3

Sociodemographic risk factors

Individual sociodemographic risk factors for being overweight at age 3 are shown in Appendix Table A13.1 (adapted from Hawkins et al, 2008).

Children of black ethnicity, and those whose mothers were lone parents, were at increased risk of being overweight, while children of Pakistani or Indian ethnicity were at reduced risk. There were no statistically significant associations between the child being overweight and the following characteristics when taken separately: the child's gender, the family income or the mother's socioeconomic status (SES), highest academic qualification, age at MCS birth or first live birth.

Modifiable risk factors

Dietary factors

Although the UK government currently recommends exclusive breastfeeding for the first six months (WHO, 2002), the WHO recommendation in place at the time the infants in this cohort were born was to breastfeed until 4-6 months of age, before introducing solid foods (DH, 1994). Seventy per cent of the mothers in this cohort initiated breastfeeding and, of those who initiated, 62% stopped before 4 months. Additionally, 36% of all mothers introduced solids before 4 months. These infant feeding practices were significantly associated with overweight status at age 3. Children were more likely to be overweight if they were never breastfed, and the risk of being overweight reduced significantly with increasing duration of breastfeeding (see Appendix Table A13.2). This association remained after adjusting for a range of sociodemographic factors in combination in a multivariate analysis (see Table 13.2). Similarly, children were more likely to be overweight if they were introduced to solid foods before 4 months compared to those for whom this was delayed to age 4 months or older (see Appendix Table A13.2 and Table 13.2 for bivariate and multivariate results, respectively).

Sedentary behaviour

Television viewing is another modifiable lifestyle factor frequently examined in relation to obesity. As reported by parents in the second MCS survey at age 3, television viewing was associated with a significantly increased risk of being overweight, especially among those watching television for three hours or more a day at age 3 (odds ratios: 1.24; 95% confidence interval [CI]: 1.06, 1.43)

Table 13.2: Associations between infant feeding and sedentary behaviour and overweight at age 3 in separate multivariate models

	% of total (n)	% overweight or obese	Multivariate OR (95 % CI)
Model 1: Breastfeeding duration**			
Never breastfed	30 (4,182)	25	1
< 4 months	42 (5,497)	23	0.91 (0.81, 1.01)
≥ 4 months	28 (3,441)	20	0.76 (0.66, 0.87)
Total %	100		
Missing *n*	8		
Model 2: Introduction of solid foods**			
< 4 months	36 (4,614)	26	1.21 (1.09, 1.35)
≥ 4 months	64 (8,503)	22	1
Total %	100		
Missing *n*	11		
Model 3: Television viewing at age 3 (hours daily) (NS)			
< 1	23 (3,053)	21	1
≥ 1 and < 3	60 (7,728)	23	1.13 (1.01, 1.27)
≥ 3	17 (2,346)	25	1.17 (0.99, 1.37)
Missing *n*	1		

Notes: Base: 13,128 children (see text for sample description).

Percentages weighted using MCS 2 UK weights.

Adjusted for child's gender, child's ethnicity, maternal SES, maternal highest academic qualification, family income, lone motherhood status, age at MCS and first live birth.

Adjusted Wald test: ** *p*<0.05, NS = not significant

(see Appendix Table A13.2). However, the overall associations attenuated after adjustment for factors such as family income and maternal education, reflecting the fact that television viewing was more prevalent in poorer families and in children of less educated mothers (see Table 13.2). However, television viewing is measured at the same time as BMI, so a causal relationship between television viewing at age 3 and being overweight or obese at age 3 cannot be inferred.

Overweight and obesity at age 5

Sociodemographic risk factors

Sociodemographic factors, when examined individually, were also associated with overweight status at age 5 (see Appendix Table A13.3). While there was no evidence for gender differences in overweight at age 3, by age 5 significant differences had emerged when 23% of girls were overweight compared to 19% of boys. Similarly, the risk of being overweight for black children persisted and had strengthened by age 5, although there were no other significant differences in risk by ethnic group. The risk of being overweight by age 5 was separately and inversely associated with maternal SES, maternal educational qualifications and family income, and was higher in the offspring of lone mothers. Although the risk of being overweight was not significantly associated with maternal age at the cohort child's birth, there was a bimodal association with maternal age at first motherhood, with children of mothers aged 20-24 years or older than 35 years at first motherhood at increased risk of being overweight at age 5.

Modifiable risk factors

Dietary factors

Similar associations between infant feeding patterns and the risk of being overweight were found at age 5 as at age 3 years; breastfeeding was associated with a lower, and introduction of solids before 4 months with a higher, risk of the child being overweight (see Table 13.3 and Appendix Table A13.4). Eating at regular meal times at age 3 was not significantly associated with overweight at age 5 (see Appendix Table A13.4 and Table 13.3). More detailed information on dietary habits was collected at age 5, including frequency of eating breakfast, eating and drinking between meals and fruit consumption. At present we can only examine cross-sectional associations between these dietary behaviours and being overweight. The findings of these cross-sectional analyses suggest an association at age 5 between not eating breakfast every day and being overweight (see Appendix Table A13.4). Although at age 5 children eating cakes or sweet biscuits between meals were less likely, and those eating yoghurt between meals more likely, to be overweight, these findings could be explained by dietary controls imposed in response to the child's weight rather than as causative per se. There were no

Table 13.3: Associations between infant feeding, dietary habits and overweight at age 5 in separate multivariate models

	% of total (n)	% overweight or obese	Multivariate OR (95% CI)
Model 1: Breastfeeding duration[a] **			
Never breastfed	29 (3,823)	23	1
< 4 months	42 (5,233)	22	0.94 (0.84, 1.06)
≥ 4 months	29 (3,291)	18	0.78 (0.67, 0.91)
Total %	100		
Missing *n*	7		
Model 2: Introduction of solid foods[a] **			
< 4 months	36 (4,401)	24	1.24 (1.12, 1.37)
≥ 4 months	64 (7,943)	20	1
Total %	100		
Missing *n*	10		
Model 3: Regular meal times at age 3[a] (NS)			
Never	2 (249)	19	1
Sometimes	6 (866)	23	1.52 (1.0, 2.33)
Usually	45 (5,374)	21	1.38 (0.95, 2.02)
Always	47 (5,864)	21	1.45 (0.97, 2.16)
Total %	100		
Missing *n*	1		

Notes: Base: 12,354 children (see text for sample description).

Percentages weighted using MCS 3 UK weights

[a] Adjusted for child's gender, child's ethnicity, maternal SES, maternal highest academic qualification, family income, lone motherhood status, age at MCS and first live birth and an indicator of physical activity behaviour at age 5: hours of television viewing or computer use.

Adjusted Wald test: ** $p < 0.05$, NS = not significant

significant associations between weight status and parentally reported drinks between meals or fruit consumption.

Physical activity and sedentary behaviour

Although television viewing at age 3 was significantly associated with obesity at age 5 in bivariate analyses (see Appendix Table A13.4), this attenuated and became non-significant after adjustment for confounding factors, particularly after adjusting for regularity of breakfast consumption (see Table 13.4).

Children who watched television/used a computer for at least two hours per day at age 5 were more likely to be overweight (see Appendix Table A13.4) and this was also independent of diet and other confounding factors. Children whose most common mode of transport to school at age 5 was via a vehicle (that is, public transport, school or local authority bus, minibus or coach, car or other vehicle) were also more likely to be overweight at age 5 than children

Table 13.4: Associations between physical activity or sedentary behaviours and overweight at age 5

	% of total (n)	% overweight or obese	Multivariate OR[a] (95% CI)
Television viewing (hours daily) at age 3*			
< 1	23 (3,053)	19	1
≥ 1 and < 3	60 (7,728)	22	1.16 (1.01, 1.32)
≥ 3	17 (2,346)	23	1.19 (1.00, 1.44)
Total %	100		
Missing *n*	1		

Notes: Base: 12,354 children (see text for sample description).

Percentages weighted using MCS 3 UK weights.

[a] Adjusted for child's gender, child's ethnicity, maternal SES, maternal highest academic qualification, family income, lone motherhood status, age at MCS and first live birth and number of days child ate breakfast at age 5.

** $p \leq 0.05$.

who walked or cycled to school in multivariate analyses. However, in both of the above significant correlations, because children's behaviour is measured at age 5, the same age as their BMI, we cannot infer that there is a causal relationship here. Participation in sport or physical activity classes or clubs, such as swimming, gymnastics, football or dancing reported at age 5 was not associated with overweight status at age 5 in either bivariate (see Appendix Table A13.4) or multivariate analyses.

Summary of key findings

Female sex and lower maternal SES status, lower maternal education and lower family income were all associated with an increased risk of being overweight at age 5. Children of lone mothers were at increased risk of being overweight at ages 3 and 5, as were children at age 5 whose mothers were under 24 or over 35 years at first motherhood.

The evidence for sex differences in the risk of being overweight as a child is inconsistent in the literature, perhaps reflecting country or cultural differences. While some studies have found no differences (Salsberry and Reagan, 2005), others have reported boys as more at risk (Dubois and Girard, 2006) and yet others report that girls were at greater risk (Wake et al, 2006).

At age 3, children of Pakistani or Indian ethnicity were at reduced risk of overweight. In contrast, black children were at the greatest risk of being overweight: this may reflect patterns of weight gain in infancy. We have previously reported that black MCS babies experienced the highest weight gain between birth and 9 months of age (Tate et al, 2006).

Infant feeding practices were strongly associated with risk of being overweight at both 3 and 5. Mothers who breastfed at all, who breastfed for longer than 4 months or who deferred the introduction of solids to 4 months or later, were less likely to have children who became overweight during the pre-school years, even after allowing for the maternal sociodemographic factors known to be associated with infant feeding practices. This observation is consistent with additional research on breastfeeding suggesting these practices have a protective effect (Arenz et al, 2004; Harder et al, 2005; Owen et al, 2005). There is also more limited evidence that transferring from milk to solid foods at an early stage is associated with childhood obesity (Hawkins and Law, 2006).

Children's television viewing at age 3 was positively associated with being overweight at age 5, with increased viewing provoking greater risk, consistent with other studies in young children (Hawkins and Law, 2006). However, in our analyses these associations were confounded by socioeconomic factors. Cross-sectional analyses indicated positive associations between dietary behaviours (irregular breakfast consumption, consumption of certain snacks between meals), sedentary behaviours (television viewing, computer use, travelling by vehicle to school) at age 5 and overweight at age 5. We will be able to examine the association of such factors with weight status at age 7 when the fourth MCS survey of the cohort is completed.

Conclusions

In this chapter we examined individual and familial factors associated with children being overweight and obese at ages 3 and 5. We found significant levels of early childhood overweight among this nationally representative cohort of contemporary British children, with 23% overweight or obese at age 3 and 21% at age 5. This risk is socially patterned, with cohort child's sex and ethnicity, maternal SES status, education and age at first motherhood, family income and lone parenthood all significantly associated with the risk of early childhood overweight. Importantly, modifiable factors such as infant feeding practices and indicators of dietary and physical activity behaviours were also significantly associated with early childhood overweight, suggesting the need for further investigation using longitudinal data that will become available for MCS children at age 7.

Some, but not all, of the factors examined in this chapter are amenable to change through policies for children, parents, services and communities. Interventions to change infant feeding practices, dietary and sedentary behaviours as well as engagement in physical activity are needed. However, there have been few evaluations to determine the extent to which policies or interventions are supporting the adoption of these healthy behaviours or of their impact on the risk of becoming overweight.

Our findings are consistent with the continued need to promote breastfeeding initiation and duration and adherence to recommendations regarding optimal age for the introduction of solid foods in infancy in the UK. They also provide more limited support for enhanced nutritional programmes, such as the school fruit and vegetable scheme (DH, 2006) and for the current recommendation for all children to participate in one hour of moderate intensity physical activity each day (DH, 2004).

The recent government Foresight report (Government Office for Science, 2007) highlighted the complexity of the causal pathways to obesity. Evidence from longitudinal epidemiological studies will enhance our understanding of these pathways, and, through later follow-up, allow the consequences of overweight and obesity of early childhood onset to be characterised.

The MCS is the fourth nationwide cohort study in the UK. Obesity and physical activity are a strategic priority and future analyses will provide invaluable insights into the pathways to obesity and overweight in a large contemporary and multiethnic cohort of children and enable us to compare these experiences with those of children living in the 20th century and participating in earlier cohort studies. These analyses will contribute to the development of appropriate interventions and policies to prevent and reduce childhood obesity.

Appendix

Table A13.1: Sociodemographic risk factors for overweight at age 3

	% of total (n)	% overweight or obese	Bivariate OR (95% CI)
Child's gender (NS)			
Male	50 (6,634)	22	1
Female	50 (6,494)	24	1.07 (0.97, 1.18)
Total %	100		
Missing *n*	0		
Child's ethnicity**			
White	87 (11,087)	23	1
Mixed	3 (359)	23	1.00 (0.75, 1.34)
Indian	2 (335)	10	0.35 (0.24, 0.49)
Pakistani	3 (581)	19	0.76 (0.62, 0.93)
Bangladeshi	1 (205)	21	0.89 (0.61, 1.30)
Black (Caribbean, African, Other)	3 (373)	30	1.42 (1.08, 1.86)
Other ethnic group	1 (161)	21	0.85 (0.50, 1.44)
Total %	100		
Missing *n*	27		
Maternal socioeconomic circumstances (at first contact) (NS)			
Managerial and professional occupations	31 (3,757)	23	0.94 (0.83, 1.06)
Intermediate occupations	18 (2,292)	21	0.84 (0.73, 0.97)
Small employers and own account workers	4 (472)	19	0.75 (0.58, 0.96)
Lower supervisory and technical occupations	5 (720)	23	0.93 (0.75, 1.16)
Semi-routine and routine occupations	35 (4,593)	24	1
Never worked and long-term unemployed	7 (1,135)	23	0.91 (0.75, 1.10)
Total %	100		
Missing *n*	159		
Maternal highest academic qualification (at first contact) (NS)			
Degree	18 (2,284)	22	0.86 (0.72, 1.02)
Diploma	9 (1,199)	23	0.91 (0.75, 1.11)
A/AS/S-levels	10 (1,281)	21	0.79 (0.65, 0.96)
O-levels/GCSE grades A-C	35 (4,469)	23	0.92 (0.80, 1.05)
GCSE grades D-G	11 (1,349)	26	1.06 (0.88, 1.28)
Other academic qualifications	2 (323)	23	0.89 (0.61, 1.30)
None of these qualifications	15 (2,196)	25	1
Total %	100		
Missing *n*	27		

(continued)

Table A13.1: Sociodemographic risk factors for overweight at age 3 *(continued)*

	% of total (n)	% overweight or obese	Bivariate OR (95% CI)
Family income (at age 3) (NS)			
£0–£11,000 per annum	22 (3,037)	24	1.18 (1.01, 1.37)
£11,000–£22,000 per annum	28 (3,851)	24	1.18 (1.02, 1.36)
£22,000–£33,000 per annum	23 (2,780)	24	1.17 (1.00, 1.36)
£33,000+ per annum	27 (3,156)	21	1
Total %	100		
Missing *n*	304		
Lone motherhood status (at first contact)**			
Non-lone mother	86 (11,166)	23	1
Lone mother	14 (1,962)	26	1.22 (1.06, 1.40)
Total %	100		
Missing *n*	0		
Mother's age at first live birth (years) (NS)			
14-19	18 (2,391)	23	1.02 (0.89, 1.17)
20-24	25 (3,470)	25	1.08 (0.94, 1.24)
25-29	30 (3,736)	23	1
30-34	20 (2,444)	21	0.88 (0.75, 1.01)
35+	6 (722)	23	1.01 (0.81, 1.26)
Total %	100		
Missing *n*	365		
Mother's age at MCS birth (years) (NS)			
14-19	7 (974)	23	0.95 (0.78, 1.14)
20-24	16 (2,294)	23	0.95 (0.82, 1.10)
25-29	28 (3,648)	24	1
30-34	31 (4,023)	22	0.91 (0.81, 1.03)
35+	17 (2,185)	23	0.97 (0.85, 1.11)
Total %	100		
Missing *n*	4		

Notes: Base: 13,128 children (see text for sample description).

Adjusted Wald test: NS = not significant, ** $p < 0.05$

Table A13.2: Bivariate associations of overweight at age 3 with infant feeding and sedentary behaviour

	Bivariate OR (95% CI)
Breastfeeding duration**	
Never breastfed	1
< 4 months	0.88 (0.80, 0.98)
≥ 4 months	0.75 (0.66, 0.85)
Introduction of solid foods**	
< 4 months	1.25 (1.14, 1.38)
≥ 4 months	1
Television viewing at age 3 (hours daily)**	
< 1	1
≥ 1 and < 3	1.14 (1.02, 1.27)
≥ 3	1.24 (1.06, 1.43)

Notes: Adjusted Wald test: ** *p*<0.05

Table A13.3: Sociodemographic risk factors for overweight at age 5

	% of total (n)	% overweight or obese	Bivariate OR (95% CI)
Child's gender**			
Male	51 (6,304)	19	1
Female	49 (6,050)	23	1.30 (1.17, 1.43)
Total %	100		
Missing *n*	0		
Child's ethnicity**			
White	89 (10,627)	21	1
Mixed	3 (320)	23	1.11 (0.83, 1.47)
Indian	2 (287)	19	0.87 (0.60, 1.26)
Pakistani	3 (468)	17	0.77 (0.59, 1.01)
Bangladeshi	1 (174)	21	1.02 (0.66, 1.55)
Black (Caribbean, African, Other)	2 (329)	36	2.10 (1.52, 2.85)
Other ethnic group	1 (122)	14	0.63 (0.34, 1.16)
Total %	100		
Missing *n*	27		

(continued)

Table A13.3: Sociodemographic risk factors for overweight at age 5 *(continued)*

	% of total (n)	% overweight or obese	Bivariate OR (95% CI)
Maternal SES (at first contact)**			
Managerial and professional occupations	32 (3,701)	20	0.83 (0.73, 0.94)
Intermediate occupations	19 (2,204)	19	0.77 (0.68, 0.89)
Small employers and own account workers	4 (459)	21	0.89 (0.69, 1.15)
Lower supervisory and technical occupations	5 (690)	21	0.88 (0.69, 1.11)
Semi-routine and routine occupations	34 (4,227)	23	1
Never worked or long-term unemployed	6 (934)	21	0.88 (0.69, 1.12)
Total %	100		
Missing *n*	139		
Maternal highest academic qualification (at first contact)**			
Degree	19 (2,237)	17	0.69 (0.57, 0.82)
Diploma	10 (1,184)	21	0.89 (0.73, 1.09)
A/AS/S-levels	10 (1,252)	19	0.79 (0.64, 0.97)
O-levels/GCSE grades A-C	35 (4,217)	22	0.94 (0.81, 1.10)
GCSE grades D-G	11 (1,271)	25	1.08 (0.88, 1.32)
Other academic qualifications	2 (270)	21	0.91 (0.59, 1.40)
None of these qualifications	14 (1,899)	23	1
Total %	100		
Missing *n*	24		
Family income (at age 5)**			
£0-£13,000 per annum	20 (2,711)	22	1.27 (1.09, 1.49)
£13,000-£26,000 per annum	33 (4,214)	22	1.27 (1.10, 1.48)
£26,000-£36,400 per annum	19 (2,318)	22	1.29 (1.10, 1.52)
£36,400+ per annum	27 (2,997)	18	1
Total %	100		
Missing *n*	114		

(continued)

Table A13.3: Sociodemographic risk factors for overweight at age 5 *(continued)*

	% of total (n)	% overweight or obese	Bivariate OR (95% CI)
Lone motherhood status (at first contact)**			
Non-lone mother	87 (10,580)	21	1
Lone mother	14 (1,774)	25	1.29 (1.11, 1.51)
Total %	100		
Missing *n*	0		
Mother's age at first live birth (years) **			
14-19	17 (2,148)	22	1.09 (0.93, 1.27)
20-24	25 (3,195)	23	1.17 (1.03, 1.34)
25-29	31 (3,610)	20	1
30-34	21 (2,405)	19	0.91 (0.78, 1.06)
35+	6 (693)	22	1.10 (1.00, 1.35)
Total %	100		
Missing *n*	303		
Mother's age at MCS birth (years) (NS)			
14-19	7 (845)	21	1.02 (0.82, 1.25)
20-24	16 (2,074)	21	1.05 (0.89, 1.23)
25-29	28 (3,439)	21	1
30-34	32 (3,885)	21	1.02 (0.90, 1.16)
35+	18 (2,109)	22	1.10 (0.95, 1.26)
Total %	100		
Missing *n*	2		

Notes: Base: 12,354 children (see text for sample description).

Adjusted Wald test: ** *p*<0.05, NS = not significant

Table A13.4: Bivariate longitudinal and cross-sectional associations between infant feeding, dietary habits and physical activity or sedentary behaviours and overweight at age 5

		Bivariate OR (95% CI)
Breastfeeding duration**		
	Never breastfed	1
	< 4 months	0.90 (0.80, 1.01)
	≥ 4 months	0.73 (0.64, 0.85)
Introduction of solid foods**		
	< 4 months	1.24 (1.12, 1.37)
	≥ 4 months	1
Regular meal times at age 3 (NS)		
	Never	1
	Sometimes	1.33 (0.90, 1.99)
	Usually	1.14 (0.80, 1.64)
	Always	1.19 (0.81, 1.73)
Number of days child eats breakfast at age 5**		
	7 days	1
	6 days or less	1.56 (1.30, 1.87)
What child mainly eats between meals at age 5**		
	Crisps or similar snacks	1.18 (1.01, 1.38)
	Cakes and sweet biscuits	0.82 (0.69, 0.98)
	Fruit or vegetables	1
	Bread or similar items	0.96 (0.77, 1.20)
	Sweets, chocolate or ice cream	0.99 (0.81, 1.22)
	Yoghurt	1.25 (1.05, 1.48)
	Other dairy (cheese or eggs)	1.07 (0.76, 1.50)
	Other	0.97 (0.61, 1.56)
	Does not eat between meals	1.46 (0.98, 2.17)
What child mainly drinks between meals at age 5 (NS)		
	Sweetened drinks	1.14 (0.99, 1.32)
	Artificially sweetened drinks	1.17 (1.00, 1.37)
	Unsweetened or pure fruit juice	1.11 (0.95, 1.30)
	Water	1
	Milk	1.02 (0.85, 1.21)
	Other	0.90 (0.62, 1.31)
Consumption of fruit portions per day at age 5 (NS)		
	0 or 1	1.00 (0.87, 1.15)
	2	1.03 (0.91, 1.15)
	≥ 3	1

(continued)

Table A13.4: Bivariate longitudinal and cross-sectional associations between infant feeding, dietary habits and physical activity or sedentary behaviours and overweight at age 5 *(continued)*

	Bivariate OR (95% CI)
Television viewing (hours daily) at age 3**	
< 1	1
≥ 1 and < 3	1.19 (1.05, 1.35)
≥ 3	1.30 (1.09, 1.55)
Television viewing or computer use at age 5 (hours daily)**	
< 1	1
≥ 1 and < 2	1.15 (0.93, 1.41)
≥ 2 and ≤ 4	1.32 (1.09, 1.60)
> 4	1.37 (1.10, 1.72)
No of days per week child participates in sports/activities at age 5 (NS)	
≥ 3	1
2	0.82 (0.67, 1.00)
1	0.93 (0.78, 1.10)
Less often or not at all	0.98 (0.83, 1.16)
Mode of transport to school at age 5 (NS)	
Walk or cycle	1
Vehicle	1.09 (0.98, 1.21)

Notes: Adjusted Wald test: ** *p*<0.05, NS = not significant

FOURTEEN

Resilience in children's development

Ingrid Schoon, Helen Cheng and Elizabeth Jones

Introduction

The aim of this chapter is to assess early childhood influences on the cognitive and behavioural development of children in the Millennium Cohort Study (MCS) at age 5. In particular we consider the role potential protective factors in the family environment may play and whether they can ameliorate some of the disadvantages known to influence children's development, such as family financial hardship.

The association between limited family material resources and poor child and adolescent development is well documented (Duncan and Brooks-Gunn, 1997; Bradley and Corwyn, 2002; Engle and Black, 2008). Children growing up in circumstances characterised by socioeconomic disadvantage are at greater risk of developing cognitive and behavioural adjustment problems during childhood, which in turn have consistently been found to influence later outcomes regarding education, employment, health and social integration (Rutter and Madge, 1976; Essen and Wedge, 1978; Duncan and Brooks-Gunn, 1997; Schoon, 2006). Persisting social inequalities in children's behaviour and development are of ongoing concern for policy makers and social scientists, as indicated, for example, in the *Every Child Matters* framework (HM Treasury, 2003) and *The Children's Plan* (DCSF, 2007).

The UK has been identified as a highly privileged country, according to the United Nations (UN) Human Development Index, measured in terms of longevity, knowledge and income (UNDP, 2001). Nonetheless about one million British children (8%) were living in severe poverty at the turn of the millennium (ie poor on three possible counts, Adelman et al, 2003). 21% of children lived in households with an equivalised household income (before housing costs [BHC]) below 60% of the median (DWP, 2003). A report by the UN suggests that poverty rates for children in the UK were several times higher than those in most Western industrialised countries (UNICEF, 2007), although the situation appears to have improved since then (OECD, 2008). Given the persistence of poverty even in highly developed countries it is essential (a) to develop strategies to reduce poverty in the first place, and (b) to learn more about the impact of material hardship on children's early development, and to identify factors that enable successful development in the face of adversity.

Not all children are affected by adversity in the same way, and some children adjust well despite the experience of childhood poverty. The process of withstanding the negative effects of adversity, or succeeding against the odds, is described by the notion of resilience, which is associated with features of the children, their parents and the wider social context that enable positive adjustment despite the experience of adversity (Luthar, 1999; Masten, 2001; Rutter, 2006; Schoon, 2006). Although key features and protective factors promoting resilience could be identified in previous research, we do not have a great understanding of the potential protective factors and processes that can buffer against or reduce the negative influences from exposure to family adversity and hardship during the early years. Although the effects of material hardship on child outcomes seem to be strongest during the pre-school and early school years (Duncan and Brooks-Gunn, 1997), there are relatively few studies on young children or infants. Using data from children born in the millennium, following their development from birth to age 5 years, we will help to close this evidence gap.

This chapter investigates the relationship between family economic resources, parental and child characteristics in shaping children's developmental outcomes at age 5. We are interested in whether family and child characteristics have a moderating influence on the effects of family hardship on young children. Moderating influences refer to the mechanisms through which adversity influences on child adjustment can be buffered or reduced. The key outcomes of concern are indicators of cognitive and behavioural development. We link the children's developmental outcomes to indicators of family financial hardship, parental characteristics and children's development since birth, using a series of multiple regression models. The following questions will be tested:

- First, to what extent does family adversity influence children's cognitive and behavioural development at age 5? Is family adversity a risk factor for obstructing development? In particular, we focus on the role of family financial hardship (operationalised through the family being in receipt of state benefit at either age 9 months, age 3, or age 5, or at some combination of these times). Based on earlier studies, we expect persistent hardship to be associated with lower levels of children's development, after controlling for other demographic background factors such as mother's age and education.
- Second, we want to assess whether parental characteristics, such as mother's depression, mother's self-esteem and the quality of the parent–child relationship moderate the association between family financial hardship and child development, that is, do these characteristics moderate the influence of adversity onto the children? For example, do parental psychological characteristics, such as mother's positive self-esteem and the quality of the parent–child relationship reduce the influence of adversity onto the children? The role of parental psychological well-being and parent–child interactions in shaping the association between the experience of material hardship and child development has been established in previous studies (Elder and Caspi, 1988; Conger et al, 1992; McLoyd, 1994).
- In addition, we assess the association between earlier developmental outcomes and cognitive and behavioural adjustment at age 5, after controlling for earlier

and contemporary family financial hardship and parental characteristics collected at 9 months and age 3. Do earlier developmental outcomes play a role in shaping later cognitive and behavioural adjustment in addition to family-related experiences? There may be virtuous (or vicious) circle effects from having good development indicators at an earlier age. In particular we examine three sets of associations: first, between school readiness and early language skills (British Ability Scales [BAS] naming vocabulary) assessed at age 3 and developmental outcomes at age 5; second, between behavioural adjustment (Strengths and Difficulties Questionnaire [SDQ]) at age 3 and cognitive and behavioural development at age 5; and third, between the delay in gross and fine motor development at age 9 months and developmental outcomes at age 5.

All models control for original characteristics of the child, such as gender, ethnicity, birth weight and age of the child at interview. The separate associations between each of these characteristics and developmental outcomes at age 5 are described in more detail in a descriptive account of the third MCS survey (Jones and Schoon, 2008).

Assessment of cognitive ability in the MCS data

Cognitive abilities at age 5 have been measured with three sub-scales of the BAS second edition (BAS II): naming vocabulary, picture similarities and pattern construction, capturing core aspects of verbal, pictorial reasoning and spatial abilities (Elliott, 1996; Hill, 2005) (see Box 1.1 in Chapter 1, this volume). In our analyses the sub-tests are used as a composite measure, giving information about the general cognitive ability of the child.

One of the sub-scales, naming vocabulary, has already been used among the MCS children at age 3, enabling us to establish longitudinal stability of expressive verbal ability (see also Box 1.1 in Chapter 1, this volume).

Another indicator of early cognitive ability was the Bracken School Readiness Assessment (BSRA) (Bracken, 1998), which had been included in the MCS child's assessments at age 3 (George et al, 2007; Jones and Schoon, 2008). Scores were age-standardised in relation to the US norm sample, with a high score reflecting greater school readiness. Comparison of the BAS sub-scales collected at age 3 and 5, as well as the BSRA will be used in this analysis of MCS children to examine interrelationship between measures of cognitive ability over time.

About 15,000 MCS children completed the cognitive assessments at age 5, although the exact number varied depending on the sub-scale used. For 14,853 children we have complete data on all three BAS sub-scales at age 5. At age 3 we have fewer respondents, as only 12,096 children's completed the BAS naming vocabulary sub-test and only 11,553 the Bracken assessment test. All cohort members who completed the assessments at age 5 are included in analyses; no one has been excluded. To get a better understanding of the child's general cognitive ability, we carried out a principal component factor analysis (PCA) of the positively correlated scores from the three sub-tests (Jones and Schoon, 2008). The existence of highly correlated coefficients between sub-sets of variables suggests that those variables are measuring the same underlying dimension. These underlying dimensions are also known as factors (or latent variables). By reducing the size of a dataset from a group of interrelated variables into a smaller set of factors, PCA achieves parsimony by explaining the maximum amount of variance in a correlation matrix using the smallest number of explanatory concepts (Dunteman, 1989).

PCA analysis of the three BAS sub-scales used in MCS 3 confirmed the presence of a general underlying cognitive ability factor, traditionally dubbed *g* (Carroll, 2006). The underlying factor accounted for 56% of the total variance among the three tests. The loading of each of the sub-tests on the underlying factor was 0.57 for picture similarities, 0.57 for naming vocabulary and 0.59 for pattern construction. These loadings can be thought of as the Pearson correlation between the latent factor and the observed variables, that is, the measured sub-tests.

We saved *g* scores for each participant, based on the underlying factor score from the PCA. The scores indicating general cognitive ability (*g*) were standardised to a mean of 100 and a standard deviation of 15.

MCS girls generally performed better than boys in the cognitive ability tests at age 5, as in the teacher assessments described in Chapter 12 (this volume). There is also evidence of variation in cognitive ability test scores by ethnicity (Jones and Schoon, 2008; and Chapter 10, this volume). White children achieved the highest test scores, followed by children of mixed ethnicity.

When examining variation in cognitive ability by socioeconomic family background, the findings suggest that children with more educated parents achieve higher cognitive scores than children with less educated parents. When looking at children's adjustment in relation to family income, we found that children living in families receiving below the 60% median family income, known as the poverty line, scored eight points below children from households earning above this line, and children growing up with two natural parents had higher scores than those growing up in single-parent households, or in reconstituted families

Figure 14.1: General cognitive ability: factor loadings

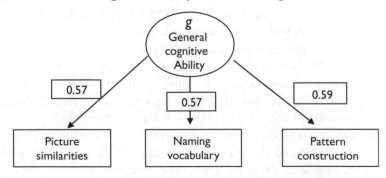

at age 5 (for more details, see Jones and Schoon, 2008). In the current analysis, we applied an indicator for family poverty by looking at families in receipt of certain state benefits at up to three time points: Income Support, Jobseeker's Allowance and Tax Credits. This is a broader definition of means-tested benefits than that used in Chapter 2 (this volume) which also applied the condition of receiving Housing Benefit or Council Tax Benefit to exclude those with the highest incomes among recipients of Tax Credits and Jobseeker's Allowance. All of these benefits are income tested. For the rest of the chapter we refer to the receipt of 'income benefits'. The approach in this chapter to measuring material circumstances helps us to identify whether MCS children were living in persistent poverty (at all three MCS surveys) or medium-term poverty (at two out of three MCS surveys) or in short-term poverty (at only one MCS survey). The measure does not enable us to identify the timing of poverty, and it could be that being in receipt of income benefits on only one of the three occasions will be at the age 5 interview. This is not ideal since receiving income benefits for these cases is being measured at the same time as children's development, and cannot be argued to have a predictive or causal effect on development. However, such cases are in the minority in the sample.

Assessment of behaviour adjustment

Behavioural adjustment of the MCS children at age 3 and 5 was measured with the SDQ via parental report, usually from the mother (see Box 1.2, Chapter 1, this volume for more detail). For the following analysis an overall difficulties mean score for the whole sample was computed by summing replies to the four sub-scales indicating problematic behaviour, that is, conduct problems, hyperactivity, emotional symptoms and peer problems. We obtained scale scores for each of the four sub-scales, as well as a summary score of total behaviour problems. In addition, we computed a score indicating mothers' reports of pro-social behaviour, to assess positive adjustment. Complete SDQ data were obtained for 12,511 children at age 5 and for 12,018 at age 3. The range of the total difficulties score is between 0 and 40. Scores between 14 and 16 are classified as borderline and scores of 17 and above are classified as abnormal (Goodman, 2001). The total scores for the whole MCS sample range from 0 to 34 at age 5, with 92% of children scoring below 14, 4.5% of children scored within the borderline range and 4.0% of children scored 17 or more. The scores were standardised when used in regressions.

MCS girls were reported by their mothers to show fewer behaviour problems than boys and received higher scores on the pro-social sub-scale, in line with teacher ratings on the personal, social and emotional (PSE) scale of the Foundation Stage Profile (FSP) (described in Chapter 12, this volume). Comparing behavioural adjustment among ethnic groups suggests that mothers of Indian and black African children reported the least behaviour problems, followed by mothers of white children. For all other ethnic groups we find scores higher than the sample mean, with Pakistani children reported to show the most behaviour problems (for more details see Jones and Schoon, 2008). In interpreting these findings, it has to be kept in mind that behavioural adjustment was assessed via the parental report, and that there might be ethnic differences in parental language skills, item interpretation or reporting. The total difficulties score was higher for children in homes where no English was said to be spoken at MCS 1 compared to those in homes speaking only English. Children growing up in bilingual homes (other than Welsh-speaking) fall in between these two groups, although children from bilingual families overall scored significantly lower than children from English-speaking-only families.

Children described by their parent as having relatively few behavioural problems were those living with two natural parents, those with more educated parents or children in families where there were two employed adults. Children of higher educated parents also were reported to show slightly higher levels of pro-social behaviour than those of less educated parents. Otherwise there were no significant differences in pro-social behaviour, suggesting that there were few systematic variations in positive behaviour among 5-year-olds.

Predicting developmental outcomes at age 5

A series of regression models were run to assess the relative influence of family financial hardship, early developmental adjustment and parental characteristics on developmental outcomes at age 5. All models control for child's age (to the precision of days), birth weight, prematurity, child's gender and ethnicity, the mother's age at the first interview and the mother's highest qualification, as well as country (England, Wales, Scotland and Northern Ireland). All analyses took account of the clustered sample design and allowed for its stratification and attrition by applying the appropriate weights.

There were significant correlations between variables used in the analyses with correlation coefficients ranging from 0.027 to 0.600. Their sizes suggest that collinearity is not a problem in the data. The highest correlations were found between the indicators of cognitive and behavioural development over time, confirming the consistency of developmental trajectories. High cognitive ability at age 5, as assessed with the BAS, is significantly correlated with school readiness ($r = 0.476$) and with naming vocabulary ($r = 0.430$), both assessed at age 3. Behaviour problems at age 5 show significant association with behaviour problems at age 3 ($r = 0.600$). Pro-social behaviour at age 5 is significantly linked to pro-social behaviour at age 3 ($r = 0.428$), indicating the stability, in relation to change, of children's behaviour over two years. Our first findings point to there being virtuous (or vicious) circles in children's development. Where children are doing well in their cognitive development at age 3, many will tend to continue their good progress through to age 5. Where children are starting to display behaviour problems at age 3, they will also tend to continue to display behaviour problems at age 5. One might argue that having a good start in terms of cognitive and behaviour adjustment can have a protective influence on children as they grow older.

Predicting cognitive ability at age 5

We now investigate the influence of financial hardship on cognitive ability at age 5 using a multivariate regression model (model 1 in Table 14.1). Financial hardship was measured by a variable indicating whether the family was in receipt of income benefits at any of the MCS interviews at age 9–10 months, 3 years or at 5 years. We focused only on recipients of means-tested income benefits, which is a more restrictive definition of poverty than that used in Chapter 2 (this volume). A set of dummy variables were created differentiating: (1) families never in receipt of income benefits at any of the three MCS surveys, the reference group; (2) families receiving income benefits once; (3) receiving income benefits twice; or (4) receiving income benefits at all three consecutive interviews. The

Table 14.1: Predicting general cognitive ability at age 5

	Model 1			Model 2			Model 3		
	B	SE	t	B	SE	t	B	SE	t
Financial hardship at MCS 1, 2, 3									
Income benefits once	-1.818**	0.399	4.56	-1.749**	0.404	4.33	-0.813**	0.355	2.29
Income benefits twice	-3.777**	0.454	8.32	-3.710**	0.460	8.06	-2.149**	0.427	5.03
Income benefits thrice	-5.211**	0.512	7.47	-5.040**	0.520	7.07	-2.749**	0.473	4.40
Parental characteristics									
Malaise at MCS 1				0.070	0.106	0.66	0.106	0.096	1.11
Self-esteem at MCS 1				0.069	0.067	1.02	0.065	0.063	1.03
Pianta at MCS 2				0.096**	0.024	3.95	-0.021	0.024	0.86
Earlier development outcomes									
Gross motor delay (9 months)							-1.012**	0.224	4.51
Fine motor delay (9 months)							-0.647**	0.272	2.38
Behaviour problems (age 3)							-0.132**	0.041	3.23
Pro-social behaviour (age 3)							-0.029	0.088	0.33
Bracken (age 3)							0.243**	0.012	20.88
Vocabulary (age 3)							0.267**	0.016	16.25
R^2		0.150			0.152			0.289	
Number of strata = 9 Number of PSUs = 398	Unweighted *n* values = 10,711			Unweighted *n* values = 10,711			Unweighted *n* values = 10,711		
Design *df* = 389 F-statistic	$F(20,370) = 62.42$ $p < 0.0001$			$F(23,367) = 56.17$ $p < 0.0001$			$F(29,361) = 101.88$ $p < 0.0001$		

**$p < 0.05$.

Notes: Analysis is weighted using sampling weights and non-response adjusted weights. Standard errors (SEs) corrected for cluster sample design. All models are controlled for age and gender of the cohort child, birth weight, ethnicity, mother's age and education at MCS 1, and country. Almost all the estimates in this and subsequent tables in this chapter are significant < 0.001.
PSU = primary sampling unit

majority of families either did not receive any income benefits at any one of the MCS interviews (52%) or received it at only one of the interviews (23%), two of the interviews (14% of families) or at all three interviews (10%). Our analyses showed that children growing up in families receiving income benefits had significantly lower cognitive ability scores than their more privileged peers. This was especially the case for those children living in families in receipt of income benefits at all three interviews, despite controls that included mother's age, education and ethnicity.

Second, we examine the role of parent psychological characteristics in moderating the influence of financial hardship on cognitive development (model 2, Table 14.1). An additional set of explanatory variables were included in this second model which might be regarded as protective factors arising from parental characteristics, the absence of psychological distress for the mother when the child was aged 9 months, a measure of mother's self-esteem at the same time and a measure of the quality of the parent–child relationship when the child was aged 3. The measure of mother's psychological distress was derived from questions based on a shortened version (nine items) of the malaise inventory (Dex and Joshi, 2004). The malaise inventory is a self-completion instrument, measuring depression, anxiety and psychosomatic illness (Rutter et al, 1970). The shortened scale has acceptable internal consistency (Cronbach's alpha = 0.73) for mothers, and correlates significantly with previously diagnosed and currently treated depression, which were also collected in the MCS interviews. Mother's self-esteem was measured, also in the first survey when the child was aged 9-10 months, using a revised version of the Rosenberg self-esteem scale comprising six items (Bachman and O'Malley, 1977) to assess how the mothers felt about themselves. The six items show satisfactory internal consistency (Cronbach's alpha= 0.79) and higher scores show more positive self-esteem. The quality of the parent–child relationship at age 3 was assessed using 15 items from the Pianta scale (Pianta, 1992) answered by the mother (for example, 'I share an affectionate, warm relationship with my child'; 'if upset, my child will seek comfort from me'; 'dealing with my child drains my energy'). Responses were summed, with a high score indicating a better relationship (Cronbach's alpha = 0.77). Except for the Pianta scale, describing the quality of the parent–child relationship, none of the assessments of psychological well-being were significantly associated with general cognitive ability of the child at age 5 years in addition and above the indicators of family financial hardship and the control variables included in the model. Nonetheless, the association between family financial hardship and child cognitive ability appears to have reduced slightly, suggesting that a warm and supportive parent–child relationship can buffer at least some of the negative effects associated with financial hardship.

Model 3 (Table 14.1) introduced further explanatory variables into the analysis, assessing their influence in addition to those of financial hardship and parental characteristics. This model included earlier developmental outcomes and indicators of delay in gross and fine motor development at age 9 months (Schoon et al, 2005), behavioural adjustment assessed with the SDQ at age 3, school readiness assessed at age 3 with the Bracken BSRA and the BAS naming vocabulary sub-test assessing expressive language development at age 3. Not surprisingly the results showed that earlier assessments of cognitive ability, such as school readiness and early language skills, were strongly and significantly associated with cognitive ability at age 5, in addition and above family financial hardship and parental characteristics. We can also see that a delay in gross and fine motor development, assessed at 9 months, is significantly associated with cognitive development later on. The influence of earlier behavioural adjustment, but not early pro-social behaviour, is significant after controlling for financial hardship, parental characteristics and the other indicators of early developmental adjustment, suggesting that early behaviour adjustment shapes cognitive development in addition and above the other variables included in the model. So, in terms of protective factors, it is only the virtuous circle of the child having displayed higher levels of school readiness, expressive language ability and better behaviour adjustment in the pre-school years that counters some of the effect of family hardship on children's age 5 cognitive scores. However, where family hardship is only short term (at one MCS survey only), the effect of more advanced cognitive development or better behaviour at age 3 substantially reduces its negative effect by age 5. The introduction of the age 3 development terms in model 3 for cognitive scores roughly halves the coefficients of income poverty. This suggests that there is a mixture of processes going on. Some of the variation in age 3 outcomes reflects the influence of financial hardship (and reduces the estimate of its direct impact), but some of it seems to be independent of income poverty, and may be thought of as reflecting an independent element of 'resilience' persisting from sweep to sweep and contributing positively to the explanation of variation in the outcome.

Predicting behavioural adjustment at age 5

We now investigate the predictors of children's behaviour at age 5. In the first instance we examine the influence of financial hardship on behaviour problems (model 1, Table 14.2). The results suggest that the association between financial hardship and behavioural adjustment is not as strong as it is with cognitive development. Nonetheless, the exposure to continuous financial hardship undermines positive behaviour adjustment, and parents of young children experiencing serious and persistent financial hardship were found to be more likely to report behaviour problems in their children.

Model 2 (Table 14.2) introduced additional explanatory variables, indicators of parental psychological well-being and the quality of the parent–child relationship, into the model. Adding these variables, in addition to those measuring financial hardship, reduced the size of association between financial hardship and behavioural development, the largest reduction occurring in the case of the association for persistent financial hardship and behavioural adjustment. The strongest statistical association from the additional variables is found for the indicator of a warm and

Table 14.2: Predicting behaviour problems at age 5

	Model 1			Model 2			Model 3		
	B	SE	t	B	SE	t	B	SE	t
Financial hardship at MCS 1, 2, 3									
Income benefits once	0.506**	0.110	4.58	0.315**	0.103	3.07	0.149	0.010	1.50
Income benefits twice	0.800**	0.130	6.15	0.510**	0.123	4.13	0.242**	0.116	2.08
Income benefits thrice	1.276**	0.175	7.28	0.755**	0.158	4.77	0.301**	0.147	2.04
Parental characteristics									
Malaise at MCS 1				0.235**	0.032	7.36	0.201**	0.031	6.54
Self-esteem at MCS 1				-0.091**	0.018	5.19	0.060**	0.015	3.90
Pianta at MCS 2				-0.192**	0.010	25.48	-0.100**	0.007	14.85
Earlier development outcomes									
Gross motor delay (9 months)							0.105	0.067	1.56
Fine motor delay (9 months)							0.024	0.069	0.35
Behaviour problems (age 3)							-0.337**	0.015	22.28
Bracken (age 3)							-0.013**	0.003	3.86
Vocabulary (age 3)							-0.013**	0.005	2.70
R^2	0.072			0.196			0.287		
Number of strata = 9 Number of PSUs = 398	Unweighted *n* values = 10,711			Unweighted *n* values = 10,711			Unweighted *n* values = 10,711		
Design *df* = 389 F-statistic	F (20,370) = 27.66 p <0.0001			F (23,367) = 72.17 p <0.0001			F (28,362) = 89.58 p <0.0001		

**p<0.05.

Notes: Analysis is weighted using sampling weights and non-response adjusted weights. Standard errors (SEs) are corrected for cluster sample design. All models are controlled for age and gender of the cohort child, birth weight, ethnicity, mother's age and education at MCS 1 and country,

supportive parent–child relationship, that is, scores on the Pianta scale. The next strongest predictors of children's behaviour at age 5 are those of the mother's psychological well–being and positive self-esteem. The findings suggest that these indicators of protective factors are moderating the influence of financial hardship on behavioural adjustment.

After including additional indicators to the model, i.e. those of early developmental (but not behavioural) adjustment (model 3, Table 14.2), the association between short-term financial hardship became insignificant, and intermediate and persistent financial hardship (that is, receipt of income benefits at two or all three interviews) fell to only border-line significance, being reduced considerably in size. In addition and beyond the significant influence of earlier developmental adjustment, mother's psychological well-being and positive self-esteem, and particularly a positive parent–child relationship have maintained a significant role in shaping behavioural adjustment of the 5-year-old child. Regarding the indicators of earlier developmental adjustment, we found a strong statistical association with earlier and current behaviour problems, and there was also a significant association between school readiness and early expressive language at age 3. These results point, therefore, to protective factors in the family environment being able to partly offset the negative effects of financial hardship on children's development at age 5. Also, that when earlier cognitive and behaviour adjustment are added in, as a virtuous circle, the effects of financial hardship can be more or less attenuated. However, the attenuation of the financial terms in model 3 for behaviour problems suggests that there might be other independent unmeasured protective or resilient elements embodied in early development terms.

Predicting pro-social behaviour at age 5

Lastly we examined the predictors of the measure of the child's pro-social behaviour at age 5 using a multivariate regression model. As before, measures of financial hardship as explanatory variables were entered first, along with controls (model 1, Table 14.3). The results show that only the experience of persistent financial hardship was associated negatively with the development of pro-social behaviour to any extent. Neither is the association as strong as with the other two, cognition and behaviour problems and developmental outcomes.

As a second step, measures of the mother's psychological well-being and the quality of the parent–child relationship were included as additional explanatory variables into the model (model 2, Table 14.3). The findings suggest that mothers' characteristics appear to fully moderate the association between persistent financial hardship and pro-social behaviour at age 5, as the statistical association became insignificant after mothers' characteristics were included. A strong influence on pro-social behaviour is displayed through the positive results for the quality of the parent–child relationship and mothers' self-esteem.

Model 3 adjusts for earlier developmental outcomes in addition to financial hardship and mother's characteristics (see Table 14.3). The results suggest that key predictors of enhanced pro-social behaviour at age 5 were earlier indication of pro-social behaviour, no early delays in fine and gross motor development, a warm and supportive parent–child relationship and positive mother's self-esteem. These variables appear to be vital in fully moderating the negative association between financial hardship and the child's psychosocial adjustment. Pro-social behaviour does show evidence, therefore, of being influenced by protective factors in the family environment, sufficient to eliminate the negative effects of financial hardship. However, pro-social behaviour appeared to be less negatively associated with financial hardship in the first place. Under these circumstances it makes less sense to seek evidence of resilience to financial hardship.

Table 14.3: Predicting pro-social behaviour at age 5

	Model 1			Model 2			Model 3		
	B	SE	t	B	SE	t	B	SE	t
Financial hardship at MCS 1, 2, 3									
Income benefits once	-0.007	0.047	0.16	0.041	0.046	0.90	0.037	0.043	0.86
Income benefits twice	-0.061	0.058	1.05	-0.002	0.056	0.04	0.020	0.053	0.37
Income benefits thrice	-0.160**	0.060	2.68	-0.037	0.059	0.63	-0.009	0.056	0.16
Parental characteristics									
Malaise at MCS 1				-0.003	0.011	0.31	0.004	0.010	0.44
Self-esteem at MCS 1				0.043**	0.008	5.32	0.032**	0.007	4.37
Pianta at MCS 2				0.058**	0.003	19.57	0.034**	0.003	11.27
Earlier development outcomes									
Gross motor delay (9 months)							-0.050**	0.026	1.92
Fine motor delay (9 months)							-0.123**	0.035	3.53
Pro-social behaviour (age 3)							0.302**	0.011	26.73
Bracken (age 3)							0.001	0.001	0.72
Vocabulary (age 3)							0.003	0.002	1.67
R^2	0.031			0.092			0.193		
Number of strata = 9 Number of PSUs = 398	Unweighted *n* values = 10,711			Unweighted *n* values = 10,711			Unweighted *n* values = 10,711		
Design *df* = 389 F-statistic	$F_{(20,370)} = 17.85$ $p < 0.0001$			$F_{(23,367)} = 41.29$ $p < 0.0001$			$F_{(28,362)} = 65.53$ $p < 0.0001$		

**$p < 0.05$.

Notes: Analysis is weighted using sampling weights and non-response adjusted weights. Standard errors (SEs) are corrected for cluster sample design. All models are controlled for age and gender of the cohort child, birth weight, ethnicity, mother's age and education at MCS 1, as well as by country.

Conclusions

The findings from the analyses of MCS children's development at age 5 suggest, as found in other studies, that persistent financial hardship undermines cognitive as well as behavioral adjustment of young children at this age, and is thus a significant risk factor for development. The negative impact of poverty appears to be strongest on children's cognitive development, although both behavioural development and the emergence of pro-social behaviour are negatively related. Children exposed to financial hardship at three interviews were most severely touched by its effects. The findings suggest that hardship has differential effects on specific child outcomes, with poverty exhibiting stronger effects on cognitive development than behavioural adjustment, confirming previous findings (Conger et al, 1994; Linver et al, 2002; Schoon et al, 2007). As a result, we need to know more about the configurations of associations among hardship indicators that are most salient for different individuals, and about variations in children's susceptibility to environmental influence. Our lack of understanding of *how* the experience of hardship influences child development across domains has hampered the ability of policy makers to design effective interventions to improve child well-being.

However, there is also evidence that protective factors in the family environment can moderate the negative effects of financial hardship in some of the measures and that virtuous circles of development can also help to protect children. A positive mother–child relationship plays a significant beneficial role for both cognitive and behavioural development in economically constrained conditions. The findings thus highlight the important role of parent–child interactions in promoting positive child development and assisting resilience in children who face financial adversity, a point noted in earlier studies, but found here to be operating at a very young age (Elder and Caspi, 1988; Conger et al, 1992; McLoyd, 1994). A mother's psychological well-being and positive self-esteem also appear to moderate the negative association of financial hardship with behavioural adjustment. However, mothers' characteristics were not significant in shaping cognitive development once income poverty and other control variables were included. It has to be kept in mind, however, that cognitive development appears to be most strongly affected by the exposure to financial hardship. It is also worth noting that the negative effects on children's development of single episodes of financial hardship appeared to be more easily offset by protective factors in the family environment, partly because the size of the negative effects were lower for single than for persistent episodes of financial hardship.

There are also interesting associations between earlier physical and cognitive developmental adjustment and outcomes at age 5. Cognitive development at 5, for example, appears to be significantly associated with expressive language ability and school readiness at age 3. A virtuous circle appears to operate where children start off well. However, a vicious circle also operates where children experience early delays in fine and gross motor development at age 9-10 months. These findings suggest that attention to delay in fine and gross motor development might be a crucial screening procedure for the promotion of later cognitive development. Delay in gross motor development is also a significant predictor of age 5 behavioural adjustment (in addition and over and above all other variables included in the model). Again, this finding highlights the importance of early screening for developmental delay at ages under 1 year, as a tool to promote positive child development. If there were some way of setting children off on a virtuous path, then that too would have benefits.

In interpreting the findings one has to keep in mind that further analysis should examine in more detail the interactions between the variables included in the model, and assess, more rigorously, the causal pathways linking financial hardship, parental well-being, and children's developmental adjustments over time. It might well be that there are reciprocal effects, that is, that the experience of poverty early in life influences children's developmental adjustment which in turn influences parent's mental health, their self-esteem and the quality of the parent–child relationship – and vice versa. In any case, the findings provide insights into the multidimensional influences on child development early in life, pointing to the need for any policy interventions aiming to promote positive development of children to provide support for both parents and children. Parents exposed to persistent poverty might themselves be affected negatively, their mental health and self-esteem being undermined by the experience of enduring hardship, which in turn could affect their parenting and interactions with the child.

Further, it can be seen from the three sets of models, as noted earlier, that although all models have significant estimates, the variance explained for each model are relatively low, ranging from 26% to 40%. Other factors such as family structure may also play some role in shaping children's early cognitive development and behaviour adjustment; for example, lone versus two-parent families, experience of separation or divorce (see Chapters 4, 5 and 10, this volume), number of siblings, parental relationship quality (see Chapter 4, this volume), social support, adverse life events for the parents, child abuse, teenage pregnancy, childhood neglect, parent ill health (see Chapter 15, this volume), experience of early education and day care (see Chapter 12, this volume) and children's physical well-being. There are multiple factors and processes enabling resilience in young children, not all of which have been measured explicitly here. In their analysis of earlier 1958 and 1970 cohort studies Feinstein (2003) and Schoon (2006) found that socially disadvantaged children who were initially displaying resilience had to struggle to maintain their relative position as they passed through the school years. Whether this will apply to the children of the millennium is something that can be traced in future surveys. Further investigations are required in order to explore the complex pathways and multiple influences shaping children's cognitive development and behaviour adjustment in the face of socioeconomic adversity.

Acknowledgements

The analysis and writing of this chapter were supported by grants from the Nuffield Foundation and the UK Economic and Social Research Council (ESRC): RES-225-25-2001 and RES-594-28-0001. Data from the Cohort Studies were supplied by the ESRC Data Archive. Those who carried out the original collection of the data bear no responsibility for its further analysis and interpretation.

FIFTEEN

Parental and child health

Yvonne Kelly and Melanie Bartley

Introduction

Healthy development in early childhood encompasses physical health, socioemotional behaviour and cognitive ability. Early to mid-childhood is a crucial time in the life course, with concurrent rapid development and transition into formal education. Markers of early childhood health and development have been found to be socially patterned, with children from advantaged backgrounds doing better compared with their disadvantaged peers. A range of environmental factors influences early childhood health and development, including the health of their parents, suggesting possible intergenerational transmission of health. However, little is known about the pathways via which the health of parents influences child health and developmental outcomes. This chapter examines the Millennium Cohort Study (MCS) for evidence on a number of alternate pathways for parents' health to influence children's health and development, assessing the contribution of parents' psychosocial and health-related behavioural factors to children's outcomes.

Existing literature

A large body of research has linked parental health-related behaviours to markers of child health and development including smoking, alcohol consumption (Jones et al, 1973; Kelly et al, 2008) and body mass index (BMI) (Owen et al, 2005; Sharma et al, 2005). Parental health reflects contemporary circumstances as well as the accumulation of lifetime influences. Parental health status, as opposed to health behaviours, is less frequently investigated, although the effects of parental illness is an obvious pathway for the transmission of risks in the close environment from adults to children.

There are also socioeconomic factors that affect early childhood health and development including household income, parental occupation and education, nutrition, environmental stimulation, parenting, family relationships, housing, social networks and residential area (McLoyd, 1998; Evans, 2004; Duncan and Magnuson, 2005; Grantham-McGregor et al, 2007; Irwin et al, 2007). The underlying pathways by which environmental factors influence child health and development vary according to the particular marker of child health and development under consideration. Social gradients are evident for markers of childhood health and development including obesity (Jotangia et al, 2005), illness and morbidity (Aber et al, 1997; Berntsson and Kohler, 2001; Chen et al, 2002; Spencer and Coe, 2003), socioemotional behaviour (Meltzer et al, 2000; Kelly et al, 2001) and cognitive test scores (Evans, 2004; Duncan and Magnuson, 2005; George et al, 2007; Jones and Schoon, 2008; also discussed in Chapters 9, 10, 12 and 14, this volume). The mechanisms behind these social health inequalities may be directly due to material living standards or run through self and social esteem, so-called 'psychosocial' pathways, as elaborated by Marmot and Wilkinson (2005) and their contributors. Also, understanding early child ill health is important for understanding later life (Spira and Fischel, 2005).

Pathways to child health

This chapter considers four possible pathways for parental health to influence child health and development:

1) Parental health-related behaviours affect both parents' and children's health (lines marked A on Figure 15.1).
2) Association between parents' and children's health is due to the repercussions of parents' psychological distress, on health and development of children: the 'psychosocial' pathway (B).
3) Socioeconomic background plays a role in explaining both parents' mental and physical health and thereby influences early childhood health and development (C).
4) Although both parental health and child outcomes are socially patterned, socioeconomic circumstances have a direct role in child health and development regardless of parental health, the psychosocial environment or behaviours (D).

Figure 15.1: Hypothesised pathways linking parental and child health

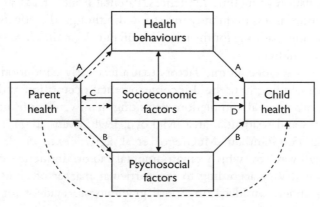

MCS data

We analysed data on cohort members who participated in the MCS 1 and 3 surveys. We considered four markers of early childhood health and development as dependent variables: parent-rated fair/poor health, limiting longstanding illness, children's socioemotional behaviour and childhood obesity.

Child's general health

During interviews the main respondent was asked to rate the child's general health and in particular, whether the cohort member had a longstanding illness that limited their activities.

Child's socioemotional health

We used an indicator of whether the child was displaying clinically relevant behavioural difficulties. When cohort members were around the age of 5 at the MCS 3 interview, the mother figure was asked to complete the Strengths and Difficulties Questionnaire (SDQ) (see Box 1.2, Chapter 1, this volume). Scores from the conduct problems, hyperactivity, emotional symptoms and peer problems sub-scales were summed to construct the total difficulties score, with a range of 0–40. The clinically relevant cut-point for problem behaviours (≥ 17) applied to the top 10% of all MCS children with SDQ data at age 5.

Childhood obesity

During home visits height and weight were measured in a standard manner. Obesity was defined using age and sex-specific cut-points as recommended by the International Obesity Taskforce (IOTF) (for more details see Chapter 13, this volume) (Cole et al, 2000).

Explanatory factors

The independent variables of parental health were available for both mother and father figures who were asked questions about their health at each survey. In this chapter we use answers from MCS 1 and 3 questions on general health (dichotomised as good/poor, including 'fair' with poor), and whether or not they had a limiting longstanding illness to construct a parental health score, as follows:

0 = general health was 'good' and no limiting longstanding illness
1 = general health was 'poor' and no limiting longstanding illness
2 = general health was 'good' and some limiting longstanding illness
3 = general health was 'poor' and some limiting longstanding illness

Only main and partner respondents with data for both MCS 1 and 3 were given a score. Scores for MCS 1 and 3 surveys were summed to give a score with a range of 0–6, and we constructed a three-category variable for use in the analysis: a score of 0 signified 'very good health'; scores of 1–3 signified 'average health'; and scores of 4 or more signified 'poor health'.

Other parental background measures that were hypothesised to confound or mediate the relationship between parental health and child outcomes were also examined: parents' health-related behaviour, psychosocial well-being and their socioeconomic position. Whether or not these factors confound or mediate relationships between parent and child outcomes is likely to depend on the particular marker of child health and development under consideration. Mediation means identifying a pathway through which a causal relationship works; confounding occurs when two factors are not themselves causally related, but have a common association with other factors that may be. For example, health behavioural factors might mediate the relationship between parental health and child obesity, while socioeconomic and psychosocial influences may confound the relationship. There is also the possibility of reverse causation from the child outcome to the variables used as predictors, such as child health affecting family income, both measured at age 5, which is not explored here.

Parental psychosocial markers were the current mental health of mother and father figure respondents from MCS 3 (Kessler et al, 2002). Parent health-related behavioural markers, all from MCS 3, were current parental smoking (Yes/No) and current alcohol consumption (Yes/No). In addition, we considered markers of the obesogenic environment: parental BMI at MCS 3, the child's patterns of eating at age 5 (eating fruit, regular meal times and skipping breakfast) and the level of the child's physical activity at age 5 (frequency of structured exercise, visits to the playground, computer and television use) in relation to child obesity. Of course the use of age 5 markers of the obesogenic environment limits the ability to make causal inferences on age 5 outcome measures, as observations are cross-sectional, and importantly, reverse causation may play a part in shaping features of the obesogenic environment, for example physical activity and eating habits.

The measures of socioeconomic background used were: the highest occupational group in the family when the child was age 9–10 months (MCS 1) (professional and managerial, intermediate, small employer and self-employed, supervisory, semi-routine and routine, never worked); highest educational qualification in the couple (from MCS 3: NVQ Levels 0-5, overseas, none); income poverty score from MCS 1 (net family income, equivalised on Organisation for Economic Co-operation and Development [OECD] scale greater than or equal to 60% of the national median household income, compared with income below this poverty line); and housing tenure at age 5 (owning, renting or other type of tenure).

Data analysis

We included all singleton infants who participated in MCS 1 and 3 surveys ($n=14,478$). Socioemotional outcome data on problem behaviour were available for up to 13,878 and obesity data for 14,242 cohort members. When we considered mother figure health scores, missing data for explanatory factors reduced the sample from 14,383 to 13,484 (93.7%) for socioemotional outcomes and for obesity to 11,401 (79.3%). For models considering partner respondent health scores, missing data for explanatory factors reduced the sample from 8,708 to 8,200 (94.2%) for socioemotional outcomes and for obesity to 8,000 (91.9%). Multivariate analyses are based on the cases with complete data on relevant variables using Stata version 9.2 (Stata Corporation, 2006). The Stata svy command was used throughout to take account of the clustered sample design and the unequal probability of being sampled.

For the investigation of children's socioemotional difficulties and obesity, logistic regression models were used. Model A adjusts for health-related behavioural markers; model B adjusts for a marker of the psychosocial environment; model C adjusts for socioeconomic factors; and model D simultaneously adjusts for all factors.

Findings

The proportion of mother figure respondents with very good health (score of 0) was 69%, with average health (score of 1–3) 23% and poor health (score of 4 or more) 7.9%. Father figure respondents were more likely to have very good health (72.7%), 20.9% had average health and 6.4% had poor health. It should be noted that some of the main respondents had no partners in the data, either because they were lone parents or because partners who were present did not respond.

Table 15.1 shows that parental health scores are socially patterned, for example 78% of mother figure respondents with an NVQ Level 5 qualification had very good health compared with 52% with no qualifications. Similar patterns were seen for occupations, poverty and housing tenure in both main and partner respondents. Of mother figure respondents who were current smokers, 58% had very good health compared with 74% of non-smokers, while 72% of mother figure respondents who currently drank had very good health compared with 59% who did not drink alcohol. Socioeconomically advantaged mother figure respondents and their partners (managerial and professional occupations) were over-represented among the group with very good health. Mother and father figure respondents with overall better health were more likely to be current drinkers and less likely to be current smokers compared with respondents in worse overall health (see Table 15.2).

Table 15.1: Distribution of parental health by socioeconomic, psychosocial and health behavioural factors

	Mother figure health score				*Father figure health score*			
	n	*Very good*	*Average*	*Poor*	n	*Very good*	*Average*	*Poor*
Parental socioeconomic measures								
MCS 1 Highest occupational classification in the household								
Managerial and professional	2,832	78.6	17.5	4.0	2,113	81.4	15.8	2.8
Intermediate	1,658	76.5	18.0	5.5	1,045	77.5	18.8	3.7
Small employer and self-employed	1,178	75.5	18.5	6.0	910	73.7	20.4	5.9
Low supervisory and technical	1,426	66.1	25.5	8.4	977	70.4	21.9	7.7
Semi-routine and routine	6,488	62.4	27.3	10.4	3,571	65.9	25.0	9.2
Refused/missing	801	59.1	29.8	11.2	92	57.1	24.5	18.5
MCS 1 Family poverty (OECD equivalence scales)								
Above 60% national median	8,899	73.8	20.4	5.8	6,608	76.0	19.2	4.8
Below 60% national median	4,331	57.6	29.4	13.0	1,490	56.9	28.5	14.6
Missing	1,153	67.4	25.2	7.5	610	68.1	24.5	7.4
MCS 3 Housing tenure								
Owns/mortgage	9,407	74.9	19.8	5.3	7,054	76.5	18.9	4.6
Rents	4,566	56.8	29.9	13.3	1,477	55.3	30.1	14.6
Other	399	65.9	26.6	7.6	156	63.2	25.8	11.0
MCS 3 Highest academic qualification in the household								
NVQ Level 5	1,958	77.8	18.9	3.3	1,482	79.2	17.2	3.6
NVQ Level 4	4,490	75.1	19.1	5.8	3,421	76.9	18.3	4.8
NVQ Level 3	2,311	68.3	23.3	8.4	1,463	72.2	22.1	5.8
NVQ Level 2	3,338	64.3	26.0	9.7	1,656	64.3	25.8	9.9
NVQ Level 1	766	58.9	30.9	10.2	240	58.6	29.5	11.9
Overseas	337	56.2	29.8	14.1	146	54.7	30.3	15.0
None	1,174	51.6	33.0	15.4	300	52.6	29.8	17.5
Parental psychosocial measure								
MCS 3 Kessler 6								
Normal	12,213	73.0	21.3	5.7	7,768	75.4	19.8	4.8
Possible depression	948	44.3	37.3	18.4	413	43.1	35.1	21.8
Highly likely to be depressed	497	26.2	37.6	36.3	180	31.3	36.2	32.5
Behavioural measures								
MCS 3 Parent smokes	4,099	58.2	29.6	12.2	2,415	61.1	27.4	11.5
MCS 3 Parent drinks alcohol	11,286	71.3	22.0	6.7	7,577	74.2	20.1	5.7

(continued)

Table 15.1: Distribution of parent health by socioeconomic, psychosocial and health behavioural factors *(continued)*

	Mother figure health score				Father figure health score			
	n	Very good	Average	Poor	n	Very good	Average	Poor
MCS 3 Parental BMI								
Underweight	305	59.9	27.8	12.3	71	63.2	32.7	4.1
Normal weight	6,547	75.0	19.1	5.9	2,880	76.0	18.6	5.4
Overweight	3,243	67.7	24.7	7.7	3,902	76.0	19.4	4.7
Obese	1,994	55.2	30.9	13.9	1,525	59.7	28.2	12.1
MCS 3 Mean activity score	14,374	2.5	2.7	2.9	8,687	2.4	2.6	2.8
MCS 3 Mean eating score	14,364	0.6	0.7	0.8	8,681	0.5	0.6	0.7

Table 15.2: Distribution of socioeconomic, psychosocial and health behavioural factors by parental health

	Mother figure health score			Father figure health score		
	Very good	Average	Poor	Very good	Average	Poor
	n=9,732	n=3,478	n=1,173	n=6,336	n=1,822	n=550
Socioeconomic measures						
MCS 1 Highest occupational classification in the family						
Managerial and professional	24.4	16.1	10.8	29.1	19.6	11.5
Intermediate	13.8	9.7	8.7	13.8	11.6	7.7
Small employer and self-employed	9.5	6.9	6.6	11.0	10.6	10.1
Low supervisory and technical	9.3	10.6	10.4	10.7	11.6	13.3
Semi-routine and routine	38.9	50.6	56.8	34.6	45.5	54.8
Refused/missing	4.0	6.0	6.7	0.7	1.1	2.7
Total %	100	100	100	100	100	100
MCS 1 Family poverty (OECD equivalence scales)						
Above 60% national median	70.3	57.8	48.5	82.7	72.8	7.3
Below 60% national median	22.6	34.3	44.6	11.4	19.9	59.4
Missing	7.1	7.9	7.0	5.9	7.4	33.3
Total %	100	100	100	100	100	100
MCS 3 Housing tenure						
Owns/mortgage	71.5	56.4	44.2	85.7	73.6	58.5
Rents	25.9	40.5	53.2	12.8	24.2	38.5
Other	2.6	3.1	2.6	1.5	2.2	3.1
Total %	100	100	100	100	100	100

(continued)

Table 15.2: Distribution of socioeconomic, psychosocial and health behavioural factors by parental health *(continued)*

	Mother figure health score			Father figure health score		
	Very good	*Average*	*Poor*	*Very good*	*Average*	*Poor*
	n=9,732	*n=3,478*	*n=1,173*	*n=6,336*	*n=1,822*	*n=550*
MCS 3 Highest parental academic qualification						
NVQ Level 5	15.3	11.1	5.8	18.3	13.8	9.6
NVQ Level 4	35.8	27.1	24.1	43.3	35.8	30.7
NVQ Level 3	15.5	15.7	16.7	16.3	17.3	14.8
NVQ Level 2	22.2	26.7	29.5	17.3	24.2	30.3
NVQ Level 1	4.4	6.9	6.7	2.0	3.6	4.7
Overseas	1.6	2.5	3.5	0.9	1.8	2.9
None	5.2	9.9	13.7	1.9	3.6	7.0
Parental psychosocial measure						
MCS 3 Kessler 6						
Normal	94.5	83.6	67.7	96.4	88.5	72.4
Possible depression	4.3	10.9	16.2	2.7	7.7	16.2
Highly likely to be depressed	1.3	5.5	16.1	0.9	3.8	11.4
Total %	100	100	100	100	100	100
Behavioural measures						
MCS 3 Smokes	23.6	35.6	43.6	22.8	35.5	48.6
MCS 3 Drinks alcohol	84.5	77.5	70.1	91.8	86.5	80.9
MCS 3 Parental BMI						
Underweight	2.2	3.1	4.0	0.6	1.1	0.5
Normal weight	59.8	46.8	42.2	35.7	30.6	29.5
Overweight	25.4	28.4	25.6	49.0	43.9	35.1
Obese	12.6	21.7	28.2	14.7	24.4	34.9
Total %	100	100	100	100	100	100
MCS 3 Mean child activity score	2.5	2.7	2.9	2.4	2.6	2.8
MCS 3 Mean child eating score	0.6	0.7	0.8	0.5	0.6	0.7

Child's general health

Poor parental health was related to the increased likelihood of the cohort child having fair/poor health and limiting longstanding illness at age 5. Fair/poor cohort child health was socially patterned with a two-and-a-half fold increase in likelihood for children in families where the highest occupation was semi-routine/routine compared with those in managerial/professional families. The likelihood of limiting longstanding illness appeared more weakly associated with socioeconomic markers (see Table 15.3).

Table 15.3: Markers of child health and development by parental health and explanatory factors

	SDQ	Child's BMI	General health	
	% total difficulties	% obese	% fair/ poor health	% limiting longstanding illness
Mother figure health score				
Very good	5.9	4.9	2.2	4.6
Average	13.1	7.0	6.1	7.2
Poor	20.5	7.3	12.6	12.4
Total *n*	13,862	14,165	14,382	14,376
Father figure health score				
Very good	5.1	4.3	2.5	4.5
Average	7.5	5.4	4.1	6.2
Poor	13.4	6.8	8.2	8.2
Total *n*	8,446	8,626	8,690	8,687
Socioeconomic background				
Managerial and professional	2.5	4.2	1.8	5.2
Intermediate	6.2	4.5	3.4	4.4
Small employer and self employed	4.5	4.4	2.8	4.6
Low supervisory and technical	7.7	5.6	4.2	5.6
Semi-routine and routine	12.6	6.3	5.1	6.5
Refused/missing	19.6	9.2	6.9	8.9
Total *n*	13,878	14,242	14,408	14,402
MCS 1 Family poverty (OECD equivalence scales)				
Above 60% indicator	9.5	5.9	2.8	4.9
Below 60% indicator	5.6	4.7	6.7	7.6
Missing	16.2	7.4	4.4	7.2
Total *n*	13,878	14,242	14,408	14,402
MCS 3 Housing tenure				
Owns/mortgage	5.0	4.8	2.9	5.0
Rents	16.4	7.0	6.2	7.5
Other	11.5	6.0	2.8	5.5
Total *n*	13,875	14,179	14,392	14,386
MCS 3 Highest academic qualification in the family				
NVQ Level 5	3.5	3.6	2.1	4.7
NVQ Level 4	4.6	4.4	2.7	5.0
NVQ Level 3	8.4	5.6	3.7	6.2
NVQ Level 2	11.1	6.7	5.5	6.4
NVQ Level 1	16.5	6.5	5.1	5.7
Overseas	19.8	13.3	7.1	10.7
None	23.8	7.6	7.1	7.9

(continued)

Table 15.3: Markers of child health and development by parental health and explanatory factors *(continued)*

	SDQ	Child's BMI	General health	
	% total difficulties	% obese	% fair/ poor health	% limiting longstanding illness
Total *n*	13,870	14,231	14,398	14,392
Psychosocial factor				
Mother figure MCS 3 Kessler 6 score				
Normal	6.2	5.4	3.3	5.4
Possible depression	22.8	5.7	6.1	7.3
Highly likely to be depressed	36.1	6.8	12.0	11.5
Total *n*	13510	13489	13672	13667
Father figure MCS 3 Kessler 6 score				
Normal	5.7	4.8	3.0	4.9
Possible depression	12.9	7.6	6.9	9.4
Highly likely to be depressed	14.9	4.8	5.7	5.5
Total *n*	9,365	9,468	9,533	9,529
Behavioural measures				
Mother figure MCS 3 smoking				
No	6.5	4.9	3.2	5.3
Yes	14.3	7.1	6.0	7.2
Total *n*	13,878	14,186	14,402	14,396
Father figure MCS 3 smoking				
No	4.7	4.4	3.0	5.0
Yes	10.9	6.5	4.6	5.8
Total *n*	9,705	9,926	10,000	9,996
Mother figure drinks alcohol				
Never	14.0	8.8	7.0	7.4
Yes	7.6	4.8	3.3	5.4
Total *n*	13,877	14,185	14,400	14,394
Father figure drinks alcohol				
Never	13.5	7.7	5.6	6.8
Yes	5.7	4.7	3.2	5.0
Total *n*	9,703	9,924	9,998	9,994
Mother figure MCS 3 BMI				
Underweight	12.0	1.9	4.0	7.6
Normal weight	6.9	3.2	3.5	5.2
Overweight	8.8	6.4	3.9	5.7
Obese	11.0	11.2	4.9	6.9
Total *n*	11,726	11,931	12,102	12,097

(continued)

Table 15.3: Markers of child health and development by parental health and explanatory factors *(continued)*

	SDQ	Child's BMI	General health	
	% total difficulties	% obese	% fair/ poor health	% limiting longstanding illness
Father figure MCS 3 BMI				
Underweight	11.5	0.6	3.8	8.1
Normal weight	7.3	3.1	3.4	5.1
Overweight	5.3	4.7	2.9	4.8
Obese	7.6	9.5	4.6	6.8
Total *n*	9,285	9,461	9,531	9,527
Child behaviours age 5				
Activity score				
0	5.0	3.7	1.2	4.5
1	5.9	4.5	2.4	5.3
2	7.0	5.2	3.7	5.9
3	9.2	6.3	4.0	5.6
4	13.7	6.1	5.8	6.6
5	11.8	5.9	6.3	6.6
Total *n*	13,871	14,179	14,399	14,393
Eating score				
0	5.6	4.7	3.0	5.6
1	9.5	5.9	4.0	5.2
2	20.2	8.6	8.2	9.3
3	33.8	6.3	11.7	12.8
Total *n*	13,863	14,170	14,385	14,379

Child's socioemotional health

The magnitude of association between parental health and the likelihood of clinical levels of behavioural difficulties appeared larger for the mother figure's health compared with the father figure's health (see Table 15.4). Children whose main carer had poor health were over four times more likely to have high behavioural difficulties scores than those with main carers in the best health group. The largest attenuation of the relationship between health of the main respondent and child SDQ score was seen on adjustment for the Kessler score, measuring the parents' psychological well-being. The largest attenuation in the relationship between the father figure's health and the child's SDQ score was seen on adjustment for parental socioeconomic background. Parental socioeconomic and psychosocial markers appeared to explain substantial portions of the association, and this is consistent with previous reports that indicate the importance of parental socioeconomic and psychosocial environments for a child's socioemotional health (Meltzer et al, 2000;

Table 15.4: Odds ratios (95% CI) for clinically relevant scores on SDQ total difficulties by parental health

	Unadjusted		Model A		Model B		Model C		Model D	
Mother figure health (n=13,484)										
Very good										
Average	2.40	[2.09 to 2.75]	2.11	[1.83 to 2.44]	1.95	[1.67 to 2.27]	1.86	[1.60 to 2.15]	1.56	[1.32 to 1.85]
Poor	4.12	[3.44 to 4.95]	3.28	[2.72 to 3.95]	2.42	[1.96 to 2.99]	2.73	[2.24 to 3.32]	1.77	[1.42 to 2.20]
Father figure health (n=8,200)										
Very good										
Average	1.51	[1.17 to 1.95]	1.28	[0.99 to 1.66]	1.41	[1.08 to 1.83]	1.13	[0.87 to 1.46]	1.02	[0.78 to 1.34]
Poor	2.87	[2.00 to 4.09]	2.14	[1.49 to 3.07]	2.28	[1.57 to 3.30]	1.69	[1.18 to 2.41]	1.39	[0.95 to 2.03]

Notes: Model A adjusts for health-related behaviours: current smoking and current drinking.

Model B adjusts for a psychosocial factor: Kessler 6 depression.

Model C adjusts for socioeconomic factors: NS-SEC, poverty, qualifications and home ownership.

Model D adjusts for current smoking, current drinking, Kessler 6, NS-SEC, poverty, qualifications and home ownership.

All variables are from MCS 3 except NS-SEC and poverty which are from MCS 1.

Kelly et al, 2001, 2008). The relationship between father figure respondent's health and the risk of the child displaying socioemotional difficulties was attenuated on adjustment for the full range of explanatory factors. The child's socioemotional health was heavily socially patterned with children from disadvantaged economic and psychosocial circumstances more likely to have difficulties compared with their advantaged counterparts (see Table 15.3).

A clear limitation of the data on children's socioemotional health is that they were only available from a parent's report and it has been shown that multi-informant measures are more reliable for clinical identification of problem behaviours (Goodman et al, 2000). Parents with poor mental health are more likely to report socioemotional problems in their children. Nevertheless, parent-reported data on a child's socioemotional health are widely used to indicate children most likely to have problem behaviours. Therefore, as shown here, estimates of association between environmental influences, such as parental health, on child socioemotional outcomes are more robust when account is taken of parental mental health.

There is replicated evidence that behavioural and social problems can be reliably and validly diagnosed in early childhood (Egger and Angold, 2006), and that the core construct is the same as for older children. Therefore, identifying behavioural problems in early childhood is important, and these measures have been shown to predict health and well-being into adolescence and adulthood (Spira and Fischel, 2005).

Child obesity

Poor parental health was related to increased likelihood of child obesity. Adjustment for health-related behaviours and markers of the obesogenic environment appeared to explain these relationships for both main and partner respondents (see Table 15.5), with mothers' BMI independently associated with the likelihood of obesity (data not shown). Obesity was also strongly patterned according to markers of the obesogenic environment, such as child's eating and physical activity indicators (the higher the scores the more negative the environment), as well as by parental socioeconomic background measures (Table 15.3). These results suggest that the 'obesogenic' environment and behaviours are the route through which parental health affects/mediates child obesity. An alternative explanation could be that the markers observed at age 5 might have been affected by the child's weight, with causation running in the other direction.

The rise in the prevalence of child overweight and obesity in recent decades in the UK and elsewhere (Lobstein et al, 2004) is a major public health concern. Child obesity tracks into adulthood and is associated with chronic disease risk (Parsons et al, 1999; Freedman et al, 2001). In simple terms, obesity is a consequence of an imbalance in (over)-nutrition and energy expenditure. However, the antecedents of nutritional intake and energy use are highly complex in nature, with influences

Table 15.5: Odds ratios (95% CI) for child obesity (not including overweight) by parental health

	Unadjusted		Model A		Model B		Model C		Model D	
Mother figure health (n=11,401)										
Very good										
Average	1.48	[1.22 to 1.79]	1.09	[0.87 to 1.37]	1.53	[1.25 to 1.86]	1.34	[1.10 to 1.62]	1.11	[0.88 to 1.40]
Poor	1.55	[1.17 to 2.05]	0.98	[0.73 to 1.32]	1.52	[1.12 to 2.06]	1.31	[0.99 to 1.74]	0.93	[0.67 to 1.29]
Father figure health (n=8,000)										
Very good										
Average	1.27	[0.99 to 1.64]	1.00	[0.76 to 1.30]	1.23	[0.94 to 1.61]	1.20	[0.93 to 1.5]	0.96	[0.73 to 1.27]
Poor	1.65	[1.07 to 2.56]	1.12	[0.71 to 1.76]	1.53	[1.00 to 2.33]	1.49	[0.98 to 2.27]	1.10	[0.72 to 1.68]

Notes: Model A adjusts for health-related behaviours: current smoking, current drinking, parent BMI, and child activity and eating habits.

Model B adjusts for a psychosocial factor: Kessler 6 depression.

Model C adjusts for socioeconomic factors: NS-SEC, poverty, qualifications and home ownership.

Model D adjusts for current smoking, current drinking, parent BMI, child activity and eating habits, Kessler 6, NS-SEC, poverty, qualifications and home ownership.

All variables are from MCS 3 except NS-SEC and poverty, which are from MCS 1.

working across generations, and throughout the life course, and these are sensitive to macro-level contexts (Parsons et al, 1999; Lobstein et al, 2004; Law et al, 2007).

There are many plausible points in the life course at which to intervene in order to tackle obesity and associated health risks. However, a recent review article points to the lack of success of individual level interventions aimed at reducing obesity (Lawlor and Chatuvedi, 2006). Given this, interventions that aim to reduce parent and child BMI through behaviour change programmes appear unlikely to succeed. Perhaps a more fruitful avenue will be the identification of broader environmental and societal influences that are amenable to change and effective policy developments, for example on transport infrastructure, safe outdoor spaces and the availability of affordable 'healthy' foods (Lobstein et al, 2004).

Child cognitive scores

Parental health was also associated with children's cognitive test scores to a similar order of magnitude for both main and partner respondents (results not shown). For example, children in families where mother or father figure respondents had poor health had naming vocabulary scores 3.7 and 3.5 points (around one third of a standard deviation) lower respectively compared with children living in families where main and partner respondents had very good health. Similar patterns were observed for test score differences on the British Ability Scales (BAS) pattern construction and picture similarities sub-scales, although absolute differences were smaller in magnitude compared with those seen for the naming vocabulary sub-scale, reflecting overall variation in these measures. Adjustment for health-related behaviours appeared to explain little of the relationship between parental health and child cognitive test scores, perhaps due to the opposing social distribution of these markers. Adjustment for socioeconomic markers appeared to explain the largest proportion of the relationship between both main and partner respondent health and children's cognitive test scores. Associations between main and partner respondent overall health and cognitive test scores were rendered statistically non-significant on adjustment for the full range of explanatory factors. However, all the estimates for the parents in the worst health category would still tend to be negative, despite having confidence limits that span zero.

Conclusions

Parental health is related to measures of early childhood health and development, but these relationships appear to have different underlying explanations. Family socioeconomic circumstances appear particularly important in explaining the link between parental health and poor cognitive and socioemotional outcomes. For children's socioemotional outcomes, in terms of problem behaviour, the parent's mental well-being (the 'psychosocial environment') is also important in understanding the links between the child's and parents' health. For obesity, parental health–related behaviours and markers of the obesogenic environment appear to account for the link with parental health.

So-called downstream policies and interventions aimed at the individual level appear fairly limited in terms of long-run impacts on health and development (Hunter, 2003). Our findings suggest that family socioeconomic circumstances and parental psychosocial factors are important in explaining the relationship between parental health and a child's socioemotional difficulties, and to a lesser extent the likelihood of childhood obesity. Also important for the risk of childhood obesity are features of the obesogenic environment that are themselves socially patterned, although the data do not allow for causal interpretation. Therefore, perhaps more promising in the longer term for parental health and child health and development are upstream policies aimed at tackling societal inequalities that shape the circumstances in which people live.

SIXTEEN

Conclusions

Heather Joshi, Kirstine Hansen and Shirley Dex

To round off this collection of contributions we pick out some themes that have emerged from the different aspects of the children's lives covered in the Millennium Cohort Study (MCS). We then draw together a few implications for the future.

The threads running through this volume and this study tell of diversity, mobility and intergenerational transmission. The diversity of the points from which the MCS children have started out on life include inequality in their family origins, while variation and inequality are beginning to emerge in the development paths of the children themselves. On mobility, the longitudinal data permits a view of the fluidity of the families' situation over the first five years in almost as many dimensions: family composition, poverty, parental employment, location and childcare. The study also provides an important building block to assess secular change in intergenerational social mobility, and detailed evidence on the various routes through which parents transmit well-being and also social advantage to their children.

Diversity and equality

Taking a view over five years, it may be surprising that so many families of these young children have been touched by inadequate income at some time. On one measure of income poverty available from the MCS data, 39% of MCS families and their children have been affected. If subjective accounts of financial stress are included, nearly two thirds have not had enough financial resources on at least one of the three MCS surveys. The MCS shows that low income goes along with a number of other indicators: workless lone parenthood, workless couples, low parental education, low social class in terms of occupations, social housing, disadvantaged neighbourhoods or poor parental health. These are all different facets of socioeconomic disadvantage, which also tend to be associated with poorer outcomes for children, as measured at ages 3 and 5, on learning and behaviour ratings. This is illustrated by the figures in Chapter 9 (this volume) and replicated in many other chapters of this volume.

Ethnic diversity can be thought of as another dimension of inequality. It has become an important feature of life in the UK. The MCS was designed to allow for this, by over-sampling areas with high minority ethnic populations, which has indeed resulted in sufficiently large samples of the more sizeable minority ethnic groups to analyse separately. Findings in this volume show that, to an important extent, belonging to one of these larger minority ethnic groups represents an economic disadvantage, although there is diversity across (and within) minority ethnic groups. It is shown in Chapter 10 that much of the generally poorer vocabulary scores for minority children (particularly Bangladeshi and Pakistani children), by age 5 are accounted for largely by measures of socioeconomic position. There remains an otherwise unexplained shortfall on vocabulary scores for black African and black Caribbean children at age 5, after allowing for the socioeconomic setting and various parental behaviours. In the parallel analysis of behaviour problems, there remained at age 5 particularly high rates of behaviour difficulties reported, by mothers, for Pakistani and black Caribbean children. Some reasons behind ethnic differences and their economic disadvantages may be found in this volume. Chapter 3 reports the varied histories of immigration behind each community, their settlement patterns within (mostly) urban England, access to family members, religious and cultural affiliations, other social capital and use of the English language. Chapter 5 examines ethnic patterns in family forms and Chapter 6 in parental employment. The experiences of racism reported by some minority ethnic mothers (especially black mothers) constitute a disadvantage in themselves while possibly limiting access to jobs, housing and services, also reinforcing economic disadvantage.

Other dimensions of inequality running through these pages include *gender* and *age*. Although no chapter is explicitly devoted to examining differences between girls and boys in the cohort, the variables collected do reflect emergent gender differences. For example, at age 5 girls are slightly more likely to be overweight, and to record internalising emotional problems, but they have higher cognitive scores on the British Ability Scales (BAS) and the Foundation Stage Profile (FSP) (even in mathematics, where they had not been ahead in the second generation children of the National Child Development Study birth cohort assessed in 1991). How far these differences will stabilise, converge or widen as the children go through school remains to be seen, as do the long-term consequences for gender roles and equality in adolescence and adulthood, when these beginnings will be instructive. The study also provides evidence of gender differences and inequalities among the parents. Very few of the MCS children not living with two parents are living with a lone father (72 out of 3,021 lone parents at MCS 3; Hansen, 2008, Table 18). Lone mothers of children at this age are mostly coping with parental responsibility by not having paid work and living on benefit. Mothers in couples are seldom the main breadwinner when their children are this age. Most MCS mothers reported being in part-time employment, while fathers worked full time and reported not having enough time with their child. Because we are aware of pressures on fathers' time, there was not as much data collected from MCS fathers as from MCS mothers and indeed there are not as many fathers responding to the survey. Yet fathers' testimonies can be found in, for example, their views on the quality of their relationship with the MCS child's mother in Chapter 4, and their reports of their own health, height, weight smoking and drinking in Chapter 15.

The child's age reflects another accident of birth with consequences for inequality. The study was designed to investigate the possibility that season of birth makes a difference to a child's progress, particularly in education. Although the main age 5 interview took place around the 5th birthday, the teacher assessments applied to the end of the child's first year of school, when the earlier, autumn-born children would (mostly) have been older, and the summer-born would have been youngest. The picture is more complicated in Scotland and Northern Ireland where the cohort spans more than one school year. The results of these teacher ratings by age in months clearly show an advantage on all the Foundation Stage Ratings (0.05–0.08 standard deviations per month) which would put the oldest child in an academic year between 0.6 and 1.0 standard deviations ahead of the youngest.

The parents' ages are other variables making an impact in the background of the analyses. Where they are in a couple, ages of mother and father tend to go together. There is particular interest in younger mothers who tend to be found in the less advantaged homes, and to have come from such homes themselves, to be least educated, have the lowest incomes, lowest labour force participation, highest benefit dependency and fewer partners at the outset (Chapters 2, 5 and 6). They have the most unstable partnerships over these years (Chapter 5) and most moves of home (Chapter 7) and least desirable neighbourhoods. None of this bodes well for the child, and at least calls for greater building of resilience (Chapter 14). There appears to be a developmental 'penalty' to having a mother who was young at first birth, which is mostly linked to her likely low educational attainments. However, there is some additional disadvantage to the child of being born to a mother who was under 25 at her first child that might be attributable to her immaturity per se (Hansen et al, 2009). These authors, using the MCS data, also show there is very little association of child outcomes with the mother's employment, once education is controlled. The finding that mother's employment does not feature prominently as a predictor of child development is replicated in this volume, once her education has been controlled. While there is abundant evidence of adversity associated with teenage motherhood, there is little research that marks out the oldest mothers as particularly different from those who had their first child around age 30. One exception is that mothers who were over 35 at their first birth are more likely to have a child who was overweight, but so also are those who were 20-24 (Chapter 13).

Mobility

Following families over time provides a moving picture, the strength of longitudinal studies. Transitions between geographical places of residence or different statuses illustrate the dynamics and continuities of family life, which need to be understood if policy interventions are to be effective. This volume shows that the child's first five years saw a move of home for around one in two of them, although often the move was not far and not to a very different sort of home. Although there was a small net improvement in surroundings, there were as many moves where the neighbourhood rating associated with the area deteriorated as where it improved. The same goes for moves in 'poverty space', with families falling below the poverty line matching in numbers those who rose above it, 'churning' the population with some experience of poverty. There was also rotation among the mothers who had paid jobs, and not unconnected, somewhat less speedy turnaround in the number of mothers who had partners. We also present some evidence of mobility within the children's own attributes between the two surveys where they have been assessed. There was some movement between the normal, overweight and obese categories of body mass, and changes in relative position on cognitive and behavioural scores, around strong continuities. Findings from earlier cohorts by Feinstein (2003) and Schoon (2006) are replicated in MCS. Children with high cognitive achievement growing up in low-status families tended to fall back as they aged; and the low achievers from high-status families tended to catch up, using two scales of social advantage (Chapter 9). However, it is too early to see if the delayed starters from advantaged homes actually overtake those with early promise from less promising backgrounds as they did by age 10 in the 1958 and 1970 cohorts.

The sort of mobility and immobility for which a longitudinal birth cohort study is especially well suited to record is the intergenerational continuity and discontinuity between parent and child that are commonly labelled 'social mobility'. A central chapter of this book (Chapter 9) offers an important piece of the jigsaw to answer the question about current trends in social fluidity and equality of opportunity. Although we cannot yet see how closely the MCS children's adult attainment will be correlated with their parents' attainment, a first step is to see how well children's cognitive (and softer skills) at age 5 are predicted by their parents' socioeconomic positions. In cohorts that have already reached adulthood, that attainment in the early years lays the foundation for attainments in adulthood. Chapter 9 looks at three sets of parents and children around age 5 in 1991, 2004 and 2006, using data from three cohorts. It demonstrates that the associations between parental income and both children's vocabulary and behaviour problem scores have remained stable across this period. They conclude that the Early Years element of social immobility has changed little for generations born since 1985. This is not the same thing as saying we expect no social mobility on the basis of scores at age 5. There is more variation between children that is not explained by any of the models in this volume than is explained, so we should expect individuals to be forging their own pathways around the main routes that will tend to be more systematically trodden. This raises questions about the impact of the post-1997 Labour government's attempts to reduce inequalities among children, to be discussed later.

Transmission

It is not self-evident why the children of richer parents do better. Is it because money buys better housing, neighbourhoods, garden space, food, clothing and other services, such as childcare? Or is it because of 'what parents do' (Ermisch, 2008), in terms of parenting practices? Are people who have more ability and education themselves and are more successful in the labour market also more successful at childrearing? On the other hand, is it possible that good parenting can overcome the disadvantages associated with low economic resources? The studies in this volume tend to answer yes to both questions. Breastfeeding, a good home learning environment, warm relations with the child, authoritative discipline and regular meals and bed times are among good practice that does not necessarily require high income, but that nevertheless seems to be facilitated by it. Equally, as the Good Childhood® Inquiry pointed out, lack of money is not the only source of misery among children, who can suffer, for example from family breakdown or the pressures on time in high income as well as low-income families (Layard and Dunn, 2009). There is some evidence on the former pathway in Chapters 4 and 5.

There is also an intergenerational continuity in the tendency for children who were obese by age 5 to have an obese parent (Chapter 15). This may partly be the result of genetic heredity, making the control of appetite more difficult for example, as noted in Wardle et al (2008). It could also reflect a shared 'obesogenic environment' of unsuitable food and low exercise, transmitting this particular trait, although the analyses in this volume are not able to identify causal impacts. Poor parental health, especially poor mental health, also tends to be reflected in lower development scores of children, although the pathway seems to be strongly associated with social deprivation and there may be reciprocal relationships involved (Chapter 15).

Parents are not alone in providing the resources and care needed by a growing child. The National Health Service officiated at virtually all of the births and provided healthcare for mothers and children, in principle regardless of family resources. A few families living in disadvantaged areas benefited from the early Sure Start. The evaluation of the Sure Start programme, of which the MCS was a part, found that there were some positive effects of this intervention on children by age 5 (Melhuish et al, 2008). Child Benefit offered a cash benefit to all mothers and the series of tax credits and means-tested benefits supplemented cash incomes to needier families. The early education system was also designed to break the link between family poverty and disadvantage in children. As we saw in Chapter 8, the National Childcare Strategy brought high-quality day care within reach of those disadvantaged families who did send their 3-year-old to a formal setting. However, formal early education was not then the near universal experience it was becoming (even when the MCS children reached age 4) and the general quality of the provision left room for improvement. Grandparents formed an important source of childcare at very early ages. Hansen and Hawkes (2009) report that the outcomes for children were mixed.

The purchase of private schooling is another way in which parents, who can afford it, invest in their child's future, although this is uncommon except in London. The right to choose a school within the state sector was intended to help raise standards for all through the beneficial stimulus of competition, but there has been concern that it may polarise educational opportunities between income groups. Chapter 11 presents evidence on parents' participation in choosing schools, but time will tell whether the outcome was a sorting of the socially advantaged into good schools, or indeed whether the existing sorting by neighbourhood has the same result.

Policy

The dilemma for public policy towards Early Years is how to help parents do their best in the private business of bringing up their own children while ensuring that 'every child' develops to full potential. Despite the unprecedented outlay on Early Years services which was beginning during this cohort's first five years, there are still strong socioeconomic patterns in the indicators of child development we have collected: poverty rates, high by international standards, and stagnation in the interim indicator of the Early Years stage of social mobility. Does this mean that the New Labour agenda to give every child a better start has failed? Is it too early to expect to see impacts from that on the millennium children who were the guinea pigs for the interventions? Or is it that these policies have been swimming against a tide of socially polarising forces? Perhaps these forces for increased inequalities were encouraged by the free rein given to market forces and a culture of 'excessive individualism' (Layard and Dunn, 2009). Since 2006, policies towards Early Years provisions have been consolidated (Chapter 8) and family–friendly employment continued to improve (Chapter 6), so children born a little later in the new century should have expected to see an even more favourable public policy context to their pre-school years. This would be expected to have some benefits for children of school age, which this cohort has become. However, the economic environment does not consist only of policies affecting services for children. The global economic downturn in 2008, just as fieldwork for MCS 4 was ending, will change the landscape considerably. Crevasses are appearing in what were expected to be smooth highways. Some parents will lose their jobs, and some their homes. The number of mothers with paid work, the government's intended route out of family poverty, is more likely to go down than up. There may be cuts to services like leisure facilities, if not expenditure on schools and health services. The 'Cinderella' services such as mental health have low prospects of expanding. Given the importance of employment in keeping income above the poverty line, it is likely to be all the more difficult for families to stay out of poverty. It is also likely that the recession will make it more difficult to turn the tide of economic inequalities. But it may, on the other hand, have a silver lining in so far as it enables parents and children to spend more time together in a way they can enjoy, although the uneven distribution in working hours across families may intensify.

Data collection since 2006 and record linkage

While the future course of policy, politics and the world economy remains somewhat speculative, the next steps for the MCS are well mapped out. Data were collected on 7-year-olds during 2008, from their parents, the children themselves and their teachers. The 7-year-old children did their own questionnaire about themselves as well as cognitive tests. For those who sat Key Stage 1 (in England) their first official educational assessments will be linked in. Administrative data on children's and parents' encounters with the health services and benefit system will also be attached to the survey records to widen the range of data available to researchers, while limiting the burden on our very helpful MCS respondents. After that, the next visit to the MCS families will be in 2012 when the children are 11. Schools as well as families will have had a chance to make their mark on the children's progress, in a way that may either compensate or consolidate the inequalities in endowment seen here from their homes. The children themselves will have consolidated their personalities and many of them will defy prediction.

As should be apparent from the contributions to this volume the scope for using the material already collected and that to come is very broad. We hope our readers have learned a lot about early years of life in the early years of the new century, and that some of them will be inspired to search further.

References

Aber, J.L., Bennett, N.G., Conley, D.C. and Li, J. (1997) 'The effects of poverty on child health and development', *Annual Review of Public Health*, vol 18, pp 463-83.

Acock, A.C. and Demo, D.H. (1994) *Family diversity and well-being*, Sage Library of Social Research (195), London: Sage Publications.

Adelman, L., Middleton, S. and Ashworth, K. (2003) *Britain's poorest children: Severe and persistent poverty and social exclusion*, London: Save the Children.

Allen, R. and Vignoles, A. (2007) 'What should an index of school segregation measure?', *Oxford Review of Education*, vol 33, no 4, pp 669-77.

Allen, R. and West, A. (2008) 'Religious schools in London: school admissions, religious composition and selectivity?', mimeo, London: Department of Quantitative Social Science, Institute of Education.

Andersson, G. (2002) 'Children's experience of family disruption and family formation: evidence from 16 FFS countries', *Demographic Research*, vol 7, no 7, pp 343-64.

Arenz, S., Ruckerl, R., Koletzko, B. and von Kries, R. (2004) 'Breastfeeding and childhood obesity a systematic review', *International Journal of Obesity*, vol 28 pp 1247-56.

Bachman J.G. and O'Malley, P.M. (1977) 'Self esteem in young men: a longitudinal analysis of the impact of educational and occupational attainment', *Journal of Personality and Social Psychology*, vol 35, pp 365-80.

Bartington, S., Griffiths, L.J., Tate, A.R., Dezateux, C. and the Millennium Cohort Study Child Health Group (2006) 'Are breastfeeding rates higher among mothers delivering in baby friendly accredited maternity units in the UK?', *International Journal of Epidemiology*, vol 35, no 5, pp 1178-86.

Belsky, J., Barnes, J. and Melhuish, E. (2007) *The National Evaluation of Sure Start: Does area-based early intervention work?*, Bristol: The Policy Press.

Berntsson, L.T. and Kohler, L. (2001) 'Long-term illness and psychosomatic complaints in children aged 2-17 years in the five Nordic countries. Comparison between 1984 and 1996', *European Journal of Public Health*, vol 11, pp 35-42.

Bhattacharyya, G., Ison, L. and Blair, M. (2003) *Minority ethnic attainment and participation in education and training: The evidence*, DfES Research Topic Paper RTP01-03, London: DfES.

Blanden, J. and Machin, S. (2008) 'Up and down the generational income ladder: past changes and future prospects', *National Institute Economic Review*, vol 205, pp 101-16.

Blanden, J., Gregg, P. and Macmillan, L. (2008) 'Accounting the intergenerational persistence: non-cognitive skills, ability and education', *Economic Journal*, vol 117, pp C43-C60.

Boheim, R. and Taylor, M. (2002) 'Tied down or room to move? Investigating the relationships between housing tenure, employment status and residential mobility in Britain', *Scottish Journal of Political Economy*, vol 49, pp 369-92.

Boyle, P.J., Kulu, H., Cooke, T.J., Gayle, V. and Mulder, C.H. (2008) 'Moving and union dissolution', *Demography*, vol 45, pp 209-22.

Bracken, B.A. (1998) *Bracken basic concept scale – Revised*, San Antonio, TX: The Psychological Corporation.

Bradley, R. and Corwyn, R. (2002) 'Socioeconomic status and child development', *Annual Review of Psychology*, vol 53, pp 371-99.

Bradley, S., Johnes, G. and Millington, J. (2001) 'The effect of competition on the efficiency of secondary schools in England', *European Journal of Operational Research*, vol 135, no 3, pp 545-68.

Bradshaw, J. and Finch, N. (2003) 'Overlaps in dimensions of poverty', *Journal of Social Policy*, vol 32, no 4, pp 513-25.

Bradshaw, J. and Holmes, J. (2008) *Family poverty assessed at three years old*, CLS Working Paper 2008/7, August, London: Centre for Longitudinal Studies, Institute of Education, University of London (www.cls.ioe.ac.uk/publications. asp?section=0001000100060009).

Bradshaw, J. and Richardson, D. (2009) 'An index of child wellbeing in Europe', *Child Indicators Research* (April) [for summary see www.cpag.org.uk/info/ ChildWellbeingandChildPoverty.pdf].

Bradshaw, J., Mayhew, E., Dex, S., Joshi, H. and Ward, K. (2005) 'Socioeconomic origins of parents and child poverty', in S. Dex and H. Joshi (eds) *Children of the 21st century: From birth to nine months*, Bristol: The Policy Press, pp 71-108.

Brewer, M., Clark, T. and Goodman, A. (2003) 'What really happened to child poverty in the UK under Labour's first term?', *Economic Journal*, vol 113, pp F240-F257.

Brody, G., Arian, I. and Fincham, F. (1997) 'Linking marital and child attributions to family processes and parent–child relationships', *Journal of Family Psychology*, vol 10, pp 408-21.

Buehler, C. and Gerard, J.M. (2002) 'Marital conflict, ineffective parenting, and children's and adolescents' maladjustment', *Journal of Marriage and Family*, vol 64, pp 78-92.

Buehler, C., Anthony, C., Krishnakumar, A., Stone, G., Gerard, J. and Pemberton, S. (1997) 'Interparental conflict and youth problem behaviours: a meta-analysis', *Journal of Child and Family Studies*, vol 6, no 2, pp 233-47.

Burchinal, M., Howes, C. and Kontos, S. (2002) 'Structural predictors of child-care quality in child-care homes', *Early Childhood Research Quarterly*, vol 17, pp 89-107.

Burchinal, M., Nelson, L., Carlson, M. and Brooks-Gunn, J. (2008) 'Neighbourhood characteristics and child care type quality', *Early Education and Development*, vol 19, no 5, pp 702-25.

Burgess, S. and Slater, H. (2006) *Using boundary changes to estimate the impact of school competition on test scores*, CMPO Discussion Paper 06/158, Bristol: CMPO, University of Bristol.

Burgess, S., Briggs, A., McConnell, B. and Slater, H. (2006) *School choice in England: Background facts*, CMPO Discussion Paper 06/159, Bristol: CMPO, University of Bristol.

Burgess, S., McConnell, P., Propper, C. and Wilson, D. (2004) *Sorting and choice in English secondary schools*, CMPO Working Paper Series No 04/111, Bristol: CMPO, University of Bristol.

Bynner, J. and Joshi, H. (2007) 'Building the evidence base from longitudinal data: the aims, content and achievements of the British Birth Cohort Studies', *Innovation: The European Journal of Social Science Research*, vol 20, pp 159-79.

Carneiro, P. and Heckman, J.J. (2003) *Human capital policy*, IZA Discussion Paper No 821, Bonn, Germany.

Carneiro, P. and Heckman, J.J. (2005) 'Human capital policy', in J.J. Heckman and A. Krueger (eds) *What role for human capital policies?*, Cambridge, MA: MIT Press.

Carroll, J. (2006) *Human cognitive abilities: A survey of factor-analytical studies*, New York, NY: Cambridge University Press.

Chen, E., Matthews, K.A. and Boyce, W.T. (2002) 'Socioeconomic differences in children's health: how and why do these relationships change with age?' *Psychological Bulletin*, vol 128, pp 295-329.

CLG (Communities and Local Government) (2007) *Indices of multiple deprivation, 2004* (www.communities.gov.uk/archived/general-content/communities/indicesofdeprivation/216309/).

Coldron, J. and Boulton, P. (1991) 'Happiness as a criterion of parental choice of school', *Journal of Education Policy*, vol 6, no 2, pp 169-78.

Cole, T.J., Bellizzi, M.C., Flegal, K.M. and Dietz, W.H. (2000) 'Establishing a standard definition for child overweight and obesity worldwide: international survey', *British Medical Journal*, vol 320, pp 1240-3.

Coleman, J.S. (1988) 'Social capital in the creation of human capital', *American Journal of Sociology*, vol 94, pp S94-S120.

Coleman, J.S. (1994) *Foundations of social theory*, Cambridge, MA: Belknap Press.

Coleman, M., Ganong, L. and Fine, M. (2000) 'Reinvestigating remarriage: another decade of progress', *Journal of Marriage and the Family*, vol 62, no 4, pp 1288-307.

Conger, R.D., Ge, X., Elder, G.H., Lorenz, F. and Simons, R.L. (1994) 'Economic stress, coercive family process, and developmental problems of adolescents', *Child Development*, vol 65, pp 541-61.

Conger, R.D., Conger, K.J., Elder, G.H., Lorenz, F.O., Simons, R.L. and Whitbeck, L.B. (1992) 'A family process model of economic hardship and adjustment of early adolescent boys', *Child Development*, vol 63, no 3, pp 526-41.

Cullis, A. (2008) 'Neighbourhood and well being in the earlier years', PhD thesis, Institute of Education, University of London.

Dale, A., Shaheen, N., Kalra, V. and Fieldhouse, E. (2002) 'Routes into education and employment for young Pakistani and Bangladeshi women in the UK', *Ethnic and Racial Studies*, vol 25, no 6, pp 942-68.

Dale, A., Lindley, J. and Dex, S. (2008) 'Ethnic differences in women's employment', in J. Scott, S. Dex and H. Joshi (eds) *Changing patterns of women's employment over 25 years*, Cheltenham: Edward Elgar, pp 81-106.

Dearden, L., Mesnard, A. and Shaw, J. (2006) 'Ethnic differences in birth outcomes in England', *Fiscal Studies*, vol 27, no 1, pp 17-46.

Dearden, L., Sibieta, L. and Sylva, K. (2010) *The socio-economic gradient in early childhood outcomes: Evidence from the UK*, IFS Working Paper, London: Institute for Fiscal Studies.

DCSF (2007) *The Children's Plan* (www.dcsf.gov.uk/publications/childrensplan/).

DCSF (2008) *Early Years Foundation Stage*, Research Report, Nottingham: DCSF Publications.

Dex, S. (1984) *Women's work histories: An analysis of the Women and Employment Survey*, Department of Employment Research Paper No 46, London: Department of Employment.

Dex, S. (2003) *Families and work in the twenty-first century*, Bristol and York: The Policy Press and Joseph Rowntree Foundation.

Dex, S. (ed) (2007) *Millennium Cohort Study – A user guide focusing on families in Scotland*, Edinburgh: Scottish Government.

Dex, S. and Joshi, H. (eds) (2004) *Millennium Cohort Study first survey: A user's guide to initial findings*, London: Centre for Longitudinal Studies, Institute of Education, University of London.

Dex, S. and Joshi, H. (eds) (2005) *Children of the 21st century: From birth to nine months*, Bristol: The Policy Press.

Dex, S. and Smith, C. (2002) *The nature and patterns of family-friendly employment policies in Britain*, Bristol and York: The Policy Press and Joseph Rowntree Foundation.

Dex, S. and Ward, K. (2004) 'Childcare', in S. Dex and H. Joshi (eds) *Millennium Cohort Study first survey: A user's guide to initial findings*, London: Centre for Longitudinal Studies, Institute of Education, University of London, pp 219-226 (www.cls.ioe.ac.uk/studies.asp?section=0001000200010005).

Dex, S. and Ward, K. (2007) *Parental care and employment in early childhood: Analysis of the Millennium Cohort Study (MCS) sweeps 1 and 2*, Research Series, Manchester: Equal Opportunities Commission.

DfEE (Department for Education and Employment)/QCA (Qualifications and Curriculum Authority) (1998) *Meeting the childcare challenge*, London: DfEE.

DfEE/QCA (2000) *Curriculum guidance for the Foundation Stage*, London: QCA.

DfES/Sure Start (2003) *Birth to three matters: An introduction to the framework*, London: The Stationery Office.

DH (Department of Health) (1994) *Weaning and weaning diet*, Report on Health and Social Subjects No 45, London: HMSO.

DH (2004) *At least five a week: Evidence on the impact of physical activity and its relationship to health*, A report from the Chief Medical Officer, London: The Stationery Office.

DH (2006) 'School fruit and vegetable scheme' (www.5aday.nhs.uk/sfvs/default.aspx).

Donnison, D. and Ungerson, C. (1982) *Housing policy* (*The government of housing*, revised), London: Penguin.

Dorsett, R., Campbell-Barr, V., Hamilton, G., Hoggart, L., Marsh, A., Miller, C., Phillips, J., Ray, K., Riccio, J.A., Rich, S. and Vegeris, S. (2007) *Implementation and first-year impacts in the UK employment retention and advancement (ERA) demonstration*, Research Report No 412, Sheffield: Department for Work and Pensions.

Downey, G. and Coyne, J.C. (1990) 'Children of depressed parents: an integrative review', *Psychological Bulletin*, vol 108, no 1, pp 50-76.

Dubois, L. and Girard, M. (2006) 'Early determinants of overweight at 4.5 years in a population-based longitudinal study', *International Journal of Obesity*, vol 30, pp 610-17.

Duncan, G.J. and Brooks-Gunn, J. (1997) *Consequences of growing up poor*, New York, NY: Russell Sage Foundation Press.

Duncan, G.J. and Magnuson, K.A. (2005) 'Can family socioeconomic resources account for racial and ethnic test score gaps?', *The Future of Children*, vol 15, pp 35-54.

Dunn, J., Deater-Deckard, K., Pickering, K., O'Connor, T.G. and Golding, J. (1998) 'Children's adjustment and prosocial behaviour in step-, single-parent, and non-stepfamily settings: findings from a community study', *Journal of Child Psychology and Psychiatry*, vol 39, no 8, pp 1083-95.

Dunteman, G.H. (1989) *Principal components analysis* (Quantitative Applications in the Social Sciences series, Volume No 69), Thousand Oaks, CA: Sage Publications.

DWP (Department for Work and Pensions) (2003) *Measuring child poverty*, London: DWP.

DWP (2006) *Households Below Average Incomes 1994/95–2004/05*, London: The Stationery Office.

DWP (2008) *Households Below Average Incomes 1994/95–2006/07*, London: The Stationery Office.

DWP (2009) *Households Below Average Incomes 1994/95–2007/08*, London: The Stationery Office.

Dwyer, C., Modood, T., Sanghera, G., Shah, B. and Thapar-Bjorket, S. (2006) 'Ethnicity as social capital? Explaining the differential educational achievements of young British Pakistani men and women', Paper presented at the 'Ethnicity, Mobility and Society' Leverhulme Programme Conference, Bristol: University of Bristol.

Egger, H.L. and Angold, A. (2006) 'Common emotional and behavioral disorders in preschool children: presentation, nosology, and epidemiology', *Journal of Child Psychology and Psychiatry*, vol 47, pp 313-37.

Elder, G.H. and Caspi, A. (1988) 'Economic stress in lives – developmental perspectives', *Journal of Social Issues*, vol 44, no 4, pp 25-45.

Elliott, C.D. (1996) *The British Ability Scales II*, Windsor: nferNelson Publishing Company.

Elliott, C.D., Smith, P. and McCulloch, K. (1996) *British Ability Scales second edition (BAS II): Administration and scoring manual*, London: nferNelson.

Engle, P.L. and Black, M.M. (2008) 'The effect of poverty on child development and educational outcomes', *Annals of New York Academy of Sciences*, vol 1136, no 1, pp 243-56.

Erel, O. and Burman, B. (1995) 'Interrelatedness of marital relations and parent–child relations: a meta–analytic review', *Psychological Bulletin*, vol 118, pp 108-32.

Ermisch, J. (2008) 'Origins of social immobility and inequality: parenting and early child development', *National Institute Economic Review*, vol 205, pp 62-71.

Essen, J. and Wedge, P. (1978) *Continuities in disadvantage*, London: Heinemann.

Evans, G.W. (2004) 'The environment of childhood poverty', *American Psychologist*, vol 59, pp 77-92.

Feinstein, L. (2003) 'Inequality in the early cognitive development of British children in the 1970 cohort', *Economica*, vol 70, no 277, pp 73-98.

Feinstein, L. (2004) 'Mobility in pupils' cognitive attainment during school life', *Oxford Review of Economic Policy*, vol 20, no 2, pp 213-29.

Feinstein, L. and Duckworth, K. (2006) *Development in the early years: Its importance for school performance and adult outcomes*, Wider Benefits of Learning Report No 20, London: Centre for Research on the Wider Benefits of Learning, Institute of Education.

Feinstein, L., Lupton, R., Hammond, C., Mujtaba, T., Salter, E. and Sorhaindo, A. (2008) *The public value of social housing: A longitudinal analysis of the relationship between housing and life chances*, London: The Smith Institute.

Freedman, D.S., Kettel, K.L., Serdula, M., Srinivasan, S. and Berenson, G. (2001) 'BMI rebound, childhood height and obesity among adults: the Bogalusa Heart Study', *International Journal of Obesity*, vol 25, pp 543-9.

George, A., Hansen, K. and Schoon, I. (2007) 'Child behaviour and cognitive development', in K. Hansen and H. Joshi (eds) *Millennium Cohort Study second survey: A user's guide to initial findings*, London: Centre for Longitudinal Studies, Institute of Education, University of London, pp 94-109.

Gerard, J.M., Krishnakumar, A. and Buehler, C. (2006) 'Marital conflict, parent–child relations, and youth maladjustment: a longitudinal investigation of spillover effects', *Journal of Family Issues*, vol 27, no 7, pp 951-75.

Gewirtz, S., Ball, S.J. and Bowe, R. (1995) *Markets, choice and equity in education*, Buckingham: Open University Press.

Gibbons, S. and Machin, S. (2006) 'Paying for primary schools: supply constraints, popularity or congestion', *The Economic Journal*, vol 116, pp 77-92.

Gibbons, S., Silva, O. and Wilson, J. (2006) *Urban density and pupil attainment*, Discussion Paper, London: Centre for the Economics of Education.

Gibson, M. (2000) 'Situational and structural rationales for the school performance of immigrant youth: three cases', in H. Vermeulen and J. Perlmann (eds) *Immigrants, schooling and social mobility*, London: Macmillan, pp 72-102.

Gonzales, N.A., Pitts, S.C., Hill, N.E. and Roosa, M.W. (2000) 'A mediational model of the impact of interparental conflict on child adjustment in a multiethnic, low-income sample', *Journal of Family Psychology*, vol 14, pp 365-79.

Goodman, R. (1997) 'The Strengths and Difficulties Questionnaire: a research note', *Journal of Child Psychology and Psychiatry*, vol 38, no 5, pp 581-6.

Goodman, R. (2001) 'Psychometric properties of the Strengths and Difficulties Questionnaire', *Journal of the American Academy of Adolescent Psychiatry*, vol 40, pp 1337-45.

Goodman, R., Meltzer, H. and Bailey, V. (1998) 'The Strengths and Difficulties Questionnaire: a pilot study on the validity of the self-report version', *European Child and Adolescent Psychiatry*, vol 7, pp 125-30.

Goodman, R., Ford, T., Simmons, H., Gatward, R. and Meltzer, H. (2000) 'Using the Strengths and Difficulties Questionnaire (SDQ) to screen for child psychiatric disorders in a community sample', *British Journal of Psychiatry*, vol 177, pp 534-9.

Gordon, D., Adelman, L., Ashworth, K., Bradshaw, J., Levitas, R., Middleton, S., Pantazis, C., Patsios, D., Payne, S., Townsend, P. and Williams, J. (2000) *Poverty and social exclusion in Britain*, York: Joseph Rowntree Foundation.

Government Office for Science (2007) *Foresight tackling obesities: Future choices – Project report*, London: Government Office for Science.

Granovetter, M. (1973) 'The strength of weak ties', *American Journal of Sociology*, vol 78, no 6, pp 1360-80.

Grantham-McGregor, S., Cheung, Y.B., Cueto, S., Glewwe, P., Richter, L. and Strupp, B. (2007) 'Developmental potential in the first 5 years for children in developing countries', *The Lancet*, vol 369, pp 60-70.

Griffiths, L.J., Dezateux, C., Cole, T.J. and the Millennium Cohort Study Child Health Group (2007b) 'Differential parental weight and height contributions to offspring birthweight and weight gain in infancy', *International Journal of Epidemiology*, vol 36, no 1, pp 104-7.

Griffiths, L.J., Tate, A.R., Dezateux, C. and the Millennium Cohort Study Child Health Group (2005) 'The contribution of parental and community ethnicity to breastfeeding practices: evidence from the Millennium Cohort Study', *International Journal of Epidemiology*, vol 34, no 6, pp 1378-86.

Griffiths, L.J., Tate, A.R., Dezateux, C. and the Millennium Cohort Study Child Health Group (2007a) 'Do early infant feeding practices vary by maternal ethnic group?', *Public Health Nutrition*, vol 10, pp 957-64.

Hagenaars, A., de Vos, K. and Zaidi, M.A. (1994) *Poverty statistics in the late 1980s: Research based on micro-data*, Luxembourg: Office for Official Publications of the European Communities.

Hakim, C. (2000) *Work–lifestyle choices in the 21st century: Preference theory*, Oxford: Oxford University Press.

Halpern, D. (2005) *Social capital*, Cambridge: Polity Press.

Hansen, K. (ed) (2008) *Millennium Cohort Study: First, second and third surveys – A guide to the datasets* (3rd edn), London: Centre for Longitudinal Studies, Institute of Education, University of London (www.cls.ioe.ac.uk/text.asp?section=000100200010015).

Hansen, K. and Hawkes, D. (2009) 'Early childcare and child development', *Journal of Social Policy*, vol 38, no 2, pp 211-40.

Hansen, K. and Joshi, H. (eds) (2007) *Millennium Cohort Study second survey: A user's guide to initial findings*, London: Centre for Longitudinal Studies, Institute of Education, University of London.

Hansen, K. and Joshi, H. (2008) *Millennium Cohort Study third survey: A user's guide to initial findings*, London: Centre for Longitudinal Studies, Institute of Education, University of London (www.cls.ioe.ac.uk/studies.asp?section=0001000200010012).

Hansen, K., Hawkes, D. and Joshi, H. (2009) 'The timing of motherhood, mother's employment and child outcomes', in J. Stillwell, E. Coast and D. Kneale (eds) *Fertility, living arrangements, care and mobility: Understanding population trends and processes – Volume 1*, Dordrect, Heidelberg, London and New York: Springer, pp 59-80.

Hansen, K., Joshi, H. and Verropoulou, G. (2006) 'Childcare and mothers' employment: approaching the millennium', *National Institute Economic Review*, vol 195, pp 84-99.

Harder, T., Bergmann, R., Kallischnigg, G. and Plagemann, A. (2005) 'Duration of breastfeeding and risk of overweight: a meta-analysis', *American Journal of Epidemiology*, vol 162, pp 397-403.

Harms, T., Clifford, M. and Cryer, D. (1998) *Early Childhood Environment Rating Scale (ECERS-R)* (revised edn), Vermont, VT: Teachers College Press.

Hastings, J.S., Kane, T.J. and Steiger, D.O. (2005) *Parental preferences and school competition: Evidence from a public school choice program*, NBER Working Paper 11805, Cambridge, MA: National Bureau of Economic Research.

Hawkins, S.S. and Law, C. (2006) 'A review of risk factors for overweight in preschool children: a policy perspective', *International Journal of Pediatric Obesity*, vol 1, pp 195-209.

Hawkins, S.S., Griffiths, L.J., Dezateux, C., Law, C. and the Millennium Cohort Study Child Health Group (2007) 'The impact of maternal employment on breast-feeding duration in the UK Millennium Cohort Study', *Public Health Nutrition*, vol 10, no 9, pp 891-6.

Hawkins, S.S., Cole, T.J., Law, C. and the Millennium Cohort Study Child Health Group (2008) 'An ecological systems approach to examining risk factors for early childhood overweight: findings from the UK Millennium Cohort Study', *Journal of Epidemiology and Community Health* [published online 18 September 2008, doi: 10.1136/jech.2008.077917].

Heckman, J.J., Stixrud, J. and Urzua, S. (2006) 'The effects of cognitive and noncognitive abilities on labor market outcomes and social behavior', *Journal of Labor Economics*, vol 24, pp 411-82.

Heikkila, M., Moisio, P., Ritakallio, V.M., Bradshaw, J., Kuivalainen, S., Hellsten, K. and Kajoja, J. (2006) *Poverty policies, structures and outcomes in the EU 2: Report to the Fifth European Round Table on Poverty and Social Exclusion*, Helsinki: Stakes (www.stm.fi/Resource.phx/eng/subjt/inter/eu2006/round/round1.htx.i1153. pdf).

Heinen, T. (1996) *Latent class and discrete latent trait models: Similarities and differences*, London: Sage Publications.

Hill, V. (2005) 'Through the past darkly: a review of the British Ability Scales second edition', *Child and Adolescent Mental Health*, vol 10, pp 87-98.

Hills, J. (2007) *Ends and means: The future roles of social housing in England*, CASEreport 34, London: London School of Economics and Political Science.

HM Government (2007) *PSA delivery agreement 12: Improve the health and wellbeing of children and young people*, London: The Stationery Office.

HM Treasury (2003) *Every Child Matters*, Cm 5860, London: The Stationery Office.

HM Treasury (2004) *Choice for parents, the best start for children: A ten-year strategy for childcare* (www.hm-treasury.gov.uk/d/pbr04childcare_480upd050105.pdf).

Hogarth, T., Hasluck, C., Pierre, G., Winterbotham, M. and Vivian, D. (2000) *Work–life balance 2000: Baseline study of work–life balance practices in Great Britain*, Warwick: Institute for Employment Research, University of Warwick.

Hoxby, C. (2000) 'Does competition among public schools benefit students and taxpayers?', *American Economic Review*, vol 90, no 5, pp 1209-38.

Hills, J. (2007) *Ends and means: The future roles of social housing in England*, CASE report 34 (http://sticerd.lse.ac.uk/dps/casc/cr/CASEreport34.pdf).

Hughes, G., Ketende, S. and Plewis, I. (2007) 'Housing, neighbourhood and community', in K. Hansen and H. Joshi (eds) *Millennium Cohort Study second survey – A user's guide to initial findings*, London: Centre Longitudinal Studies, Institute of Education, University of London, Chapter 2 (www.cls.ioe.ac.uk/studies.asp?section=0001000200010004).

Hunter, D.J. (2003) *Public health policy*, Cambridge: Polity Press.

Irwin, L.G., Siddiqi, A. and Hertzman, C. (2007) *Early child development: A powerful equalizer*, Washington, DC: World Health Organization.

Jackson-Leach, R. and Lobstein, T. (2006) 'Estimated burden of paediatric obesity and co-morbidities in Europe. Part 1. The increase in the prevalence of child obesity in Europe is itself increasing', *International Journal of Pediatric Obesity*, vol 1, no 1, pp 26-32.

Jenkins, S.P. (2008) *Marital splits and income changes over the longer term*, ISER Working Paper, Colchester: Institute for Social and Economic Research, University of Essex.

Jenks, C. (2001) 'Zeitgeist research on childhood', in P.M. Christiansen and A. James (eds) *Research with children: Perspectives and practice*, London: Routledge, pp 62-76.

Jones, E.M. (2008) 'Childcare', in K. Hansen and H. Joshi (eds) *The Millennium Cohort Study third survey: A user's guide to initial findings*, London: Centre for Longitudinal Studies, Institute of Education, University of London, pp 76-87.

Jones, E.M. and Schoon, I. (2008) 'Child behaviour and cognitive development', in K. Hansen and H. Joshi (eds) *Millennium Cohort Study third survey: A user's guide to initial findings*, London: Centre for Longitudinal Studies, Institute of Education, University of London, pp 118-44.

Jones, K.L., Smith, D.W., Ulleland, C.N. and Streissguth, A.P. (1973) 'Pattern of malformation in offspring of chronic alcoholic mothers', *The Lancet*, vol 301, pp 1267-71.

Joshi, H., Dodgeon, B. and Hughes, G. (2008) *A profile of population change in rural England*, CLS Working Paper 2008/4, London: Centre for Longitudinal Studies, Institute of Education, University of London.

Jotangia, D., Moody, A., Stamatakis, E. and Wardle, H. (2005) *Obesity among children under 11*, London: Department of Health.

Karney, B.R. and Bradbury, T.N. (1995) 'The longitudinal course of marital quality and stability: a review of theory, method, and research', *Psychological Bulletin*, vol 118, no 1, pp 3-34.

Kawachi, I., Kennedy, B.P. and Glass, R. (1999) 'Social capital and self-rated health: a contextual analysis', *American Journal of Public Health*, vol 8, pp 1187-93.

Kelly, Y.J., Nazroo, J.Y., McMunn, A., Boreham, R. and Marmot, M. (2001) 'Birthweight and behavioural problems in children: a modifiable effect?', *International Journal of Epidemiology*, vol 30, pp 88-94.

Kelly, Y.J., Sacker, A., Gray, R., Kelly, J., Wolke, D. and Quigley, M.A. (2008) 'Light drinking in pregnancy, a risk for behavioural problems and cognitive deficits at 3 years of age?', *International Journal of Epidemiology* [doi:10.1093/ije/dyn230].

Kessler, R.C., Andrews, G., Colpe, L.J., Hiripi, E., Mroczek, D.K., Normand, S.L., Walters, E.E. and Zaslavsky, A.M. (2002) 'Short screening scales to monitor population prevalences and trends in non-specific psychological distress', *Psychological Medicine*, vol 32, no 6, pp 959-76.

Kessler, R.C., Barker, P.R., Colpe, L.J., Epstein, J.F., Gfroerer, J.C., Hiripi, E., Howes, M.J., Normand, S.L., Manderscheid, R.W., Walters, E.E. and Zaslavsky, A.M. (2003) 'Screening for serious mental illness in the general population', *Archives of General Psychiatry*, vol 60, no 2, pp 184-9.

Ketende, S.C. (ed) (2008) *Millennium Cohort Study: Technical report on response* (2nd edn), London: Centre for Longitudinal Studies, Institute of Education, University of London (www.cls.ioe.ac.uk/studies.asp?section=00010002000100110004).

Ketende, S.C. and Joshi, H. (2008) 'Income and poverty', in K. Hansen and H. Joshi (eds) *Millennium Cohort Study third survey: A user's guide to initial findings*, London: Centre for Longitudinal Studies, Institute of Education, University of London, pp 234–58 (www.cls.ioe.ac.uk/studies.asp?section= 0001000200010011).

Ketende, S.C. and McDonald, J.W. (2008) 'Housing, neighbourhood and residential mobility', in K. Hansen and H. Joshi (eds) *Millennium Cohort Study, third survey: A user's guide to initial findings*, London: Centre for Longitudinal Studies, Institute of Education, University of London, ch 13.

Kiernan, K.E. (1997) *The legacy of parental divorce: Social, economic and demographic experiences in adulthood*, STICERD-LSE-ESRC Centre for the Analysis of Social Exclusion, CASEpaper 1, London: London School of Economics and Political Science (http://sticerd.lse.ac.uk/dps/case/cp/paper1.pdf).

Kiernan, K.E. (2002) 'Demography and disadvantage: chicken and egg?', in J. Hills, J. Le Grand and D. Piachaud (eds) *Understanding social exclusion*, Oxford: Oxford University Press, pp 84–96.

Kiernan, K.E. (2004) 'Cohabitation and divorce across nations and generations', in P.L. Chase-Lansdale, K.E. Kiernan and R. Friedman (eds) *The potential for change across lives and generations: Multidisciplinary perspectives*, Cambridge: Cambridge University Press [also available as CASEpaper 65, http://sticerd.lse.ac.uk/dps/case/cp/CASEpaper65.pdf].

Kiernan, K.E. (2006) 'Non residential fatherhood and child involvement: evidence from the Millennium Cohort Study', *Journal of Social Policy*, vol 35, no 4, pp 651-69.

Kiernan, K.E. and Estaugh, V. (1993) *Cohabitation: Extra-marital childbearing and social policy*, York: Joseph Rowntree Foundation/Family Policy Studies Centre.

Kiernan, K.E and Huerta, M.C. (2008) 'Economic deprivation, maternal depression, parenting and children's cognitive and emotional development in early childhood', *British Journal of Sociology*, vol 59, no 4, pp 783-806.

Kiernan, K.E. and Mensah, F.K. (2009) 'Poverty, maternal depression, family status and children's cognitive and behavioural development in early childhood: a longitudinal study', *Journal of Social Policy*, vol 38, no 4, pp 569–88.

Kiernan, K.E. and Pickett, K.E. (2006) 'Marital status disparities in maternal smoking during pregnancy, breastfeeding and maternal depression', *Social Science and Medicine*, vol 63, no 2, pp 335-46.

Kiernan, K.E. and Smith, K. (2003) 'Unmarried parenthood: new insights from the Millennium Cohort Study', *Population Trends*, vol 114, pp 23-33.

Kimm, S.Y. and Obarzanek, E. (2002) 'Childhood obesity: a new pandemic of the new millennium', *Pediatrics*, vol 110, no 5, pp 1003-7.

Kopelman, P. (2007) 'Health risks associated with overweight and obesity', *Obesity Reviews*, vol 8 (Suppl 1), pp 13-17.

Krishnakumar, A. and Buehler, C. (2006) 'Interparental conflict and parenting behaviors: a meta-analytic review', *Family Relations*, vol 49, pp 25-44.

La Valle, I., Clery, E. and Huerta, M.C. (2008) *Maternity rights and mothers' employment decisions*, DWP Research Report No 496, London: Department for Work and Pensions.

Lauglo, J. (2000) 'Social capital trumping class and cultural capital', in S. Baron (ed) *Social capital: Critical perspectives*, Oxford: Oxford University Press, pp 142-67.

Lavy, V. (2006) *From forced bussing to free choice in public schools: Quasi-experimental evidence of individual and general effects*, NBER Working Paper 11969, Cambridge, MA: National Bureau of Economic Research.

Law, C., Power, C., Graham, H. and Merrick, D. (2007) 'Obesity and health inequalities', *Obesity Reviews*, vol 8 (Suppl 1), pp 19-22.

Lawlor, D. and Chatuvedi, N. (2006) 'Treatment and prevention of obesity: are there critical periods for intervention?', *International Journal of Epidemiology*, vol 35, pp 3-9.

Layard, R. and Dunn, J. (2009) *A good childhood: Searching for values in a competitive age*, London: The Children's Society and Penguin.

Levacic, R. (2004) 'Competition and the performance of English secondary schools: further evidence', *Education Economics*, vol 12, no 2, pp 179-94.

Lindley, J., Dex, S. and Dale, A. (2006) 'Ethnic differences in women's employment: the changing role of qualifications', *Oxford Economic Papers*, vol 58, no 2, pp 351-78.

Linver, M.R., Brooks-Gunn, J. and Kohen, D.E. (2002) 'Family processes as pathways from income to young children's development', *Developmental Psychology*, vol 38, no 5, pp 719-34.

Lobstein, T., Baur, L. and Uauy, R. (2004) 'Obesity in children and young people: a crisis in public health', *Obesity Reviews*, vol 5 (Suppl 1), pp 4-85.

Lupton, R., Tunstall, R., Sigle-Rushton, W., Obolenskaya, P., Sabates, R., Meschi, E., Kneale, D. and Salter, E. (2009) *Growing up in social housing in Britain: A profile of four generations, 1946 to the present day*, York: Joseph Rowntree Foundation (www.jrf.org.uk/sites/files/jrf/social-housing-britain-FULL.pdf).

Luthar, S.S. (1999) *Poverty and children's adjustment*, Thousand Oaks, CA: Sage Publications.

McCulloch, A. (2003) 'An examination of social capital and social disorganisation in neighbourhoods in the British Household Panel Study', *Social Science and Medicine*, vol 56, pp 1425-38.

McCutcheon, A.L. (1987) *Latent class analysis*, London: Sage Publications.

McLoyd, V.C. (1994) 'The strain of living poor: parenting, social support, and child mental health', in A.C. Huston (ed) *Children in poverty*, Cambridge: Cambridge University Press, pp 105-35.

McLoyd, V.C. (1998) 'Socioeconomic disadvantage and child development', *American Psychologist*, vol 53, pp 185-204.

Macran, S., Joshi, H. and Dex, S. (1996) 'Employment after childbearing: a survival analysis', *Work Employment and Society*, vol 10, no 2, pp 273-96.

Marmot, M. and Wilkinson, R. (eds) (2005) *Social determinants of health*, Oxford: Oxford University Press.

Martin, J. and Roberts, C. (1984) *Women and employment – A lifetime perspective*, London: HMSO.

Masten, A.S. (2001) 'Ordinary magic – resilience processes in development', *American Psychologist*, vol 56, no 3, pp 227-38.

Mathers, S. and Sylva, K. (2007) *National evaluation of Neighbourhood Nurseries Initiative: The relationship between quality and children's behavioural development*, London: Department for Education and Skills.

Mathers, S., Sylva, K. and Joshi, H. (2007) *Quality of childcare settings in the Millennium Cohort Study*, London: Department for Education and Skills.

Mayer, S. (1997) *What money can't buy*, Cambridge, MA: Harvard University Press.

Mayhew, E. and Bradshaw, J. (2005) 'Mothers, babies and the risks of poverty', *Poverty*, vol 121, pp 13-16.

Melhuish, E.C. (2002) 'Prospects for research on the quality of the pre-school experience', in W.W. Hartup and R.K. Silbereisen (eds) *Growing points in developmental science*, Hove: Psychology Press, pp 85-101.

Melhuish, E.C., Belsky, J., Heyland, A.H., Barnes, J. and the National Evaluation of Sure Start Research Team (2008) 'Effects of fully-established Sure Start local programmes on 3-year-old children and their families living in England: a quasi-experimental observational study', *The Lancet*, vol 372, pp 1641-7.

Meltzer, H., Gatward, R., Goodman, R. and Ford, T. (2000) *The mental health of children and adolescents in Great Britain*, London: The Stationery Office.

NICHD (National Institute for Child Health and Development) (2003) 'Does quality of child care affect child outcomes at age 4½?', *Developmental Psychology*, vol 39, no 3, pp 451-69.

NISRA (Northern Ireland Statistics and Research Agency) (2005) *Multiple Deprivation Measure 2005*, Belfast: NISRA, May.

NNI (Neighbourhood Nurseries Initiative) Research Team (2007) *National Evaluation of the Neighbourhood Nurseries Initiative: Integrated report*, London: Department for Education and Skills.

Norris, S. (2005) 'Segregation or not?', *Society Today*, Swindon: Economic and Social Research Council.

O'Brien-Caughy, M., O'Campo, P.J. and Muntaner, C. (2003) 'When being alone might be better: neighbourhood poverty, social capital and child mental health', *Social Science and Medicine*, vol 57, no 2, pp 227-37.

OECD (Organisation for Economic Co-operation and Development) (2008) 'Growing unequal? Income distribution and poverty in OECD countries' (www.oecd.org/els/social/inequality).

OPCS (Office of Population Censuses and Surveys) (1997) *Birth statistics: Historical series*, London: The Stationery Office.

Owen, C.G., Martin, R.M., Whincup, P.H., Smith, G.D. and Cook, D.G. (2005) 'Effect of infant feeding on the risk of obesity across the life course: a quantitative review of published evidence', *Pediatrics*, vol 115, pp 1367-77.

Parsons, T.J., Power, C., Logan, S. and Summerbell, C.D. (1999) 'Childhood predictors of adult obesity: a systematic review', *International Journal of Obesity*, vol 23 (Suppl 8), pp S1–S107.

Paull, G. (2008) 'Children and women's hours of work', *Economic Journal*, vol 118, no 526, pp F8–F27.

Paull, G. and Taylor, J. (with A. Duncan) (2002) *Mothers' employment and childcare use in Britain*, London: Institute for Fiscal Studies.

Peach, C. (1996) 'Does Britain have ghettoes?', *Transactions of the Institute of British Geographers*, vol 21, pp 216–35.

Peach, C. (2006) 'Islam, ethnicity and South Asian religions in the London 2001 census', *Transactions of the Institute of British Geographers*, vol 31, pp 353–70.

Pearce, A., Elliman, D., Bedford, H. and Law, C. (2008) 'Residential mobility and uptake of childhood immunisations: findings from the UK Millennium Cohort Study', *Vaccine*, vol 26, pp 1675–80.

Peisner-Feinberg, E. and Burchinal, M. (1997) 'Relations between pre-school children's child care experiences and concurrent development: the Cost, Quality and Outcomes Study', *Merrill–Palmer Quarterly*, vol 43, pp 451–77.

Petterson, S.M. and Albers, A.B. (2001) 'Effects of poverty and maternal depression on early child development', *Child Development*, vol 72, no 6, pp 1794–813.

Pevalin, D.J. and Goldberg, D.P. (2003) 'Social precursors to onset and recovery from episodes of common mental illness', *Psychological Medicine*, vol 33, no 2, pp 299–306.

Phillipsen, L., Burchinal, M., Howes, C. and Cryer, D. (1997) 'The prediction of process quality from structural features of child care', *Early Childhood Research Quarterly*, vol 12, pp 281–304.

Pianta, R.C. (1992) *Child–parent relationship scale*, Charlottesville, VA: University of Virginia.

Plewis, I. (ed) (2007) *The Millennium Cohort Study: Technical report on sampling* (4th edn), London: Centre for Longitudinal Studies, Institute of Education, University of London (www.cls.ioe.ac.uk/studies.asp?section=0001000200010010).

Plewis, I. and Ketende, S.C. (2006) *Millennium Cohort Study: Technical report on response* (1st edn), London: Centre for Longitudinal Studies, Institute of Education, University of London.

Plewis, I., Ketende, S.C., Joshi, H. and Hughes, G. (2008) 'The contribution of household mobility to sample loss in a birth cohort study: evidence from the first two waves of the UK Millennium Cohort Study', *Journal of Official Statistics*, vol 24, pp 365–85.

Portes, A. (1998) 'Social capital: its origins and applications in modern sociology', *Annual Review of Sociology*, vol 24, pp 1–24.

Portes, A. and Rumbaut, R.G. (2001) *Legacies: The story of the immigrant second generation*, Berkeley, CA: University of California Press.

Prout, A. (ed) (2004) *The future of childhood*, London: Routledge.

Putnam, R.D. (1993) *Making democracy work: Civic traditions in modern Italy*, Princeton, NJ: Princeton University Press.

Putnam, R.D. (2007) '*E Pluribus Unum*: diversity and community in the twenty-first century', *Scandinavian Political Studies*, vol 30, no 2. [[pages known?]]

Qvortrup, J., Bardy, M., Sgritta, G. and Wintersberger, H. (eds) (1994) *Childhood matters: Social theory, practice and politics*, Aldershot: Avebury.

Reilly, J.J., Methven, E., McDowell, Z.C., Hacking, B., Alexander, D., Stewart, L. and Kelnar, C.J. (2003) 'Health consequences of obesity', *Archives of Disease in Childhood*, vol 88, no 9, pp 748-52.

Reiter, J.P., Zanutto, E.L. and Hunter, L.W. (2005) 'Analytical modeling in complex surveys of work practices', *Industrial Labor Relations Review*, vol 59, pp 82-100.

Riccio, J.A., Bewely, H., Campbell-Barr, V., Dorsett, R., Hamilton, G., Hoggart, L., Marsh, A., Miller, C., Ray, K. and Vegeris, S. (2008) *Implementation and second-year impacts in the UK Employment Retention and Advancement (ERA) demonstration*, DWP Research Report No 489, Sheffield: Department for Work and Pensions.

Rindskopf, D. (2002) 'Infinite parameter estimates in logistic regression: opportunities, not problems', *Journal of Educational and Behavioural Statistics*, vol 27, no 2, pp 147-61.

Roberts, T. and Ketende, S. (2008) 'Parental health', in K. Hansen and H. Joshi (eds) *Millennium Cohort Study third survey: A user's guide to the initial findings*, London: Centre for Longitudinal Studies, Institute of Education, University of London, pp 170-202.

Rogers, B. and Pryor, J. (1998) *The development of children from separate families: A review of the research from the United Kingdom*, York: Joseph Rowntree Foundation.

Rutter, M. (2006) 'Implications of resilience concepts for scientific understanding', *Annals of the New York Academy of Science*, vol 1094, no 1, pp 1-12.

Rutter, M. and Madge, N. (1976) *Cycles of disadvantage: A review of research*, London: Heinemann Educational Books.

Rutter, M., Tizard, J. and Whitmore, K. (1970) *Education, health and behaviour*, London: Longman.

Salsberry, P.J. and Reagan, P.B. (2005) 'Dynamics of early childhood overweight', *Pediatrics*, vol 116, pp 1329-38.

Sampson, R.J., Morenoff, J.D. and Earls, F. (1999) 'Beyond social capital: spatial dynamics of collective efficacy for children', *American Sociological Review*, vol 64, pp 633-60.

Sandstrom, F.M. and Bergstrom, F. (2005) 'School vouchers in practice: competition will not hurt you', *Journal of Public Economics*, vol 89, pp 351-80.

Sandstrom, M.J. (2007) 'A link between mothers' disciplinary strategies and children's relational aggression', *British Journal of Developmental Psychology*, vol 25, pp 399-407.

Schoon, I. (2006) *Risk and resilience. Adaptations in changing times*, Cambridge: Cambridge University Press.

Schoon, I., Hope, S. and Ross, A. (2007) *Material hardship, family processes, and school readiness*, Longview Seminar Series, London: Nuffield Foundation.

Schoon, I., Sacker, A., Hope, S., Collishaw, S. and Maughan, B. (2005) 'Children's development in the family environment', in S. Dex and H. Joshi (eds) *Children of the 21st century: From birth to nine months*, Bristol: The Policy Press, pp 159-74.

Schuller, T., Baron, S. and Field, J. (2000) 'Social capital: a review and critique', in S. Baron, J. Field and T. Schuller (eds) *Social capital: Critical perspectives*, Oxford: Oxford University Press, pp 1-38.

Scottish Government (2004) 'Scottish Index of Multiple Deprivation 2004', June (www.scotland.gov.uk/Publications/2004/06/19421/38085).

Sharma, A.J., Cogswell, M.E. and Grummer-Strawn, L.M. (2005) 'The association between pregnancy weight gain and childhood overweight is modified by mother's pre-pregnancy BMI', *Paediatric Research*, vol 58, p 1038.

Shonkoff, J. and Phillips, D.A. (2000) *From neurons to neighborhoods: The science of early child development*, Washington, DC: National Academy Press.

Simons, L.G. and Conger, R.D. (2007) 'Linking mother–father differences in parenting to a typology of family parenting styles and adolescent outcomes', *Journal of Family Issues*, vol 28, no 2, pp 212-41.

Simpson, L. (2007) 'Ghettoes of the mind: the empirical behaviour of indices of segregation and diversity', *Journal of the Royal Statistical Society A*, vol 170, no 2, pp 405-24.

Smith, M. (2004) 'Parental mental health: disruptions to parenting and outcomes for children', *Child and Family Social Work*, vol 9, no 1, pp 3-11.

Social Justice Policy Group (2006) *The state of the nation report: Fractured families* (www.centreforsocialjustice.org.uk/client/downloads/BB_family_breakdown.pdf).

Söderström, M. and Uusitalo, R. (2005) *School choice and segregation: Evidence from an admission reform*, IFAU Working Paper 2005:7 (www.ifau.se/upload/pdf/se/2005/wp05-07.pdf).

Spencer, N. and Coe, C. (2003) 'Parent reported longstanding health problems in early childhood: a cohort study', *Archives of Disease in Childhood*, vol 88, pp 570-3.

Spira, E.G. and Fischel, J.E. (2005) 'The impact of preschool inattention, hyperactivity, and impulsivity on social and academic development: a review', *Journal of Child Psychology and Psychiatry,* vol 46, pp 755-73.

Stamatakis, E., Primatesta, P., Chinn, S., Rona, R. and Falascheti, E. (2005) 'Overweight and obesity trends from 1974 to 2003 in English children: what is the role of socio-economic factors?', *Archives of Disease in Childhood*, vol 90, pp 999-1004.

STATA Corporation (2006) STATA software release 9.2, College Station, Texas: STATA Corporation.

STATA Corporation (2007) STATA software release 10, College Station, Texas: STATA Corporation.

Stata Library, 'Analyzing correlated (clustered) data' (www.ats.ucla.edu/stat/stata/library/cpsu.htm).

Sylva, K. and Pugh, G. (2005) 'Transforming the early years in England', *Oxford Review of Education*, vol 31, no 1, pp 11-27.

Sylva, K. and Roberts, F. (2009) 'Quality in early childhood education: evidence for long-term effects', in G. Pugh and B. Duffy (eds), *Contemporary issues in the early years* (5th edn), London: Sage, pp 47-62.

Sylva, K., Siraj-Blatchford, I. and Taggart, B. (2003, revised 2006) *Assessing quality in the early years: Early Childhood Environment Rating Scale – Extension (ECERS-E): Four curricular subscales*, Stoke-on Trent: Trentham Books.

Sylva, K., Melhuish, E.C., Sammons, P., Siraj-Blatchford, I. and Taggart, B. (2004) *The Effective Provision of Pre-School Education (EPPE) Project: Final report*, London: Department for Education and Skills/Institute of Education, University of London.

Sylva, K., Melhuish, E.C., Sammons, P., Siraj-Blatchford, I. and Taggart, B. (2008) *Effective Pre-school and Primary Education 3-11 Project (EPPE 3-11): Final report from the primary phase: Pre-school, school and family influences on children's development during Key Stage 2 (Age 7-11)*, Research Report, Nottingham: DCSF Publications.

Sylva, K., Siraj-Blatchford, I., Melhuish, E.C., Sammons, P., Taggart, B., Evans, E., Dobson, A., Jeavons, M., Lewis, K., Morahan, M. and Sadler, S. (1999) *The Effective Provision of Pre-School Education (EPPE) Project: Technical paper 6*, London: Department for Education and Skills/Institute of Education, University of London.

Tate, A.R., Dezateux, C. and Cole, T.J. (2006) 'Is infant growth changing?', *International Journal of Obesity*, vol 30, no 7, pp 1094-6.

Tate, A.R., Dezateux, C., Cole, T.J. and the Millennium Cohort Study Child Health Group (2005) 'Factors affecting a mother's recall of her baby's birth weight', *International Journal of Epidemiology*, vol 34, pp 688-95.

UK Parliament (2006) *The Childcare Act*, London: The Stationery Office.

UNDP (United Nations Development Programme) (2001) *Human development report*, New York, NY: UNDP.

UNICEF (United Nations Children's Fund) (2007) *Child poverty in perspective: An overview of child well-being in rich countries*, Florence: Innocenti Research Centre, UNICEF.

Verropoulou, G., Joshi, H. and Wiggins, R.D. (2002) 'Migration, family structure and children's well-being: a multi-level analysis of the second generation of the 1958 Birth Cohort Study', *Children & Society*, vol 16, pp 219-31.

Vu, J.A., Jeon, H.J. and Howes, C. (2008) 'Formal education, credential, or both: early childhood program classroom practices', *Early Education and Development*, vol 19, pp 479-504.

WAG (Welsh Assembly Government) (2005) *The Welsh Index of Multiple Deprivation 2005, WIMD*, Cardiff: WAG.

Wake, M., Hardy, P., Canterford, L., Sawyer, M. and Carlin, J.B. (2006) 'Overweight, obesity and girth of Australian preschoolers: prevalence and socio-economic correlates', *International Journal of Obesity*, vol 31, pp 1044-51.

Walton, S., Bedford, H. and Dezateux, C. (2006) 'Use of personal child health records in the UK: findings from the Millennium Cohort Study', *British Medical Journal*, vol 332, no 7536, pp 269-70.

Ward, K., Sullivan, A. and Bradshaw, J. (2007) 'Income and poverty', in K. Hansen and H. Joshi (eds) *Millennium Cohort Study second survey: A user's guide to initial findings*, London: Centre for Longitudinal Studies, Institute of Education, University of London, pp 170-80.

Wardle, J. and Boniface, D. (2008) 'Changes in the distributions of body mass index and waist circumference in English adults, 1993/1994 to 2002/2003', *International Journal of Obesity*, vol 32, no 3, pp 527-32.

Wardle, J., Carnell, S., Howard, C.M.A. and Plomin, R. (2008) 'Evidence for a strong genetic influence on childhood adiposity despite the force of the obesogenic environment', *American Journal of Clinical Nutrition*, vol 87, no 2, pp 398-404.

West, A. and Pennell, H. (1999) 'School admissions: increasing equity, accountability and transparency', *British Journal of Educational Studies*, vol 46, pp 188-200.

West, A., Hind, A. and Pennell, H. (2004) 'School admissions and "selection" in comprehensive schools: policy and practice', *Oxford Review of Education*, vol 30, no 3, pp 347-69.

Whitebook, M., Howes, C. and Phillips, D. (1990) *Who cares? Child care teachers and the quality of care in America. National Child Care Staffing Study*, Oakland, CA: Child Care Employee Project.

WHO (World Health Organization) (2002) *Global strategy for infant and young child feeding*, Geneva: WHO.

Wigfield, A. and Eccles, J.S. (2000) 'Expectancy-value theory of achievement motivation', *Contemporary Educational Psychology*, vol 25, pp 68-81.

Wolff, J. and De-Shalit, A. (2007) *Disadvantage*, Oxford: Oxford University Press.

Woodland, S., Simmonds, N., Thornby, M., FitzGerald, R. and McGee, A. (2003) *The second work–life balance study*, Employment Relations Research Series No 22, London: Department of Trade and Industry.

Zimet, D.M. and Jacob, T. (2001) 'Influences of marital conflict on child adjustment: review of theory and research', *Clinical Child and Family Psychology Review*, vol 4, no 4, pp 319-35.

Index

Note: Page numbers followed by *fig* or *tab* indicate information is to be found only in a figure or table.

17

7 DAY
BOOK